THE FORGI

MW00989426

This book revolutionises our understanding of race. Building upon the insight that races are products of culture rather than biology, Colin Kidd demonstrates that the Bible-the key text in Western culture-has left a vivid imprint on modern racial theories and prejudices. Fixing his attention on the changing relationship between race and theology in the Protestant Atlantic world between 1600 and 2000, Kidd shows that, while the Bible itself is colour-blind, its interpreters have imported racial significance into the scriptures. Kidd's study probes the theological anxieties which lurked behind the confident façade of white racial supremacy in the age of empire and race slavery, as well as the ways in which racialist ideas left their mark upon new forms of religiosity. This is essential reading for anyone interested in the histories of race or religion.

COLIN KIDD is Professor of Modern History at the University of Glasgow and Fellow of All Souls College, Oxford. He has previously written *Subverting Scotland's Past: Scottish Whig Historians and the Creation of an Anglo-British Identity, 1689–1830* (1993) and *British Identities Before Nationalism: Ethnicity and Nationhood in the Atlantic World, 1600–1800* (1999).

THE FORGING OF RACES

Race and Scripture in the
Protestant Atlantic World, 1600–2000

COLIN KIDD

CAMBRIDGE
UNIVERSITY PRESS

CAMBRIDGE UNIVERSITY PRESS
Cambridge, New York, Melbourne, Madrid, Cape Town, Singapore, São Paulo

Cambridge University Press
The Edinburgh Building, Cambridge CB2 2RU, UK

Published in the United States of America by Cambridge University Press, New York

www.cambridge.org
Information on this title: www.cambridge.org/9780521797290

First published 2006

Printed in the United Kingdom at the University Press, Cambridge

A catalogue record for this publication is available from the British Library

Library of Congress Cataloguing in Publication data
Kidd, Colin.
The forging of races: race and scripture in the Protestant Atlantic world, 1600 – 2000 / Colin Kidd.
p. cm.
Includes bibliographical references and index.

1. Race – Biblical teaching.
2. Race – Religious aspects – Christianity.
3. Bible – Criticism, interpretation, etc. I. Title.
BT734.k53 2006
270.8089–dc22
2006005396

ISBN-13 978-0-521-79324-7 hardback
ISBN-10 0-521-79324-6 hardback

ISBN-13 978-0-521-79729-0 paperback
ISBN-10 0-521-79729-2 paperback

Contents

Acknowledgements

I should like to thank all those who agreed to look at the draft typescript: Brian Young, Charles Webster and Noel Malcolm. As ever I owe an enormous debt to Scott Mandelbrote, who was a fund of bibliographical knowledge. At an early stage Professor David Livingstone kindly passed on various helpful offprints, and I should like to signal my gratitude for the enormous help I derived from his pioneering overviews of the nineteenth-century debate on pre-Adamism. I am also indebted to the anonymous readers for Cambridge University Press who made such helpful suggestions and at the press itself to William Davies, Michael Watson and Isabelle Dambricourt, as well as Karen Anderson Howes, who once again took on the task of copy-editing my work. Caroline Erskine helped with the preparation of the text for delivery to the press, and Valerie Wallace did a valiant job compiling the index. Lucy, Susan and Adam did their bit.

I should also like to thank librarians at various institutions: the Glasgow University Library and its inter-library loan service; the Mitchell Library, Glasgow; the National Library of Scotland; New College Library, Edinburgh; the Bodleian Library; the Library of Congress; and the New York Public Library and its uptown outpost, the Schomburg Center for Research in Black Culture, Harlem.

Finally, it seems appropriate to pay tribute to the memory of my grandfather, Andrew Kidd, who died in 1976. After his small fruit business collapsed during the Second World War, he became a coach driver, and in the late spring of 1969 he drove a party of Mormon missionaries around the United Kingdom. At the conclusion of the trip they presented him with a copy of the Book of Mormon, which I have in my possession. Its tantalising presence on my bookshelves provided an inspiration for part of what follows.

CHAPTER I

Prologue: Race in the Eye of the Beholder

The scriptures do not immediately present themselves as a racial battle-ground. Nor is race usually associated with theology. Yet it is the argument of this book that interpretations of the Bible and certain branches of the discipline of theology have played an influential role in shaping racial attitudes over the past four centuries. The focus of the book is not on religion as a social movement, but upon the intellectual history of the ways in which scripture has been mobilised in the pursuit of certain theories of race, ethnic identities, racial prejudices and anti-racist sentiments. Some aspects of this history show Christian theologians in a very positive light, but others exhibit pernicious exploitation of the scriptures to advance obnoxious strategies of racial subjugation. Indeed, much of what follows will seem shocking to most readers.

Nevertheless, history is not a straightforward matter of distributing praise or blame to our forebears. We of the present are no smarter than our ancestors; we differ from them rather in that we have been raised and live with a different set of cultural expectations. Readers who suspect that a vacuum of moral relativism lurks at the heart of this book are wrong; but a reticence about pronouncing judgement on the evils of the past is one of the proprieties of historical discourse which, it is hoped, the future will similarly accord the present. The role of the historian is to understand the intellectual universe which justified slavery, segregation and imperialism, however much he or she might deplore these phenomena; similarly, the historian hopes that his or her own generation will not be demonised by future generations for eating meat, say, or despoiling the environment – or some other offence of which the present is barely conscious. Indeed, if history shows anything, it is the failure of past generations to predict which aspects of their moral life future generations will find intolerable.

While it would seem helpful to offer clear definitions of race and racism at the outset of this study, the temptation needs to be resisted. It is unhelpful for either the author or the reader to start out with a set of rigidly defined concepts. In the work that follows the reader will perceive that race has sometimes been conceived over the past four centuries in terms of outright physical appearance, at others in terms of the assumed common descent of a group. Of course, these categories often overlapped significantly, but they neither were, nor are, ever entirely congruent. Moreover, the ethnic turn in the modern scholarship on race emphasises the distinction between race-as-ethnicity and an older emphasis upon race-as-biology. But people in the past did not make this same distinction. For instance, as Michael O'Brien has noted in his encyclopedic study of Southern intellectual life before the American Civil War, nineteenth-century conceptions of race were 'more loose jointed' than the hard-and-fast distinctions found in the modern literature on race, embracing both 'race-as-ethnicity' and 'race-as-biology'.[1] To pinpoint our subject matter too precisely at this stage with an overly tight definition of race would risk losing sight of a moving and fuzzy target. Similarly, racism or racial prejudice includes both an unthinking, instinctive dislike of other races as well as a more thought-out, reflective, doctrinal racialism. The reader will encounter both of these types of racism in the course of this work, as well as positions combining elements of both conventional xenophobia and more sophisticated kinds of racial theory. Indeed, racial theory did not always move in tandem with racist attitudes, and readers will come across some decidedly unexpected positions on race, which combine antipathy to racial hatred or oppression with a belief in the scientific reality and importance of racial distinctions.

Most accounts of race and racism focus upon power. They emphasise the ways in which people of one race fail to acknowledge the full humanity of peoples of different colour or physical appearance, and, as a result, come to oppress, enslave or dispossess the victims of racial prejudice. By contrast, the historical analysis that follows takes a very different tack. The subject matter of this book concerns not so much the physical powers of coercion enjoyed by one race over another as the ways in which the apparent 'facts' of race threatened the intellectual authority of Christian scripture. This involves re-centring the narrative of race, with the power of the Word displacing power relations as the focal point of our story. For example, my focus will not be on the nature of the encounters between white Christendom and the peoples beyond Europe, but on the questions of whether and how far such encounters compelled reinterpretations of scripture.

Nevertheless, it is important to enter a vital qualification at this point. The subject matter of this book is not the Bible itself, but its human interpreters. The Bible itself is largely colour-blind: racial differences rarely surface in its narratives. The Bible tells us very little about the racial appearance of the figures and groups who feature within it. Even in the Old Testament which is, of course, preoccupied with the doings of the people of Israel, there are very few attempts to engage – except on the level of religious observance – with the ethnic differences between the nation of Israel and the peoples and cultures of the surrounding world.

This prompts a further caveat, a significant matter of definition which does need to be clarified at the outset of this volume, and indeed provides the marrow of this very necessary prologue. Just as the Bible says nothing about race, and functions, in this respect, merely as a screen on to which its so-called interpreters project their racial attitudes, fears and fantasies, so race itself is a construct, an interpretation of nature rather than an unambiguous marker of basic natural differences within humankind.

Race is in the eye of the beholder; it does not enjoy a genuine claim to be regarded as a fact of nature. This assessment will probably surprise many readers. However much we might despise racial prejudice and the non-sensical boasts of racial superiority that accompany it, one might honestly reason, surely we observe real, natural racial differences around us all the time. Can we not trust our senses when we notice the obvious physical differences between a white European, say, and a black African? Clearly, there are physical differences between a typical white European and a typical African, but to divide humanity into clearly demarcated races upon that basis would be to build a system of classification on a biological mirage. This is because the biologist finds those observable racial differences which seem so obvious to the layperson to be superficial and misleading. A wide range of evidence drawn from the biological and medical sciences directly contradicts the layperson's assumption that external indicators of race are biologically meaningful. Race is quite literally no more than skin deep, as well as scientifically incoherent.

It turns out that by employing human characteristics other than colour, facial configuration and hair type – the mainstays of racial certainty – quite different 'racial' mappings begin to materialise. Fingerprints, for example, which enjoy considerable respect among the general public as an aid to criminal investigation, tell a story which runs counter to popular assumptions about race. It turns out that there are distinctive geo-graphical variations in the patterns of loops, whorls and arches found in fingerprints. Loops are more common among most Europeans, black Africans and east Asians; whorls among groups such as Mongolians and

Australian Aborigines; and arches among the native Khoisans of southern Africa and some central Europeans. The geographical map of fingerprint patterns confounds our expectations of racial classification.[2]

Cerumen – or ear wax – provides another decisive challenge to conventional racial categories. There are two distinctive types of human ear wax: a wet and sticky type controlled by a dominant gene, and a dry and flaky type determined by a recessive gene. A majority of Asians (80–90 per cent) have the dry type. On the other hand, ear wax once again unexpectedly groups together most Europeans and Africans as members of the 'race' of wet, sticky ear wax people. The biologist Stanley Garn recognised the peculiar racial significance of cerumen: 'earwax polymorphism', Garn realised, 'separates east from west, and unites black and white Americans'.[3]

Alternatively – and more visibly than ear wax – body hair presents another quite different test, whereby a hairy 'race' based upon the hirsuteness of the male body would group together the unlikely combination of Europeans, Australian Aborigines and the Ainu people of northern Japan. Nor is body hair linked, it seems, in any straightforward way to climate. We might expect the peoples of cold climates to have more body hair than those of warm climates. But the peoples of the Middle East tend to have quite a lot of body hair, while Eskimos and the indigenous people of Tierra del Fuego tend to have little. By contrast, male baldness is also common among the hairy peoples of Europe and the Middle East, but is rare among black Africans, Asians and native Amerindians. Moreover, as Daniel Blackburn notes, 'hair color transcends contemporary racial divisions'. Blond hair can be found among the Berbers of North Africa and Aborigines of central Australia, Papua New Guinea and Melanesia; nor, warns Blackburn, is this a product of 'European admixture'. The form of hair also varies unpredictably: a taxonomy based on the straightness or curliness of hair would distinguish a 'race' of people with helical, or loosely curled, hair, including Europeans, Inuit and Ainu, from the straight-haired race of eastern Asians and native Amerindians and from a race of people with tightly curled hair drawn from sub-Saharan Africa, southern Arabia, India, Malaysia, the Philippines and New Guinea.[4]

Other tests further complicate matters. Possession of the lactase enzyme – which permits the digestion of the lactose in milk – is more common among milk-drinking peoples. Adult lactase is a feature of the populations of northern and central Europe, Arabia and the north of India, as well as some milk-drinking peoples in Africa, such as the Fulani, but does not tend to be found as commonly among other black African peoples or among the peoples of southern Europe, or among east Asians, Australian Aborigines or native Amerindians. As the biologist Jared Diamond has argued, 'races defined by body chemistry don't match races defined by skin color', Swedes, for example, belonging, in this instance, with the Fulani of West Africa in a 'lactase-positive race'. Even the study of urinary excretion provides unusual racial groupings. While east Asians tend to excrete a lot of the non-protein amino acid beta-aminoisobutyric acid in their urine, it is rarely excreted in any appreciable amount by Europeans or by Australian Aborigines.[5]

The map of blood groupings demonstrates the flimsy and subjective nature of conventional racial classification. One early survey of populations according to the A/B/O system of blood grouping led to some very odd conjunctions. The study classified populations according to the frequency found within them of the A and B groups, placing less emphasis upon the O grouping which is found to be common throughout the world. While Amerindian populations tended to monopolise the categories of 'low A, virtually no B' and 'moderate A, virtually no B', populations classified as 'high A, little B' included the Baffin Eskimo, Australian Aborigines, Basques, Polynesians and the Shoshone of Wyoming; 'fairly high A, some B' embraced English, Icelanders and Lapps as well as Melanesians from New Guinea; and 'high A, high B' encompassed Welsh, Italians, Thai, Finns, Japanese, Chinese and Egyptians. Such classifications defy easy racial categorisation. Moreover, Richard Lewontin's later study of variation in blood groups and other variations detected in serum and blood cells showed that most variation occurred not between regions of the world, but within single populations. Such studies explode notions of 'white blood', 'black blood' and the like which are the common currency of racialist rhetoric. Indeed, scientists are aware of a wide range of human blood-group typologies beyond the A/B/O system – such as the MNS, Rh, Kell, Kidd, Duffy, Diego and Lutheran blood-group systems, which further complicates any sense – other than in ill-informed colloquialism and metaphor – of a connection between blood and race.[6]

The sickle-cell gene mutation, which provides resistance against malaria, is another invisible criterion for mapping human populations. It is common in Arabia, southern India and tropical Africa where malaria is found, but the sickle-cell gene is much rarer among the black population of southern Africa, such as the Xhosa, and absent, less surprisingly, in northern Europe. Once again, as with classification based upon the possession of lactase, component groupings of the presumed black

African race are easily realigned with populations supposedly belonging to other races. Any notion of black African racial homogeneity does not withstand scientific scrutiny. After all, if stature, one of the more visible human traits, were proposed as a test of race, Africa would be found to contain some of the shortest people in the world – pygmies of four and half feet – as well as some of the tallest, the Nilotic peoples in East Africa having average heights of six and a half feet. Indeed, less visibly and more conclusively, geneticists have shown that there is more genetic variation within Africa than there is in the rest of the world put together. In this case, according to Diamond, 'the primary races of humanity' should then 'consist of several African races' – the Khoisan for one, and a few other groupings of African blacks and pygmies – 'plus one race to encompass all peoples of all other continents', with 'Swedes, New Guineans, Japanese and Navajo' all belonging to the same racial group. Other such tests similarly debunk the notion of a distinct Asiatic race. Epicanthic folds over the corners of the eye are found, for example, not only in the Far East, but also among the Khoisan of southern Africa, while the shovel-shaped incisors common in the front teeth of Asiatic populations are also found in Sweden. The world's major racial groupings begin to look somewhat arbitrary and unscientific. Nor should we forget intra-racial variations within the indigenous population of the Americas. Contrast, for example, using the obvious criterion of body size, the heavy build of the Papago people of southern Arizona with the slender people found in the rainforests of South and Central America.[7]

Just as the study of DNA demolishes any notion of a particular black 'African' race, so too this field lays down a decisive challenge to the scientific legitimacy of race in general. According to the eminent geneticist Kenneth Kidd, 'no human population is genetically homo-genous – high levels of genetic variation are ubiquitous, even in small, isolated populations'. Such findings demolish the notions of racial purity much insisted upon by generations of racists. The examination of data on genetic variation between populations does, however, generate a pattern of geographical clustering. Nevertheless, the variations being mapped in this way are not abruptly discontinuous in their distribution and thus do nothing to validate the concept of race. Kidd concludes that 'no definitive boundaries exist among the myriad variations in DNA', and that, therefore, no 'dramatically distinct "races" exist among human beings'. Generally speaking, according to Steve Olson, today's genetic scientists estimate that approximately '85 per cent of the total amount of genetic variation in humans occurs within groups and only 15 per cent between groups'. Moreover, it seems likely that only a very small proportion of the genetic variation within human DNA is responsible for skin colour and other visible features of racial difference. It becomes easier to understand why a biologist such as Alain Corcos might argue – at first sight, implausibly – that races are mere 'figments of our imagination'. Common sense about races turns out on closer inspection to be a 'myth' of race.[8]

Although colour differences are real, of course, these turn out to be trivial and to constitute something of a red herring in the investigation of human populations. As the geneticist Steve Jones notes, 'colour says little about what lies under the skin'. There are myriad sorts of human variation – of which visible racial differences amount to only a small proportion. Moreover, the different types of variation do not move in parallel; much less do they generate any consistent sort of racial patterning. Colour is only one among the many biological variations found among humans. A chorus of commentators takes the view that, whatever the visible features of race, these do not conform to the various other improbable patterns and groupings which surface within the biological and medical sciences. James Shreeve concludes that 'there are no traits that are inherently, inevitably associated with one another. Morphological features *do* vary from region to region, but they do so independently, not in packaged sets.' Blackburn summarises the scientific evidence in a very similar way: 'Patterns of overlapping variation prevent the classification of humans into biological units, unless a very limited number of features are arbitrarily chosen.' Even if we resort to the traditional benchmarks of race, we still end up with confusion rather than a clear pattern. According to Martin Lewis and Karen Wigen, 'The global map of skin color . . . bears little resemblance to the map of hair form or to the map of head shape. One can thus map races only if one selects one particular trait as more essential than others.' The selection of any one particular trait as the test of racial difference is intrinsically subjective. From a biological perspective, the evidence is so cross-grained that arbitrariness is intrinsic to any system of racial classification. Race, so the consensus runs, belongs firmly in the realm of human culture.[9]

The world of racial classification is, to all intents and purposes, a realm not of objective science, but of cultural subjectivity and creativity, for 'race' involves the arbitrary imposition of discontinuities on the continuous physical variation of the world's peoples. Nowhere is the disjunction between superficially objective science and cultural creativity more telling than in the calculus of – supposed – 'blood' fractions. Consider the fantasia of racial hybridity which Médéric Louis Elie Moreau de Saint-Méry

(1750–1819) set out with mathematical exactitude in his *Description topo-graphique, physique, civile, politique et historique de la partie française de l'isle Saint-Domingue* (composed between 1776 and 1789, and published in 1797). Saint-Méry produced a spectacularly detailed survey of the nuances of colour found among the mixed-race coloureds in what was then the French colony of Saint-Domingue, later to become Haiti. He started with the assumption that a pure white and a pure black was each composed, respectively, of 128 units of white blood or black blood. Between these ranges Saint-Méry traced a complex asymmetric gradation of racial classes composed of varying proportions of white and black blood. A 'sacatra', for example, was the class of mixed race which approximated closest to a pure black and was composed of 16 units of white blood, 112 of black; a 'griffe' came next with 32 units of white, 96 of black blood; then a 'marabou' with 48 units of white, 80 of black; a 'mulâtre' with equal shares of 64 units of both white and black blood; next a 'quarteron' with 96 units of white, 32 of black; a 'métif' with 112 units of white, 16 of black; a 'mamelouc' with 120 units of white and 8 of black; then, finally, with infinite care devoted to the detection of the minutest strains of black inheritance, a 'sang-mêlé', with 126 units of white and only 2 of black. With painstaking precision Saint-Méry also described the various pathways by which such racial classes might be formed. For example, he described twelve different combinations which resulted in a 'mulâtre', twenty different sorts of union which would result in a 'quarteron'. Nevertheless, such combinations revealed the crudity of the system: of the six combinations of métif, the component parts ranged between 104 and 112 parts white, and between 16 and 24 parts black; or, of the five ways of becoming a 'mamelouc', the end-product covered a spectrum between 116 and 120 parts white, and 8 and 12 parts black. Similarly, within such grey areas the child of a 'sacatra' and a 'négresse', for example, would be composed of 8 units of white and 120 units of black; or the union of a 'marabou' and a 'griffonne' would yield offspring comprising 40 units of white, 88 of black; or a 'sang-mêlé' and a 'négresse' would fall just to one side of inter-racial equilibrium, with 63 units of white inheritance, 65 of black. Without apparent irony, Saint-Méry apologised for the crude approximation of his system: 'l'on ne peut offrir que les approximations que j'ai établies'.[10]

Of course, this system stands at the extreme end of racialist fantasy, but it is – at bottom – no more ludicrous as science than the basic racial distinction between black and white. All theories of race – from the simplest and most obvious to the most sophisticated and contorted – are examples of cultural construction superimposed upon arbitrarily selected features of human variation. All racial taxonomies – whether popular or scientific – are the product not of nature but of the imagination combined with inherited cultural stereotyping as well – to be fair – as the empirical observation of genuine (though superficial, trivial and inconsequential) biological differences.

If it has seemed to most people an obvious matter of common sense that races exist as a fact of biology, then it should be equally obvious how many races there are. Tellingly, there has been no consensus among race scientists as to the number of races of humanity. The answers range from three to over a hundred races. Three was, of course, long a common answer, as one of the most influential taxonomies of race was the tripartite scheme derived from the story of Noah and his three sons. However, alongside this biblical model a wide range of 'naturalistic' systems of racial classification have sprung up since the age of the Enlightenment.

One of the first writers to pose an alternative to the biblical scheme of racial taxonomy was the French traveller François Bernier, who proposed instead four or five races. Similarly, the pioneering Swedish scientist Carl Linnaeus categorised mankind into four basic races: Americanus, Europeus, Asiaticus and Afer. He also included additional categories for monsters and feral wild men, though he did not consider them properly 'races' as such. The leading racial theorist of late eighteenth-century Europe was the Göttingen anatomist Johann Friedrich Blumenbach (1752–1840), who began his career by subscribing to a four-part division of humanity similar to that of Linnaeus (1707–78). However, by the third edition of his canonical work of racial classification, *De generis humani varietate*, he had divided mankind into five basic racial types: Caucasian, Mongolian, Ethiopian, Malay and American. The Caucasian, Blumenbach argued, had been the original racial form of mankind, of which the four later types were degenerations. The Ethiopian and the Mongolian stood at the two extremes of degeneration, with Malays intermediate between Caucasians and Ethiopians, and Americans, similarly, a point of racial degeneracy midway between the white Caucasian norm and the extreme of Mongolian degeneration. The influential nineteenth-century German ethnologist Oscar Peschel (1826–75) divided mankind into seven racial groups: Australasians, Papuans, Mongoloids, Dravidians, Bushmen of southern Africa, Negroids and Mediterraneans. For some ethnologists, even the white people of Europe did not form a homogenous mass. W. Z. Ripley (1867–1941), the eminent American anthropologist and economist, distinguished three different races in Europe – the Nordic or Teutonic, the Alpine and the Mediterranean.[11]

Among modern scientists who retained some adherence to the notion of racial classification there is no consensus. Stanley Garn listed nine 'geographical races' – 'Amerindian, Polynesian, Micronesian, Melanesian-Papuan, Australian, Asiatic, Indian, European, African' – and no less than thirty-two 'local races' – 'Northwest European, Northeast European, Alpine, Mediterranean, Iranian, East African, Sudanese, Forest Negro, Bantu, Turkic, Tibetan, North Chinese, Extreme Mongoloid, Southeast Asiatic, Hindu, Dravidian, North American, Central American, Caribbean, South American, Fuegian, Lapp, Pacific Negrito, African Pygmy, Eskimo, Ainu, Murrayian Australian and Carpenterian Australian, Bushmen and Hottentots, North American Colored, South African Colored, Ladino, Neo-Hawaiian'. On the other hand, William Boyd disaggregated humanity into thirteen races in seven groups. Boyd's European group included the Early European, Lapp, North-West European, East and Central European and Mediterranean races; outside Europe the other races were the African, Asian, Indo-Dravidian, American Indian, Indonesian, Melanesian, Polynesian and Australian races.[12]

Clearly, scientific observers of race have never been able to agree about the number of different races of humankind, nor about the characteristics that determine such groupings. Such disagreements do not mean that the scientific taxonomy of races is a holy grail which has still to be achieved, but that such a quest is, in fact, a fool's errand. Luigi Cavalli-Sforza, a leading pioneer in the application of genetics to the study of 'race' and ethnicity, writes of the 'absurdity of imposing an artificial discontinuity on a phenomenon that is very nearly continuous'. Racial taxonomy is, of course, a scientific chimera.[13]

Even bureaucracies, which tend to be associated in public opinion with rigorous and rational approaches to matters of social policy are, when it comes to issues of racial classification, no less prone to creative and unscientific whimsy than other institutions or indeed than the public at large. The racial classifications employed by the United States government in its decennial censuses bear eloquent witness to the instability of racial categories. Subcontinentals from India were classed as 'Hindu' in three censuses between 1920 and 1940, in the following three counts as white, and from 1980 as 'Asian'. Mexicans were counted as white before 1930 when they were given their own category, which led to protests from the Mexican government; as a result they were once again enumerated as whites, though from 1970 a new ethnic category of Hispanic was added to the census. Today, the census includes five primary race categories – white, black, Hawaiian/Pacific islander, Asian, native American/Alaskan – with a supplementary ethnic category of Hispanic. Whereas mulattoes formed a separate census category between 1850 and 1930, it was only in 2000, in the face of a rising multiracial movement which urges government to recognise the fact of inter-racial sexual unions, that a new generation of mixed-race Americans were able to tick more than one primary race category on the return. Procedures of racial classification have not only been oppressive in their social consequences, but have also been ludicrous in their judgements, by any standards. Even the South African apartheid bureaucracy found itself stymied by the daunting task of reconciling rigid man-made racial categories with the stubborn complexities of natural difference. In 1966, for example, its Race Classification Board deemed an eleven-year-old girl to be 'coloured' despite the fact that her siblings as well as her parents were all classified as 'white'.[14]

Nor have law courts been any more consistent than scientists or bureaucracies in the classification of races. Consider the example of the United States, where the legal classification of race has been popularly understood to operate in terms of hypodescent, or the 'one-drop' rule. Under the one-drop rule any visible sign of black ancestry was often sufficient for a person to be classified as 'black'. Nevertheless, this picture of the place of race in American jurisprudence is itself something of an oversimplification, for the one-drop rule was not a consistent feature of American law. Hypodescent appears to have been a widespread custom, especially in the South, but was slow to be formally enshrined in legal codes. By 1910 Tennessee was the only state where the one-drop rule had been codified, and Virginia did not introduce until 1924 its notorious law of hypodescent which defined a white person as having 'no trace whatsoever of any blood other than Caucasian'. Case law reveals even greater complexity and a variety of unexpected contingencies in the legal formulation of racial categories and divisions. For instance, the theory of blood fractions could, on occasions, run counter to perceptions of racial colour. Although, generally, there would be considerable overlap between race determined by blood fractions and race determined by physical appearance, each category was underpinned by a quite different logic of racial classification. Consider the case of *People* v. *Dean* which wound its way up the Michigan Supreme Court in 1866. This revolved around the electoral franchise which under the state constitution restricted voting rights to 'white male citizens or inhabitants, and certain *civilized* [my italics] male inhabitants of Indian descent'. William Dean, whose qualification to vote in Nankin Township, north of Detroit, had been challenged, claimed to be of Indian descent but – not being a member of a tribe – civilised, and therefore entitled to vote. The state, on the other hand, argued that Dean's African-American ancestry precluded any rights to the franchise. At the initial trial court a physician who examined Dean's skin, hair and 'cartilages of the nose' on behalf of the prosecution concluded that Dean had African blood in him, but 'very much diluted, not exceeding one-sixteenth part'. The state also contended that Dean, who had been born in Delaware, had been known there as a mulatto, of mixed white and African blood. Curiously, the Michigan Supreme Court neglected Dean's claim to be a 'civilized Indian'. Instead Dean's blackness became the issue at hand. Justice James V. Campbell, writing for the Michigan Supreme Court's majority opinion, employed two distinct criteria of racial classification in his judgement, the empirical but somewhat vague test of colour and the genealogical mathematics of blood fractions. Although Campbell noted that it had 'never been the case that any one having visible tokens of African descent has been regarded by the community generally as a white person', he nevertheless concluded that the facts of genealogy must trump appearance, that 'persons of precisely the same blood must be treated alike, although they may differ in their complexions'. Campbell proposed a quarter-blood standard, by which those who had less than a quarter African heritage might have a 'reasonable claim to be called white', with Dean falling on the white side of the new one-fourth rule.[15]

Even more bizarre in its unmasking of the shifting and unstable fantasies which underpinned apparently objective legal definitions of race was the case of *United States* v. *Bhagat Singh Thind*, decided in 1923. Thind was a Punjabi who had come to the United States in 1913, had enlisted in the army and had successfully petitioned in 1920 to become an American citizen. This petition before the Ninth Federal Circuit Court in Portland, Oregon, had been a tricky matter for his lawyers, as under naturalisation provisions dating back to 1790, only 'free white persons' could become naturalised citizens of the United States. Were Asians white? Thind's legal case rested on the anthropological consensus that the Caucasian race embraced two groups, the Aryans and the Semites, of which the former embraced not only most of the peoples of Europe, but also many of the peoples of northern India from which Thind originated. Thind, it appeared, was racially Aryan and Caucasian, and therefore surely met the whiteness test laid down in 1790. Although the Circuit Court agreed with this line of argument, its decision was overturned when the US Supreme Court upheld the challenge of the Bureau of Immigration and Naturalization that Thind was a 'Hindoo', and therefore was neither white nor worthy of citizenship. In 1923 the US Supreme

Court ruled that Thind might be ethnologically 'Caucasian', but as a 'Hindoo' – actually Thind was a Sikh, a distinction beyond the wit of the authorities – was not 'white'. Contemporary racialism rested upon sciences of race which confidently bandied around terms such as 'Caucasian' and 'Aryan' as synonyms for white; but a racialist jurisprudence adopted other criteria for whiteness when ethnological classifications of this sort opened up the danger of the unrestricted immigration and naturalisation of Caucasian Asians. The racial casuistry adopted by the US Supreme Court on this occasion depended upon the attainment of modern western modes of civilisation as a test of potential assimilability to white American standards. Neither descent from a common racial ancestry, such as the Aryan family, nor colour itself provided a reliable test in this regard. Indeed, the Supreme Court deemed dark-skinned Europeans to be white under this new dispensation.[16]

Having no real substance in nature or in science, 'races' are inherently unstable, liable to change their definition and composition from one society to the next, and within the same society from one era to the next. Adjacent cultures have classified races in staggeringly different ways. Just because the 'facts of race' appear to be obvious to the average person, and the assumptions about what constitutes racism appear to be similarly clear, it does not therefore follow that the concepts either of race or of racism can be extrapolated cavalierly back into past societies as unproblematic tools of analysis. Cultures do not all read 'nature' in the same way. Nor do they notice the same things about human 'Otherness'. The 'Other' has assumed distinct, often surprising and sometimes unpredictable forms in different places, times and cultures, not all of them racial. As Frank M. Snowden Jnr has shown in his classic study *Before color prejudice* (1983), the world of Greco-Roman antiquity seems to have had little sense of colour-based racial difference, notwithstanding the practices of slavery within those cultures and indeed the sharp ethnocentric distinctions made between civilised and barbarian societies.[17] This kind of xenophobia was not predicated on anything like biological racism. Even more unexpected patterns emerge in Joyce Chaplin's *Subject matter* (2001), her magisterial study of the early encounters between English colonists and native peoples in North America. Chaplin shows that it was the natives' susceptibility to disease, not the outward physical features of race or even any sense of cultural or technological superiority (which was surprisingly absent in the early phase of contact), which served as the primary marker of differentiation.[18] Furthermore, even when race is the benchmark of Otherness, it proves less portable than one might imagine. The idea of race transfers only with superficial ease from one culture or era to another. Like other products of culture, racial taxonomies necessarily vary from place to place. The child of one black and one white parent, for instance, would be classified as 'white' in Brazil; as 'coloured' in South Africa; as 'black' in the United States. Gloria Marshall argues that skin colour plays no role in Japanese racial classification. The outcast Burakumin, for example, are physically identical to other Japanese, but are considered to be racially inferior. On the other hand, perceptions of something as natural as skin colour might themselves be culturally determined. In 1940 the Chinese scientist Zhu Xi classified the races of mankind into ten distinct categories based on colour, including three distinct varieties of yellowness: pure white, red-white, ash-white, red-brown, black-brown, deep brown, black, dark yellow (native Americans, Indo-Malaysians, Polynesians), yellow-brown (Malaysians) and pure yellow (the Chinese alone). If race were a part of nature rather than a product of culture, then racial benchmarks should be static and relatively stable. Nothing could be further from the truth. Cultures have disagreed not only over the boundaries but also over the basic constituents of such apparently self-evident groupings as the white race.[19]

'When did your ancestors become white?' The question is almost certainly impolite, but not far removed from the surprising realities of cultural history. This is because research has shown that classification by colour is not quite as obvious as the layperson thinks. In North America and in Britain, people of Irish stock are now regarded as unambiguously white. But scholars have shown that this has not always been the case, and that it is only in the relatively recent past that the Irish, as it were, became 'white'. By contrast, native Americans were once thought of as 'white' and were later reconceptualised as 'redskins'. If anything, 'whiteness' – something perhaps taken for granted by most 'whites' today – has been just as mutable – and, not least for those at the margins who wished to be considered 'white', perilously unstable – as the shifting cultural differences between ethnic groups. Today's United States possesses a more capacious category of whiteness which includes groups who now pass as 'white' yet were once seen as racially inferior. Along parallel lines, L. P. Curtis Jnr has shown that Irish immigrants in Victorian Britain were routinely depicted with simian features, most particularly by nineteenth-century cartoonists, and were generally seen as an ape-like race quite distinct from the peoples of Britain only a short voyage away across the Irish Sea. Whiteness – a counter-intuitive, but persuasive body of argument now runs – was 'invented'.[20]

The most sophisticated exposition of this phenomenon comes in Matthew Frye Jacobson's wonderfully insightful book *Whiteness of a different color* (1998). Jacobson reminds us that today's 'visual economy and racial lexicon' are recently coined and contingent. Past generations of Americans did not see races as today's Americans see them, nor did they deploy quite the same nomenclature. Moreover, the passing of old racial taxonomies and vocabularies has intellectual as well as social consequences, for people of today are oblivious of the racial differences once so apparent in the past: 'entire races have disappeared from view, from public discussion, and from modern memory, though their flesh-and-blood members still walk the earth'. Where, for example, asks Jacobson, are the Teutonic, Celtic, Iberic and Mediterranean races, 'races' which were so obvious to nineteenth-century Americans? The history of 'race', according to Jacobson, is a narrative of shifting 'public fictions'. In particular, he points to a prevailing system of racial classification in the nineteenth century whereby 'one might be both white and racially distinct from other whites'. The Anglo-Saxon American response to mass European immigration between the 1840s and 1924 meant that this period of American history 'witnessed a fracturing of whiteness into a hierarchy of plural and scientifically determined white races'. Only towards the end of this period was racial whiteness 'reconsolidated', as 'probationary' white groups at the margins were granted full scientific status as 'Caucasians'. The key expression in Jacobson's analysis is 'the alchemy of race', the somewhat mysterious process by which apparently white European immigrants who were not recognised as such by 'white' Anglo-Saxon Protestant Americans became transformed into 'whites'.[21]

A similarly unexpected taxonomy of race is observable on the other side of the Atlantic. Whereas the people of twentieth- and twenty-first-century Scotland tend to be proud of their national identity as Scots and also consider themselves as part of a Celtic fringe – Scotland, Ireland, Wales – which sits at the northern and western peripheries of Saxon England, their nineteenth-century forebears, at least in the Scottish Lowlands, took a fundamentally opposing view, boasting instead of their Anglo-Saxon racial identity and their ethnological affinity with the people of England; the people of Ireland, Wales and the Scottish Highlands they deemed to be parts of an inferior, albeit white, race of Celts. Race had a spectacularly different range of meanings for Scots of the Victorian era compared to that held by their descendants in the second half of the twentieth century. The very term was itself unstable, with 'race' often used to denote what we might now call nations or ethnic groups, as well as peoples of different colours or widely differentiated physical features. Nineteenth-century Britons imagined racial differences between white Saxons and white Celts, deluding themselves that Irish Celts bore traces of simian characteristics.[22]

As well as being subjective, colour was in recent centuries only one among several benchmarks which have defined race for – so-called – scientific racists. Historians of racial attitudes know that there is more to race than colour. Indeed, skin colour has not always been the prime determinant of racial difference. Cranial capacity, the facial angle and the cephalic index all held out the prospect to scientists of apparently objective, accurate measurement, whereas colour by itself could not.

From the late eighteenth century the most fashionable means of determining race was the calculation of the 'facial angle', a method devised by the Dutch anatomist Petrus Camper (1722–89). The facial angle was calculated at the intersection of two lines, one running from the forehead to the front point of the lips, the other from the ear to the nostrils. Although Camper was by no means as committed a racist as he is sometimes portrayed, the facial angle became a tool for scientific racists throughout the nineteenth century. The angle of the average European was about eighty degrees, the average for an African about seventy degrees; the facial angle of an orang-utan was about fifty-eight degrees. This appeared to suggest that there was a hierarchy of racial intelligence from the animal world up through the lower races to the higher races. Nineteenth-century racial commentators coined the terms prognathous and orthognathous to describe racial types based upon the facial angle.[23]

During the nineteenth century there was a general fixation upon the cranium, but the various schools of racial science which flourished at this time adopted different ways of relating the cranium to race. Some craniologists simply measured the capacity of the skull, whereas phrenologists found this much too crude an indication of character. Instead, phrenologists produced a map of the skull divided into thirty-seven different zones, each representing a localised faculty or phrenological organ. For instance, at the front of the skull the phrenologists tended to locate various intellectual faculties, including 'calculation', 'comparison' and 'causality'; at the crown of the skull some of the higher ethical elements of character, including 'conscientiousness' and 'hope'; and towards the base of the skull some of the more instinctive characteristics such as 'combativeness' and 'amativeness'. The cranial conformations of different racial groups were assessed and compared against this plan of the phrenological faculties. The Swedish craniologist Anders Retzius also coined the 'cephalic index' as a means of classifying skulls into long-headed (dolichocephalic) and wide-headed (brachycephalic) types.[24]

Or might the key to racial classification reside in a quite different part of the anatomy far removed from the cranium? Around 1800 the length of the forearm became a major issue in British anthropological debates about racial difference between whites and blacks. More bizarrely, the nineteenth-century French scientist Etienne Serres (1786–1868) constructed a hierarchical racial taxonomy based on variations in the position of the navel and umbilical cord in the embryos of different human types. Some racial benchmarks were even more eccentric. For instance, the British entomologist Andrew Murray (1812–78) studied variations in human lice gathered from people in different countries and concluded from tests that body lice were racially specific and could not survive on the bodies of other races. Or take the case of the distinguished British anatomist and evolutionist Sir Arthur Keith (1866–1955), who began his career with a detailed study of the external configuration of the ear. The shape of the ear, Keith believed, provided a decisive clue to racial identity. Between 1895 and 1897 Keith carried out examinations of 15,000 ears, with the aim of garnering evidence of racial characteristics. This analysis of the outer shape of the ear now seems somewhat misguided; though, as we now know, the ear wax within might have yielded some interesting results of racial differences. During the nineteenth century there was also considerable interest in eye and hair colour. John Beddoe (1826–1911) deployed an authoritative-looking mathematical formula to calculate the 'Index of Nigrescence' in the populations of the regions of Britain and Ireland: $D + 2N - R - F$ (or the dark-haired plus twice the black-haired – doubled, according to Beddoe, 'in order to give its proper value to the greater tendency to melanosity shown thereby' – minus the red-haired and the fair-haired, with brown hair neutral). Nor should we forget that during the nineteenth century and the rise of Aryan linguistics, language – mistakenly conflated with matters of anatomy and physiology – became a central determinant of racial categories.[25]

Sometimes colour trumped other racial characteristics; sometimes race scientists insisted upon the incontrovertibly objective mathematics of cranial measurement as a substitute for the subjectivity associated with the study of complexion; sometimes the 'facts' of physical appearance found themselves at odds with the 'facts' of genealogical blood fractions; sometimes – as with some, though not all, Aryan philologists – language was considered a more decisive test than the superficial appearance of anatomy; sometimes a whole battery of tests, including hair type, eye colour, bodily constitution and the like, were deployed in the quest for 'race'. The historian of race becomes, inevitably, a connoisseur of polymorphous perversity.

Race, it should be clear by now, exists as a property of *our minds*, not of *their bodies*. It is a bogus scientific category rather than a fact of nature, and belongs not so much to the realm of objective biology as to the quite distinct realm of human subjectivity. Attitudes to race are determined both by real – but inconsistent – physical features and by the symbolic universes, the cultures, in which humans translate the misleading facts of physical difference into racial ideologies, stereotypes and folklores. If race, then, is more properly a social and cultural construct, what are the social and cultural factors that have shaped its construction?

CHAPTER 2

Introduction: Race as Scripture Problem

Given that race is a cultural construct, it should occasion little surprise that the dominant feature of western cultural life – Christianity – should have exerted an enormous influence on its articulation. The book of Genesis has played a very large role in the cultural construction of race. Nevertheless, scholarly discussion of racial constructs has tended, on the whole – though there are important exceptions – to drift into the territorial waters of sociology. Race is contextualised alongside issues of status and class, and the social relations of power are, reasonably enough, accorded pride of place in interpretations of the rise of racism. That race is also a theological construct has hitherto attracted much less attention, though it has occasionally intruded at the margins of the more scrupulous studies of race – albeit as a somewhat anomalous factor. It is one of the central arguments of this book that, although many social and cultural factors have contributed significantly to western constructions of race, scripture has been for much of the early modern and modern eras the primary cultural influence on the forging of races. 'Race-as-theology' should be an important constituent of the humanistic study of racial constructs alongside accounts of 'race-as-biology', 'race-as-ethnicity' and 'race-as-class or -caste'. On the other hand, this study also investigates the extent to which the dethronement of scripture from its dominant position in western intellectual life in the centuries following the Enlightenment has contributed to a reconfiguration of racial attitudes. It asks how far a decline in the authority of scripture opened up an ideological space for the uninhibited articulation of racialist sentiments. An appreciation of the theological inflections of racial discourse is essential to a proper parsing of the early modern and modern histories of race.

Although the Bible is itself colour-blind with regard to racial difference, the book of Genesis offers a compelling explanation of the origins of mankind, the peopling of the world after the Flood by the sons of Noah and their

19

offspring, and the confusion of languages (and consequent division of humanity) that accompanied God's displeasure at the Tower of Babel. According to the Bible, the whole of humanity descends from Adam and Eve, by way of Noah and his wife and their three sons – Ham, Shem and Japhet – and their wives, the only human survivors of a universal Flood. Genesis sets out in some detail the lineages which descend from the sons of Noah; but there is no discussion of the ethnicity of the peoples listed. Among the very few exceptions to the invisibility of matters of race and colour in the scriptures is the remark found in Jeremiah 13:23 – 'Can the Ethiopian change his skin, or the leopard his spots?' The ultimate insignificance of ethnicity and race surfaces in the New Testament. Acts 17:26 sets out a clear statement of the unity of humankind – 'And [God] hath made of one blood all nations of men for to dwell on all the face of the earth.'

Thus the Bible is a text which treats of issues apparently pertinent to race and ethnicity, but in a manner oblivious of the fact of racial difference. It describes, for example, the peopling of the world, but ignores the racial identity of the detailed lineages it describes which originated with Noah's sons. It is this very incongruity between the Bible's significance for an understanding of ethnicity and its silence on matters of race that has tempted theologians and other readers of scripture, including anthropologists, race scientists and ideologues of all sorts, to import racial meanings and categories into the Bible.

The most influential passage of scripture came in Genesis 10. This appeared to provide a map of ethnic filiation, which set out the families of the sons of Noah and claimed that 'by these were the nations divided in the earth after the Flood'. The sons of Japhet were listed as Gomer, Magog, Madai, Javan, Tubal, Meschech and Tiras. In addition, scripture also specified the sons of Gomer – namely Ashkenaz, Riphath and Togormah – and those of Javan – that is, Elishah, Tarshish, Kittim and Dodanim. The sons of Ham were identified as Cush, Mizraim, Phut and Canaan, while further details were given of the sons of Cush, Mizraim and Canaan. Similarly, the children of Shem were Elam, Asshur, Arphaxad, Lud and Aram, with a great deal of further detail, for the bulk of the Old Testament constituted, of course, the history of the lineage of Shem through Arphaxad, the distant direct progenitor of the Abrahamic line. Such genealogical listings seemed to have been accorded ethnological significance. The sons of Shem, it was announced in Genesis 10:31, were set out 'after their families, after their tongues, in their lands, after their nations'. Chapter 11 then sets out the story of the Tower of Babel and the confounding of the world's languages. To all intents and purposes, for orthodox readers of scripture, Old Testament genealogy was the essential point of departure for understanding the races, linguistic groups, ethnicities and nations of the world.

Seventeenth- and early eighteenth-century antiquaries usually identified Celts as the offspring of Gomer, the son of Japhet, and the Germanic peoples as a particular line of descent from Gomer's son Ashkenaz. Whereas Germans and Celts were identified for much of the early modern period as closely related ethnic groups, during the nineteenth century they were seen by many commentators as distinct and discrete racial groups who shared very little in common and exhibited sharply contrasting racial characteristics. This shift in attitudes is explained, in large part, by the emergence of a more secularised ethnology whose point of departure was no longer the Table of Nations set out in Genesis 10.[1]

Of course, Old Testament anthropology runs into the sand. There is a huge gap – or perhaps not so huge, depending upon one's scheme of chronology – between the facts of ethnicity set out in Genesis and the appearance of ethnic groups in the historical and ethnographic works of Greece and Rome. From which of Noah's sons came the Scythians, say? A great deal of early modern anthropology involved the reconstitution of the lineages of peoples between the petering out of scriptural ethnography and the start of the classical record.

Whereas race depends on a – supposedly – naturalistic perception of racial difference as a 'biological fact', the reliance of most early modern and some modern ethnological theories on the irrefutable historical testimony of the Old Testament transmutes the concept of 'race' into the neighbouring, but qualitatively distinct, category of 'lineage'. In general, when, under biblical inspiration, race is collapsed into lineage, this should inhibit racial prejudice. This is because the interpretation of the supposed biological 'facts' of racial difference through the lens of scripture tends to result in the ascription of the racial Other to some part of the Noachic family tree, however distant from the Japhetite branch to which the white race was customarily assigned. Scripture has the benign capacity to render racial Otherness as a type of cousinage or remote kinship.

Unfortunately, scriptural notions of lineage also possessed a more sinister capacity to encourage the importation of divinely authorised categories of blessed and cursed – and by extension objective moral categories of good and evil – into the reading of the ethically neutral differences between races. Most obviously, the Bible was capable of exacerbating negative attitudes towards the racial Other by ascribing, say, the blackness of Africans to the divine curse placed on the descendants of

Ham, or to the mark placed upon the murderous Cain (and presumably inherited by his descendants). The central issue was not so much one's possession of a particular colour of skin as one's membership of a particular lineage singled out in the Old Testament for special favour or disfavour. The idea of race-as-lineage is capable of generating pronounced tensions between the notion of a family of races underpinned by the sacred anthropology of the Old Testament and the universal message of the New, and the idea of cursed and blessed lineages. In these respects the Bible serves, confusingly, both to diminish and to exacerbate racism.

Crucial evidence of the intimate connection between scripture lineages and the discourse of race can be found in the very terminology of race and ethnology, which is saturated with theological and biblical terms. Terms of abuse and technical expressions alike bear witness to the scriptural provenance of the race question whether in the low-level discourse of the public bar or in the more rarefied conversations of the intelligentsia. The concept of the 'ethnic' is itself an emblem of the religious saturation of the language of ethnicity. Johnson's *Dictionary* (1755) defined 'ethnick' as 'heathen; pagan; not Jewish; not Christian', and also included an entry for 'ethnicks', meaning 'heathens; not Jews; not Christians'. Other dictionaries reiterate the same broad definition of ethnic as 'heathenish'. Thomas Blount's *Glossographia* of 1656 defined 'ethnick' as 'heathenish, ungodly irreligious: And may be used substantively for a heathen or gentile'. In Nathaniel Bailey's *Universal etymological dictionary* (6th edition, 1733), 'ethnick' is given a similar definition: 'heathenish, of or belonging to heathens'. This usage can be traced throughout the early modern British world. There has been a subtle but significant shift in the meaning of 'ethnic' over the past couple of centuries, from an original association with religious Otherness – although early modern pagans would tend not to be white Europeans – towards a more secular description of racial, national or cultural distinctiveness.[2]

Sacred history left its mark most indelibly in the field of linguistics, whose nomenclature – 'Semitic', 'Hamitic' – betrays a scriptural provenance. Associations with Noah's other son, Japhet, have in the long run proved less enduring; but they were common until the end of the nineteenth century in philological writings. In 1767 the English antiquary James Parsons (1705–70) published an influential work on the relationships of the ancient languages of Europe entitled *Remains of Japhet*. Even the Indo-Europeanist transformation of philological classification did not disturb this established identification of the lineage of Japhet with Europe.

During the nineteenth century, as we shall see, Japhetite was a common synonym for Aryan or Indo-European, and part of the success of this new philological concept appears to stem from its ease of incorporation within an established biblical genealogy for the world's cultures and peoples. The boundaries between quite distinct systems of nomenclature – biblical and philological – were fuzzy and permeable. Examples of category fusion abounded. The distinguished American scientist Alexander Winchell (1824–91) wrote of the 'early dispersion of the Japhetites or Indo-Europeans – called also Aryans'. Similarly, the Irish anthropological writer and lawyer Dominick McCausland (1806–73) claimed that one of the leading families of the Caucasian race 'has been designated by historians as the Aryan, by philologists as the Indo-European, and by religionists as the Japhetic – all denoting one and the same people'. For example, Sanskrit was the 'language of the eastern Japhetites', according to McCausland, who described India's dominant ethnic group as 'Hindu Aryan Japhetites'.[3]

Noachic categories persisted limpet-like in the field of ethnology, even cohabiting on occasions with a subversive irreligious intent. Somewhat improbably, the deistic French polygenist, Bory de Saint-Vincent (1780–1846), who believed that the earth's human population was composed of fifteen distinct species of humanity, had recourse at times to a conventional biblical nomenclature, naming the species found in Europe, for example, the 'Japetic'. The legacy of the supposed curse upon Ham long survived in South Africa, particularly in the Western Cape, where 'Gam' – alluding to Ham – has been employed as a 'pejorative label for the coloured labouring poor'. However, Noachic nomenclature in the sphere of ethnology and linguistics sometimes led to a degree of confusion. When terms like 'Semitic' and 'Hamitic' were used to describe families of languages, these terms created the impression that such languages were quite distinct, belonging to the divergent dispersals of the descendants of Shem and Ham. The German biblical scholar Friedrich Gesenius (1786–1842) was the first scholar to show that the supposed Semitic language family included languages conventionally described as Hamitic. The nineteenth-century British ethnologist James Cowles Prichard (1786–1848) also ventured into the philological no man's land where Semitic and Hamitic languages appeared to overlap. Hebrew, he believed, belonged to the Canaanitish or Hamitic family of languages, not to the Syrian, or Semitic proper, grouping. To avoid inaccuracy, Prichard preferred a regional description of the latter grouping, deploying the term 'Syro-Arabian' rather than Semitic.[4]

African history and anthropology were long in thrall to the 'Hamitic hypothesis', the notion that everything of value in the culture of sub-Saharan Africa had been brought there by the Hamites, a Caucasoid people (surprisingly enough given the associations of Ham with blackness). According to Edith Sanders, the Hamitic hypothesis emerged during the nineteenth century as a scholarly by-product of theological concerns. In particular, the argument that only Canaan had been cursed as a punishment for the disrespect shown by his father Ham seemed to imply that the rest of Ham's progeny had escaped – white and uncursed. The Egyptians were considered to belong to the non-Canaanite descendants of Ham, and it suited nineteenth-century ethnologists and Egyptologists to emphasise that the high civilisation of Egypt had been white and Caucasoid. Africanists speculated on the diffusion of high culture from Egypt to central and southern Africa by way of a race of Hamitic nomadic pastoralists. Despite the supplanting of theology by science, the Hamitic idea survived into twentieth-century anthropology. Curiously, the term 'Hamite' was to be replaced by another ethnic label, which was also of biblical provenance, though, perhaps, less embarrassingly so: the 'Hamites' of nineteenth-century ethnological speculation tended to become the 'Southern Cushites' of mid-twentieth-century African anthropology. In this way, a residue of a much older theological debate survived into twentieth-century theories about the ethnology of Africa.[5]

The term 'Caucasian', which in common currency denotes the physical characteristics of the – supposed – white European race, is also indirectly indebted to scripture and the Noachic story. As Hannah Augstein has shown, the anthropological classification of a 'Caucasian' race had its roots in the study of biblical geography, in particular the quest by sacred geographers to locate the final resting place of the Ark, and hence presumably of the post-diluvial beginnings of humankind. Some late eighteenth-century ethnologists claimed that the Caucasus Mountains abounded in sea shells. Did this confirm speculation that humanity had dispersed from its Caucasian navel? Or did it suggest rather that the Caucasus too had been inundated and that the centre of humanity might well be found in the higher regions of the Himalayas? As an ethnological term, Caucasian provides only the merest hint of its provenance in a contested field of biblical scholarship; nor does it now possess the monogenist, Eurasian associations of its first coinage.[6]

However, the connection between race and scripture goes *much* deeper than the words used to denote racial, linguistic and ethnic groups. The logical coherence of Christian theology depends upon a certain reading of the significance of race. Conversely, race has the potential to undermine some of the central doctrines of Christianity. This book contends that between the seventeenth and nineteenth centuries intellectuals confronted race primarily as a theological problem. Indeed, race – as we shall see in more detail in later chapters – started out as a theological problem in the early modern period. In particular, the unity of the human race was fundamental to Christian theology. If mankind did not spring from a single racial origin, then theologians were confronted with a scenario that undermined the very essence of the Christian story. The sacred drama of Fall and redemption rests upon assumptions of mankind's common descent from Adam. Otherwise, the transmission of original sin from Adam would not have polluted the whole human race. In the second place, Christ's atonement – however limited the scope for election – would not apply to the whole of mankind. This issue will recur throughout the book. A monogenist theory of race is inextricably inter-woven with some of the central tenets of Christian doctrine. The over-riding importance of the unity of mankind for the biological transmission of original sin and indeed for defending the historical truths set out in Genesis meant that Christian commentators on race were inclined to refuse the apparent fact of distinctive races or racial types for fear of endorsing the destructive heresy of polygenesis. So much discussion of race was framed by the question of monogenesis that it distorted western ethnology in an anti-pluralist direction. Theology tended to inhibit a full acceptance of racial diversity.

It is a central argument of this book that the construction of race has been significantly restricted in its articulation and meanings by theolo-gical imperatives. At times theological considerations have run against the grain of biological understandings and sociological uses of race. On occasions, theology has constrained the expression of racialist sentiments, though the capacity of the Bible to yield multiple and sometimes con-tradictory readings means that Christianity has rarely been sufficient in itself to prevent acts of racial oppression when whites – however staunchly Christian – have found themselves presented with tempting opportunities to obtain wealth or power. Nevertheless, social realities notwithstanding, constructions of race tended not to follow a sociological logic, but con-formed to theological imperatives.

Cross-cultural comparisons help to foreground the Christian inflec-tions of European racial thought. In the cultures beyond Christendom, racial speculation was framed somewhat differently. Frank Dikotter notes that monogenesis was an alien concept imported into China in the seventeenth century by Christian missionaries, and that it never obtained the same dominance in the East. Instead, polygenesis exercised an uncontroversial purchase in the non-Christian cultures of China and Japan, and bigenism – the notion that mankind arose from two distinct origins (a single origin for the yellow race and a separate source for the other races of the world) – was more pronounced in the racialist theories of late nineteenth- and early twentieth-century Chinese intellectuals than in the West which, Darwinism and secularisation notwithstanding, retained a preference for some form of monogenist explanation.[7]

Indeed, it seems probable that the influence of theology on the construction of race was most profound not when it served to inscribe obvious scriptural patterns on the taxonomy of race, but when it acted as an obstacle to the exaggeration of racial difference. As we shall see, in the early modern period, during the Enlightenment, and even at the high noon of nineteenth-century racialism, theological imperatives drove the conventional mainstream of science and scholarship to search for mankind's underlying unities. The emphasis of racial investigation was not upon divisions between races, but on race as an accidental, epiphenomenal mask concealing the unitary Adamic origins of a single, extended human family. The deepest impact made by theology on the construction of race was thus, arguably, of a negative kind; quietly, subtly and indirectly, theological needs drew white Europeans into a benign state of denial, a refusal to accept that human racial differences were, literally, anything other than skin deep. Obviously, this negative inhibitory influence is hard to measure; but, as we shall see throughout this book, the ongoing defence of monogenesis tended over the course of early modern and modern history to direct the focus of racial analysis away from differences towards similarities. Theological factors, more than any others, dictated that the proof of sameness would be the dominant feature of western racial science.

The defence of monogenist orthodoxy dictated that the discourse of race as often as not became fixated not upon the empirical facts of human difference, but upon ways to reconcile such differences with the deeper truth (and theological necessity) of aboriginal human unity. Theological pressures encouraged many Christian ethnologists to dismiss skin colour or other physical characteristics as superficial traits which might be explained away in environmentalist terms. The principal objective of the Christian ethnologist was to search for the underlying commonalities which would confirm the biological unity of mankind. Theological perspectives on the question of race promoted the notion that ultimately race was a matter of delusive appearances.

Distorted in a benign fashion, generally speaking, by theological anxieties, the western discourse of race focused less than might be imagined upon visible signs of ethnic variety and more upon the invisible Adamic sameness which must, according to the revealed Word of scripture, lie beneath the apparent Otherness of the world's peoples. The demands of Christian theology meant that western observers of race were encouraged to view the phenomenon through the wrong end of the telescope. Christianity – for reasons of orthodoxy, principally, rather than out of philanthropy – saw through the outer anatomical and epidermal cladding of the races of the world, concerned only to establish their ultimate Adamic pedigree. This was a distortion of truth, though it erred, possibly by chance, in the direction of philanthropy.

Despite the rise of a more secular worldview in recent centuries, the legacy of scriptural authority continues to leave its mark on the field of race and ethnology. Within the world of science in general (and ethnology in particular), there endured archaic survivals from a biblicist culture. The anthropologist Audrey Smedley has argued against a crude distinction between naturalistic knowledge and supernatural beliefs. Rather, she argues, these were often 'intertwined'. According to Smedley, 'certain theologically based assumptions and propositions survived undiluted in scientific thought'. The rise of science was accompanied by unchallenged beliefs in the 'Judeo-Christian idea of a single creation and the Noachian explication of human diversity'.[8]

Even as the nineteenth-century science of race slipped its biblical moorings and abandoned the scriptural genealogy of peoples set out in Genesis, residual patterns derived from scripture continued to shape the study of race. Indeed, George Stocking, the pre-eminent historian of anthropology, has argued persuasively that in nineteenth-century Britain the new science of ethnology emerged as an 'outgrowth' of biblical scholarship, notably from a monogenist tradition concerned with the nature of man, the origins of language and the peopling of the world. Just how 'scientific' was the dominant monogenist racial science of the nineteenth century, with its genealogical and 'migrationist' paradigms of aboriginal human unity and differentiation? The spectre of Genesis haunted the birth of ethnology. Similarly, although many ethnologists and biologists no longer traced racial pedigrees back to Noah's three sons, Ham, Shem and Japhet, several scientists nevertheless retained a curious attachment to a triadic division of races. Scientists were slow to jettison the conventions of Genesis, despite the strong affinities between their theories of racial types and the hypothesis of multiple creations. The leading French naturalist Georges Cuvier (1769–1832) was a Protestant who subscribed to the story of man's common descent but was dissatisfied with several elements in the Genesis story, including its system of chronology. Cuvier conserved a very weak version of monogenesis (verging on polygenesis), but argued that three subspecies of mankind – Caucasian, Mongolian and Ethiopian – had diverged at a very early stage in human history and had developed in isolation from one another. In Britain, Cuvier's disciple, the soldier and naturalist Charles Hamilton Smith (1776–1859), appeared to combine a monogenist position with an adherence to a tripartite scheme of races in his *Natural history of the human species* (1848). Hamilton Smith conjectured that man had originated in three basic aboriginal types, which nevertheless sprang initially from a common zone near the Gobi desert. Similarly, the French racial theorist Count Gobineau (1816–82), a proponent of racial hierarchy whose arguments were underpinned by a theory of racial types, appeared to mimic the book of Genesis in his division of mankind into three races – the white, the black and the yellow. Moreover, while Gobineau's system of racial typology seemed to lead logically to polygenist conclusions, he felt constrained nonetheless by Christian norms, and instead fastened his racial typology somewhat unconvincingly to ultimate monogenist beginnings. Throughout the nineteenth century – if not beyond – inherited biblical patterns lurked within the workings of racial science, acting as a powerful brake on the shift towards new theories – whether polygenist or evolutionary – in the biological sciences.[9] Even in today's secularised academy, as we have already seen, the legacy of the scriptures has not been totally erased from the human sciences, though such survivals now exist only in the form of an inherited nomenclature and no longer distort basic disciplinary paradigms.

Besides the central theological problem generated by Europe's encounter with the racial Other, there are a number of sub-problems or puzzles which have arisen from attempts to reconcile scriptural interpretation with the apparent 'facts' of race. What did the flesh-and-blood peoples of the Bible look like? To which races did the main characters of the scriptures belong? The various puzzles which follow are indicative of the rich interplay of racial and theological discourses in a variety of contexts. Nevertheless, these puzzles are presented here – largely shorn of context – both as a means of introducing the reader to these themes and also as a way of demonstrating the persistence of these issues (albeit in various formulations) in different periods, cultures, geographical settings, social structures and racial environments.

WAS ADAM WHITE OR BLACK?

Speculation about the colour of Adam, the first man, arises not only from a natural human curiosity but from a deeper concern about the racial identity of the first human. Of what colour was mankind originally? In particular, if Adam were created in God's likeness, does this confer a divine sanction upon a particular hue? However, more was at stake than just racial pride. Other weighty issues depended in some measure upon the colour of Adam. Indeed, the maintenance of Christianity as a viable intellectual system depended upon the assumption that the racial diversity of the world could be reconciled with the Genesis narrative of Adam, the first man. The expansion of white Europe across the globe led to a growing realisation that the extremes of racial variation posed a potential threat to the authority of the Bible, which says that all mankind is descended from Adam. Moreover, the whole Christian scheme of Fall, transmission of original sin and redemption through Christ, if it has a valid claim to universality, seems logically to require that all humans are descended from the first parents Adam and Eve. This is the position known as monogenesis, that all the peoples of the world, regardless of race, spring from a common origin. On the other hand, some observers have been so overwhelmed by the huge differences in physique, colour and visage which appear to separate races that they have posited an alternative – and heretical – notion of polygenesis, that humankind takes its rise from more than one set of original parents. One solution to this problem, which besets theology as well as science, is to conjecture how different environmental conditions might have transformed the physical appearance of the descendants of Adam and Eve, resulting in a chain of subtle gradations of hue which might eventually encompass all the racial features found across the globe. However, the plausibility of such a monogenist solution is determined by its point of departure. It is harder to suspend disbelief in the progressive environmental mutation of descendants of a white Adam into blacks (or vice versa) than in that of the descendants of an intermediately tawny Adam into both blacks and whites. But, of course, there are other factors to consider besides scientific plausibility. In particular, a solution to this problem must take into account the conventional assumption of white Christians that the Bible from start to finish is populated by whites. Thus there were two quite distinct issues in the ongoing problem of Adam's colour. One was scientific: was it easier for intellectuals committed to the biblical truth of the unity of the human species to explain the transformation of an aboriginal whiteness into racial blackness, or the other way round, to provide an acceptable scientific account of how an original black colouring became lighter, or to posit some other aboriginal hue for Adam? The other question was racial. White and black racialists alike tended to believe that theirs was the aboriginal and authentic colour of mankind. The issues were technically quite separate, but their reverberations travelled beyond the fields of science, race and theology.

The scientific issue first assumed prominence during the Enlightenment of the eighteenth century, when there was a serious attempt to explain the racial composition of the world in naturalistic terms. However, while a few daring *philosophes* were only too happy to cock a snook at the shibboleths of old-time religion, the generality of scientists, particularly in the British and American Enlightenments, tried to produce theories that did not overstep the bounds of Christian orthodoxy.

The most obvious answer which occurred to enlightened white writers on racial matters was to assume that Adam had been white like themselves. In his *Universal system of natural history* (1794–1803), the astrologer and medical scientist Ebenezer Sibly (d. 1800) came to the predictable conclusion that 'we must consider white as the stock whence all others have sprung. Adam and Eve and their posterity, till the time of the deluge, were white; in the first age of the world no black nation was to be found on the face of the earth.' Indeed, Sibly believed that no humans had reached Africa till after the dispersal from Babel, that the continent's first inhabitants had been white and that Africans had become dark only as a result of the actions of the climate there over successive generations.[10] Nevertheless, for some commentators an intermediate colour like red seemed to fit more persuasively with naturalistic explanations of racial diversification from an original hue. Was it not more plausible to trace the emergence of the full racial spectrum as a sequence of modifications of shade from a colour which stood midway between the extremes of white and black? In mid-eighteenth-century Virginia, John Mitchell (1690?–1768), a British physician interested in racial questions who lived in the colony between 1735 and 1746, argued that 'an intermediate tawny colour', found among Asiatics and native Amerindians, had been the 'primitive and original complexion' of mankind.[11] Similarly, in his *Anthropologia: or dissertations on the form and colour of man* (1808),

Thomas Jarrold (1770–1853), a Manchester physician, hazarded a solution to this vexing question of 'the colour of our first parents'. If it could be 'fully ascertained' that it was a reddish colour, then 'this would remove many difficulties; for redness is so much a medium colour, that it was well adapted for the descendants of our first parents to have commenced their migrations with'.[12]

Unsurprisingly, the identification of Adam as reddish or copper-coloured held out another kind of significance for native Amerindians. The link with Adam was seized upon by William Apess (1798–1839), a part-Pequot. Apess grew up in hardship, and was indentured for a while to white families. He then converted to Christianity and eventually became a Methodist minister. Apess had a keen sense from his own upbringing of the subordinate status of his own people, and supported campaigns to gain recognition for Amerindian rights. In his writings he also tried to boost native American self-worth and dignity. In *A son of the forest*, Apess boasted of the racial connection between Amerindians and Adam: 'I humbly conceive that the natives of this country are the only people under heaven who have a just title to the name, inasmuch as we are the only people who retain the original complexion of our father Adam.' Reinforcing this point, Apess also took the line that the native peoples of North America were of Semitic stock, being descended from the Ten Lost Tribes of Israel. Hence, it seemed unsurprising to Apess that Amerindians might more closely resemble the original Adamic appearance than Europeans, who were more distantly related, he believed, to the original Semitic line.[13]

This identification also held some appeal for black writers, who saw an opportunity here to undermine white pretensions. In his *Principia of ethnology* (1879), the black American writer Martin Delany also argued that Adam had been of a reddish complexion:

It is, we believe, generally admitted among linguists, that the Hebrew word Adam (ahdam) signifies red – dark-red as some scholars have it. And it is, we believe, a well-settled admission, that the name of the Original Man was taken from his complexion. On this hypothesis, we accept and believe that the original man was Adam, and his complexion to have been clay color or yellow, more resembling that of the lightest of the pure-blooded North American Indians. And that the peoples from Adam to Noah, including his wife and sons' wives, were all of one and the same color, there is to our mind no doubt.[14]

This position – that neither white nor black was the natural or aboriginal colour of mankind – was not uncommon among black writers.

However, another, more promising option was also open to black writers. In the medical science of the Enlightenment era, there had also sprung up another intellectually respectable tradition, which reasoned that the first man had been black. The celebrated Scottish doctor John Hunter (1728–93) took the line that modifications of colour in the natural world were 'always ... from the dark to the lighter tints'. Hunter speculated whether where there were 'specimens of a particular kind, entirely black, the whole have been originally black'. Looking at humanity, Hunter noted that few people were 'perfectly white'. Hunter redefined the 'fair man or woman' in strict terms as 'a spotted or variegated animal'.[15] Behind such generalised and discursive comments about racial colouring in mankind lurked the controversial – if not quite heretical – probability of a black Adam.

A version of this line was adopted by James Cowles Prichard, mentioned above, the leading figure in British ethnology during the first half of the nineteenth century and a stout defender of monogenesis. Prichard detected three varieties of colour in man – melanic, albino and xanthous. He went on to argue that the 'melanic' – or black – was the 'complexion generally prevalent' among most of mankind, and that 'it may be looked upon as the natural and original complexion of the human species'. Prichard made much of the phenomenon of white negroes. He also claimed that the xanthous – or yellow – variety springs up out of every melanic race. Whiteness and yellowness were offshoots of an aboriginal blackness. The implication was clear to his readers, though he did not spell it out: Adam had been black.[16]

Indeed, by the mid-nineteenth century the idea of a coloured Adam had become less distasteful to scientists worried by the need to reconcile scripture with the science of racial diversity. The Scottish Free Churchman, geologist and journalist Hugh Miller (1802–56) concluded that Adam must have stood somewhere among the many intermediate types found between the two racial extremes – according to Miller, the Goth and the Negro. If Adam – or indeed Noah – had been of 'the mingled negroid and Caucasian type – and who shall say they were not? – neither the Goth nor the negro would be so extreme a variety of the species as to be beyond the power of natural causes to produce'.[17]

But there was another less conventional solution. Examining the evidence drawn both from scripture and from the sciences, the American scientist Alexander Winchell concluded that, if Adam had been the father of all humanity, then he had not been white. On the other hand, Winchell believed it more likely that Adam had been merely the parent of the white race alone, a race preceded by pre-Adamite races of other hues. Thus, a way was found of securing the whiteness of Adam, though at the cost of downgrading him from his conventional status as the father of all humanity.[18]

WAS CAIN BLACK? WHICH RACE DID HE ENCOUNTER IN THE LAND OF NOD?

The curious story of Cain in Genesis provides a number of riddles surrounding the issues of race and the origins of mankind. Cain is now generally remembered by the public at large as the first murderer. The outline of the story ran as follows. Having been informed by God that his offering of corn to God was less acceptable to the Deity than Abel's sacrifice of sheep, Cain got into a quarrel with his brother Abel and then killed him. However, there are other aspects of the Cain narrative which have puzzled generations of interpreters. After his crime, Cain was cast out as a fugitive to wander the earth, and he was somehow marked by God, apparently for Cain's own protection. In the words of Genesis 4:15 – 'And the Lord set a mark upon Cain, lest any finding him should kill him.' What was the mark of Cain? Was it, as some racial commentators believed, blackness? However, the mystery deepens – more puzzling still were the verses which followed:

And Cain went out from the presence of the Lord, and dwelt in the land of Nod, on the east of Eden. And Cain knew his wife; and she conceived, and bare Enoch: and he builded a city, and called the name of the city after the name of his son, Enoch. (Genesis 4:16–17)

Having been cast out from the family of Adam and Eve, whom did Cain marry and which people did he recruit to follow him and to help him build the city of Enoch? Was the land of Nod, perhaps, already populated? Were any races Cain encountered there descended from someone other than Adam? Or did Cain commit incest by marrying one of his sisters? John Painter, for example, concluded that Adam's thirty-three sons and twenty-three daughters (a traditional reckoning of Adam's progeny) had intermarried with one another; but that, in the circumstances of the time, this had not been a sin: 'The sons of Adam must have married their sisters and nieces, and the second generation their first cousins: in marrying thus they committed no wickedness, seeing that it was a case of necessity.'[19] Other commentators were much less sanguine about the probability that incest was intrinsic to the biblical history of man. Morally, the best solution seemed to be some form of exogamy.

However, the alternative to a story of sin was a narrative encompassing something even more horrific – heresy, in particular the belief that there had existed pre-Adamites, men before Adam, a separately created race unmentioned in Genesis. This solution threatened to undermine the essential logic of the scriptures which told of man's Fall in Adam, the biological transmission of original sin to his descendants and then Christ's redemption of mankind on the cross. However, the rise of biblical criticism in the nineteenth century – damaging as it was to certain conventional understandings of the Bible – suggested a solution to the puzzle of Cain's marriage. Now Old Testament scholars came to recognise that there were two separate accounts of the creation of man in the first and second chapters of Genesis. While the mainstream of biblical critics took the view that these were different accounts of the same supposed event drawn from multiple sources, some orthodox literalists saw the possibility that these creation accounts might refer to two distinct, indeed historically separate, creation processes – first of the pre-Adamites, described in the first chapter of Genesis, and then of an Adamite race, detailed in the following chapter. There was, moreover, the further riddle of how to interpret the sixth chapter of Genesis. According to Genesis 6:2, after the gradual multiplication of peoples on earth, the 'sons of God' had intermarried with 'the daughters of men'. Did the 'sons of God' and 'daughters of men' refer to distinct pre-Adamite and Adamite races? In addition, Genesis 6:4 pointed out that there were 'giants in the earth in those days'. Might the existence of these different races of 'sons of God', 'daughters of men' and 'giants' provide a watertight solution to the puzzle of Cain's marriage? Cain had not committed incest and it was not necessary to advocate heresy in order to evade that conclusion, for polygenesis, however long overlooked, was implicit in the scriptures themselves.[20]

For many commentators, the mark of Cain also portended a more particular racial significance. Some, such as the author of *Clearer light*, an anonymous English tract of 1874 which dealt, among other things, with the problem of race in the scriptures, claimed that Cain was the primal ancestor of all black people: the mark upon Cain should be read as a racial transformation which included changes to the texture of his hair and the blackening of his skin. This author also maintained that at this time Adam and Eve had no other surviving children but, even if there had been, it would have been extremely unlikely that Cain had gone on to marry any of his sisters, not least because they would have been reluctant to marry their brother's murderer. Therefore the compelling conclusion was that there had been two distinct racial creations of mankind, one distinct from Adam and Eve into whose body Cain had married. Indeed, *Clearer light* proposed that the early Bible history of mankind told the story of three distinct races: the white race whose creation was mentioned in Genesis 1:27; the descendants of Adam and Eve (excluding Cain who now bore his mark) who were 'red or copper-coloured, resembling the Asiatic nations'; and the black negroid descendants of Cain.[21] By contrast, John Overton (1764–1838), the English genealogist of Christ, had identified Cain as the father of the Chinese race, a people whose very high antiquity suggested that in their east Asian remoteness they had escaped the Deluge which had engulfed the rest of the known world in the age of Noah.[22] This line persisted later in the nineteenth century in the influential work of Dominick McCausland.[23]

Champions of black pride transformed the curse of Cain. Surely white was the mark of evil? In particular, the black nationalist leader Marcus Garvey (1887–1940) inverted the white racist version of the mark of Cain. Garvey argued that Adam and Eve had been black as had their sons Cain and Abel. The subsequent whiteness of Cain and his descendants – down to modern Europeans – was a punishment for sin: 'When Cain slew Abel and God appeared to ask for his brother he was so shocked that he turned white, being the affliction of leprosy and as such, he became the progenitor of a new race out of double sin. The white man is Cain transformed, hence his career of murder from Cain to Mussolini.'[24]

WERE NOAH AND HIS SONS THE FOUNDERS OF THE GREAT RACIAL DIVISIONS OF MANKIND?

The Bible does not tell us what Noah looked like. However, in the non-canonical Apocrypha the Book of Enoch appears to describe Noah as an albino. Recording the birth of Noah the son of Lamech (106:10), it stated that 'the colour of his body is white as snow ... and the hair of his head is whiter than white wool'. Disregarding the Book of Enoch and the lack of any account in Genesis of Noah's racial characteristics or the details of his movements after the Flood, some scholars began to speculate that Noah had ended up in China, where he was remembered under another name as Fohi, the founding father of Chinese civilisation.

The identification of Fohi as Noah helped to resolve one of the trickiest areas of early modern apologetics, the difficulty encountered in

synchronising sacred history with the high antiquity of Chinese civilisation. This generated not only a complex mathematical calculation, but
also posed an acutely pressing problem for Christian chronology. How
could China's great antiquity be reconciled with the orthodox position
that the earth had been created around about 4000 BC? There was scope
to fudge the issue. Although Archbishop Ussher (1581–1656) famously
dated the Creation with some precision to 23 October 4004 BC,
chronological orthodoxy permitted a bit of leeway.[25] As a result, there
developed a line of argument that Noah himself had very promptly settled China in the immediate aftermath of the Flood. Samuel Shuckford
(d. 1754), in his *Sacred and prophane history of the world* (1728–37)
rebutted the explosive claim that Chinese history was older than the
Mosaic past, by claiming that Fohi, the first king of China, had lived
about the time of Noah around 2952 BC and indeed was a corrupted
memory of Noah himself. Shuckford found confirmation of this in
Chinese associations of Fohi with a rainbow, which had featured prominently in the Bible story of the Flood, and in the Chinese boast that
Fohi had been parentless, a rendering of the notion, according to
Shuckford, that Noah had been 'the first man in the post-diluvian world'.
Although now obscure, Shuckford's work long enjoyed some wide
influence among scholars, going through at least eight editions in Britain
and the United States up to 1858.[26] In a similar vein, Simon Berington
argued that it was not clear just where Ararat was and went on to speculate that the Ark might have come to rest in central Asia; while many of
Noah's descendants had travelled west, Berington believed that Noah
himself had gone to the East where he had established many of the
excellences in government and culture of Chinese civilisation. Indeed,
Berington contended that the utter distinctiveness of the Chinese language, which sounded 'more like the pipping of young turkeys, than a
human speech', rendered it likely that it had been the primeval language
belonging to those eastern descendants of Noah who had avoided the
confusion of tongues at Babel.[27] This identification of a Chinese
Noah finds an echo in the medical researches of the eighteenth-century
Virginian doctor, John Mitchell, who reckoned that Noah and his sons
had been 'of a complexion suitable to the climate where they resided' and
had therefore been of 'a dark swarthy, a medium betwixt black and
white', the colour of 'the southern Tartars of Asia, or northern Chinese'.[28]

Nevertheless, the sons of Noah presented a much more significant
problem than the identity of Noah himself. Ham, Shem and Japhet were
traditionally considered to be the fathers of the different divisions of

mankind, Ham of the Africans, Shem of the Hebrews, Japhet of the Europeans. Did the progeny of Noah look different, and if so why? So influential were scriptural readings of racial difference that even those scientists who wished to treat the subject of race in a naturalistic manner, detached from its biblical moorings, would long find it necessary to do battle on theological terrain. During the Enlightenment, the sceptical French biologist Claude-Nicolas Le Cat (1700–68) argued that the racial myth of the three sons of Noah – 'l'un étoit blanc, le second basané, et le troisième noir' – had been formulated in a culture unaware of the existence of the 'Red Indians' of the New World; otherwise the Book of Genesis would have told the story of the four sons of Noah. Nevertheless, Le Cat doubted whether even this number of sons was requisite to explain the wide range of colour types found across the earth:

Les auteurs de cette tradition – là ne sçavoient pas qu'il y avoit une quatrième race d'hommes couleur de cuivre, car ils auroient assurément donné à Noé quatre fils, dont chacun auroit été d'une de ces couleurs; et j'ai lieu de craindre encore que ces quatre frères n'eussent pas suffi à fournir toutes les espèces d'hommes reconnues sur la surface de la terre.

Indeed, Le Cat concluded, even if the number of Noah's sons had matched the number of racial colourings found in the world, then this still left the further puzzle, of how if Noah and his wife had been white – as tradition had it – they had produced offspring of different races: 'comment de Noé et de sa femme, qui étoit blancs, ont pu naître tous ces enfans de diverses couleurs'.[29]

The nineteenth-century American ethnologist Josiah Priest (1788–1851) took a curious – but, as we shall see, ultimately sinister – line on the providential emergence of racial divisions. Priest believed that Noah, like his ultimate ancestor, Adam, had been reddish in complexion. From the reddish race there had emerged white and black variants. However, these had not arisen as a result of gradual, natural changes, but by way of two sudden heavenly interruptions of the course of nature. Priest argued that God had intervened 'in an extraordinary and supernatural manner' to alter the skin colour of two of the babies of Noah's wife while they were still in the womb. God had given to these two sons – Ham and Japhet – 'such forms of bodies, constitutions of natures, and complexions of skin, as suited his will'. As a result, Japhet was born white, and Ham was born black. Priest was a convinced anti-abolitionist and his theory of the miraculous changes which had been wrought upon the embryonic Ham in particular was designed to refute the abolitionist notion that 'in the veins of Adam, the first man and great father of all mankind, the blood of the negro race, as well as the blood of the other races, flowed free and full'. If the abolitionists were right, then this seemed to justify the equality of races. However, Priest insisted that there was 'never any negro blood in the veins of Adam'. 'Negro blood' had been created specially by divine intervention in the embryonic Ham, on account of which Ham had been 'born a negro with all the physical, moral, and constitutional traits, which mark and distinguish that race of men from the other two races'. So far so good for the racialist Priest; but, to his alarm, he was nearly hoist on his own petard. By Priest's own reasoning, the Adamic line which passed through Shem was reddish in colour, which carried the further implication that Christ had therefore come of copper-coloured stock. Priest was adamant that the 'Saviour of mankind, though born of a Jewish copper colored woman, was nevertheless a white man'. Christ, Priest insisted, had been of a 'bright, fair complexion', with hair of a 'yellow or golden color', eyes of a 'hazel or blue cast' and with a forehead which was 'high, smooth and broad'. Christ's racial identity – as we shall see below – constituted another critical issue for Christian ethnologists, but one which was not always easily reconciled with the racial science of the Old Testament.[30]

The identification of the Noachids with the division of races came to be adopted by other cultures when they came into contact with Christianity. India provides a fascinating example of the encounter of Old Testament templates and the indigenous imagination. British scholars in India sought to reconcile Indian religion with sacred history, on the assumption that the mythologies of other cultures were misremembered or corrupted versions of the shared early history of mankind found in the first eleven books of Genesis. Their Indian amanuenses were encouraged to look out for parallels between the legends of Indian antiquity and the early part of the Old Testament. This had some unfortunate results, as in the case of Francis Wilford (1761?–1822). An apparently serendipitous Orientalist, Wilford found himself deceived by an all-too-helpful pandit who had interpolated a Noah-figure, Satyavarman, and his three sons S'arma (Shem), Kharma (Ham) and Jyapati (Japhet) into a manuscript of the Padma Purana.[31]

On the other hand, in nineteenth-century New Zealand the Maori assimilated this tripartite division of the races of the world and used it for their own purposes. The earth, they noted, had been peopled by the descendants of Taapeta (Japhet), Heema (Shem) and Hama (Ham).

Maori patriots insisted upon their ethnic origins in the noble lineage of Shem, identifying themselves closely with ancient Israel; by contrast they located the *pakeha*, or whites, as the offspring of Japhet. Moreover, the Maori also went on to fashion pedigrees for their native aristocracies out of the genealogies of prophets found in the Old Testament.[32]

DID THE CURSE UPON HAM TURN HIM AND HIS POSTERITY BLACK?

One element in the story of Noah and his sons drew particular attention from writers on racial topics. In the ninth book of Genesis is the curious tale of how Noah planted a vineyard, drank of the wine it yielded and, drunk, collapsed in his tents, his garments awry, thus accidentally exposing himself. Ham chanced upon his father in this state and gossiped about Noah's nakedness to his brothers, Shem and Japhet, who loyally covered up their father. When Noah realised what had happened, he was angry with Ham and pronounced an anathema on Ham's lineage, or to be more exact, on the line of Ham's son Canaan:

Cursed be Canaan; a servant of servants shall he be unto his brethren.
And he said, Blessed be the Lord God of Shem; and Canaan shall be his servant.
God shall enlarge Japheth, and he shall dwell in the tents of Shem; and Canaan
    shall be his servant.   (Genesis 9:25–7)

This passage appeared to justify race slavery, for the line of Ham was associated with Africa, and the passage seemed to indicate that at least some of Ham's descendants through Canaan were condemned by this patriarchal curse to be the servants of the lighter-skinned descendants of Shem and Japhet.

The curse of Ham managed to hold its own alongside naturalistic explanations of colour during the age of Enlightenment. James Boswell (1740–95) in his *Life of Johnson* (1791) records a lively discussion at Clifton's eating-house in Butcher-row on Saturday, 25 June 1763:

Johnson and an Irish gentleman got into a dispute concerning the cause of some part of mankind being black. 'Why, Sir, (said Johnson), it has been accounted for in three ways: either by supposing that they were the posterity of Ham, who was cursed; or that God at first created two kinds of men, one black and another white; or that by the heat of the sun the skin is scorched, and so acquires a sooty hue. This matter has been canvassed among naturalists, but has never been brought to any certain issue.'[33]

In 'The Ordination', the Scots poet Robert Burns (1759–96) encapsulates the story of Ham in a couplet describing a well-known biblical text to be expounded from a Scots Presbyterian pulpit:

> How graceless Ham leugh at his Dad,
> Which made Canaan a niger.[34]

Despite the insensitive frivolity of Burns's tone, the story of Ham had immense staying power and was put to very serious and sinister ends.

Some theologians questioned folkloric misunderstanding of the significance of the curse. In *Negro slavery unjustifiable* (1804), the Reformed Presbyterian pastor of New York city and uncompromising opponent of slavery, the Reverend Alexander McLeod, exposed the fragile chain of logic upon which apologists for slavery depended when they invoked the curse upon Ham's son Canaan:

In order to justify Negro slavery from this prophecy, it will be necessary to prove four things, 1. That all the posterity of Canaan were to suffer slavery. 2. That African Negroes are really descended of Canaan. 3. That each of the descendants of Shem and Japheth has a moral right to reduce any of them to servitude. 4. That every slaveholder is really descended from Shem or Japheth. Want of proof in any of these particulars will invalidate the whole objection.[35]

Nevertheless, such a precise reading tended to have less impact than the conventional misreading of the curse. According to Thomas Peterson, the story of Ham was 'certainly among the most popular defenses of slavery, if not the most popular' in the American South in the decades before the American Civil War.[36]

The legend of the curse of Ham remained a vital influence on racial attitudes into the twentieth century. In apartheid South Africa theologians of the Dutch Reformed Church – the church of 42 per cent of the white population of South Africa – still felt the need to pronounce on the question of the curse of Ham. The significance of the curse upon Ham featured in *Human relations and the South African scene in the light of scripture*, an authoritative report approved by the General Synod of the Dutch Reformed Church in October 1974. The curse, the report noted, was limited to Canaan and was 'later fulfilled in that the Canaanites became servants of the Israelites'. There was, the report pointed out firmly, 'no scriptural foundation on which the subordinate position of some present-day peoples, which is the result of all sorts of historical and cultural factors, can be related to the curse on Canaan'. However, notwithstanding this non-racialist reading of the story of Ham, the Dutch Reformed Church did not reject the authority of the book of Genesis for modern-day society. Instead it found justification for separate development in the story of the Tower of Babel. The true message of the Babel story, according to the church, lay in the unspiritual and arrogant assumption of early mankind that its destiny lay in a united body of humanity which spoke a single language, as described in Genesis 11:6. God's punishment, the confounding of languages and the scattering of peoples across the globe, was a welcome corrective, which highlighted man's true destiny in a providentially ordered pluralism, a world of separate nations and communities.[37]

DID MOSES PROVIDE A PRECEDENT FOR MISCEGENATION?

Behind white America's fear of the black male there lurked an abhorrence of miscegenation. However, on this particular point scripture presented some problems for racialists, for the Bible itself appeared to endorse miscegenation. In Numbers 12:1 the scriptures seemed to describe the marriage of Moses to a black African woman: 'And Miriam and Aaron spake against Moses because of the Ethiopian woman whom he had married: for he had married an Ethiopian woman.'

Discussion of the racial significance – or rather racial insignificance – of this passage had a long pedigree. The seventeenth-century English scholar and physician Sir Thomas Browne (1605–82) thought that the description of Moses' wife as an Ethiopian was somewhat misleading: 'the wife of Moses translated in scripture an Ethiopian, and so confirmed by the fabulous relation of Josephus, was none of the daughters of Africa, nor any Negro of Ethiopia, but the daughter of Jethro, prince and priest of Madian, which was a part of Arabia the stony, bordering upon the Red Sea'. Richard Kidder (1633–1703), an Anglican cleric working along parallel tracks, claimed that Miriam and Aaron's complaints did not concern race per se. Rather the issue at hand was the fact that Moses 'had married a stranger, and not one of the stock of Israel'. Thomas Stackhouse (1677–1752) in his *New history of the Holy Bible* (1733) noted the quarrel between Moses and his siblings over his marriage. Inter-racial marriage, however, did not seem to be the prime cause of concern. Was the bride of Moses really black? Did the term 'Ethiopian' strictly denote someone of Negroid complexion? Stackhouse thought not. He read the passage to mean that Moses had married an 'Ethiopian, or rather Arabian woman', and did not suggest that the cause of the quarrel was the issue of race, but rather a religious question of whether it was appropriate for Moses to marry into an idolatrous nation.[38]

Race loomed larger for later centuries. Opponents of exclusively white Caucasian interpretations of scripture sometimes pointed to Moses' intermarriage with another race as evidence of the anti-racial message of scripture. For instance, the Reverend J. B. Clifford of Bristol denounced the racialist interpretations of scripture which had become so pronounced during the last third of the nineteenth century. To confound racialists, Clifford claimed that the Bible itself provided numerous examples of racial intermixture, including most spectacularly the case of Moses who 'married an Ethiopian woman, descended from Ham'. The anti-racialist Clifford took tremendous comfort from such examples of ethnic intermarriage: it was 'as if God would pour contempt on all the pride of national genealogy and ancestry; and reiterate by facts, as well as by words, that Christ is the Seed, in whom alone all the nations of the earth are to be blessed'.[39] Even the Dutch Reformed Church of South Africa in its report of 1974 conceded that Moses had in fact married a black woman. The marriage was 'obviously between persons of different racial origin'. Indeed, these scrupulous literalists conceded that scripture does not in fact pronounce against mixed marriages.[40]

By contrast, some racists resorted to awkward casuistry in the face of Moses' marriage. Josiah Priest, an American critic of abolition and, of course, of miscegenation, produced the argument that Moses had contracted his marriage to the Ethiopian woman in ignorance of God's will, as the marriage had taken place about forty years before the law had been given to Moses at Mount Sinai, which placed a divine ban upon racial intermarriage. On the other hand, the leading Southern clergyman, the Belfast-born Presbyterian Dr Thomas Smyth (1808–73) of Charleston, argued of the Midianites 'from whom Moses selected his wife' that they 'could not have been negroes'.[41]

While some black theologians now take pride in the fact that Moses married a Cushite, other black nationalist commentators – particularly those who dislike racial integration as much as white racialists – question whether Moses himself had been white and whether his marriage had indeed been across racial lines. A racially ambiguous Moses, or Musa, features prominently in the doctrines inherited by the black nationalist religion, Nation of Islam. Fard Muhammad, whose teachings inspired Nation of Islam, identified Moses, or Musa, as a mulatto prophet sent by Allah to assist in the civilising of the barbaric white race.[42] The influential black nationalist minister Albert Cleage (1911–2000) also advanced the line that the marriage of Moses to the Midianite was the uncomplicated union of two blacks, Moses being the leader of the ancient black nation of Israel and, in Cleage's words, 'unquestionably all non-white'. Indeed, Cleage turned the whole notion of Mosaic miscegenation on its head. The marriage of Moses was evidence of black Israelite separatism: even when marrying out of the immediate ethnic group, the nation of Israel had deliberately avoided contact with white people.[43]

WHICH RACE CONSTITUTES THE SURVIVING REMNANT OF THE LOST TRIBES OF ISRAEL?

Perhaps the most influential of all the racial puzzles drawn from the Bible which have surfaced in the cultural and scholarly traditions of the West concerns the search for the Ten Lost Tribes of Israel.[44] The Old Testament records twelve original tribes in the Jewish nation, associated with the various sons of the patriarch Jacob: the tribes of Reuben, Simeon, Levi, Issachar, Zebulun, Dan, Naphtali, Gad, Asher, Judah, Benjamin and Joseph. The distribution of the tribes was somewhat complicated. The Levites, who functioned as a hereditary priesthood, were diffused among the other tribes, while the tribe of Joseph was split into two, the tribes of Manasseh and Ephraim. Furthermore, the tribes did not comprise a single political unit, but were divided into two distinct Jewish kingdoms. The southern kingdom of Judah included the tribes of Judah and Simeon and most of the tribe of Benjamin, while the northern kingdom of Israel was composed of the ten remaining tribes, including Ephraim and Manasseh. Between 732 BC and 721 BC, the Assyrians invaded the northern kingdom of Israel, and the ten northern tribes were removed to the lands of Assyria and Media.

Where had the Ten Lost Tribes gone? Which modern-day communities, wondered theologians, constituted the descendants of the Ten Lost Tribes? The quest was significant, for the Bible identified the Lost Tribes as the future beneficiaries of certain divine promises and blessings. The Apocrypha appeared to offer a clue as to the location of the Lost Tribes. In II Esdras 13:40–6 it was recorded that the Lost Tribes had sought security in a remote inhospitable land far beyond the narrow passages of the Euphrates river:

these are the ten tribes who were taken captive from their land in the days of King Hoshea, whom Shalmaneser, the king of the Assyrians, led away into captivity and transported them across the river; thus it was that they transferred into another land. But they decided to leave the multitude of peoples and proceed to a more remote region where no human species ever lived, and there perhaps observe their ordinances which they did not observe in their land. So, when they passed through the narrow entrances of the Euphrates River, the Most High performed miracles for them and held back the courses of the river until they had crossed over. The way through that country, which is called Arzareth, required a long trek of a year and a half. Since they have lived there . . .

A number of commentators suspected that the Ten Lost Tribes were to be found in the remoteness of Afghanistan, or in adjacent areas.[45] However, another influential strain of literature appeared during the early modern period, which identified the native American peoples of the New World as the Lost Tribes of Israel.[46] The myth of the Lost Tribes of Israel has in fact enjoyed a global resonance. Almost every culture or ethnic group on the planet has put forward some claim or other to be the genuine descendants of the Ten Lost Tribes.[47] In the mid-nineteenth century, the bizarre ideology of the British Israelites gained ground and became firmly entrenched in Protestant religious culture on both sides of the Atlantic. This was the notion that the Anglo-Saxon peoples of Britain and North America were the descendants of the Ten Lost Tribes and, more significantly, the heirs of the prophecies associated with the tribes. Thus the story of the Lost Tribes provided a justification for racial empire: it was foretold in scripture; therefore, it was argued, it was divinely sanctioned.[48]

Even more pernicious, of course, and offensive to Jewish people, was the idea that various non-Judaic peoples were true descendants of ancient Israelites and that modern Jewry was somehow of less importance in the divine dispensation. The scholarly quest for the Ten Lost Tribes displayed at different times and in different hands various combinations of genuine philo-Semitism and anti-Semitism, but at all times manifested an insensitivity towards contemporary Judaism. Eventually, the twentieth-century heirs of the British Israelites, the Christian Identity movement in North America, would exploit the puzzle of the Ten Lost Tribes to justify an openly anti-Semitic and virulently racist agenda.[49]

WAS JESUS WHITE OR BLACK?

The central figure in the New Testament, God's son, Jesus Christ, partakes both of a divine and a human nature, his human incarnation encouraging – and, to some extent, legitimising – speculation about his racial features. However, the Bible itself is silent on this question. The Bible does not describe Christ's physical appearance. Nevertheless, in a sense, most people seem to have a fixed mental image of what Christ looked like, which draws on depictions of Christ within the western tradition in art and, even more influentially today, on Hollywood depictions of Jesus on the screen. These various images – both artistic and cinematic – usually conform to a stereotype, but one ungrounded in any serious research on the historical Jesus or the ethnology of New Testament Palestine. Our image is, by definition, a bogus one, received second- or third-hand from a spurious, but resilient, canon of images. According to William Telford, 'The canonical Gospels do not tell us what Jesus looked like and so film-makers . . . have been dependent on a secondary imagined, one might even say specious misrepresentation of Jesus in art and painting.' What art has bequeathed Hollywood is 'the icon of the blond, bearded, long-haired, blue-eyed, white-robed Aryan'. This image became standard in motion pictures from Cecil B. DeMille's *The King of Kings* (1927). Sometimes Jesus is literally Nordic, as in Max von Sydow's portrayal of Christ in George Stevens's film, *The Greatest Story Ever Told* (1965). Even in Martin Scorsese's otherwise controversial motion picture, *The Last Temptation of Christ* (1988), Christ is still played by a very European-looking Willem Dafoe. Hence the shock value – for a mainstream white audience, at least – of a truly subversive film such as *Dogma* (1999), the work of a provoca-tive Roman Catholic writer-director, Kevin Smith, which suggests that Christ was black and that this fact has been obscured by the dominant white cultural tradition.[50]

Christ's racial identity became a matter of some import for modern American racists. The American anthropologist and champion of the Nordic race Madison Grant (1865–1937) read racial significance into traditional European depictions of Christ: 'In depicting the crucifixion no artist hesitates to make the two thieves brunet in contrast to the blond Saviour. This is something more than a convention, as such quasi-authentic traditions as we have of the Lord strongly suggest his Nordic, possibly Greek, physical and moral attributes.'[51] However, for the mid-nineteenth-century American defender of race slavery Buckner Payne (1799–1883), it was not enough simply to prove that Christ had been white, but to show that 'the Saviour of the world was of a white slave-holding nation'.[52]

Numerous challenges have been made to the dominant assumption of a white Christ. In the late eighteenth and early nineteenth centuries, British Orientalists turned to Indian antiquities in the hope of finding there some independent verification of the revealed truths of the Judaeo-Christian tradition. The credulous Francis Wilford appeared to have

alighted upon a Hindu folk memory of Christ when he encountered the
tale of Salivahana, the son of a virgin, who had been crucified on a
Y-shape plough.[53] But might Indian corroboration of the gospel not turn
out on closer inspection to be a more damaging Hindu Ur-narrative from
which the story of Christ was itself derivative? One English theologian
did contemplate a Christ of various racial hues, black and white and
yellow. The Reverend J. B. S. Carwithen (1781–1832) in *A view of the
Brahminical religion and its confirmation of the truth of the sacred history*
(1810) kept an open mind concerning the claims of both Christianity and
Hinduism to 'an origin equally divine'. Carwithen went on to raise the
possibility 'that Christ, the only-begotten of the Father, has probably
appeared, at different periods of time, in different parts of the world,
under various denominations, and in different forms of humanity'.[54]
However, some other scholars began not only to trace the origins of the
Christ story in Indian antiquity and legend, but also to draw out the
racial implications of an Indian prototype Christ. One of the first scholars
to suggest that Christ had not been white was the eccentric English
Orientalist Godfrey Higgins (1773–1833). In *Anacalypsis* (1836), Higgins
suggested that Christ was a distorted folk memory of a more ancient
eastern deity representative of solar power. Christ was a derivative of
'Cristna', later 'Krishna', the god of a black race in India. Proclaimed
Higgins, 'The Romish Christ of Europe is the Cristna of India', who were
both in their turn, ultimately, 'renewed incarnations of the same Being,
and that Being the solar power'. Moreover, the Christ of Europe, it
seemed, had inherited the dark racial features of Cristna. Higgins contended that 'in all the Romish countries of Europe . . . the God Christ, as
well as his mother, are depicted in their old pictures and statues to be
black'.[55] Working along parallel lines, the American mythographer Sarah
Titcomb (1841–95) claimed that depictions of Christ's appearance owed
more to ancient Aryan symbolism than to any biological reality. Christ's
reddish-blonde, wavy and abundant hair constituted the symbolic
representation of a sun-god.[56] Another version of such speculations surfaced in the work of the French mythographer Louis Jacolliot (1837–90),
who argued that the roots of biblical Christianity were to be found much
longer before in ancient India. Christianity was derivative of ancient
Indian religion. The Trinity, for example, drew upon the three creative,
preserving and spiritual principles found, respectively, in the principal
Hindu deities Brahma, Vishnu and Siva. Christ himself was borrowed from
the ancient Indian incarnated redeemer-deity Christna – also named Jezeus,
meaning 'pure divine essence' – born of a virgin named Devanaguy.[57]

Twentieth-century black America is far from convinced by white representations of a Nordic Christ. In his 1920 miscellany *Darkwater*, the black American leader and prolific writer on behalf of black causes W. E. B. DuBois (1868–1963) published a short story entitled 'Jesus Christ in Texas'. Here a Christ – whose 'hair hung in close curls far down the sides of his face and his face was olive, even yellow' – puts in appearances on both sides of the racial divide in the American South. Conventional Southern racists are troubled by the presence of this mysterious figure of indeterminate race: 'Why, the man was a mulatto, surely; even if he did not own the Negro blood, their practised eyes knew it.'[58] In 1929 another black writer, Countee Cullen (1903?–46), published a volume of poetry in which the central piece was 'The Black Christ'.[59]

Much more explicit was George Alexander McGuire (1866–1934), a disillusioned black Episcopalian priest who became active within Marcus Garvey's Universal Negro Improvement Association and primate of the related African Orthodox Church. In a sermon at the UNIA convention in 1924, Bishop McGuire rejected the traditional image of the Caucasian Christ:

If God be our Father, and we bear His image and likeness, why should we not teach our children that their Father in Heaven resembles them even as they do Him? Why should we permit the Caucasians to constantly and indelibly impress upon their youthful minds that God is white? Why should not this race, which bore the Cross of the Man of Sorrows up Mount Calvary and has borne it ever since, not claim Him as their own, since He carried in His veins the blood of Ham as well as the blood of them?

McGuire argued that 'at least two' of Christ's forebears were of 'Hamitic descent', Tamay, the mother of Phares (who was the son of Judah) and Rahab, the mother of Boaz (who was the great-grandfather of David). Jesus Christ, so McGuire's argument ran, was a lineal descendant of both Phares and Boaz, each of whom had Hamitic – and presumably black – ancestors. Mary, the mother of Christ, was of this same lineage herself. McGuire urged those responsible for mediating images of the Madonna to be true to her ethnic roots, as McGuire interpreted them: 'When, therefore, our Negro artists, with brush, chisel or otherwise, portray the Madonna for their race, let them be loyal to truth, and present the Blessed Virgin Mother and her Most Holy Child in such manner as to reveal both the Hamitic and Semitic blends.' But theology, it seemed to McGuire, remained silent on the great issues of race. He proclaimed that had Christ lived in the American South of McGuire's own era Jesus would have been a victim of its vile code of racial discrimination, a subject which Christianity tended to skirt around: 'If the Man of Sorrows lived today in Dixie with his pedigree known as it is, the color line would be drawn against Him. Why may we not write the facts down in our theology?'[60]

The mainstream Christian position that Christ's racial background is irrelevant in the light of Christ's universal colour-blind message did not go far enough for champions of the black Christ. The most influential proponent of black liberation theology, Professor James H. Cone, rudely dismissed the anxious liberal cry that 'surely Christ is above race' as a species of white liberalism which would only serve to perpetuate the ugly racist legend of a white Christ:

White liberal preference for a raceless Christ serves only to make official and orthodox the centuries-old portrayal of Christ as white. The 'raceless' American Christ has a light skin, wavy brown hair, and sometimes – wonder of wonders – blue eyes. For whites to find him with big lips and kinky hair is as offensive as it was for the Pharisees to find him partying with tax-collectors. But whether whites want to hear it or not, *Christ is black, baby*, with all of the features which are so detestable to white society.[61]

Cone has been a powerful voice in the campaign to rid theology of its unconscious as well as conscious racial assumptions. Ultimately, however, for Cone, Christ's blackness stands as a metaphor for Christ's identification with the oppressed of the earth. Other leading proponents of black theology, such as Albert Cleage, the author of *The black Messiah* (1968), were more explicit, and took the view that Jesus Christ was quite literally black. Cleage, indeed, insisted that Jesus was black and the leader of a revolutionary movement against white Roman oppression.[62]

WAS JESUS ARYAN OR SEMITIC?

Quite apart from the question of Christ's colour, there has been considerable speculation, not least from anti-Semites, about Christ's ethnic background. Some anti-Semitic Christians have found it hard to reconcile their religious commitment to Christianity with the notion that Jesus Christ was Jewish. For most people the insensitive, but unthinking, message of art and film that Jesus is white may have some subliminal influence on their racial attitudes; but, in general, it does not turn them into full-blown racists. On the other hand, as we shall see, the coincidence of the rise of racial anthropology in nineteenth-century European intellectual life alongside a shift in Christological interpretation away from a supernatural Messiah of universal significance to the immediate and particular worldly context of the historical Jesus raised, in somewhat sinister form, the issue of Jesus' racial background.

Nowhere was this more apparent than in the German world, but the racialist reading of Christ which would emerge in late nineteenth-century Germany fed on earlier developments in France. Here the renegade former seminarian Ernest Renan (1823–92), presented in his popular *Vie de Jésus* a human and historical Jesus drained of Judaic significance,[63] and, more directly, Emile Burnouf (1821–1907) distanced the origins of Christianity from the distinctive characteristics of the Semitic race and suggested that Jesus' homeland of Galilee had been an Aryan region somewhat different from the rest of Semitic Palestine. Burnouf tried to reduce the phenomenon of religion to a science, but a science whose key was racial. The story of Christianity, he argued, could be understood properly only by way of an analysis of the relative proportions of con-flicting Aryan and Semitic elements in its formation. Burnouf claimed that historically the Jewish community had been composed of two dis-tinct coexisting racial elements. While the bulk of the ancient Israelite nation had been Semitic, there was a minority based north of Jerusalem, around Galilee, which was 'probably' Aryan. Burnouf attributed the Aryan character of the Christian religion in good part to the role played by the Galilee region in the earliest days of Christianity and to the fact that Christ had spent only a short time in the undoubtedly Semitic city of Jerusalem. A racial pattern also emerged, as it appeared to Burnouf, in the chequered reception of the Christian message in its earliest days. The fact that Jesus had not been Semitic helped to explain not only the fact that Christianity's 'earliest enemies were the Semites of Judaea [who] killed Jesus', but also that Aryan Greeks and Hellenised Jews in neighbouring lands had been prominent in adopting Christ's faith and in setting up the first Christian churches.[64]

Under the influence of Aryan ethnology, Christian anti-Semites could console themselves that there was nothing Jewish about Jesus. Nobody did more to popularise the Aryan interpretation of Christ than Houston Stewart Chamberlain (1855–1927), a Germanophile Englishman who had assimilated to his adopted country with the zeal of the Germanophile convert; indeed he had become Wagner's son-in-law. In his major work *The foundations of the nineteenth century* (1899), Chamberlain asked directly whether Christ was a Jew by race. A crucial part of the answer concerned the composition of Galilee. Chamberlain claimed that the northern districts of Palestine had been home to aboriginal non-Israelites, and that these peoples had kept themselves somewhat apart from the rest of the region. Moreover, he also drew attention to the transmission of 'purely Aryan blood' into Galilee by means of Phoenician and Greek migration as well as Assyrian colonisation. The result was 'a strong admixture of non-Semitic blood'. Moreover, the Galileans, it seemed, did not speak Hebrew. Chamberlain concluded that it was a strong probability, if not a near certainty, that Jesus had not been Jewish. Race mattered in this instance, as Chamberlain believed that the form of the skull within a race community determined its basic thought patterns. Chamberlain sharply contrasted the mental characteristics of the Jews and their materialistic idolatry with the imaginative superiority of the Aryan mind, and, by extension, Aryan religion. Primitive Christianity had not, as far as Chamberlain was concerned, started its long and chequered history bearing the imprint of the Jews.[65]

Chamberlain's views were influential. Abroad, the American racial theorist Madison Grant claimed that 'the Jews apparently regarded Christ as, in some indefinite way, non-Jewish'.[66] At home Chamberlain's views were amplified by German biblical scholars and theologians during the first half of the twentieth century. Moreover, Christ became a totem of Aryan manliness among pro-Christian Nazi ideologues. Artur Dinter, Gauleiter of Thuringia and a bestselling writer under the acknowledged influence of Chamberlain, was emphatic on the subject of Christ's Aryanhood. Furthermore, Dietrich Klagges, a friend of Goebbels, argued that Christ had led his fellow Galileans against Jewish hegemony in the region, portraying Christ as a sturdy opponent of Judaism.[67]

On the other hand, there was also a decisively pagan alternative to the Aryan reading of Christ. During the late nineteenth and early twentieth centuries there were intimate and ideologically important connections in Germany between theories of the occult and the promotion of racial purity. Many thinkers dabbled in the occult, especially in supposedly ancient pagan mysteries which were identified as the religious worship of their Aryan ancestors. One branch of this racialist mysticism involved the debunking of Christ as a recent impostor, superimposed upon a more remote Germanic deity, Krist. Behind the supposed 'Christ', figures such as Rudolf Gorsleben and Karl Maria Wiligut identified an ancient Aryan Krist religion.[68]

There were marked tensions between proponents of Aryan paganism and Aryan Christianity. Indeed, the Nazi ascendancy marked a potential crisis for even the most racist German Christians, for there was no clear Nazi consensus on the subject of religion. Christians were forced on to the defensive when confronted with the claims of some leading Nazi ideologues that Christianity was quintessentially Jewish and un-German, and ought to be replaced with a pagan religion native to the German *Volk*. The alternatives were to jettison Christianity or to refurbish it as an acceptable Aryan religion. Similarly, what policy, German Christians wondered, should they adopt with regard to the Old Testament? Should it be discarded as a relic of Jewish religion or preserved as an integral feature of Aryan Christianity? Between 1939 and 1945 the Institute for the Study and Eradication of Jewish Influence on German Church Life, based at Eisenach in Thuringia, worked under its director, Professor Walter Grundmann, to revive an authentic Christianity purged of its alien Judaic corruptions. Grundmann published a life of Jesus in which he argued that Jesus had been a Galilean and, hence, most probably Aryan. Other scholars within the German scholarly tradition had pronounced the Galilee of Jesus' time to be either *judenrein* or Jewish only in so far as its non-Semitic inhabitants had been forced to convert to Judaism. To describe Christ as Jesus of Galilee or Jesus the Galilean was to employ a racially loaded nomenclature. Professor Susannah Heschel concludes that by this stage German New Testament scholarship was no longer simply committed to a quest for the historical Jesus but had become deeply implicated in justifications of anti-Semitism and the legitimation of Nazi ideology.[69]

Adolf Hitler himself absorbed elements of the tradition of the Aryan Christ. It mattered enormously to the leader of Nazism that Christ had not come from Semitic stock. In his table talk Hitler discussed Christ's Galilean background and its ethnological significance: 'Galilee was a colony where the Romans had probably installed Gallic legionaries, and it's certain that Jesus was not a Jew. The Jews, by the way, regarded Him as the son of a whore – of a whore and a Roman soldier.' This is a reference to the legend, found in the second-century pagan philosopher Celsus and in rabbinical sources, that Christ's father had been a Gallo-Roman legionary called Panthera, or Pandera. Hitler blamed St Paul for the Semitic corruption and 'decisive falsification' of the Galilean's anti-Jewish message into a species of Judaeo-Bolshevism: 'If the Jew has succeeded in destroying the Roman Empire, that's because St Paul transformed a local movement of Aryan opposition to Jewry into a super-temporal religion, which postulates the equality of all men amongst themselves, and their obedience to an only god.'[70]

At first glance some of these puzzles seem esoteric, antiquarian and the insignificant stuff of theologians' parlour games. Nevertheless, the

intimate association between German repudiations of Jesus' Jewishness
and the regime responsible for the Holocaust serves as a warning that
questions of racial identity, even concerning the identities of remote
biblical characters, can have serious social and political consequences. The
Nazi regime provides only the most obvious and obnoxious example of
the ideological salience of such puzzles. The strategy of African-American
leaders and writers to challenge complacent white assumptions that the
Bible was peopled by white Europeans and that Jesus was of a blond,
Nordic appearance has had ramifications well beyond the realm of
theology in boosting black American self-confidence and political, as well
as religious, activism. After all, on the other side of the racial divide,
slaveholders and their apologists had utilised the curse upon Ham to
justify to a Christian society the enslavement of generations of African-
Americans. Even today the movement of 'white nationalist' reaction in
the United States against the achievement of civil rights for blacks and
what is considered to be a Jewish-controlled mainstream media draws
considerable inspiration from the literature of the search for the Ten Lost
Tribes of Israel.

The remit of the study which follows has been limited to Protestantism
within the Atlantic world.[71] The emphasis that Protestantism places on
the individual's freedom to interpret scripture has generated an enormously rich literature on the question of the Bible's racial significance.
Indeed, in some cases this has triggered an intense engagement with the
words, logic and narrative coherence of scripture, leading interpreters into
positions which were conventionally assumed to be heretical. Subjected to
certain impeccably Protestant strategies of close reading, scripture
appeared to yield the presence on earth of men before Adam – in the eyes
of the orthodox, surely phantom pre-Adamites whose very being ran
counter to the consensus of Christian tradition and whose hypothesised
existence must have originated in hermeneutic error. Such findings not
only posed problems for defenders of biblical authority and the systems of
theology that flowed from acceptance of the scriptures, but also had an
impact on the significance, relationships and genealogy of races. Moreover, on the fringes of the Protestant world, particularly in the United
States, some religious groupings – as we shall see in chapter 7 – came to
stake their claims to biblical truth and denominational distinctiveness on
interpretations of those portions of scripture from which an ethnological
or racialist message might conceivably be drawn. Both 'Protestantism'
and the 'Atlantic world' have been broadly and generously defined, with

the latter not excluding, for example, British discussions of the races and religions found in its vast empire to the east in India. More controversially, perhaps, 'Protestantism' is justifiably stretched to embrace groupings whose origins (if not their primary identities) lie within Protestant culture, including, for example, Mormonism, black Hebrews and even Nation of Islam. Such a blanket definition is not intended in any way to indicate disrespect towards these religions, merely to point out the influence of a Protestant culture of hermeneutic freedom in shaping the extra-Christian fringe of religiosity, particularly in the United States. New religions coined in the nineteenth and twentieth centuries bore an imprint from the Protestant norms of the surrounding culture, as well as, in some cases, from the racial attitudes of the culture in which they emerged. It should also be stressed that, as no one scholar is now capable of mastering even the North American literature on race between 1600 and 2000, the historical investigations which follow are meant to be suggestive rather than exhaustive or comprehensive.

CHAPTER 3

Race and Religious Orthodoxy in the Early Modern Era

Race was not a central organising concept of intellectual life or political culture during the early modern era. Ironically, during the age of European expansion, when so many indigenous peoples of the New World and transported slaves from Africa suffered at the hands of exploitative white Europeans, white domination did not rest on articulate theories of white racial superiority. Other arguments – whether derived from the Christian imperative to spread the Word of God through missions or from theories of natural law concerning the connection between proper use of the land and rights to its ownership – were used to justify European superiority and expropriation.[1] Racial identity was subliminal, though no less potent in its effects. 'Whites' conquered the world without any overt ideology of white superiority.

Although doctrinal racism was not a feature of the early modern Atlantic world, the absence of racialist doctrine did not mean that racist prejudice was similarly invisible. Racist attitudes existed, but, significantly, did not rest upon clearly articulated theories of racial difference. Race – like ethnicity and even national consciousness (as distinct, say, from allegiance to one's monarch) – was a matter of second-order importance behind primary commitments to church and state.[2] Political and confessional alignments were more prominent than pride in ethnic or racial identities.

Forms of early modern racism did exist, but they should not be parsed anachronistically in terms of modern expectations about their sources, idioms or resonance. There were intellectual limits to racial consciousness. Strictly speaking, the disciplines of ethnology or linguistics did not exist in anything like their forms in the nineteenth century, when systems of classifications emerged to categorise physical races and language families.[3] During the early modern era there were some attempts to classify languages, but nothing on the scale of what was to follow Sir William Jones's breakthrough in the late eighteenth century.[4] Commentators did of course note empirical differences between peoples; but they did not possess the intellectual equipment to taxonomise 'peoples' into 'races'. Instead race occupied a marginal position in early modern intellectual discussion, except as it related to the theological problems associated with the origins and distribution of mankind. In so far as the intelligentsia of early modern Europe marshalled forces to tackle the issue of race, it was primarily to defuse the explosive potential of racial difference as a weapon in the hands of religious heterodoxy.

Indeed, we should not exaggerate the self-confidence of an expanding white Christendom. The age of European discovery generated a peculiar set of intellectual and psychological problems for white Christendom, as well as the more obvious material opportunities for exploitation, plunder and conquest. Race, as we shall see throughout much of this book, not only fostered a sense of innate superiority in the dominant white race; it also functioned, at different periods and in various ways, as an incubator of anxieties. These anxieties had little to do with the ways in which white people compared themselves to peoples of other races, but nonetheless touched upon a crucial sense of self. This was because race threatened to undermine the scriptural foundations of Christian religion. Not only was race a matter of apparent 'fact' about which the Bible had nothing directly to say, but the discoveries of new races and civilisations seemed in certain respects to call into question the authority of the scriptures.

Race constituted but one of a number of intellectual problems generated by the outside world, and especially by the expanding world beyond the former horizons of medieval Christendom, which early modern defenders of Christianity needed to accommodate to the ultimate fact of Christian orthodoxy. These discordances included the vast disparity in the chronologies of the pagan and Christian worlds; the very existence of apparently civilised cultures which flourished in the absence of Christian revelation; and the claims to divinity of non-Christian godheads. Why did the Bible say nothing about America? How was it peopled? How could the author of Genesis, Moses, be so sure about the global extent of the Flood and its universal impact on an erring mankind if he were ignorant of the wider geography of the continents beyond the Middle East? Moreover, the sheer diversity of the world's races, as well as their religions and languages, proved something of an Achilles heel for generations of Christian theologians. How could scholars account for such differentiation from common origins within a chronology that stretched back only to 4004 BC or thereabouts?[5]

Attempts to make sense of racial differences belonged mainly to the province of para-theology, those auxiliary regions of theology which included sacred history, sacred geography, sacred geology and a pejorative strain of comparative religion whose rationale was the reconciliation of paganism to the ultimate, universal and only truth of Christianity. Sacred geography, for example, was a vital branch of a nascent discipline of geography which was far removed from its secularised modern-day successor: in realising the full sense of scripture it was important to calibrate place names and tribal groupings mentioned in the Bible with modern-day locations, toponyms and ethnic names. Every question in the sphere of ethnology was examined principally in the light of its relationship to theological orthodoxy.[6] The peopling of the New World was first and foremost a theological conundrum, and only secondarily an ethnological question which might be settled on its own terms. This outlook would remain respectable in the highest circles of intellectual life well into the age of Enlightenment. In 1773 master's candidates at Harvard tackled the thorny issue 'Were the aborigines of America descended from Abraham?'; and decided that they were.[7]

Nor did science in the early modern era constitute a separate sphere of intellectual life wherein the topic of race might be investigated free of religious constraints. Despite the trend towards experimentation, early modern science remained a discipline rooted in textual exegesis, whether of the ancients, such as Aristotle, or the Bible. Indeed, as Peter Harrison has shown, one of the characteristic features of science within the early modern Protestant world was the decline of the textual authority of the likes of Aristotle, the 'pope' of pre-Reformation scholasticism, and the rise in the scientific authority of the Bible. Critical humanist scholarship came to value not only the most pristine texts of the ancients, but the de-Catholicised text of the Bible as a supremely reliable ancient source. The humanist turn *ad fontes* enhanced the status of the Bible in the academic mainstream of science and scholarship, at least until the advent of the Higher Criticism in the nineteenth century. Far from the scientific revolution of the seventeenth century contributing to the demise of scripture, warns Harrison, the emergence of early modern science went hand in hand with a positive reappraisal of the scientific value of the Bible. Indeed, Protestant scientists read the Bible and the natural world – God's book of nature – in tandem as complementary 'texts'. In addition, Harrison also notes that early modern Protestant exegesis witnessed a marked retreat from symbolic and allegorical readings of scripture towards a more literal treatment of the Bible. To be sure, Protestant exegesis did consider typological readings of scripture in which some events or characters in the Old Testament were seen to prefigure developments in the New Testament; but Harrison makes clear that these approaches were quite distinct from allegorical readings and were not out of step with a literal interpretation of the Bible as a reliable guide in the fields of science and history. The Old Testament set out, in plain terms and unmediated by allegory – so early modern Protestant scholars believed – the creation of the world, the origin of humankind and the ancient history of the world from earliest times. In parallel, the realm of nature too was denuded of symbolic significance. Nature and scripture consisted of facts, not of signs and symbols.[8]

Equally, the Old Testament lay well within the realm of scientific discourse. Indeed, it appeared to invite biological investigation. Early modern scientists explored the biological consequences of the Fall, the Flood and the confusion at Babel. One major source of perplexity was the remarkable longevity of Old Testament patriarchs relative to humanity in the early modern era. Might some of the events described in Genesis have wrought significant changes in the constitution of the human body? Indeed, some wondered whether the stature of man had been diminished by the trauma of the Flood. Patriarchal man had also enjoyed other physical advantages, according to Richard Cumberland (1632–1718), the bishop of Peterborough, who argued against the supposed impossibility that Noah and his three sons and their wives had peopled the whole world after the Flood. Back in patriarchal times, Cumberland argued, men were more virile than today and enjoyed greater longevity; thus, 'the constitution of such long-lived men must needs be much stronger than ours is, and consequently more able and fit to propagate mankind to great numbers than men can and now do'.[9]

However, such curiosities from the bizarre borderlands which overlapped the zones of biology and theology serve as a reminder of the wider ideological significance of the peopling of the whole world from the loins of Noah and his family. During the early modern era theological concerns helped to inhibit – and at the very least to circumscribe – the articulation of racial prejudices and the formulation of identities based upon race. The orthodox belief in common biological origins transmuted what might be viewed in different circumstances as ethnic Otherness into a form of ethnic cousinage, however distant. All genealogies led back to the patriarch Noah. To suggest that racial distinctions were innate and the gulf between races unbridgeable was to risk courting accusations of heresy.

Seventeenth- and eighteenth-century Protestant ethnologists did not conceive of race and ethnicity in terms of innate, aboriginal differences between groups. Rather, they related the apparent differences, dissimilarities and distances among the world's races and peoples to the basic knowledge revealed in the Old Testament that the population of the world constituted a family, the lineage of Noah. Thus, scripture dictated that beneath the world's ethnic diversity there was a web of family relationships. The focus of early modern ethnology was on filling in gaps in mankind's family tree. Genesis 10 and other parts of scripture, including stray references in chapters 27 and 38 of Ezekiel, provided snatches of ethnological information regarding the connections between different groups, but the Bible provided only fragments of the possible family tree which scholars, using linguistic and other techniques (including the calibration of these findings against the Old Testament narrative), might attempt to reconstitute. Early modern Christian anthropologists did not immediately presume an unbridgeable gulf between the white European self and the non-European Other, but were led by scriptural imperatives to explore how the Other might fit with the knowledge of the dispersion of peoples found in Genesis 10 and 11; whether any particular Other might belong to the lineages of Ham, Shem or Japhet and their descendants, as set out in Genesis 10; and how the religious practices of the Other might be related to the original common religion of Noah. In the orthodox mainstream of early modern Protestant anthropology all lines of enquiry led back to Noah. Ultimately, race and ethnicity involved questions of pedigree: did an ethnic group descend from the line of Ham or Shem or Japhet?

According to the English Baptist minister and biblical commentator John Gill (1697–1771), the Table of Nations in Genesis 10 served several important purposes:

> to show the original of the several nations of the world, from whence they sprung, and by whom they were founded; and to confute the pretended antiquity of some nations, as the Egyptians, Chaldeans, Chinese, and others; and to point out the particular people, which were to be the seat of the church of God for many ages, and from whom the Messiah was to spring.[10]

The generality of seventeenth- and eighteenth-century commentators on anthropological questions upheld the line taken in *The ancient patriarchs' peregrination* (1600) that Noah, his wife and his sons, Ham, Shem and Japhet, and their wives had made up the entirety of mankind in the aftermath of the Flood.[11] This remained an orthodox tenet of belief and the necessary starting point for enquiries into the origins of races and nations.

To those who patrolled the outworks and external ramparts of biblical authority against infidel assailants, the origins of nations constituted an issue which also fell within their remit. It featured prominently in the concerns of Francis Lee (1661–1719), a one-time mystical Philadelphian who turned to a more conventional high church piety. Lee's *Apoleipomena* (1752) constituted a stalwart defence of the authority of the Mosaic scriptures against the cavils of contemporary deists and freethinkers as well as errors inherited from the deluded mythologies of pagan antiquity. Lee insisted that a proper understanding of ethnic origins must proceed from the historical truths set out by Moses in Genesis. It was a particular bugbear of Lee's that so many ancient nations – including the Egyptians, the Scythians and the Pelasgians of Greece – had propounded the gratifying national vanity of their self-origination. On top of the delusion of autochthonous origins, Lee also noticed that many nations had claimed to have a pedigree that stretched back beyond the orthodox limits of biblical chronology. Such pretensions were not only absurd, but contrary to the clear word of scripture. Indeed, the Bible provided a potent antidote to the errors that arose from national pretensions. What the scriptures revealed, according to Lee, was a web of relationships amongst all the peoples of the world. Moreover, ethnography seemed to confirm the message of scripture about the common origins of the world's peoples. How, asked Lee, could one account for the 'very remarkable concord and conformity among nations, even the most distant, in some particular customs, sacred and civil'? Communication between far-flung cultures would have been an impossibility. In addition, some of these cultural similarities were too 'arbitrary' – tales of universal deluges, for example – to be explicable in terms of universal reason. Only the Mosaic narrative of the origins of peoples made sense of the core of commonality found in the various cultures and religions of the world. The Old Testament underpinned Lee's proclamation of the 'general consanguinity of all the nations of the earth'. Yet this sense of universal consanguinity did not preclude the sense of a special affiliation with a particular lineage, whether from Ham, Shem or Japhet. Lee maintained that there was 'no nation, at this day, upon the earth, but it is very possible to show how they might be descended from one of the three heads of mankind; and to which of these three they are more related than the other two'.[12]

However, this is not to suggest that the demands of theological orthodoxy totally cramped intellectual curiosity, scepticism or combative disagreement. There was plenty of scope for argument and disputation within the permitted boundaries of theological orthodoxy. There was nothing monolithic, for example, about the ethnological literature on the Tower of Babel. The historicity of the Tower of Babel was believed to be well established; on the other hand, there were disputes about just what had happened to language at Babel. One burning issue concerned the number of languages into which the universal tongue had been confounded at Babel. Estimates ranged from seventy-five languages to as low as fifteen, though most calculations tended to cluster around seventy. The English geographer Peter Heylyn attacked as a vain 'conceit' the traditional speculation that seventy languages had sprung up suddenly at Babel, twenty-six in the line of Shem, fourteen in that of Japhet and a further thirty Hamitic languages. In Heylyn's reckoning, the linguistic changes at Babel had been much more limited.[13]

There was room for considerable divergence and sometimes significant nuance in renderings of the tragic confusion of tongues which had followed Babel. Simon Patrick (1626–1707), the bishop of Ely, wondered whether the Semites had been involved in the building of Babel, and contemplated the possibility that they had escaped punishment, thus retaining their ancient language, Hebrew. Similarly, the eastern descendants of Noah might well have escaped the trauma of Babel. Patrick also took a very narrow view of the confounding of languages. God, he claimed, had not made 'every one speak a new different language, but they had such a confused remembrance of the original language which they spake before, as made them speak it very differently'. As a result of variations in 'inflections, terminations, and pronunciations', these dialects had become as distinct as the romance languages were to Latin.[14] By contrast, John Webb (1611–72), the English Sinologist (who is better remembered as an architect), took the view that Chinese was the primitive language of mankind. Predictably, Webb's Sinology was shaped more by Christian theological imperatives than by any desire to understand China on its own terms. What mattered to Webb was how the linguistics and ethnology of China might help to solve problems in the interpretation of scripture.[15] Similarly, Simon Berington indicated that Chinese had a much better claim than Hebrew to have been the original tongue.[16] While many commentators traced the underlying unity of the world's languages back to a hypothesised Ur-language which had been corrupted at Babel, others, most prominently William Wotton (1666–1727), took the line that such was the huge and inexplicable variety of the world's languages that only a providential miracle such as had occurred at Babel could account for it. Yet even Wotton perceived patterns which connected languages. The Japhetic languages, he noted, 'agreed in some common principles'.[17]

Such was the relatively low profile of race in the public discourse of the early modern era that sometimes elements in sacred history that to later generations appeared replete with obvious racial significance summoned forth decidedly non-ethnological interpretations. Joseph Charles (1716–86), vicar of Wighton in Norfolk, eschewed ethnological and philological speculation in his treatise *The dispersion of the men at Babel considered* (1755). Instead Charles advanced a spiritual and prophetic interpretation of the dispersion at Babel, arguing that the miracle of the confusion of tongues was intended to effect wholly religious purposes. The Hebraic line of Shem, Charles contended, had been separated from the rest of humanity after Babel, in order more easily to preserve the true religion for posterity. The purity of worship of the one true God was more likely to be maintained among a single isolated community than among the undifferentiated mass of humanity. Thus, although the miracle at Babel had brought about the separation of peoples, Charles insisted that its ethnological effects were secondary and instrumental to ulterior religious purposes. In general, race mattered less to early moderns than their twenty-first century descendants imagine.[18]

Early modern ethnology was dominated by the troubling intellectual consequences which flowed from the discovery of the 'New World'. Why had the Bible made no mention of this continent? More worrying, how had this land a distant ocean away been peopled from the Old World after the Flood? Indeed, had the universal deluge described in scripture covered a far-flung continent of which Moses – the supposed author of Genesis – had appeared to have no knowledge? The truth of Christianity and the coherence of its theological system depended crucially on the question of how America had been settled. If the people of America turned out to be an autochthonous race which had sprung up separately from the rest of humanity, then the universality of original sin and of the corresponding gospel promise of redemption was a nonsense.

Commentators employed a number of strategies and lines of explanation to reconcile the peopling of America with the norms of sacred history. Might the natives of North America be descendants of the Lost Ten Tribes of Israel, or perhaps seafarers, whether Vikings or Carthaginians, or even wandering Tartars from northern Asia? Amerindian ethnography was strongly inflected by theological anxieties about the real identity of native Americans. Observers paid less attention to understanding native

Americans as they were than to reconciling what was known about them to the culture, beliefs, languages and appearance of other ethnic groups in the Old World from whom they might have been descended. The beginnings of comparative ethnology owe a debt of sorts to monogenist concerns. Comparison was a means of fitting Amerindian peoples within the permitted parameters of sacred history.[19]

However, not all intellectuals were convinced. Instead there were intimations of polygenesis from various quarters, including the pioneering German scientist Paracelsus (1493–1541) and the subversive Italian friar, Giordano Bruno (1548–1600).[20] However, these sporadic rumblings had been drowned out by the chorus of explanation recounting the possible Old World origins of the population of the New World. Nevertheless from the mid-1650s this issue assumed enormous proportions, and was, arguably, for a while at least, the dominant concern of theologians across Europe. The otherwise divided clerisies of seventeenth-century Christendom united in horror at the scandalous theological speculations of Isaac La Peyrère (1596–1676). In *Prae-Adamitae* and *Systema theologica ex praeadamitarum hypothesi pars prima*, a devastating ensemble of amateur theology which threatened the established canons of the discipline, La Peyrère opened out hitherto neglected wrinkles in scripture to reach the unwelcome conclusion that there had been men before Adam. Published anonymously in Holland in 1655, the work soon went through four reprints, as well as translations into Dutch and English. Moreover, it immediately provoked a tremendous anti-pre-Adamite backlash. By 1656 at least a dozen rebuttals had been published. La Peyrère remained a heretic to be reckoned with long after his death, and refutations of his work continued to flow from the presses during the eighteenth century. Richard Popkin, the leading historian of La Peyrère's heresy, has remarked that, notwithstanding his present obscurity, La Peyrère was 'considered the greatest heretic of his day'.[21]

Certainly, La Peyrère's close reading of scripture involved a substantial revision of the sacred narrative and, to all intents, a highly personal freestyle rendering of the main contours of Christianity. However, unlike many other open critics of Christianity, La Peyrère was a slippery, possibly accidental, heretic, and his motivations are difficult to parse. La Peyrère came from a Calvinist background in Bordeaux. It seems that he took the Protestant freedom to interpret scripture to a radical extreme. He wrestled with scripture on his own terms, and his Protestantism gave him the confidence to persist with his unorthodox speculations. If Protestantism meant anything, it meant not abasing one's God-given faculties of understanding before established canons of interpretation. But the ultimate aim, it seems, was to strengthen rather than, as it appeared to most contemporaries, to weaken the logic and authority of the Christian scriptures. La Peyrère's heresy did not verge upon atheism, but focused to an even greater extent than traditional theology on the role of the nation of Israel in the divine plan for mankind. Messianism, rather than scepticism, prejudiced La Peyrère's approach to the scriptures. The criticisms of orthodox theology and sacred history found in the *Prae-Adamitae* ran in conjunction with the messianic interpretation of the history and divine purpose of the Jewish people to be found in La Peyrère's *Du rappel des Juifs* (1634). Thus, although the pre-Adamite theory of La Peyrère was polygenist in its anthropology and daring in its adoption of a critical approach to scripture, the whole project was underpinned by La Peyrère's exaggerated respect for the leading role played by the Jews in sacred history proper. Indeed, La Peyrère divided human history into four phases, a pre-Adamite phase followed by three eras of sacred history proper, involving the election of the Jews, their rejection and their eventual recall. Polygenesis was the obverse of a Messianic and philo-Semitic reading of scripture and history, whereby the rest of mankind was assigned to a walk-on role in the divine narrative.[22]

However, La Peyrère had a most unusual point of departure. He milked to the full the apparent (though far from obvious) pre-Adamite implications of Romans 5:12–14:

As by one man sin entered into the world, and by sin, death: so likewise death had power over all men, because in him all men sinned. For till the time of the law sin was in the world, but sin was not imputed, when the law was not. But death reigned from Adam into Moses, even upon those who had not sinned according to the similitude of the transgression of Adam, who is the type of the future.

La Peyrère did not accept the conventional view that by the law was meant Mosaic law. Instead La Peyrère reached the conclusion that only with the creation of Adam had the law come into force, but that sin – though in a state of nature, and without moral significance or the formal imputation of sin – had existed before Adam. Who were these amoral pre-Adamite sinners? There must have been humans – moral beings – in this world, concluded La Peyrère, before the creation of Adam. One heretical supposition led logically to another, and then another, until very little of the basic narrative of Genesis was left intact. As a result, La Peyrère's heresies were manifold. He questioned the accuracy and integrity of extant versions of the Bible. The Bible, La Peyrère claimed, moreover, did not set out the early history of humanity as a whole: it only narrated the history of the Jews. The history of the Jews began with Adam, but there had been men before Adam. The Bible did not tell the universal history of mankind. Nor had the Flood been a universal catastrophe, being rather a local inundation which had affected Palestine, the land of the Jewish race, but whose effects had not been felt further afield in the lands of the descendants of the pre-Adamites. In this way, La Peyrère was also able to reconcile the long chronologies of pagan history with the 'truth' of the Hebrew history found in the Bible. The diverse peoples and cultures of the world need not be forced into the Procrustean bed of a supposed monogenist orthodoxy. Moreover, La Peyrère was so alert to inconsistencies in scripture that he came to another heretical conclusion, that the Pentateuch as it had been handed down to Christianity could not have been the work of Moses, but had been copied from originals.[23]

La Peyrère found himself under intense pressure. Arrested by the archbishop of Malines in the Spanish Netherlands where he had gone to escape the storm, La Peyrère converted to Catholicism and promised to recant his errors. He went to Rome, and in 1657 abjured his heresies in the presence of the pope. Catholicism provided a convenient refuge for La Peyrère: now, untroubled by the Protestant imperative to make sense of scripture for himself, he could leave the ultimate determination of the meaning of scripture to the papacy. Notwithstanding this dramatic recantation, La Peyrère continued to flirt with pre-Adamite theory and was reluctant to concede that his previous reading of scripture was inconsistent with reason. He spent his last years in a monastic retreat near Paris dabbling with Messianism and pre-Adamism, his inclination towards a Protestant-inspired root-and-branch revision of Christian tradition indulged under cover of his prudent acknowledgement of papal authority.

Regardless of the ecclesiastical contortions undergone by La Peyrère, Christian apologists from all confessions remained troubled by the pre-Adamite heresy and continued to denounce its shortcomings. According to Popkin, La Peyrère was 'one of the most frequently refuted authors of the period 1655–1800'.[24] In late seventeenth- and early eighteenth-century England, La Peyrère was as notorious a bogeyman as the homegrown heretic Thomas Hobbes. Attacks on pre-Adamism became a staple of English ethnological writings during the second half of the seventeenth century. Edward Stillingfleet (1635–99), the future bishop of Worcester, devoted a section of his mammoth *Origines sacrae* (1662) to a refutation of the pernicious pre-Adamite heresy. This kept La Peyrère and pre-Adamism in the public eye, as the work was reissued eight times by 1709.[25] Stillingfleet recognised that pre-Adamism as conceived by La Peyrère threatened not only the truth of scripture, but also some of the fundamental tenets of Christianity, including the Fall:

> the peopling of the world from Adam ... is of great consequence for us to understand, not only for the satisfaction of our curiosity as to the true origin of nations, but also in order to our believing in the truth of the scriptures, and the universal effects of the fall of man. Neither of which can be sufficiently cleared without this. For as it is hard to conceive of how the effects of man's fall should extend to all mankind, unless all mankind were propagated from Adam; so it is inconceivable how the account of things given in scripture should be true, if there were persons existent in the world before Adam was ...

Stillingfleet realised that La Peyrère's interpretation of the pre-Adamite provenance of pagan cultures made a nonsense of the universal biological transmission of original sin. As Stillingfleet recognised, the pre-Adamite heresy was not an eccentric antiquarianism which merely nibbled away at the margins of Old Testament folklore, but a threat to the very foundations of the faith. In response to La Peyrère's treatment of non-Jewish history, Stillingfleet presented his own version of the diversification of humanity from a common Adamic origin. Diversity had not preceded Adam, but arose from the progressive dispersal and cultural differentiation of the offspring of Adam's descendant, Noah, throughout the world.[26] Similarly, in *The primitive origination of mankind, considered and examined, according to the light of nature* (1677), the jurist Sir Mathew Hale (1609–76) condemned various aspects of the pre-Adamite heresy, including the theory of a local deluge and the notion that the Old Testament was coherent only as a history of the Jewish people. Rather, Hale countered, the history of the wider population of the world's continents was eminently compatible with the scheme of history set out in the Old Testament. The population of the New World did not stand as an implicit rebuke to the authority of scripture. There were, after all, various plausible explanations of how the New World had come to be peopled by the Adamite descendants of the Old.[27] The ethnic Other of the Americans was assuredly not a biological Other.

Polygenesis, moreover, was not only wrong in itself, its whole tendency lay in the direction of immorality. Monogenesis meant that inter-racial brotherhood was an ethical imperative. Several English theologians cited

Acts 17:26, which became the central text of monogenist theology. Religious doctrine did not, of course, prevent race enslavement within the British Empire, but, just as clearly, it did nothing to endorse such behaviour towards other races. According to Richard Kidder, the monogenist account found in the sacred history of the origins of mankind served to inhibit chauvinistic boasting and to encourage a philanthropic attitude towards the different races of the world:

> God thought fit to make one man to be the head and parent of the whole race of mankind, that men might not boast and vaunt of their extraction and original (as the Jews have observed) and that they might think themselves under an obligation to love and assist each other as proceeding from the same original and common parent . . . [28]

The Dissenting cleric and biblical scholar, Nathaniel Lardner (1684–1768), drew a similarly philanthropic conclusion from scriptural ethnology:

> all men ought to love one another as brethren. For they are all descended from the same parents, and cannot but have like powers, and weaknesses, and wants. Solomon says, Proverbs 27:19, 'As in water (or any other mirror), face answers to face, so the heart of man to man.' By considering ourselves we may know others: what they want, how we may relieve and comfort them. And this thought should abate exorbitant pride. For, notwithstanding some differences of outward condition, we have all the same nature, and are brethren.

But the main object of this brand of theology was not so much to spread ethical sweetness and light as to confound pre-Adamite imaginings which threatened the integrity of the faith. How could Lardner prove that 'all mankind have proceeded from one pair'? There were, he maintained, external evidences to support the truths set out in scripture: 'this account of Moses is much confirmed by the great agreement between the several nations of the earth in bodily frame, and intellectual powers, like desires, and passions, and diseases, and in universal liableness to death'.[29]

Early modern Protestant scholars with an interest in anthropological questions were not oblivious of the empirical facts of racial difference. However, they tended to approach questions of ethnicity and race with an awareness that the origins of man and the peopling of the world were areas of knowledge whose fundamentals were set out in the Old Testament. A scriptural paradigm prevailed in the sphere of proto-anthropology. Thus, according to an early modern logic, issues that would now be considered as ethnological or biological were lumped together with questions in theology, sacred history and scriptural exegesis.

Race and theology inhabited the same ideological space. In particular, racial questions overlapped with certain para-theological issues, which, while not integral to the Christian faith, derived from the orthodox claim that the Bible provided a reliable account of the origins of the world. A good example of such imbrication is to be found in Sir Thomas Browne's *Pseudodoxia epidemica* (1646), an eclectic collection of short essays exposing a range of popular errors and misconceptions, which went through six editions by 1672. These essays – including 'Of Gypsies', 'Of Pigmies', 'Of the blacknesse of Negroes' and 'Of the Jewes' – provide clear evidence that early modern Englishmen were aware of racial differences and that some vulgar racial prejudices did exist in seventeenth-century England; however, there is no evidence that such prejudices formed component parts of any coherent racialist ideology. Rather Browne's targets belong to the miscellaneous folklore of his time. In 'Of the Jewes', Browne considers the 'received opinion' that 'Jews stink naturally, that is, that in their race and nation there is an evil savour.' Browne puts forward various arguments, including an emphasis on Jewish 'commixtures' with other nations and a specific rejection of the libel that 'ill savour is a curse derived upon them by Christ' for their role in the crucifixion, in order to expose the lazy thinking which underpins the offensive belief that Jews as a group smell. In a longer series of essays 'Of the blacknesse of Negroes', Browne exposes flaws in the principal contemporary explanations of the dark skin colouring of Africans, namely that was caused either by the action of the sun or by way of the curse pronounced by Noah upon his son Ham and his posterity. With regard to the former assumption, Browne points to the fact that inhabitants of the tropical latitudes of Asia and the Americas do not possess the same dark colouring of the corresponding peoples in Africa. Moreover, even outside the tropical zone, in southern Africa, the peoples of the Cape are darker than their equivalents on other continents. Climate does not provide a straightforward or reliable answer. Nor, argued Browne, does the alternative solution of Noah's curse on Ham. Not only was the curse actually pronounced upon Ham's son Canaan rather than upon Ham himself, any attempt to relate the curse (upon the descendants of either Ham or Canaan) to skin colour soon has to confront the reality, as perceived by Browne, that many of the ethnic descendants of Ham – the peoples of Egypt, Arabia, Assyria, Chaldea – and of Canaan – Sidonians, Canaanites, Amorites – do not appear to have been black. Moreover, Browne denies that black colouring is a curse. It is not a deformity, he argues, and does not offend against the classical canons of beauty set out by Aristotle or Galen. The curse pronounced by Noah did not relate at all to skin colouring but was accomplished when the Canaanite kingdom was conquered by the Israelite descendants of Shem. Browne is unable to offer a plausible answer to the scientific-cum-biblical riddle of 'how and when the seed of Adam did first receive this tincture' of blackness. Browne considers some analogous cases. We are lucky, he concludes, that the Bible provides a clear answer to the problem of mankind's linguistic diversity: 'if the favourable pen of Moses had not revealed the confusion of tongues, and positively declared their division at Babel, our disputes concerning their beginning had been without end'. Sometimes when the biblical record was silent on a topic, one had to assume a similar kind of providential intervention: 'if you deduct the administration of angels, and that they dispersed the creatures into all parts after the Flood, as they had congregated them into Noah's ark before; it will be no easy question to resolve, how several sorts of animals were first dispersed into islands, almost how any into America'. Browne's reflections on the origins of race were framed alongside cognate perplexities regarding the populousness of the earth in the era preceding the Flood and the vexed question of whether Adam and Eve had possessed navels.[30]

Browne's approach was far from atypical. The connection between biological and biblical issues emerges vividly in the pages of the *Athenian Mercury*, a London journal founded in 1691 (initially as the *Athenian Gazette*, though it very quickly changed its name). The *Athenian Mercury* was devoted solely to answering queries sent in by readers, and as such stands representative in some measure of popular knowledge and inquisitiveness. The question-and-answer formula of the paper attracted numerous enquiries which touched upon the racial and biological dimensions of scripture. For instance, one query asked 'Whether Negroes shall rise so at the last day?' The *Mercury* acknowledged that black and white races appeared to place different values on colours, but decided in the end that black had too many negative associations: 'Taking then this blackness of the Negro to be an accidental imperfection', the *Mercury* concluded that the Negro would 'not arise with that complexion, but leave it behind him in the darkness of the grave, exchanging it for a brighter and better at his return again into the world'. A couple of readers wrote in to ask whether there were men before Adam. The journal did not entertain the pre-Adamite heresy of La Peyrère, and insisted that Adam was the first of this world and 'the father of all living'. Similarly, the journal closed down the pre-Adamite option in its answer to the question 'Who was Cain's wife?' Incest with his own sister was in this regard the theologically orthodox – if morally questionable – solution. By the same token, in answer to the query, 'Who was that Cain feared should slay him, after he had killed his brother Abel?', the *Mercury* concluded – with an implausible orthodoxy – that Cain had been afraid of his brothers who were yet to be born or their own or his own sons. A later answer to a similar query backtracked somewhat to air the possibility that Adam might have had more children than those named in scripture. In answer to the racial query, 'What is the reason some men are black, some tawny, and some white in the same climate, as in India?', the *Mercury* reviewed the range both of naturalistic and of biblical explanations for the colouring of blacks. Biblical accounts of racial colouring included not only the mark of Cain, but also a psychosomatic interpretation of how Lot's – presumably white – daughters might have conceived a dark child: 'some say Lot's daughters having upon their flight from Sodom an idea of the smoke and flames they left behind them, might very probably in the act of generation with their father, fix a similitude of colour upon conception by the power of their imaginary faculty'. However, in answer to a later query, 'What was the mark God set upon Cain?' there was no mention of race. The *Athenian Mercury* also tackled the ethnic identity and location of the Ten Lost Tribes of Israel, the various biological – including sexual – consequences of the Fall of Man, the identity of the language spoken universally before the confusion of tongues at Babel (Hebrew) and, of course, the ongoing riddle of Adam's navel.[31]

Clearly, the study of race did not exist as a coherent discipline in its own right during the seventeenth and early eighteenth centuries. Rather, racial questions belonged within the empire of theology, the dominant domain of early modern knowledge, though occupying a frontier province close to the encroaching territories of medicine and natural science. Yet the sciences, though rising rapidly in authority, had themselves still to obtain full autonomy from the realm of scriptural exegesis. Even among the leading natural scientists of the early eighteenth century, the issue of racial origins still demanded a scriptural treatment. The provincial status of race as a subject of intellectual enquiry is apparent in the very full account of racial differences produced by the Newtonian mathematician, scientist and theologian William Whiston (1667–1752) in a dissertation which he appended to his *Supplement to the literal accomplishment of scripture prophecies* (1725). In this essay, entitled 'An exposition of the curse upon Cain and Lamech: shewing that the present Africans and

Indians are their posterity', Whiston treated race – including the intermediate biological causes of difference in complexion – as an accidental
result of providential intervention in sacred history. This, as we shall see,
had two bizarrely divergent consequences: race was for Whiston both an
unimportant epiphenomenon of a deeper spiritual reality, yet, precisely
because of this assumption, non-white colouring seemed to be a mark of
religious and moral failings. Thus, although Whiston treated race as
superficial and meaningless in itself, he found it expressive – indirectly –
of spiritual (not biological) meanings, a train of logic which betrayed him
into the articulation of racist sentiments.

An orthodox monogenist, however heretical his opinions on the
Trinity, Whiston was perplexed by the variety of colourings found in the
races of the world. Assuming that the peoples of the world all descended
from the stock of Adam, Whiston argued that science on its own could
not provide a compelling solution to the riddle of racial difference:
'neither the different heat of the sun, nor change of climate, nor indeed
any other like physical cause does afford an adequate solution of this
problem'. Not that biology failed to explain exactly how blacks and
whites differed; the problem was that biology in itself could not account
for the mechanism or process by which races had come to differ anatomically. According to Whiston, anatomists had found that 'blacks have a
network tunicle between the cuticula and cutis, with small cavities full of
a black juice, more than the whites; it seems evident, to a demonstration,
that nothing else but the Author of our being could produce such an
additional tunicle and juice as these blacks have'. What made blacks black
depended upon a sort of supplementary creation, and therefore could
only be the work of the Creator himself: the 'grand distinction' of race
among mankind depended upon the 'particular interposition' of God in
the constitution of man.[32]

In accounting for race, Whiston had recourse to certain curses in the
book of Genesis, though not, it is worthy of note, to the curse upon
Ham. According to Whiston, the descendants of Ham were white or
tawny in complexion, but not black. Instead Whiston traced the non-
white races to the antediluvial descendants of Cain and of Lamech, both
of whom had been cursed by God for the grievous sin of homicide and
both of whom had had racial marks placed upon them. Whiston assumed
that Adam and Eve had been 'proper whites', as was their son Cain, 'by
birth a white'. However, after Cain's murder of his sibling Abel, God had
'changed [Cain] to the remotest species and colour of a perfect black'.
Thereafter Cain had fled to the land of Nod where he married and had a

son Enoch, whose great-great-grandson Lamech killed two men:

And Lamech said unto his wives, Adah and Zillah, Hear my voice: ye wives of
Lamech, hearken unto my speech: for I have slain a man to my wounding, and a
young man to my hurt.

If Cain shall be avenged sevenfold, truly Lamech seventy and sevenfold.

(Genesis 4:23–4)

The Cainites had begun to intermarry with the white line of Seth (Adam
and Eve's third son) after the seven generations of punishment were over.
The racial differences between the Cainite and Sethite lines were overlaid
with religious significance: whereas Whiston termed the 'seed' of Cain the
'old idolaters', the offspring of Seth he knew as the 'old worshippers of
the true God'. Whiston interpreted the seventy and sevenfold punishment inflicted upon Lamech as a racial transformation which would
persist among the descendants of Lamech for at least seventy-seven
generations, a chronology which obviously postdated the Flood, and
which, according to Whiston's calculations, stretched precisely to the era
of Jesus Christ. But how had the Lamechites survived the Flood? Whiston
held the view that the Flood had not been universal, except in so far as it
had covered the whole known ancient world. This was quite consistent
with scripture, as 'the other general expressions of Moses do not extend
beyond the world known in the days of Moses'. Therefore, the words of
Genesis properly interpreted did not present an insuperable obstacle to
Whiston's thesis that the non-white lineages of Cain and Lamech had
survived the Flood in other continents such as Africa and the Americas
which had been beyond its reach. Not that Whiston reckoned these
wicked non-white peoples had deserved to survive: 'the posterity of Cain
and Lamech were the worst part of mankind, and most of all deserved the
Deluge'. This sounds like an acceptance of genocide; though Whiston's
categories were primarily moral and spiritual, and only racial in a secondary sense. By a similar token, Whiston argued that the punishment
inflicted upon the descendants of Lamech had not only been racial, but
had also involved their 'exclusion' from 'the church and people of God',
who were, of course, Semites. The non-white Lamechite races had
remained sunk in idolatry, polytheism and superstition until the coming
of the Messiah, at the end of seventy-seven generations, at last opened up
the possibility of their readmission to the church. Thus Whiston read the
promises of the gospel found in Colossians 3:11. The curse upon the
Lamechites and its lifting were both to be read as simultaneously racial

and spiritual. Indeed, Whiston forecast, in line with the optimistic prophecy of Isaiah 66:18–19 regarding a future in-gathering of all nations,
that the colour of the Lamechite races was only a temporary affliction, not
a permanent anatomical property: 'I incline to think it will be taken off
upon their general conversion to Christianity.'[33]

However, this conversion had not yet occurred, and Whiston was able
to trace the four non-white 'species' of mankind to the four children of
Lamech, each of whom had experienced a distinctive racial metamor-
phosis, ranging from black to olive. The four non-white races, the
Africans, Amerindians, East Indians and Hottentots – the last classified
by Whiston in 'the lowest degree of human nature' – were descended
respectively from Lamech's three sons Jabal, Jubal and Tubal-Cain, and
from his daughter, Naamah. Indeed, here Whiston implicated the line of
Ham in the degeneration of the true patriarchal religion into idolatrous
superstition, by way of Naamah whom Whiston identified as the wicked
wife of Ham. Whiston also tackled other outstanding problems en route,
including the question of the peopling of America, which had become
implicated in the defence of the credibility of the Old Testament.
America, in Whiston's account, had been first peopled by Lamechites in
the era before the Flood when there had been no Atlantic Ocean to impede
overland migration. The alternative thesis of America's population from
Siberia, Whiston thought improbable on the grounds of the extreme cold
which would have seriously hampered the movement of peoples.[34]

The early modern period generated an enormous literature on the
Noachids. But during the seventeenth and eighteenth centuries the central issue at stake was not the question of the racial identities of Ham,
Shem and Japhet, but the quite different – and then more urgent –
concern about which gods the descendants of Noah had worshipped. Did
they know how the true religion had become corrupted in each strain of
Noah's descendants? In effect, comparative religion rather than racial
anthropology dominated discussions of the peopling of the world.
Comparative religion did, of course, have close affinities with biological
questions. Thomas Stackhouse, for instance, interpreted similarities in the
customs found in different cultures as evidence of an underlying blood
relationship:

there are many customs and usages, both civil and religious, which have prevailed in all parts of the world, and can owe their original to nothing else, but
a general institution; which institution could never have been, had not all

mankind been of the same blood originally, and instructed in the same common notices, before they were divided in the earth.[35]

However, notwithstanding the clerisy's resolute response to the pre-Adamite issue, in Christian apologetic the problem of racial Otherness tended to be overshadowed by a more pressing concern about pagan Otherness. What struck early modern commentators about the diversity of the world was not so much the differences in physical appearance and colours between peoples, but the curious range of pagan religions found across the globe. The primary question ethnographers asked about Asians, Africans and native Americans was not how their bodies differed from those of white Europeans, but how their apparently different religious practices and beliefs might have derived from the Judaeo-Christian tradition. The dominant mode of discourse during the early modern era in the field of ethnic difference was what would now be called comparative religion. Understanding pagan differences from Christianity was a matter of greater concern, it seemed, than making sense of physical differences from the white European norm. This is because, La Peyrère excepted, the problem posed by the religious diversity of the world presented a more obvious challenge to the self-understanding and legitimacy of Christendom. How had the various peoples of the non-European world come to acknowledge deities other than the one true God of the Judaeo-Christian tradition? The notion that there might be a plurality of genuine gods was beyond the pale of Christian possibility. It seemed much more likely that the various religions of the world were degenerate forms of an original Judaeo-Christian Ur-religion once shared by all the people of the world in the immediate aftermath of the Flood. Scholars used a number of strategies to explain the process of degeneration from a common universal monotheism into a spectacularly diverse range of pagan cults, in which polytheisms predominated. Estrangement from the Hebrew line of Shem in the dispersion of peoples, a phenomenon perhaps exacerbated by the confusion of tongues at Babel and the loss of a common language, had led to a degree of cultural disorientation among the other offspring of the Noachids. Some elements of the original patriarchal religion, scholars contended, must have endured despite the loss of contact with the principal bearers of the original religion of Noah. Nevertheless, the gradual erosion of a common cultural memory had, most likely, enabled various local beliefs and practices to flourish on top of the residual elements of the religion of Noah. Some scholars argued that the leaders of these several tribal branches of the descendants of Noah had become gods themselves, being posthumously deified by their followers. Similarly, Noah and his sons might themselves have come to find themselves revered in the pagan memory as deities. As a result, some scholars sought out vestigial traces of Noah, Ham, Shem and Japhet among the gods of different pagan religions. In such ways, it was argued, polytheism might have arisen out of an original monotheism.[36] Thomas Browne, for example, discerned a distorted memory of the sacred history of the Noachids in classical mythology:

Noah was Saturn, whose symbol was a ship, as relating unto the Ark, and who is said to have divided the world between his three sons. Ham is conceived to be Jupiter, who was the youngest son; worshipped by the name of Hamon, which was the Egyptian and African name for Jupiter, who is said to have cut off the genitals of his father, derived from the history of Ham, who beheld the nakedness of his.[37]

Curiously, one of the principal features of ethnic difference which attracted the attention of early modern Protestant anthropology was whether a non-European people exhibited triadic patterns in its culture or religious worship. Such patterns were seized upon as evidence that the ancient patriarchal religion of Noah had been Trinitarian in doctrine; and that contemporary late seventeenth- and eighteenth-century critics of the Trinity, such as Arians, Socinians and unitarians of different stripes, were wrong in their allegations that the orthodox doctrine of the Trinity was a corruption of ancient doctrine, a theological imposture insinuated within the Christian tradition.[38]

The profile of Ham in early modern discourse belonged as much to this apologetic sphere of comparative religion as it did to discussions of race and slavery. To the clerisies of the early modern world Ham was known primarily as the father of idolatry. Hamites did indeed acquire an unsavoury reputation during the eighteenth century in the field of sacred history. However, this owed little or nothing to the race issue and everything to the identification of the Hamitic line as the principal begetters of pagan polytheism. As John Pocock has noticed, in eighteenth-century discourse 'the distinguishing characteristic of the descendants of Ham is not pigmentation but idolatry'.[39] Ham, it was widely believed, had played a central role in the degeneration of the original monotheistic religion of Noah into idolatrous paganism. To be anti-Hamitic was not necessarily to be racist, but to attribute the corruption of patriarchal Christianity to a particular lineage of descent from Noah (not all of whom by any means were reckoned to be black). Indeed, (non-black) Egypt was commonly identified as the citadel of ancient idolatry. According to Gill in his mammoth and encyclopedic *Exposition of the Old Testament*, Ham did indeed suffer from a bad profile, but this had nothing to do with race. Rather Ham was known as a 'magician' and as 'the public corrupter of mankind'. In his discussion of the curse upon Ham or rather Canaan, Gill made no mention of race. Gill understood the curse – more properly applicable to Canaan who was to be a servant of Japhet – to refer to the fall of the Sidonian city of Tyre (founded by Canaanites) to Alexander the Great (the Greeks being of Japhetan descent) and to the fall of the city of Carthage (ultimately Canaanite in origin) to the Japhetan Romans. Similarly, in his remarks upon the mark of Cain, Gill notes that this has been interpreted to mean different things, including a horn in the forehead, facial leprosy, a 'wild, ghastly look' and 'a shaking and trembling in all his limbs'.[40] As late as 1825 the Anglican mythographer Matthew Bridges described Ham, or 'Cham', as 'the father of postdiluvian idolatry'.[41]

Nevertheless, Ham was also well known as a divine precedent for black enslavement. The curse upon Ham did attract significant comment during the early modern era, though this has to be carefully parsed. George Fredrickson has argued, persuasively, that the early modern period witnessed a sort of 'supernaturalist racism' or 'racialized religiosity', one in which religious shortcomings or other offences in the sight of God (rather than colour itself) had brought about the relegation of some peoples to a 'pariah' status. At the heart of the culture of supernaturalist racism stood, of course, the curse of Ham. Nevertheless, Fredrickson rightly reminds us that the curse of Ham had greater purchase during the early modern era at the level of popular mythology than it did as 'formal ideology'. Many serious theologians took careful note that the curse had fallen quite specifically on Ham's son Canaan, not on Ham himself or on his whole lineage. If anything, the curse of Ham would become more pronounced as an intellectually serious justification of racial subordination only in the nineteenth century. Moreover, as Fredrickson notes, supernaturalist racism was circumscribed by the universalism of the Christian gospel message. Supernaturalist racism was not in this sense, then, a direct religious precursor of the biological determinism of post-Enlightenment racialism. 'Ethnic predestination', Fredrickson surmises, would have been a step too far for the authorities of the early modern confessional state.[42]

Indeed, race slavery was in theory at first nothing of the sort, but rather the enslavement of pagans, who happened to be black. Many scholars concur in the opinion that race was a product rather than the cause of American slaveholding. Christianity, many colonial Americans believed, did away with the necessity of paternal control and made one free. Only over time did colour become the central justification of the American slave system. In the interim Protestants tied themselves in knots over the question of Christianising the pagan unfortunates of the black slave population. If Christianity made one free, then perhaps it was better not to proselytise.[43]

There was no consistent line on the ethnological significance of Ham. Peter Heylyn (1599–1662), the English High Churchman and geographer, argued, reasonably, that the heat of the sun could not be the direct cause of blackness, as many supposed. After all, Amerindians remained of lighter hues around the equatorial regions than Africans at similar latitudes. Nor did he have any truck with the bizarre notion that blackness was God's punishment for sex in the Ark. It was 'ridiculous', argued Heylyn, to suggest that Ham had been cursed because 'he had carnal knowledge of his wife when they were in the Ark'. The reasons for blackness, he concluded, were not directly vouchsafed by scripture, but were 'God's secret pleasure'; though it remained possible, he conceded, that the curse on Ham and his posterity had 'an influence on it'.[44] In the 1740s the Virginia physician John Mitchell argued that a dark skin colour was more suitable for a hot climate, and therefore could hardly be deemed a 'curse' on black people: 'the black colour of the negroes of Africa, instead of being a curse denounced on them, on account of their forefather Ham, as some have idly imagined, is rather a blessing, rendering their lives, in that intemperate region more tolerable and less painful'.[45]

Notwithstanding the occasional use of the curse upon Ham to smear peoples of African descent, blacks appear to have recognised that the Bible itself provided no warrant for the racist practices which disfigured the early modern Atlantic world. Black Afro-Britons appear to have subscribed to the same ideology of biblical monogenesis as their white counterparts. Ignatius Sancho (c. 1729–80) referred throughout his correspondence to humanity as 'the race of Adam', a formulation which was more than a conventional form of words for an eighteenth-century black Christian, not least as Sancho himself asked the question whether there were 'any blackamoors in the Ark'. More elaborately, Olaudah Equiano (c. 1745–97) worked out his identity and that of the West African people from which he sprang by the lights of scriptural ethnology. Acts 17:26 was for Equiano – as for white commentators – a shibboleth of monogenesis and of the common brotherhood of all races. More particularly, Equiano speculated that the West African tribe in which he claimed he had grown up before his enslavement and transportation had originated as an off-shoot of the Israelite nation of the Old Testament. Had they not practised male circumcision, various ritual purifications and washings and, above all, worshipped a single Creator-deity? Equiano could not 'forbear suggesting what has long struck me very forcibly, namely, the strong analogy which . . . appears to prevail in the manners and customs of my countrymen, and those of the Jews, before they reached the Land of Promise'. Analogy by itself, he confessed, 'would induce me to think that the one people had sprung from the other'. Equiano was struck by the problem of accounting for 'the difference of colour between the Eboan Africans and the modern Jews'; however, he believed that environmentalist explanations made sense of such apparently irreconcilable variations in human appearance.[46]

During the early modern period Protestant apologetic twisted ethnic Otherness – particularly pagan Otherness – into forms incapable of harming the central tenets of Christianity; but by the same token apologetic imperatives downplayed the distances between races and – in the interest of upholding Christian tenets of monogenesis – served to inhibit the emergence of racialist doctrine. This is not to deny that early modern Christian anthropology was riddled with 'prejudice'; it did indeed 'prejudge' the world's diversity. But, surprisingly, early modern Christian ethnographers were on the lookout, first and foremost, for suppressed similarities – not differences – between cultures. Significantly, what tended most to catch the early modern eye in the world's ethnic diversity was not the appearance of other races, but the religious lineaments of other cultures, and in particular the glimpses these seemed to offer of an ancient unified religious culture. Theological imperatives pointed early modern ethnographers in the direction of the unity hitherto concealed behind the diversity of the world's peoples and cultures. Apparent facts of racial, linguistic and religious difference were to be discounted as superficial distractions from the underlying unity of humankind.

Nevertheless, as Keith Thomas has rightly observed, the prevailing monogenism of the early modern era 'did not prevent the emergence of notions of racial inferiority', blackness being often considered a 'defor-mity' or a result of degeneration from a common white ancestor.[47] Early moderns were also quick to turn to the language of bestiality and bar-barity in their descriptions of peoples, but this applied as often as not to fellow whites (the Irish) and to the lower orders at home as it did to other races. Nevertheless, polygenist speculation was severely circumscribed and with it the temptation towards an intellectual ordering of the races of the world which emphasised the irredeemably alien characteristics of the Other'. Instead the bias of temptation was uniformly in the opposite direction towards rooting the 'family of man' very precisely in biblical genealogies which led back to Noah, and ultimately to Adam. Theological orthodoxy and the narratives of sacred history underpinned notions of the family of man and brotherhood of mankind, however much these notions were disregarded in practice in the imperial rush towards the possession of slaves and the dispossession of indigenous peoples.

CHAPTER 4

Race, the Enlightenment and the Authority of Scripture

The Enlightenment has traditionally been depicted as a benign era of rationalism which saw the triumph of tolerance over barbaric prejudices and superstitions. It was an era, according to conventional wisdom, when the experimental methods and less inhibited speculation of the seventeenth-century 'scientific revolution' were transferred to those branches of learning dealing with human nature and the workings of society. This process, moreover, had depended on the sympathetic assumption that the whole of humankind shared a common nature. Indeed, a philanthropic worldview appeared to be the logical consequence of a more 'enlightened' understanding of man-in-society.

In recent decades, however, the Enlightenment has begun to attract a very bad press. Adverse comment has come from several quarters, from postmodernists as well as from traditionalists, from Left as well as from Right.[1] The Enlightenment has played a central role in the culture wars and in debates over the western canon of 'dead white males' and its relevance in a world of multicultural societies intent on abandoning traditional gender roles and ethnic stereotypes. Not least among the supposed iniquities of the Enlightenment has been its association with racism. In the first place, there has been a generalised non-specific charge that the Enlightenment, the principal prop of modern western intellectual life, was the achievement of several generations of periwigged white males who complacently assumed the superiority of white European culture to the values of extra-European civilisations and gave at the very least implicit, sometimes very explicit, support to campaigns for overseas empire and colonialism.[2] Much of this is, up to a point, fair comment. After all, the Enlightenment boasted that the eighteenth-century age of reason was wiser in its insights than the benighted, unenlightened generations of Europeans which had preceded it. If eighteenth-century Europeans could articulate so openly the sense that they were brighter than their own superstitious and credulous Christian forebears, it seems unlikely that they valued the superstitions and traditions of other religious cultures. Emmanuel Chukwudi Eze claims that

the Enlightenment's declaration of itself as the 'Age of Reason' was predicated upon precisely the assumption that reason could historically only come to maturity in modern Europe, while the inhabitants of areas outside Europe, who were considered to be of non-European racial and cultural origins, were consistently described and theorized as rationally inferior and savage.[3]

The allegation laid against the Enlightenment concerns not only the perceived qualities of one culture's achievements relative to another, but also a white dismissal of the potentialities of other races. The Enlightenment, it has been suggested, bore the unmistakable imprint of white supremacy. Some figures, such as David Hume (1711–76), who achieved notoriety during the Enlightenment for their religious heterodoxy have now obtained a new kind of notoriety in recent decades for having endorsed the proposition that blacks were mentally inferior to whites.[4] While all racist statements are abhorrent, any racist statement which wins the imprimatur of a figure hitherto securely ensconced in the canon of philosophical greatness needs to be exposed and refuted. Furthermore, the very existence of this sort of statement automatically calls into question the vaunted wisdom of Hume as well as his very status within the canon.

   The case of Hume serves as a reminder of a second and much deeper hypothesised connection between race and the Enlightenment. This is because several critics and historians have identified the Enlightenment as the doctrinal fount of modern racism. They can point to a specific logic which connects secularisation to racism. If the early modern world was constrained in its attitudes to other races by the word of scripture, so the argument runs, then the Enlightenment witnessed a liberation of science and philosophy from the shackles of Christian tradition, which created the ideological space in which racist doctrines might flourish. There are plenty of examples that offer apparent confirmation of such suspicions. The high culture of eighteenth-century Europe – and its provincial outposts in such places as Virginia and Bengal – gave rise to various innovative strains of thought about race, nationhood, language and ethnicity. This world gave birth to the Indo-European idea (from which the doctrines of Aryan racialism would eventually evolve), to the concept of the 'Caucasian' (in the work of Blumenbach), to the first philosophical justification of ethnic nationalism (in the work of Herder), to a racial justification for slavery and, arguably, to a new irreligious form of anti-Judaism (in the work of Voltaire). Modern scholarly debates have also begun to rage about the relationship of the Enlightenment to the rise of Orientalism, triggered by the work of Edward Said, and about the downgrading of a backward eastern Europe by the western European Enlightenment.[5]

How integral was this dark side of Enlightenment to the Enlightenment as a whole? Were these various developments in the sphere of ethnology simply an unusual set of coincidences, or was the Enlightenment, as some scholars believe, a necessary precondition of scientific and philosophical racism? Of course, xenophobia and popular bigotry coexisted during the early modern era with the monogenist anthropology set out in scripture; yet the intellectual respectability of racism in the nineteenth and early twentieth centuries depended crucially upon the gradual withdrawal of scriptural claims to police the legitimacy of philosophical and scientific ideas, a process inaugurated during the Enlightenment. In *Towards the final solution* (1978), George L. Mosse was unequivocal, beginning his history of modern racism with its origins in the Enlightenment: 'Eighteenth-century Europe was the cradle of modern racism.' Although Mosse did recognise that Pietism – and the eventual notion of a 'racial soul' – had also made a contribution to the complicated genealogy of European racialist ideas, he assigned special significance to the Enlightenment urge towards the secular classification of races. No longer, argued Mosse, was the savage to be understood in terms of his hypothesised biblical descent. Instead scientific classification depended upon procedures of observation and measurement, whether of cranial capacities, facial angles and the like, processes which in their turn contributed to theories of mental inferiority.[6] A chorus of scholars has sung this same song, identifying either an outright revolt against Christianity or a more evasive displacement of scripture-based knowledge by new types of naturalistic and empirically grounded reasoning as the essential foundation of racialism as an intellectual programme. Hannah Augstein has suggested that the collapse of a Genesis-aligned anthropology from the late eighteenth century opened a 'playground for all sorts of racialist speculations'.[7] Moreover, naturalistic reasoning in the sciences appeared to relegate man from his special status within the biblical scheme of creation. The classification of animals into varieties was a prominent feature of natural history during the Enlightenment, and was extended to the races of humanity. George Fredrickson has assigned a central role to eighteenth-century biology in the rise of racialism: 'Whatever their intentions, Linnaeus, Blumenbach, and other eighteenth-century ethnologists opened the way to a secular or scientific racism by considering human beings part of the animal kingdom rather than viewing them in biblical terms as children of God endowed with spiritual capacities denied to other creatures.'[8] Others have argued that the Enlightenment's urge to classify knowledge led to an ethnological re-ordering of humankind. According to the Russianist Yuri Slezkine, 'the search for order within the "family of man"' was a 'principal preoccupation of the Age of Reason . . . People were organised into peoples.'[9]

Nobody has done more to explore the tantalising connections between Enlightenment and modern racialism than the late Richard Popkin. In his quest to understand the philosophical bases of modern racism, Popkin has traced the 'enlightened' provenance of two distinctive streams of racialist discourse. The Enlightenment incubated both naturalistic theories of racial degeneracy from a white norm and polygenist theories of multiple, separate origins for the races of mankind. While the former at least underpinned a science of race which made no overt attempt to dislodge the authority of scripture and the idea contained within the Bible of a common origin of all races, the latter explicitly challenged the scriptural view of human racial unity. Popkin has drawn attention to the radical and heterodox scheme of biblical criticism formulated by Isaac La Peyrère – 'the Galileo of anthropology' – as the crucial point of departure for modern theories of racial denigration. La Peyrère – as we saw in the previous chapter – was a sincere if heretical Christian, whereas his successors during the Enlightenment were openly critical of biblical authority. Where La Peyrère aimed to reinterpret the Bible in order to understand it better, the biblical critics of the radical deistic Enlightenment, such as Voltaire, followed La Peyrère's method of identifying inconsistencies in scripture, but only in order to expose the scriptures to raillery. Thus a destructive satire would wear away the authority of these ancient texts. Whatever the wider benefits to mankind of this assault on Christian authority, argues Popkin, it also paved the way for a full-blown philosophy of racial Otherness, which would have been scarcely conceivable otherwise. Similarly, Fredrickson has argued that, 'to achieve its full potential as an ideology, racism had to be emancipated from Christian universalism'. Philosophically respectable racism, it is argued, was the bitter fruit of Enlightenment.[10]

Some of these charges against the Enlightenment are warranted; but others fail to convince, in part because they foreground the radical exceptions to the Enlightenment at the expense of its more conventional rank-and-file members. Enlightenment specialists have become more sensitive in recent years to the undramatic continuities experienced by a set of regional and national Enlightenments which were, typically, much less radical in tone and substance than the bogey 'Enlightenment Project' reified by the movement's modern-day critics. In so far as there was a project, many participants in the Enlightenment, not least within the Protestant Atlantic Enlightenment of the British Isles and North America, aimed not so much to make the world anew as to effect a reconciliation between the best of the new philosophy and the core truths of Christianity. Enlightenment took place largely within churches, though until recently it was the radical extreme outside churches that attracted the most attention.[11]

On the great questions of religious authority, the Enlightenment produced two different streams of answer. The Enlightenment involved a broad spectrum of positions on religion, and supporters of the Enlightenment found themselves on both sides of the battle. The harshest critics of religion and its most sophisticated defenders belonged equally under the big tent of Enlightenment. On the one hand, the religious radicalism of a sceptical, deistic Enlightenment stressed the absurdities that appeared when scripture was held up to the light of reason; on the other hand, a moderate, clerical Enlightenment yoked reason and sophistication to the cause of religion, constructing a new strain of enlightened apologetic, a kind of supernatural rationalism, which combined scripture with science and philosophy. Both kinds of Enlightenment found themselves at odds with hidebound, traditionalist, undeviating orthodoxy, though in differing degrees. The deistic radicals challenged scripture as well as theological scholasticism, while the moderate Enlightenment aimed to conserve the basic truths of scripture and the Christian tradition, at the minimal cost of some superannuated superstitions which did not deserve houseroom in a rationally reformed Christianity. Thus for enlightened clerics and their supporters in the world of science, the primary aim was not to overthrow Christianity, but to re-establish it on firmer foundations. This meant separating the valuable wheat of the Christian tradition from its superstitious chaff. For the majority of its supporters, certainly in the Protestant world, the Enlightenment was a further wave of Reformation. It was not about the wholesale rejection of Christianity, but rather a tidying exercise which might well see untenable superstitions or inessential but problematic beliefs cast out of the churches, but only in order to conserve and bolster a purer and stronger Christianity. The intended outcome was a rational – and rationalised – Christianity better able to withstand the criticisms of deists and other dangerous radicals. As such the bulk of the Enlightenment found itself in conflict with Christian traditionalists to the Right, as well as with deists to the Left.[12]

The position of race within the mainstream of Enlightenment was equally nuanced and ambiguous. While the Enlightenment did include a radical wing which was intensely critical of scripture, and by extension of monogenesis, an unscientific doctrine tainted by its provenance in theological dogma, the dominant strain of Enlightenment within institutions, such as churches, universities, and medical and scientific societies, attempted to reformulate an independent case for monogenesis on solid naturalistic foundations. In this way the Enlightenment conserved the inner core of the early modern paradigm of ethnic theology. On the other hand, many monogenists detached their arguments from scriptural standards and formulated new scientific approaches to race, which, wrested out of their immediate contexts, would, in the longer run, become mainstays of a racialist worldview. Nevertheless, it is tempting to exaggerate the extent to which the Enlightenment witnessed the emergence of a body of science – not least in the sphere of biology – which enjoyed complete autonomy from religious presuppositions and biases.

Indeed, some of the most controversial figures in the emergence of a new racial science turn out to owe debts to both sides of the division – itself both porous and somewhat spurious – between the 'enlightened' and the 'unenlightened'. Take for example the influential work of the Dutch anatomist Petrus Camper on the facial angle. The theory of the facial angle became a staple of racialist discourse during the nineteenth century, and its formulation during the Enlightenment is conventionally regarded as a milestone in the march of scientific racism. Yet the Camper revealed by Miriam Meijer in her subtle and persuasive reconstruction of his career and academic context was not a proponent of a secular race science liberated from scripture. Instead Camper stands at the confluence of science and theology, within a conservative Enlightenment which tended to assume that the facts of the natural world uncovered by scientific research would confirm – rather than overturn – the truths of Christianity. Camper was committed to an empirical method, but, like the British Newtonians, he considered 'nature' not as an entity totally independent of religion, but as God's 'creation'. The facial angle, Meijer demonstrates, was conceived within an intellectual milieu best described as physico-theology, where natural science reveals the glory and wisdom of God by way of his other book, the book of nature. Camperian anatomy, Meijer notes, was intended as a verification of religious truth.

Moreover, it was a science that also embraced teleology, or the study of God's ultimate purposes. Unsurprisingly, there was no place within Camper's physico-theological science of anatomy for polygenesis. Ironically, given the uses to which the theory of the facial angle was put by nineteenth-century racialists, Camper was a convinced Christian monogenist, who explicitly denied the polygenist contention that blacks had not descended from the original couple, Adam and Eve. Rather, science was deployed to confirm not only the fact of monogenesis, but also the Christian message of universal philanthropy across races.[13]

The tangled roots of race science are also evident when one peers below the surface reputation of Johann Friedrich Blumenbach, a German anatomist and race scientist who also belongs to an intellectually cautious and restrained Christian Enlightenment, as does his notorious coinage – the notion of the 'Caucasian race'. Not that the enlightened Blumenbach defended scriptural science in its entirety. He queried orthodox interpretations of the Flood and mocked those absurd literalists who claimed that the entire animal world had been stocked from the Ark. How, Blumenbach wondered, had the sloth, which crawled about six feet an hour, made it from Mount Ararat to South America? Yet Blumenbach was a convinced monogenist, who steered the science of race away from unwelcome polygenist conclusions. Blumenbach discerned five different racial types in the world, four of which – Mongolian, Ethiopian, American and Malay – were degenerations from an aboriginal Caucasian type. The action of sunlight in the tropical regions, Blumenbach believed, had affected the liver, producing a blackened bile which, in turn, darkened the pigment. Although depicted as pioneer race scientists, Camper and Blumenbach subscribed to the dominant paradigm of Enlightenment in the Protestant world, a Christian Enlightenment in which non-scriptural arguments drawn from science and by analogies with nature were used to buttress the great monogenetic truth of the Old Testament.[14]

Even the dominant Francophone Enlightenment spoke in sharply contrasting accents on the subject of race. On the whole, the French Enlightened tradition was more outspokenly polygenist than its more moderate counterpart in Britain and bequeathed to the nineteenth-century a radical strain of ethnological speculation whose daring far outstripped the coy monogenism of British race science.[15] Nevertheless, polygenesis was not the whole story as far as eighteenth-century France was concerned. The influence of Voltairean scepticism within the French Enlightenment needs to be set against the biological science of

Georges-Louis Buffon (1707–88), which accorded more closely with the norms of enlightened science in eighteenth-century Britain.

A convinced polygenist, Voltaire explicitly set himself as a watchdog of Enlightenment against the theological tradition, which aimed to reconcile accounts of the peopling of America with the teachings of scripture. Rather, Voltaire concluded that the facts of humanity accorded more easily with the notion of a diversity of fixed racial types.[16] But Voltairean polygenesis faced serious challenges. By the late 1740s Buffon reasoned that recent geographical discoveries of the proximity of north-eastern Asia and the north-west of the Americas had demolished the question of how one might explain the peopling of the New World from the Old. Buffon went on to argue that the racial variations found in humanity were not to be accounted for by any notion of fixed racial types: 'Tout concourt donc à prouver que le genre humain n'est pas composé d'espèces essentielle-ment differentes entre elles, qu'au contraire il n'y a eu originairement qu'une seule espèce d'hommes.'[17] However, this monogenist position was no less 'enlightened' than the scheme of polygenesis that Voltaire advo-cated. Buffon reached his monogenist conclusions by way of an impec-cably scientific chain of reasoning. The cumulative weight of evidence seemed to suggest that originally there had been only a single strain of humankind. But as this strain had spread out over the planet its members had experienced such a wide range of environmental conditions and domestic economies, as well as having been exposed to such different sorts of localised diseases, that there seemed little need to resort to polygenesis to explain the facts of race. Intermarriage between people of different appearances, moreover, had itself produced further changes in human appearance.

Voltaire and Buffon bequeathed two diametrically opposed views of race to the wider culture of Enlightenment. On the one hand, Voltaire's polygenesis had about it a whiff of anti-scriptural notoriety for those sceptical *philosophes* who were tempted to live dangerously. On the other hand, the impeccably enlightened and naturalistic reasoning of Buffon, indebted as it was to geography and biology rather than to theological imperatives, reassured the moderate mainstream of Enlightenment in the Atlantic world that monogenesis was quite compatible with the latest scientific discoveries. Indeed Michèle Duchet argues that by the mid-eighteenth century enlightened developments in the fields of geography and biology had begun to make Voltaire's speculative polygenesis seem rather old hat: 'Après les découvertes de Béring et ses compagnons, connues dès 1747, le polygénisme voltairien aura quelque chose de désuet et d'anachronique, si on le compare aux thèses de Buffon. Tandis que Voltaire raisonne en métaphysicien, Buffon s'en tient aux faits.'[18]

Other developments in enlightened France also contributed to the long-term decline of traditional scriptural ethnology. In particular, the French Enlightenment witnessed the first significant steps in the analysis of the sources from which the book of Genesis had been composed, an insight which would later reach fruition in nineteenth-century German Pentateuchal scholarship. In 1753 Jean Astruc (1684–1766), a professor and medical scientist, published anonymously his *Conjectures sur les mémoires originaux dont il paroît que Moyse s'est servi pour composer le livre de la Genèse*. This work pointed to the duplication of narratives of the Creation and the Flood in Genesis and the puzzling use of different names for God. Astruc did not challenge outright the Mosaic provenance of Genesis, though Moses was downgraded from its author to the role of compiler. Astruc's findings were not immediately devastating to the authority of Genesis, though they contributed to its long-term textual deconstruction.[19]

Within the British Enlightenment, polygenist speculation occupied a more marginal position. In Britain daring criticisms of religion were voiced, only to be drowned out by a more stolid kind of Enlightenment which sought, at least in the field of anthropology, a concordance between the new science and the basic truths of monogenesis. The medical sciences and moral philosophy of the Enlightenment in the British world ultimately depended, no less than did Christianity, upon an assumed uniformity in human biology and human nature. Enlightenment itself rested upon monogenesis – upon the uniformity of human nature in different times, environments and conditions. How else would the new sciences of sociology operate? Monogenesis had an axiomatic importance in the intellectual realm independent even of its theological significance – not that contemporaries sought to separate these two functions.

Nevertheless, the early phase of Enlightenment in England during the 1690s had witnessed a deistic challenge to biblical authority, with a few brave freethinkers daring to probe the authority of scripture.[20] Where apparent contradictions in scripture seemed obvious, these needed to be addressed. Some of these biblical critics pretended (at least) to be orthodox in their intentions, merely resolving and tidying up problems in scripture which the complacently orthodox had neglected and allowed to fester; others seemed (certainly to their orthodox critics) to favour a deistic alternative of natural religion to what they perceived as the frauds of priestcraft and so-called revelation. While there was no clear unifying doctrine or strategy to this wave of freethinking, it marked a significant phase in the emergence of the Enlightenment and placed the Church of England on the defensive. The first decade of the eighteenth century saw the emergence of a 'Church in danger' campaign, which was, in part, prompted by fears over the spread of irreligious tracts since the 1690s, a situation compounded by the lapsing of the Licensing Act in 1695. Amidst the clamour over the wider authority of both scripture and its clerical interpreters, there were some particular challenges to the Old Testament account of the origins of mankind, which, in turn, prompted strong rebuttals from the ranks of the orthodox.

In *Oracles of reason* (1693), the freethinker Charles Blount (1654–93) complained that there were 'oftentimes great errors committed in the manner of reading scripture'. He noted that one type of error was reading the general into the particular: 'As that of Adam, whom Moses made only to be the first father of the Jews, whilst others hyperbolically make him to be the first father of all men.' Similarly, the Flood had also been localised, and thus Noah was not, according to Blount, 'the chief of mankind, but the chief of our lineage, that is, the Jews'. Blount made it clear that he regarded how the rest of the world had been peopled as an open question. Chapters 10 and 11 of Genesis did not provide the answers, which went beyond the limited scope of the story of peoples set out in the Old Testament.[21] In response, Josiah King, chaplain to the Earl of Anglesey, accused Blount of arguing for a double creation and identified him as a disciple of the pre-Adamite heresy.[22] The issue did not, of course, concern the racial implications of the question, but the way in which Blount had questioned biblical anthropology as a means of undermining the authority of scripture.

A similarly 'enlightened' challenge to the authority of scripture came from the shadowy L. P., the prudently reclusive author of *Two essays, sent in a letter from Oxford, to a nobleman in London* (1695). This radical pamphlet argued vigorously for a 'philosophic' interpretation of the Bible to match the recent developments of natural philosophy. L. P. declared, somewhat disingenuously, that he had no intention of challenging the authority of Moses. Nevertheless, he did wonder why the Old Testament – the sacred scriptures, he argued, of the Jewish rather than the Christian dispensation – should be off-limits to freethinking Christian speculation; after all, he contended, 'it can be no crime in one, who is no Jew, to comment a little upon some parts of it, with a Christian plainness, and a philosophical liberty, founded upon nature herself'. The Jewish tradition – as L. P. saw it – of a universal Flood in the time of Noah seemed acutely preposterous. Destruction on such a scale was neither 'agreeable to the usual methods of providence, nor to the wisdom of the divine nature'. If the antediluvian peoples of the world inhabited only Mesopotamia and Syria, then why was it necessary to flood the whole globe in order to eradicate the bulk of humanity? Indeed, the Flood narrative showed the deity in a bad light. It would have been ridiculous to effect the destruction of 'all the innocent dumb creatures, and the beauty of the creation, in the uninhabited parts... for the sake only of a few wanton and luxurious Asiatics, who might have been drowned in a topical Flood, or by a particular Deluge'. Something must be wrong, then, with the Flood narrative in Genesis. So, by the same token, the system of anthropology found in the Old Testament was also flawed. A lot of intractable intellectual problems flowed from the tradition 'of planting all the earth from one little spot'. The facts of human cultural, linguistic and racial diversity flew in the face of what was surely a Judaic shibboleth of monogenesis: 'The great zeal to maintain a Jewish tradition, put many learned Christians upon the rack to make it out. Every corner is searched to find out a word, a rite, or a custom, in order to derive from thence many millions of different people.' The populating of the New World presented a particular problem, given that there was no biblical or historical record of how it was originally peopled. The hypothesised Siberian–Alaskan route seemed too cold for draught animals and therefore an unlikely trajectory for inter-continental colonies. The geographical proximity of Africa and South America suggested a more plausible theory of migration across a short stretch of ocean from West Africa; 'but then the natives are most Negroes, or much blacker than the Americans, who have long hair, little or no beards, and are of an olive colour'. Accounting for the origin of the black race was equally bogged down in major difficulties:

The origin of Negroes lies very obscure; for time out of mind there hath been blacks with a woolly substance on their bodies instead of hair; because they are mentioned in the most ancient records now extant in the world. Tis plain, their colour and wool are innate, or seminal from their first beginning, and seems to be a specific character, which neither the sun, nor any curse from Ham could imprint upon them.

Many other nations who inhabited climates similar to those of black peoples were not black in appearance. Neither did whites become black in the tropics, nor blacks become white in New England or Virginia. There were also problems with the curse of Ham. Colour, L. P. argued, was 'only accidental to beauty, which consists wholly in proportion and symmetry'. Moreover, the line of Ham included Asiatics and Egyptians, who had clearly not turned black on account of the curse. The idea of universal descent from a single pair of human beings raised too many objections of this sort. It seemed hardly credible that 'all posterity, both blacks and whites, separated by vast seas, were all included actually in form within Adam and Eve.' All things considered, multiple local crea- tions, which ran counter to Mosaic (or rather – as L. P. repeatedly sug- gested – Judaic) orthodoxy, seemed the most plausible theory of accounting for the peopling of the world by its different races, at least in the current state of knowledge: 'I see no way at present to solve this new face of nature, by old arguments fetched from eastern rubbish, or rab- binical weeds, unless some new philosopher starts up with a fresh system; in the mean time let them all be aborigines.'[23] More typical of moderate enlightened opinion was L. P.'s critic, John Harris, who complained of this silly 'pother about the negroes, and the improbability of their pro- ceeding from the same stock with the fairer and whiter nations'.[24]

On racial questions, medical and scientific investigation – even within the mainstream of Enlightenment culture – was to be shaped by the ultimate imperatives of theological orthodoxy. Medical science became one of the outer defences of the Christian citadel. In 1743, for instance, John Mitchell, a doctor in Urbanna, Virginia, communicated to the Royal Society of London a substantial paper which tackled the question of how medicine might account for racial differences. This paper, 'An essay upon the causes of the different colours of people in different climates', was read to the society at several of its meetings during May and June 1744. Drawing upon his observations of blacks in Virginia and extrapolating from Newton's work on light and colours, Mitchell argued that the colour of blacks did not proceed, as some scientists assumed, from a black humour or fluid peculiar to that race, but rather from the 'thickness and density' of skin on negroid peoples. In effect, blackness stemmed from the failure of the skin to reflect light, itself brought about by the density of its texture in blacks 'which obstructs the transmission of the rays of light, from the white and red parts below them; together with their greater refractive power, which absorbs those rays; and the smallness of the particles of their skins, which hinder them to reflect any light'. As a result, Mitchell insisted, the distinct racial appearances of blacks and whites were not essentially different, but differed 'only in degree; since whiteness proceeds from a reflexion or transmission of the rays of all colours; but blackness is brought on by an extinction or suffocation of those same mixed rays'. Taking his argument a stage further, he made clear how true enlightenment served scriptural orthodoxy, for the application of the Newtonian theory of light to racial questions upheld monogenesis against its presumptuous, but uninformed, critics:

That there is not so great, unnatural, and unaccountable a difference between negroes and white people, on account of their colours, as to make it impossible for both ever to have been descended from the same stock, as some people, unskilled in the doctrine of light and colours, are very apt positively to affirm, and without any scruple, to believe, contrary to the doctrine (as it seems to be) of the sacred pages.

Nevertheless, Mitchell was no complacent defender of the descent of all mankind from a white Adam and Eve. He was well aware that 'white people . . . look on themselves as the primitive race of men, from a certain superiority of worth, either supposed or assumed', but he found that they had the 'least pretensions to it' of any race. This is because whites had degenerated further from the aboriginal 'tawny' or 'swarthy' colour of the Noachids than even 'the Indians and negroes'.[25]

Although he dissented from the notion that brown might be the aboriginal colour of man, Oliver Goldsmith (1730?–74), now better remembered as a novelist but then a prolific hack writer on historical and scientific themes, stands representative of the same strain of moderate Christian Enlightenment. In his eight-volume *History of the earth and animated nature* (1774), Goldsmith emphasised the regularity of God's influence on the natural by means of the mechanical and scientifically predictable operation of secondary causes. Monogenesis was enshrined not only in scripture, but was also a reasonable inference from scientific observation. Indeed, humanity's rich racial variety was reducible to pre-dictable patterns of regularity. Goldsmith noted that 'we have frequently seen white children produced from black parents, but have never seen a black offspring the production of two whites'. From these data, Goldsmith felt entitled to conclude that 'whiteness is the colour to which mankind naturally tends'. Indeed, his commitment to monogenesis notwithstand-ing, Goldsmith provides clear evidence of how an anti-polygenist stance, which downplayed the deep-rooted differences between races and mini-mised their biological significance, might nevertheless also incorporate crudely racialist sentiments. Not only was whiteness the aboriginal colour of mankind, argued Goldsmith, but 'all those changes which the African, the Asiatic, or the American undergo, are but accidental deformities, which a kinder climate, better nourishment, or more civilized manners, would, in a couple of centuries, very probably remove'.[26]

At the core of Enlightenment within the Atlantic world was the Scottish Enlightenment, the interconnected achievements of the moral philosophers, jurists and philosophical historians of the university cities of eighteenth-century Britain's northern province. Until the mid-1770s, monogenesis was an unspoken assumption of the distinctive strain of social enquiry associated with the Scottish Enlightenment. The emergent spheres of what came to be known as sociology, anthropology and political economy rested upon the assumed uniformity of human nature. In particular, the stadialist theory of mankind's progress through four broad stages of socio-economic development from primitive rudeness to commercial refinement was incompatible with notions of racialist differentiation; indeed it was bound up with a comparative sociology predicated upon the presumed similarity of manners in modern 'savage' and prehistoric European societies.[27]

Representative of the Scottish Enlightenment and at the forefront of theologically respectable ethnology was William Robertson (1721–93), the leader of the Moderate party in the Kirk of Scotland, the principal of Edinburgh University and one of the leading practitioners of theoretical history. In his *History of America* (1777), Robertson was confronted with the problem of how to account for the peopling of the New World, a conundrum ripe for exploitation by deistic polygenists. Robertson made it clear that he was not going to confabulate genealogies to trace the exact relationship of the Amerindian peoples to the sons of Noah; but, though lacking this detailed historical information, neither would he concede the crucial fact of monogenesis. The result was a rationalised and minimalist scheme of monogenesis, which yielded nothing of import to the cavils of deists or sceptics:

We know, with infallible certainty, that all the human race spring from the same source, and that the descendants of one man, under the protection, as well as in obedience to the command of heaven, multiplied and replenished the earth. But neither the annals nor the traditions of nations reach back to those remote ages, in which they took possession of the different countries, where they are now settled. We cannot trace the branches of this first family, or point out with certainty the time and manner in which they divided and spread over the face of the globe. Even among the most enlightened people, the period of authentic history is extremely short; and every thing prior to that is fabulous or obscure.

Robertson went on to mock those deluded antiquaries who had proposed – without the warrant of reliable evidence – transatlantic colonies of Jews, Canaanites, Carthaginians, Phoenicians and the like as a means of resolving the quandary of how America had first been peopled. Robertson banished himself from these vast, windy realms of speculation. The historian's was a 'more limited province, confined to what is established by certain or highly probable evidence'. Instead the discoveries of Bering in the area between Alaska and Siberia convinced Robertson that viable communication between the Old and New Worlds was more than a mere conjecture, but was now attested by modern exploration.[28]

Within the Scottish Enlightenment the aspiration towards a historical sociology that was universal in scope was rooted in the assumption that the basic motivations of mankind were the same in all ages and places. The same was true of medicine. In a paper to Edinburgh's Royal Medical Society, Richard Millar feared that polygenesis would bring about the 'immediate end of the arts and sciences', which were 'founded upon the analogy that we are all of the same species. The art of medicine, must above every other, be the most vain and fruitless, as it depends so completely upon a supposition of this kind'.[29] Only with the quasi-polygenist challenge posed by Lord Kames (1696–1782) in 1774 did the intellectuals of Enlightenment Scotland, particularly within the field of medical science, become more articulate about their monogenist pre-suppositions.

Until 1774 the instinctive monogenism of Enlightenment Scotland was ruffled only by David Hume's puzzling, brief and understated espousal of polygenist racialism. This lapse – if a lapse it were – has significantly damaged Hume's current reputation. Many of today's students know Hume best as the infamous white philosopher who let down his guard and uttered racist sentiments of which any thinking person, not least a philosopher, should be ashamed. Yet Hume's reputation as a racist rests on a footnote. Seldom can a footnote – a footnote indeed which runs not only against the grain of his wider *oeuvre*, but also against the argumentative thrust of the essay which it supplements – have done so much to sink a reputation. The footnote in question was added by Hume in 1753 to an essay of 1748 entitled 'Of national characters'. In this essay Hume argues that national characters are the result of moral rather than physical causes. To put the argument in modern terms, the anachronisms of language notwithstanding, ethnic and national differences belong to the realm of social and cultural construction. This is unsurprising as the edifice of Hume's moral philosophy rests on the crucial foundation of a uniform human nature. Ethnic determinism had no place in Hume's philosophy. Yet the footnote which Hume inserted into the essay in 1753 cut across the specific argument of this piece, and stands in contradiction to one of the basic premises of his philosophy. The opening sentences of the remarkable footnote run as follows:

I am apt to suspect the negroes, and in general all the other species of men (for there are four or five different kinds) to be naturally inferior to the whites. There never was a civilized nation of any other complexion than white, nor even any individual eminent either in action or speculation. No ingenious manufactures amongst them, no arts, no sciences. On the other hand, the most rude and barbarous of the whites, such as the ancient Germans, the present Tartars, have still something eminent about them, in their valour, form of government, or some other particular. Such a uniform and constant difference could not happen, in so many countries and ages, if nature had not made an original distinction betwixt these breeds of men.

Hume then goes on to admit in offensively joky terms an exception to his general thesis of black mental inferiority to whites: 'In Jamaica indeed they talk of one negroe as a man of parts and learning; but tis likely he is admired for very slender accomplishments, like a parrot, who speaks a few words plainly.' If the first part of the footnote suggests a sophisticated scheme of polygenist racialism, the latter example of the Jamaican black is more suggestive of the racist banter of the unthinking bigot. Yet Hume was far from casual in his use of words. Indeed, he was an obsessive and meticulous reviser of his own publications. By the edition of 1777, which followed his death the year before but which incorporated some final changes, Hume had amended the footnote with care, deleting from the first sentence the phrases 'and in general all other species of men (for there are four or five different kinds)', but retaining the rest of the footnote. In this way, Hume retreated from the outright heretical polygenism of the original footnote, but without sacrificing either its unequivocally racist message or the broad hint that the vast biological gulf between whites and other races might have its roots in some deep, possibly aboriginal, racial differences.[30]

The lively debate sparked off by this footnote leaves numerous questions unresolved. How integral was polygenist racism to Hume's particular Enlightenment project? Did Hume – the most devastating Enlightenment critic of Christian orthodoxy, its metaphysical underpinnings, its interpretation of history, its miraculous providences – become a racist because of his liberation from the shackles of Christian orthodoxy? Yet doubts surely remain about the philosophical significance of Hume's remarks, regardless of his careful revisions. Might even Hume's racism – confined to the nether regions of his text – have been of a vulgar, conventional and unreflective cast?

However, Hume did not stand alone within the Scottish Enlightenment as an advocate of the polygenist heresy. It also surfaced in the work of Hume's kinsman, Henry Home, a polymathic philosopher, historian and jurist, who had been elevated to the judicial bench with the title of Lord Kames. Unlike Hume, Kames was not a critic of Christianity and its shaky philosophical underpinnings. Kames appeared to be a committed Presbyterian, if anything too committed to its Calvinist precepts. His *Essays on the principles of morality and natural religion* (1751) had drawn him into an apparent denial of free will, in the midst of what had been conceived – ironically enough – as an orthodox Calvinist response to Humean philosophy. As a result, Kames had found himself by 1755–6 the target of heresy-hunters within the Kirk who found fault with his lapse into necessitarianism, a species of determinism which went beyond the permitted bounds of Calvinism. Kames was not a deist or a critic of conventional religion; but, as he had shown, he was a daring expositor of Christian philosophy, who ventured, perhaps foolishly, where its logic appeared to lead him.[31] In his anthropological survey, *Sketches of the history of man* (1774), the unfortunate Kames found himself drawn by the force of evidence and logic to a further trespass, this time on the forbidden realm of polygenist speculation.

In the sections of the *Sketches* dealing with the origins of man, Kames tried to tackle a number of disparate racial issues in biology and geography which confronted the Enlightenment. The question of black colouring, for example, presented a quite different problem from the bodily hairlessness of native Amerindians, and from the further geographical question of how America had been first settled. The peopling of Australasia presented another quite separate problem for those attempting to account for man's racial origins. It is important to note – given the undue prominence which black–white differences have assumed in the literature on race – that Kames was even more concerned with the intractable problem of native Amerindian and Australasian distinctiveness.[32]

Native Amerindians and Australasians presented particularly acute problems of racial provenance, as their respective continents seemed never to have been connected by any land passage to Europe, Africa or Asia. In the case of America, Kames did not accept the conventional argument that it had been populated from Siberia. Not only did this geographical remoteness make it unlikely that America had been peopled 'from any part of the old world', but the 'external appearance of the inhabitants' made 'this conjecture approach to a certainty'. The 'very frame of the human body', including colour, hair type and physiognomy, seemed to point to aboriginal racial differences. Nor did Kames believe that climatic variation could account for racial differences. Were not Amerindians the inhabitants of the same latitudes as peoples on other continents? Yet the bodies of the Americans were hairless, their faces were beardless and their 'copper colour' differed 'from the colour of all other nations'. Native Amerindians looked quite unlike any people of the Old World:

The external appearance of the inhabitants, makes this conjecture approach to a certainty; as that appearance differs widely from the appearance of any other known people. Excepting the eye-lashes, eye-brows, and hair of the head, which is invariably jet-black, there is not a single hair on the body of any American: not the least appearance of a beard.

Kames noted that native Amerindian children were born with 'down upon the skin', but that this disappeared by about the eighth or ninth day after birth and thereafter never grew back. This was in stark contrast to the situation in the Old World where children were born with 'skins smooth and polished' and where no down appeared until puberty. Equally difficult to explain away was the colour of native Amerindians: 'Another distinguishing mark is their copper colour, uniformly the same in all climates, hot and cold; and differing from the colour of all other nations.' The point about uniformity across climates threw a major obstacle in the way of a satisfactory environmentalist explanation of native American colouring. It could not simply be a matter of climate. Kames reasoned that 'as the copper colour and want of beard' continued 'invariably the same in every variety of climate', that these characteristics had to 'depend on some invariable cause acting uniformly; which may be a singularity in the race of people', though it could not be a consequence of the climate.[33]

Similarly, as regards Australia, Kames speculated that a 'local creation' of the aboriginal race appeared to be an 'unavoidable' conclusion from the evidence. Kames found that 'every rational conjecture' pointed towards 'a separate creation'. The biblical account of the origins of mankind from a single pair of humans struck him as incompatible with the facts of biology and geography. Kames's heterodox line of reasoning thus led to a divergence from scriptural orthodoxy, though not from a divine providentialist interpretation of the origins of humanity and its various races. America and Australia, he concluded, 'must have been planted by the Almighty with a number of animals and vegetables' of which some were 'peculiar' to these continents. Might humans also have been fitted to these strange environments? Kames wondered that 'when such care has been taken about inferior life' whether 'so wild a thought be admitted, as that man, the noblest work of terrestrial creation, would be left to chance'. Surely God had created different races of men suited to different continents and different climates?[34]

Kames challenged Buffon's environmentalist explanation of racial diversity within a unitary mankind. Neither climate, nor any other 'accidental cause', argued Kames, could account for such racial peculiarities as the copper-coloured hairlessness of native Americans, never mind those staple titillations of a white male Enlightenment, 'the prominence of the pudenda universal among Hottentot women, or the black nipple no less universal among female Samoides'. Climate seemed to be limited in its effects. Kames argued that Europeans who lived in hot climates for several years, turning brown in the process, nevertheless tended to have offspring of 'the same complexion with those in Europe'.[35]

Empirical evidence drawn from geography and biology seemed to indicate that 'God created many pairs of the human race, differing from each other both externally and internally; that he fitted those pairs for different climates, and placed each pair in its proper climate; that the peculiarities of the original pairs were preserved entire in their descendants.' But the evidence had to be misleading; for 'this opinion, however plausible, we are not permitted to adopt; being taught a different lesson by revelation, viz. That God created but a single pair of the human species'.[36]

Giving a passable impression of judicious scrupulosity, which presumably came second nature to a judge of his seniority, Kames waxed ambivalent on the quandary which he faced. The truth of the scriptures could not be questioned, but it seemed to fly in the face of the factual evidence amassed from around the world: while nobody could – or presumably should – 'doubt of the authority of Moses, yet his account of the creation of man is not a little puzzling'. Not only was there no mention in scripture of the creation of different races of men formed for different climates; but originally, *pace* scripture, Adam seemed to have been endowed with a degree of knowledge about the natural world which he had passed on to his descendants, a historical fact which seemed to be squarely contradicted by the lessons taught by historical anthropology that mankind had at first lived in the savage state, a condition which still prevailed in some corners of the globe. This 'dismal catastrophe', Kames reckoned, could be explained only by some 'terrible convulsion', such as that related in chapter 11 of Genesis as divine punishment for the human arrogance exhibited in the Tower of Babel.[37]

Thus, in lieu of endorsing a potential scriptural error, Kames resorted to a proactive approach to biblical interpretation, positing an enlarged role for chapter 11 of Genesis in the origin of races. Without in any way questioning the truth of scripture, Kames appeared to claim, he was filling a lacuna which was implicit in the biblical account of the origins and divisions of mankind. Kames inserted a racial hermeneutic into Genesis 11 which the facts of nature and the narrative logic of the Babel story both seemed to demand. A benign God could not justly send a dispersed mankind to torrid and arctic zones of the globe in which they would not survive. The author of Genesis had related the confounding of languages and the post-Babelian dispersion, but his account had not discussed either the consequent racialising of an aboriginal mankind fitted only for one climate or the process of degeneracy by which a dispersed and divided humanity lapsed into savagery.[38]

Kames appeared to agonise over the question, plumping for 'the confusion of Babel' as 'the only known fact that can reconcile sacred and profane history'. Race and degeneracy, Kames suggested, were equally products of the 'terrible convulsion' which followed the building of the Tower of Babel. In the aftermath of Babel God had not only confounded the languages of men and scattered them across the globe, as in conventional interpretations of this event, but had also fitted each separate division of mankind with a bodily constitution fit for the environment which they would inhabit. After all, Kames pondered, without such an 'immediate change of constitution', how could 'the builders of Babel' have survived 'in the burning region of Guinea' or in 'the frozen region of Lapland'? The events which followed the building of the Tower of Babel appeared to constitute not only a plausible explanation for racial diversity but also the point of departure for Kames's otherwise 'enlightened' system of stadialist anthropology set out in the *Sketches of the history of man*:

That deplorable event reversed all nature: by scattering men over the face of all the earth, it deprived them of society, and rendered them savages. From that state of degeneracy, they have been emerging gradually. Some nations, stimulated by their own nature, or by their climate, have made a rapid progress; some have proceeded more slowly; and some continue savages. To trace out that progress towards maturity in different nations, is the subject of the present undertaking.[39]

Was Kames being serious? Did he honestly regard the subject matter of historical sociology as an account of how men came to terms with the upheaval of the dispersion after Babel? This seemed a curious deviation from the naturalistic accounts of social and economic progress characteristic of the Scottish Enlightenment. Ambivalence seemed to reign. Indeed, was Kames subversively unmasking flaws and implausibilities in traditional readings of Babel? Moreover, just where *did* he stand on the vexed question of racial origins? Was Kames a co-Adamite heretic – subscribing to the notion that every race had its own equivalent of Adam and Eve – or the creative but orthodox exegete of a post-Babelian catastrophe?

As things transpired, the invocation of Babel did not fool Kames's learned audience. Few readers appear to have interpreted the *Sketches of the history of man* as a defence of monogenist Christian orthodoxy. Kames was read as the advocate of a co-Adamite system of local creations and his name became a byword for polygenesis in the later Enlightenment. Indeed, Kames would long remain something of a bogeyman in this area. Kamesian polygenesis was still of profound concern to some leading Presbyterian intellectuals, such as the Reverend Henry Cooke of Belfast, as late as 1850.[40] More immediately, the perceived polygenist thrust of Kames's *Sketches* provoked a flurry of prompt replies, as well as a steady stream of opposition over the next few decades. John Anderson delivered an anti-Kamesian paper on 'Discourses of natural and artificial systems in natural history; and of the varieties in the human kind' to the Glasgow Literary Society in 1774. Anderson argued that it was 'contrary to the whole analogy of nature' to suppose that 'different men were created with different qualities for every climate'. After all, people did not find themselves trapped as 'prisoners in particular latitudes', but were instead free, unconstrained by their bodily constitutions, to move about from one continent to another, one latitude to another. Even if it were admitted that the offspring of whites remained white, whatever the climate, and the offspring of blacks similarly retained the parental colouring in any part of the world, this was not in itself conclusive that the races of mankind descended from a plurality of Adams and Eves. Anderson insisted that 'a cause may produce an effect which will continue to produce similar effects while the first cause is removed'. Some local outbreak of disease in primitive times might have remained permanent in one strain, with 'long lasting effects upon the body which are transmitted to posterity', thus creating a distinct 'variety' of mankind. For example, the ancient inhabitants of Africa might have become black by way of some illness or environmental cause, as a result of which perhaps a 'mucus' might have 'lodged in their skin', this 'effect' remaining and being 'so wrought into the constitution as to make a variety in the human kind'.[41]

By the 1770s Scottish philosophy was dominated by the Common Sense school which had emerged as a sophisticated, liberal and self-consciously enlightened reaction to the sceptical absurdity, as its members saw it, of Hume's philosophy. Within the Common Sense school it was James Beattie (1735–1803) who reacted most vigorously to the polygenist tendencies he detected in the works of Hume and Kames. Beattie thought it no coincidence that a notorious anti-Christian philosopher such as Hume should succumb to racial bigotry and polygenesis, and in his *Essay on truth* he exposed Hume's wrong-headed and obnoxious views on anthropology. Later, in his *Elements of moral science*, Beattie engaged with Kamesian polygenesis. A Christian moral philosophy depended on a reliably monogenist account of the origins of the Amerindian and black races. Beattie reminded his readers that 'the enemies of our religion long pleased themselves with the conceit, that the Indians of America were not of the human species'. Similarly, Beattie saw that the humanity of negroes was a matter of theological importance in the Enlightenment battle between orthodoxy and its critics. Clearly, there were those who expressed 'doubt' about whether Negroes belonged to humanity proper. Beattie maintained that the rationale behind such talk was not, ultimately, a desire on the part of white men to justify their subjugation of black people, but rather a more insidious conspiracy to subvert Christian orthodoxy. Claims that Negroes were not fully human, as Beattie perceived, involved an assault on the authority of scripture: 'For this notable piece of casuistry we are, I believe, indebted to those ingenious modern philosophers, who never find any difficulty, or want of evidence, in paradoxes unfriendly to the Christian religion.'[42]

For all his enlightened sophistication, Beattie believed that scripture, ultimately, explained the racial unity of mankind: 'The only credible account extant of the origin of mankind is that which we have in scripture. And if we acquiesce in it, we must believe, that all the nations upon the earth are "of one blood", being descended of the same first parents.' The polygenists, on the other hand, lacked scriptural authority or the backing of other source materials of an equivalent venerable antiquity: 'we have no genealogical table whereby it can be made appear, that Negroes are not descended from Adam and Eve'. There was, moreover, 'nothing in the nature of the negro, in his soul, or in his body, which may not easily be accounted for, on the supposition that he and we are of the same family'. Here, somewhat tautologically, Beattie also invoked the religious sensibility of the Negroes, including their 'idea, though no doubt a very imperfect one, of a supreme being and a future state', as evidence for the unity of the species and – ultimately – the truth of scripture. The universality of a capacity for religion seemed to justify the notion that the Negro, like the white man, possessed a soul.[43]

Beattie was too conventional to concede the possibility that mankind – including Adam – had originally been black. Therefore, he had to find some way of explaining how aboriginal white men had turned dark. The curse of Ham was an abomination to this 'enlightened' enemy of race slavery; environmental conditions provided the obvious solution. To the standard objection that white European planters did not turn brown or black or red, Beattie pointed out that, unlike the original natives of Africa and the Americas, planters did not run around naked; nor did they eat the same kind of food. Moreover, it might take hundreds of years to turn white Europeans into blacks, even in the torrid zones of the equator. Quite plausibly, Beattie noted that flattish noses and thick lips of the sorts found in African populations occasionally appeared among white Europeans without 'raising any suspicion of a foreign kindred'. Reason, Beattie argued, was not at odds with scripture in the ways suggested by the enemies of religion.[44]

Racial variation also became a matter of pressing concern in late eighteenth- and early nineteenth-century Scottish medical circles. An immediate answer to Kames's racial speculations came in the 1775 Edinburgh MD thesis of John Hunter (d. 1809), *De hominum varietatibus*, a work which emphasised not only the role of climate but also the thickness of the skin in determining colour. In addition, William Charles Wells (1757–1817), South Carolina-born of a Scots loyalist family and educated at Dumfries and the Edinburgh medical school before settling in London, produced a very sophisticated account of colouring within a unitary humankind. Wells concluded from his study of a white Sussex woman whose left arm was covered in black skin, that 'great heat' was 'not indispensably necessary to render the human colour black'. He also suggested how minor variations in susceptibility to disease might operate in different climates in the primitive ages of mankind to shape distinctive – though 'accidental' – racial populations.[45]

The leading scientific society for medical students in Enlightenment Scotland, Edinburgh's Royal Medical Society, developed a feverish interest in the question of how racial differences might be reconciled with the axiomatic truths of monogenesis. Between the academic session of

1785–6 and that of 1811–12, this student society heard thirteen different papers on the topic of racial diversity, including one by the English medical student James Cowles Prichard, who would go on to dominate British monogenist race science during the first half of the nineteenth century.[46] With only two exceptions, the papers at the Royal Medical Society were roundly hostile to Kamesian polygenesis.[47] The clear majority of papers sought ways of reconciling race scientifically with the core truth of monogenesis. Indeed, several combined scientific analysis of racial differences with an open deference to Mosaic authority. This vein of Enlightenment was not about criticising religion – quite the reverse. Indeed, one of the speakers, Nicholas Pitta, challenged the notion that Enlightenment was equivalent to a critique of scripture. He opposed not only 'the hypothesis of several original species', but also 'an attachment to such a doctrine simply because it opposes a tenet of religion'. Such a stance was 'unphilosophical in the extreme'.[48] It was, in other words, unenlightened to hold a position merely because that position contradicted the supposed superstitious authority of the Bible. Moreover, of the two exceptions to the anti-Kamesian trend, one was cautiously agnostic, leaving only one open declaration of support for polygenesis. This came from Alexander Robertson, who boldly confessed that he was 'a proselyte to the opinion of Lord Kames'. Robertson concluded that there were 'different races of men, the progenitors of each of which were originally created in those climates, in which Providence intended their progeny to live'.[49] Note Robertson's invocation of providence. Although polygenesis involved a challenge to traditional readings of scripture and its logical consequences posed insuperable problems for theologians, Kamesian polygenesis, the product – however controversial – of a conservative Enlightenment, was not of itself openly irreligious or disrespectful of divinity.

The agnostic contribution to this ongoing discussion came from R. E. Taylor, who was so troubled by the lack of any clear correlation between climate and colour that he was reluctant to reach a conclusion on the topic: 'in the present state of our knowledge, I think, we are by no means authorized to conclude that mankind are originally descended from one pair'.[50] This particular problem troubled a number of other speakers, who tried to reconcile this environmentalist anomaly with the core truth of monogenesis. Various papers noted that the scientific data contradicted any complacent assumption that there was a 'regular gradation' in colour 'in proportion to latitude and temperature'.[51] How might one explain the relatively close proximity of 'the white race of

Moors' to black Africans of 'the darkest hue'? Why were there no indigenous blacks in the hottest latitudes of the Americas? It would be wrong, argued John Bradley, to assume that similar latitudes necessarily enjoyed similar climates. There were so many other geographical factors to consider: to take obvious examples, the climate at high altitudes in mountainous countries or the ways in which soil and vegetation affected climate. Bradley argued that 'larger spreading succulent plants, by exhaling their moisture to the atmosphere serve considerably to mitigate the ardor of the sun'.[52] On the other hand, sandy soil seemed to intensify the effects of the sun. Similarly E. Holme argued that hot winds made west Africa warmer than other parts of the world, including regions of a similar latitude, which explained the unusual blackness of west Africans by contrast with east Africans of the same latitude.[53] On the other hand, some speakers noted considerable colour diversity within the Jewish race despite a prohibition on intermarriage with other groups. Jews seemed to take on different hues and complexions in the different environments in which this ethnic diaspora found itself. Surely, it seemed, the case of the Jews amounted to proof that climatic and other environmental conditions provided a mechanism for explaining racial variation within populations descended from common parents?[54]

Various papers suggested that exposure to the elements explained the differences of complexion in those from higher and lower walks of life. There were social as well as physical causes to consider. Richard Millar identified three different potential causes of racial diversity which in no way depended upon a plural creation. These were exposure to the air, modes of living and the heat of the sun. Millar also drew attention to the importance of different sources of nutrition for racial colouring. For example, the fact that Greenlanders were darker in appearance than other northern peoples seemed to undermine the environmentalist theory of racial origins. But, as Millar noted, the Greenlanders used whale oil as fuel which generated a dark smoke, hence providing a potential explanation of their anomalous darkness.[55] There were also perceived linkages between the socio-economic state of a people and its colour. R. D. Mackintosh noted that savages went around naked, and that this accelerated the process of darkening.[56] According to Pitta, 'the effect of climate' on colouring was 'augmented by a savage state and corrected by a state of civilization'. An offensive circularity was at work here – even in monogenist science: black savages were black because they were savages, which is only slightly less objectionable than the familiar mid-nineteenth-century charge that black savages were savages because they were black.

Pitta, moreover, believed that white was the aboriginal colour of man. Whites became black in some circumstances, and not vice versa, because colouring took place, he believed, by way of the secretion of a 'carbonaceous pigment' on to the skin.[57] Enlightened monogenesis was less doctrinally racialist than polygenesis, but sometimes no less racist in tone.

Several of the papers at the Royal Medical Society also touched upon albinism, another phenomenon involving colour change which occurred independently of climatic factors. Albinos appeared to provide a solidly scientific basis for enlightened monogenesis. Reviewing colour differences in the natural world, particularly the phenomenon of albinism, across several animal species, Prichard concluded that there was 'an established law prevailing throughout the animal kingdom, according to which each species has a tendency to deviate from its original colour and assume varieties of hue, and that all the varieties of the human race may by the strictest analogy be referred to this cause'.[58] Mackintosh pursued an analogy between albinos and other races: if the likes of albinos and white negroes were not viewed as separate races, but merely as accidental varieties of humanity, then why should the existence of more common racial varieties – such as blacks or Amerindians – lead to a presumption in favour of polygenist or co-Adamite solutions?[59] At the other extreme, Pitta – airing a fashionable theory derived from the American monogenist Samuel Stanhope Smith (discussed further below) – compared racial differences to the phenomenon of freckling in whites, arguing that blackness might 'be justly considered an universal freckle'.[60] Colour differences, the general consensus among the medical students ran, did not provide an insuperable obstacle to monogenist explanations of human origins.

Kames's *Sketches* had emphasised the particular problem of accounting for the peopling of the New World. This issue was brought into sharp focus in a Royal Medical Society paper of 1788 by an American medical student at Edinburgh, Benjamin Smith Barton (1766–1815). In his paper 'An essay towards a natural history of the North American Indians. Being an attempt to describe, and to investigate the causes of some of the varieties in figure, in complexion etc among mankind', Barton denounced Kames's *Sketches* as a 'melancholy monument of his ignorance of natural history'. Reviewing the long history of speculation – some of it fantastical – on the peopling of the New World, Barton aligned himself with the theory of the Tartarian peopling of the New World from Siberia. This thesis had not only received geographical confirmation from the voyages of exploration undertaken by Bering and Cook, but there were similarities, it appeared, between the languages as well as the characteristics of the Tartars and native American peoples. Indeed, Barton would – as we shall see – achieve distinction back in the United States as a professor in Philadelphia and leading member of the American Philosophical Society, not only in the broad area of natural history, but also in native Amerindian linguistics and ethnography, a field which, of course, complemented his monogenist endeavours in the field of medical sciences.[61]

Barton epitomised the close two-way connections between the Scottish and American Enlightenments, not least by way of his communication of a sophisticated American response to Kames back to a Scots audience. As scholars such as Henry May have recognised, the impact of the Scottish Enlightenment was felt across the Atlantic world, most particularly in outposts of the Scots Presbyterian community in the New World.[62] In this way the shadow of Kames came to loom large over the American Enlightenment's approach to the issue of racial differences. During the late eighteenth and early nineteenth centuries, the College of New Jersey at Princeton functioned as the leading transatlantic satellite campus of the Scottish Enlightenment, and it was here that a prominent Princeton academic, Samuel Stanhope Smith (1751–1819), produced the most influential of the many responses to Kamesian polygenesis.[63] Published in Philadelphia in 1787, Smith's *Essay on the causes of complexion and figure in the human species* immediately attracted attention back in the mother country, and was published the following year in an Edinburgh edition which carried a preface by Barton. Smith's theories were common currency in the later Scottish Enlightenment, and circulated in the papers of the Royal Medical Society. A much-extended second American edition of Smith's treatise followed in 1810. In the first edition Smith propounded an environmentalist theory of racial variation, and enhanced it with an account – heavily indebted to the sociology of the Scottish Enlightenment – of the ways in which the 'state of society' further affected the impact of climatic factors on the human form. In the first place, obviously, the sun darkened the skin. However, darkening of the skin, Smith claimed, might also be brought about by the operation of excess bile upon the mucous substance underneath the outer lamella of the skin. In some situations a population might be exposed both to the full effects of the sun's rays and to a bilious constitution: 'The change of climate produces a proportionable alteration in the internal state and structure of the body, and in the quantity of the secretions. In southern climates particularly, the bile, as has been remarked, is always augmented.' Cold, on the other hand, tended to restrain the production of bile and to propel blood to the surface of the body, resulting in a clear and florid complexion. There was, however, an exception to this rule: the Eskimo peoples of the Arctic regions appeared to be darker than the peoples of the temperate zones. Extreme cold, Smith hypothesised, also operated – in a manner akin to the effects of extreme heat – to augment the production of bile. There were further anomalies to accommodate. In particular, Smith noted that 'the same parallel of latitude does not uniformly indicate the same temperature of heat and cold'. Proximity to the ocean, wind patterns, the altitude of the terrain and soil type all contributed to complicate any direct correlation between skin colour and geographical position relative to the sun. Thus Smith produced a plausible scientific solution to the conundrum of why 'the colour of the American must be much less deep than that of the African' at similar latitudes.[64]

Smith's originality lay, however, in combining physiological perspectives on the question of race with the insights of the new sociology developed in the Scottish Enlightenment, and thence exported to a wider reading public. According to Smith, 'the state of society' had a major impact in 'preserving or in changing' the appearance of a people. Whereas 'savages' necessarily underwent 'great changes by suffering the whole action and force of climate without protection', 'men in a civilized state' enjoyed 'innumerable arts by which they [were] enabled to guard against its influence'. Thus Smith added a new ingredient to the list of factors which plausibly accounted for the enormous variety found within the human species, its origins in a single human pair notwithstanding.[65]

Somewhat complacently Smith propounded the values of the moderate Christian Enlightenment. 'The most accurate investigations into the power of nature', he averred, 'ever serve to confirm the facts vouched by the authority of revelation.' 'A just philosophy' would 'always be found to be consistent with true theology'. Yet Smith's enlightened defence of monogenesis amounted to so much more than the reconciliation of core Christian truths with the cutting edge of scientific and sociological investigation. Implicit in Smith's remarks on the wider significance of anthropology was the suggestion that polygenesis was incompatible even with a thoroughly secular Enlightenment. In such a situation polygenist philosophers would find themselves hoist by their own petard, for polygenesis threatened to unravel the very fabric of Enlightenment. How could philosophers reason about the human condition or construe universal principles of morality if humankind turned out to be sprung from plural origins? Smith was unequivocal on this point – no monogenesis, no Enlightenment:

The writers who, through ignorance of nature, or through prejudice against religion, attempt to deny the unity of the human species, do not advert to the confusion which such principles tend to introduce. The science of morals would be absurd; the law of nature and nations would be annihilated; no general principles of human conduct, of religion, or of policy could be framed; for, human nature, originally, infinitely various, and, by the changes of the world, infinitely mixed, could not be comprehended in any system. The rules which would result from the study of our own nature, would not apply to the natives of other countries who would be of different species; perhaps, not to two families in our own country, who might be sprung from a dissimilar composition of species. Such principles tend to confound all science, as well as piety; and leave us in the world uncertain whom to trust, or what opinions to frame of others. The doctrine of one race, removes this uncertainty, renders human nature susceptible of system, illustrates the powers of physical causes, and opens a rich and extensive field for moral science.[66]

Smith makes it abundantly clear why thinkers of the moderate Enlightenment, who in other areas were happy to sidestep the authority of sacred history, were slow to abandon the idea of monogenesis. This crucial element in the scheme of Christian redemption also functioned as the backbone of moral philosophy and the human sciences.

Given the presence of race slavery in the southern section of the new United States and the problem of accounting for the first peopling of the New World, racial issues acquired a prominent place in the discussions of the American Enlightenment. Although the question of black–white relations – framed largely in terms of political, sociological and economic inequalities – dominates the discourse of race in the present-day United States, the issue of race had a somewhat different salience during the American Enlightenment. Then, the apparently unbridgeable gulf between the Amerindian peoples of the New World and the various races of the Old assumed as much prominence as differences between blacks and whites. Moreover, the Enlightenment construed questions on both topics in theological as much as in sociological terms. The suggestion, for instance, that blacks constituted a distinct race from whites, while it might have provided a biological justification for race slavery, also raised – as T. F. Gossett has argued – 'a much more explosive issue than the question of Negro equality', namely the authority of scripture. While the eighteenth-century forebears of modern Americans were not blind to racial issues of domination, control and inequality, the tensions of an unresolved Enlightenment generated the more pressing problem of how one reconciled the contrasting appearances of white Europeans, black Africans and copper-coloured Amerindians with the authorised account of the unitary origins of humankind set out in Genesis.[67]

Amerindian origins remained a matter of puzzlement and debate, the exploration of the northernmost reaches of the Pacific Ocean notwithstanding. Naturally, a consensus began to emerge that native Amerindians were migrant Tartars in origin, who had come into the Americas by way of some landbridge or narrow crossing between Siberia and Alaska. Nevertheless, there were alternative monogenist theories of how the American continent had first been settled. In his *History of the American Indians* (1775), James Adair dismissed the co-Adamite theories of Kames, arguing instead from an ethnographic study of Amerindian customs, laws and languages that native Americans were descended from Adam – the 'parent of all the human species' – by way of the Israelites, and that ethnically they were 'copper colour American Hebrews'. Andrew Turnbull, a Charleston physician, argued instead that Amerindians were descended from ancient seafaring Carthaginians who had crossed the Atlantic to the New World. In addition to these various monogenist positions, there were also cautiously sceptical voices which diverged from monogenist orthodoxy. The role of the deity in Creation was not in question, but there were doubts that the monogenist account of human origins retailed by Genesis captured the whole story. The Dutch-born naturalist and cartographer Bernard Romans (c. 1720–c. 1784) in his *Concise history of East and West Florida* (1775) claimed that 'God created an original man and woman in this part of the globe, of different species from any in the other parts.' In a letter of 27 May 1813 to his old political adversary John Adams, Thomas Jefferson rejected Romans's idea of a separate creation, though he had himself flirted with such solutions.[68]

In his *Notes on the State of Virginia* (1787), Jefferson touched on the origins of both native Americans and black Africans, without committing himself definitively on either. Jefferson was aware that northern Asia seemed the most plausible origin for the native peoples of America. However, the evidence of language, argued Jefferson, ran directly counter to this theory. Why, he asked, were more of the languages of America irreducible into Ur-languages than those of northern Asia? He continues:

But imperfect as is our knowledge of the tongues spoken in America, it suffices to discover the following remarkable fact: Arranging them under the radical ones to which they may be palpably traced, and doing the same by those of the red men of Asia, there will be found probably twenty in America, for one in Asia, of those radical languages, so called because if they were ever the same they have lost all resemblance to one another. A separation into dialects may be the work of a few ages only, but for two dialects to recede from one another till they have lost all vestiges of their common origin, must require an immense course of time; perhaps not less than many people give to the age of the earth. A greater number of these radical changes of language having taken place among the red men of America, proves them of greater antiquity than those of Asia.[69]

Did this mean that these Amerindians – of greater antiquity, it seemed, than the peoples of Asia – might have been created separately from the peoples of the Old World? Jefferson did not expand on this theme. Nor was Jefferson any more explicit on the possibility that blacks might have a separate origin from whites. He worked his way tentatively round the theological quicksands which safeguarded this topic from uninhibited enquiry:

I advance it, therefore, as a suspicion only, that the blacks, whether originally a distinct race or made distinct by time and circumstances, are inferior to the whites in the endowments both of body and mind. It is not against experience to suppose that different species of the same genus, or varieties of the same species, may possess different qualifications.[70]

The richness and instability of Jefferson's vocabulary are indicative of caution and uncertainty. Did blacks constitute a separate 'species' or 'variety' or merely a 'distinct race'? Jefferson's reluctance to advance a straight answer is of a very different kind from today's squeamishness on racial topics. For Jefferson, the issue that prompted circumspection was not that of racial superiority but rather the proscribed (yet eminently plausible) scenario of separate creations.

Jefferson's crab-like quasi-polygenist shuffles round the question of racial diversity need to be set against the dominant monogenist orthodoxy of the mainstream American Enlightenment. When in 1795 a debating society at Dickinson College in Pennsylvania tackled the question of the origins of races, the victors – unsurprisingly – were on the side which upheld mankind's common descent.[71] Monogenists were also delighted during the 1790s by the case of Henry Moss, a black man who turned progressively white. Moss seemed to provide some reinforcement to the argument formulated by the leading scientist Benjamin Rush (1746–1813) during the 1780s that blackness was an accidental mark of separation between the races, the enduring, but decidedly not innate, result of a form of leprosy which afflicted Africans and darkened their skin.[72] Nor was

Barton convinced by Jefferson's philological speculations on Amerindian origins. In his *New views of the origin of the tribes and nations of America* (1798), Barton took issue with Jefferson's argument that many Amerindian languages were *sui generis* and irreducible to a common stock: quite the reverse, argued Barton, who by systematic comparison traced all of the Amerindian languages he studied to a single common origin in the language of the Lenni-Lennape, or Delawares.[73]

Analysis of the place of race in the Enlightenments of Britain and America does something both to refine the general caricature of the Enlightenment as a radical and destructive force bent on criticising established institutions and doctrines, and to dismiss the particular charge that an enlightened critique of scripture paved the way for the rise of modern racialist doctrine. Nevertheless, at the margins of the British Enlightenment a sceptical probing of scripture did lead to a less circumscribed strain of polygenist racialism. Indeed the connection between polygenist racism and an enlightened distaste for scriptural authority appears all too vividly in the work of the early Scots racialist John Pinkerton (1758–1826). A Voltairean strain of anti-Semitism enabled Pinkerton to attack the scientific value of the Old Testament without openly compromising a notional adherence to Christianity. 'Judaic legends', insisted Pinkerton, were not 'binding on our faith'. Taking an ostensibly anti-Judaic, or more properly, Marcionite line – probably as tactical cover for a deeper philosophical thrust at Christian truth – Pinkerton openly rejected the authority of the Old Testament. 'What', Pinkerton asked, 'has the Christian religion, the most amiable and respectable the world has ever seen', to do with the Judaic folklore of the Old Testament? Pinkerton aligned himself with the radical Enlightenment on the limitations of scripture as a body of knowledge about history, science and anthropology:

if we have recourse to scripture for accounts of the origin of men, or of nations, we shall be shockingly deceived. The scripture is merely a doctrinal work; and it moves pity to see questions of philosophy decided by scripture, when it is well known that the Copernican system, the spherical shape of the earth, with many other matters mathematically certain, are quite opposite to scriptural accounts.

Scripture – with its obvious deficiencies, which Pinkerton tried to blame on ignorant rabbis – should not constrain scientific reasoning. 'For people to determine questions of the origin of nations' from the Old Testament, claimed Pinkerton, was as absurd as to reason from the absence of any discussion of the Americas in the scriptures that, therefore, 'America cannot exist.' He urged that observation of nature should supplant an intellectual reliance upon scripture, particularly on the un-Christian Old Testament which, he argued, had itself been superseded by the New.[74]

Nature, Pinkerton argued, not only generated different 'classes' of animals, but different 'varieties' within each class. Were there not, he estimated, about forty or fifty quite different varieties of dog? Why should mankind be any different? Arguing from 'analogy and actual observation', Pinkerton advanced what he regarded as the reasonable proposition that 'so far from all nations being descended of one man, there are many races of men of quite different forms and attributes'. Pinkerton surveyed the races of the world, including 'the olive coloured, lank-haired East Indian', 'the large-limbed, dusky Turk' and 'the florid Hibernian', and wondered whether these were of 'one race with the curl-pated black Ethiop; or with the copper-faced American'. 'To suppose all races of men descended from one parent', he concluded, 'is as absurd as to suppose that an ass may become a horse, or ouran-outan a man.'[75]

Pinkerton's purposes were somewhat unusual. He championed medieval Scots literature – mistakenly – as the language of the aboriginal Picts of Scotland, whom he further misidentified as Goths. By contrast, Pinkerton loathed the Gaelic Celts of the Scottish Highlands and what he perceived as their barbaric way of life and limited cultural achievements. To point up the contrast between the supposedly Germanic aboriginal peoples of Scotland and the Celts appears to have been the ulterior motive behind Pinkerton's polygenist speculations, which first emerged in a work devoted to the revival of poetry in Scots. Pinkerton continued his attack in his openly racialist *Dissertation on the Scythians and Goths* (1787). Nevertheless, he remained keenly aware that to venture such speculations also involved him in the sphere of biblical criticism. In this further work Pinkerton claimed that the Flood of Noah was now 'generally reputed a local event'. His position on racial origins had also undergone some slight reformulation, which brought it closer to the providential dispensation of Kamesian co-Adamitism than to outright Voltairean scepticism. Pinkerton found it

a self-evident proposition that the author of nature, as he formed great varieties in the same species of plants, and of animals, so he also gave various races of men as inhabitants of several countries. A Tartar, a Negro, an American etc differ as much from a German, as a bulldog, or lap-dog, or shepherd's cur, from a pointer. The differences are radical; and such as no climate or chance could produce: and it may be expected that as science advances, able writers will give us a complete system of the many different races of men.[76]

However much the Voltairean rhetoric had been toned down, the implications of Pinkerton's analysis remained devastating.

Contemporaries could not miss the destructive significance of Pinkerton's speculations. Pinkerton had raised the stakes. The issue of the ethnic make-up of the aboriginal inhabitants of Britain was no longer confined to the desiccated realms of antiquarianism, but was explosive in its theological implications. The Reverend William Coxe (1748–1828), an Anglican cleric, along with the Welsh antiquary William Owen Pughe (1759–1835), produced *A vindication of the Celts* (1803) in answer to the slurs of Pinkerton. As well as defending the Celts, Coxe and Pughe felt it their 'duty to combat a system, which, in its principles, rejects the authority of the holy scriptures'. Pinkerton's work, they argued, amounted to a perversion of sacred history and chronology. It was necessary, Coxe and Pughe felt, to set out an orthodox statement of scriptural ethnology, proclaiming – in the face not only of Pinkerton but his presumed inspiration, Voltaire – that 'the race of mankind is not more ancient than the era stated in the Bible, and that all the nations of the earth may have descended from a single pair'.[77]

The fullest response to Pinkerton came from another celebrated Welsh antiquary, the Reverend Thomas Price (1787–1848), in his *Essay on the physiognomy and physiology of the present inhabitants of Britain* (1829). Price took issue with 'the modern theory of original national distinctions, and of generic diversities of the human race'. What made Price particularly anxious, however, was when the issue of 'varieties of complexion' was 'made to form a basis for a system of scepticism and infidelity'. Natural science gave way to theology when scholars argued that racial colours were 'the peculiar and unchangeable properties of so many different species of creatures; that the dark and fair complexions [were] not derived from the same original parents, but [were] from their first creation totally separate and distinct'. At this point, Price suggested, the question became 'one of the most vital concern'. The theological consequences of polygenist argument were 'blasphemous' in the extreme and could not 'be too severely reprehended'. There was no scope here for religious latitude:

For whatever latitude of construction may have been conceded, in some passages of the Mosaic history of the creation, on account of the alleged indefinite meaning of the terms employed; yet, with regard to the derivation of the human race from the original parent stock, no such compromise can in the slightest degree be permitted: for in this truth of our common descent from Adam is involved the whole doctrine of the fall and redemption of man.

The 'unchangeableness' of racial types was a 'fallacy'. Price insisted that 'the difference of physiological character in the human race' was 'altogether the result of external and accidental causes'; 'climate and habit' were largely responsible.[78]

Pinkerton was not alone in using scripture to expose flaws in Christian anthropology. With a pointed and disingenuous naivety the scientist Edward King (1753?–1807) noted that 'the express words and history of Holy Writ, teach us, that there were several distinct species of men, from the creation to the flood'. King went on to describe Adam as 'the progenitor of the class or species of men, endowed with the greatest and most useful abilities'. Cain, he concluded, had 'debased his descent from Adam' by marrying into 'an inferior caste, or species of mankind'. Thereafter, King argued, only 'one branch of the principal and highest race of mankind was preserved in the Ark'.[79]

Another quarrel on the origins of races was provoked by Dr Charles White (1728–1813), an English physician, who delivered several lectures on race to the Literary and Philosophical Society of Manchester in 1795, which were subsequently published as a polygenist account of racial hierarchy in *An account of the regular gradation in man* (1799). Blacks, he argued, occupied a lower rung on the ladder of creation than whites. Their physical peculiarities left blacks, so White believed, somewhere between Europeans and the great apes in the scale of animal life. For example, the length of the forearm in blacks, White calculated, was consistently longer than in Europeans, even allowing for height differences. Nor was he prepared to accept that anomalies in colour such as albinos or 'piebald' blacks could be explained by environmentalist means of climate or differences in the state of society. Colour was, it appeared, an innate difference, a position which received clear reinforcement from the various perceptible divisions among whites and blacks and the apes on the biological ladder. However, White's offensive catalogue of purported empirical variations in cranial formation, penis size, clitoral dimensions and menstrual patterns were not in themselves sufficient to establish an enlightened scheme of polygenist racial science. White also had to confront objections to his scheme 'upon other than philosophical principles', in particular the claim that polygenist science had 'a direct tendency to discredit revelation'. Conventional readings of Genesis, White acknowledged, provided an obstacle to naturalistic reasoning in this area, and had to be dismantled. Could it be that Christians had misunderstood the significance of Genesis? White insisted that divine revelation 'was given to man for a different purpose than to instruct him in philosophy and natural history'. The Bible was not a storehouse of scientific knowledge. Indeed, most 'rational Christians', according to White, believed the Mosaic account of creation to be 'allegorical'. In addition, even if Genesis were read as 'literally true', he noticed that 'another race of mankind besides that descended from Adam, seems implied in the text'. White wondered why there was no mention anywhere in scripture of Adam and Eve having had daughters. Did this not suggest that there must have been other peoples extant of whom scripture was otherwise silent? More conclusively, White resorted to the problem of Cain's marriage. From which human lineage did Cain obtain a wife? White reckoned that if 'Cain had sisters prior to that period, from amongst whom he might have taken a wife, it is a singular circumstance that Moses should not have noticed them'.[80]

White's principal critic was Thomas Jarrold, like White a physician and a member of the Literary and Philosophical Society of Manchester. In his Glasgow MD thesis *Disputatio medica inauguralis, de longitudine brachii* (1802), Jarrold had challenged White's view that the length of the forearm was a benchmark of innate racial difference. Jarrold produced a more sustained and comprehensive challenge to White's views in his *Anthropologia: or, dissertations on the form and colour of man* (1808). Jarrold contended that in the torrid zones of Africa the onset of puberty came earlier than in temperate Europe. Thus, as black Africans continued to grow 'to as late an age as Europeans', they grew over a longer period, which explained their longer forearms, without any need to resort to theories of separate creation. Jarrold also gave careful attention to contemporary theories that attributed racial colouring to the proportion of iron in the blood. However, medical science apart, Jarrold was acutely aware that if it were shown that 'there are more than one species of men, the history given by Moses is false, for children of the same parents are necessarily of the same species'. Polygenesis was inextricably linked with the repudiation of scripture, and as such demanded to be explained away as a mistaken extrapolation from the scientific evidence.[81]

In 1800 Christian monogenesis remained as dominant a feature of British ethnology as it had in 1700.[82] How fair is it, then, to bracket off the Enlightenment experience from the rest of the long early modern history of ethnic theology? Did the Enlightenment mark a significant watershed in the history of racial doctrine? Its cautious orthodoxy notwithstanding, the British Enlightenment did witness a significant, if unheralded, departure from older canons of ethnic theology. In particular, the moderate Enlightenment quietly abandoned the details of sacred history. There is clear evidence, in some quarters at least, of a determination to establish a demarcation of race and nationhood from scriptural genealogies. In general, the early modern quest to establish detailed linkages between scriptural genealogies and the profane history of nations no longer proved quite so attractive to the enlightened vanguard of rational Christianity. This older genre of ethnological speculation did, however, continue to flourish in the groves of a less enlightened erudition; and, as we shall see, Indo-European linguistics would emerge in the British Enlightenment of Bengal out of a brilliantly inspired attempt to synthesise sacred history with a new kind of philology. Nevertheless, many of the most influential works of the moderate Enlightenment evaded the question of Noachic genealogies. It was recognised that huge gaps separated the lineages set out in Genesis and the beginnings of the historical record of distinct races and nations, and, furthermore, that it was a gross intellectual impropriety to fill the chasm with antiquarian fancy. Moreover, some enlightened Christians recognised that it was futile to defend to the last every jot and tittle of the Old Testament. In the view of Archdeacon William Paley (1743–1805), the most sophisti-cated and influential of Anglicanism's enlightened apologists, Voltaire and his deistic followers aimed to attack the authority of Christianity by way of its exposed 'Judaic' hinterland. Paley refused 'to make Christianity answerable with its life, for the circumstantial truth of each separate passage of the Old Testament'. This would only weaken the authority of Christianity. Rather, the Christian citadel of the New Testament needed to be made impregnable to sceptical raillery and nitpicking. Thus Paley insisted that 'a reference in the New Testament to a passage in the Old, does not so fix its authority, as to exclude all enquiry into its credibility'; nor, however, on the other hand, was it a legitimate demand to make of sacred Old Testament history, 'what was never laid down concerning any other', that either every individual element of it must be true, or the whole package somehow be deemed a tissue of falsehood.[83]

There was no direct assault within the clerical Enlightenment upon the folkloric aspects of the Old Testament. Scholars attempted to reorient anthropology away from an antiquarian exploration of biblical lines of descent; they were not prepared to dispense with Adam and Eve. To be sure, a crude biblical literalism did not satisfy the more rigorous standards of enlightened ethnology. Historical narratives peppered with Noachids carried less weight with enlightened audiences than generalised stadialist conjectures of the ways in which mankind might have effected the gra-dual transformation from rudeness to refinement; but it was another thing entirely to make the further leap from monogenesis to polygenesis. While the Atlantic Enlightenment embraced a naturalistic non-scriptural scheme of anthropology, practitioners of this new style of enlightened science remained openly committed in most cases to the defence of monogenesis. Race had begun what was to prove a long and gradual move from the realm of theology to the province of biology.

Indeed, from certain perspectives the idea of Enlightenment can seem a very misleading guide to eighteenth-century intellectual history. Some 'enlightened' developments owed very little to naturalistic reasoning, but sprang serendipitously from unenlightened motivations. The defence of Genesis actually contributed to genuine advances in the field of ethnology, indeed to a paradigm shift in the science of linguistics. Consider the ambiguous but undoubted achievements of Sir William Jones (1746–94) in the field of linguistic classification. Jones dethroned Hebrew from its special place as the assumed primeval language of all mankind prior to Babel. His discovery of the Indo-European language group drew attention to the relationship of European languages to Persian and Sanskrit in lieu of a previously assumed connection with a universal Hebraic Ur-language. This insight shattered an older scripturally derived paradigm of linguistic (and, by extension, ethnic) relationships. Nevertheless, Jones did not otherwise overthrow the authority of the Mosaic scheme of ethnology found in Genesis. Jones's pioneering remapping of languages was superimposed upon a traditional map of the peopling of the world by the Noachids in the aftermath of the dispersion at Babel. The comparative method in linguistics coexisted alongside, and was woven into, a sacred genealogy of races and nations.[84]

Thus Jones belongs foursquare to the Christian Enlightenment. His intended project needs to be distinguished from its enduring intellectual by-product. This is because Jones's principal aim – notwithstanding his scrupulous attention to philological comparisons – was to calibrate the sacred history found in Genesis with evidence drawn from Hindu antiquity. Jones sought independent verification of the truths of sacred history in the cultures, traditions and antiquities of the East. The science of Orientalism would be the handmaiden of an enlightened Christianity, whose authority would no longer rest exclusively on faith in the revealed Word. Not only did Jones scavenge among Hindu legends for scraps of evidence which might confirm the truth of the Christian narrative, but – in a circular argument – the Bible was used as a key to the interpretation of India's sacred history. Jones identified Menu I as Adam and Menu II as Noah. The two Menus were the two great founders of the human species, its progenitor and its restorer. Adam was derived from *adim*, which meant 'the first' in Sanskrit, while he derived Menu from Nuh 'the true name' of the patriarch Noah. Jones also conjectured that the first three avatars or descents of Vishnu related 'to an universal deluge, in which eight persons only were saved'. Chronologically speaking, Jones fixed 'the second, or silver age of the Hindus' as 'subsequent to the dispersion from Babel'.[85]

Jones identified three large divisions of mankind – the Tartarian descendants of Ya'fet, the Arab progeny of Shem and the offspring of Ham found in India: 'the whole race of man proceeded from Iran, as from a centre, whence they migrated at first in three great colonies; and that those three branches grew from a common stock, which had been miraculously preserved in a general convulsion and inundation of this globe'. However, the language of Noah, Jones believed, had been 'lost irretrievably'. There was no single word used in common by the Arabian, Indian and Tartarian peoples which could not be explained as a linguistic borrowing consequent upon Islamic conquests.[86]

Nor should we exaggerate the linguistic revolution which Jones accomplished. The sacred contours of early modern philology, although highly misleading in certain respects, did not, it seems, stifle enlightened trends towards linguistic comparisons and an interest in the shared genealogies of – quite literally – Europe's 'family' of languages. Indeed, Maurice Olender has argued that the idea of a broadly European language group, a crude prototypical version of the Indo-European hypothesis, emerged out of the notion that Europe had been settled by the descendants of Japhet, who, it was presumed, had brought with them languages whose ultimate provenance was in the Japhetic branch of the dispersal following Babel. Olender suggests that the notion of a Japhetan Europe was a useful 'conceptual tool' which 'permitted the conceptualizing of the history of a mother tongue which transformed itself over time into innumerable dialects'.[87]

By the early nineteenth century an Anglican Enlightenment had emerged which bore some similarities with other forms of moderate, conservative Enlightenment in the Atlantic world. In the field of racial origins, John Bird Sumner (1780–1862), a future archbishop of Canterbury, promoted a style of apologetic which wove powerful strands of naturalistic reasoning in the sciences together with a plausible defence of the authority of scripture. Moreover, Sumner trained the sceptical arguments of the Enlightenment – somewhat one-sidedly it should be admitted – on the novel hypothesis of polygenist origins. Did polygenesis really accord any better with the facts of science? Sumner denied the force of any scientific imperative which might compel a retreat from monogenist orthodoxy. Polygenesis, indeed, was a much leakier vessel than monogenesis, for whose seaworthiness he was confidently prepared to vouch. Polygenesis, insisted Sumner, was not a simple matter of arguing for a few – say three or four – separate creations of the basic black, white, yellow and red races. If scientists were to agree that 'features and complexion have never deviated from the mould in which they were first cast, six thousand years ago' and were therefore 'specific', then they would be faced with the further intractable problem of determining the boundaries between races. Sumner pointed to the absurdity of a polygenist theory which failed to account for the perceptible, albeit minor, differences between peoples, for example, even within southern Africa: 'a thousand different tribes in every extensive district crowd upon us, each claiming, and with almost equal right, the distinction of a separate creation. The European is not more unlike the Caffre, than the Caffre differs from the Bojesman, or the Hottentot, from whom they are separated only by a range of hills.' Just how was racial diversity to be explained?[88]

Climate alone did not provide a convincing answer in Sumner's view. The proximity of lighter and darker races in parts of Africa and the persistence of Amerindian colouring across different climatic zones in the Americas persuaded Sumner that climate provided at most only a partial solution to the riddle of human racial differences. Instead, he argued, the key to racial variation was the effect which 'local causes', including localised extremes of heat and cold, the extent of local exposure, by way of terrain and the like, to such extremes, the quality and quantity of food, and the state of civilisation, had upon the physical constitution. Here the Old Testament was invoked to reinforce Sumner's naturalistic insights, though it was reinterpreted according to the lights of the new sociological and conjectural history pioneered during the Enlightenment. Sumner speculated that in the era of early post-diluvian antiquity 'two circumstances' would have contributed to 'perpetuate those varieties which local causes might produce, and, perhaps, to fix those strong characteristic features, which, in their extremes, so widely separate the different races of mankind'. In the first place, there was the 'protracted period to which the lives of the patriarchs were extended' which would have allowed 'more scope for the operation of those causes, whatever they are, which influence the form and features'. Second, and a phenomenon typical of the sociology of Old Testament-type societies, was the 'universal custom of adhering to one family in forming matrimonial alliances'. As a consequence of these factors, Sumner suggested, distinctive racial characteristics would emerge and become 'more strongly marked'.[89]

Similarly, John Mason Good (1764–1827) provided a compelling defence of monogenesis in a series of lectures delivered at the Surrey Institution in 1811–12, which were subsequently published as *The book of nature* (1826). Good was a physician and scientist of international standing, who was elected to a fellowship of the Royal Society and accorded membership of the American Philosophical Society. In religious matters he – a Unitarian dissenter who turned to Anglicanism out of disquiet at the sceptical turn taken by Unitarianism – represented a retreat from the outer limits of fashionable non-Trinitarian dissent. Sensitive to contemporary trends in divinity as well as in science, Good was all too aware that the question of racial variety could not be divorced from theological consequences, indeed that proto-evolutionary and polygenist explanations of human origins involved challenges of one sort or another to traditional understandings of scripture. Hence a persuasive scientific survey of the field needed to incorporate exegetical as well as biological judgements. Most obviously, Good found himself conceding – as eagle-eyed polygenist readers of scripture claimed – that there were indeed two distinct references to the creation of man in Genesis. Nevertheless, Good insisted that these were simply two versions of the same narrative, a first mention followed by a fuller discussion: 'the two accounts of the creation refer to one and the same fact, to which the historian merely returns, in the seventh verse of the second chapter, for the purpose of giving it a more detailed consideration'. Nor did wrinkles in the story of Cain present insuperable objections to a monogenist reading of scripture. Such had been the fecundity of early humanity that Cain had been able to choose his wife from a pool of 'many thousand' Adamites. Once he had dispensed with scriptural objections to monogenesis, Good was able to present a scientific account of racial diversity. A 'combination of causes', including, most prominently, climate, nutrition, the manner of life and hereditary diseases, were sufficient in themselves to explain racial variation within a monogenist framework. Analogies with domesticated animals, Good believed, provided a plausible indication of how differences in mode of subsistence and manner of living could influence physical appearance. Moreover, there seemed to be a compelling wealth of scientific and medical evidence, from albinism, white negroids, piebaldness and similar dermatological anomalies, for the impermanence of skin colour – and especially of blackness which Good believed the literally skin-deep product of the sun's calorific rays.[90]

There is no single conclusion to be drawn from a study of racial ideas in the age of Enlightenment. The Enlightenment did give birth to a de-Christianised form of scientific racism; but equally the moderate form of Enlightenment taught in the Scottish universities during the eighteenth century and exported throughout the Anglophone world would be recycled as a sustaining ideology for Christian missions. All mankind, so the leading Scottish moral philosophers taught, shared the same human potential for development. In more overtly Christian cladding, the mission ideology derived from this contended that all men shared the same capacity for civilisation by way of exposure to the Word.[91] Nor did the Aryan (or Indo-European) idea radically displace an older biblical ethnology inherited from the early modern era. Rather, many traditionalists co-opted the new insights of Aryanism in order to bolster the defence of Mosaic orthodoxy.

Yet the sceptical and deistic branches of the Enlightenment undoubtedly paved the way for polygenist alternatives to the monogenist orthodoxy of biblical culture. While polygenism remained a controversial fringe viewpoint in the British world, it found a more secure foothold across the Channel in France where daring Voltairean influences lived on in the polygenist anthropology of figures such as Antoine Desmoulins (1796–1828), who argued that there had been at least eleven types of mankind, and in the work of the leading French ethnologist of the nineteenth century, Paul Broca (1824–80).[92] In the United States the influence of the Scottish Enlightenment remained strong, and there was a strong evangelical aversion to polygenist speculation. Nevertheless, American culture did remain open to French influences, and polygenist approaches would become more central to American anthropology than they proved in Britain itself.

CHAPTER 5

Monogenesis, Slavery and the Nineteenth-Century Crisis of Faith

In the nineteenth century, race became a dominant theme in western intellectual life. Not only did it become an organising concept in fields such as biology and anthropology, but ethnic differences also acquired a novel salience in fields such as history. Whereas hitherto the emphasis of history had been upon artificial groups such as empires, states and nations, now a scientific understanding of race seemed to promise a more authentic narrative based upon the facts of nature, the biological differences that existed between racial units. Racialist interpretations also became common in other areas of the humanities. Moreover, the accelerating commercial and industrial progress of the white peoples of Europe and North America and the spread of white-on-black imperialism throughout the world seemed to offer empirical vindication to the insights of racial science. Racial science – begotten, of course, in the white man's professions and universities – seemed to provide a compelling explanation of the world and the white man's place in it. Viewed from this perspective, the Victorian era reeks of a suffocating and bigoted complacency, and, no doubt, many white imperialists existed in a fug of self-righteous superiority.

However, for the intelligentsia which did so much to pioneer the science of race and to incorporate racialist perspectives into the outlook of the West, matters were not so straightforward. To the white intelligentsia of the nineteenth-century Atlantic world, race was not simply a matter of power relations. Nor, ironically, was this era of undoubted racism marked by white complacency on the subject of race. Anxiety and a concern to preserve the truth of Christian orthodoxy in the face both of troubling scientific developments and of the bewildering array of races, peoples, languages and religious beliefs complicated feelings of white superiority. Indeed, the rise of a racialist paradigm in scientific and cultural explanation ran in tandem with a quite distinct intellectual trajectory, that of the nineteenth-century crisis of faith. The arrogance of western racial superiority was tempered by a troubled sense that God was dying. In the very era when missionaries engaged in a Herculean export drive to transmit the message of Christianity to other continents, back home the intellectual authority enjoyed by Christianity over many centuries seemed to be in eclipse. Indeed, as we shall see, even missionaries in the field would find their faith tested. The unappetising fact of white racial self-confidence needs to be set against a background of persistent and troubling religious doubts, to which the problem of racial diversity itself contributed. Although Christian disillusionment arose from a variety of causes, race turns out to have been a significant, if sometimes neglected, feature in the wider ecology of religious crisis.

Other factors played, of course, more central, or more directly influential, roles in the unravelling of Christian certainties. Uniformitarian geology and evolutionary biology in the sciences, together with radical new approaches to biblical criticism, constituted the primary challenges confronting Christian apologetics. Nevertheless, the rise of evolution was closely – albeit indirectly – connected to the emerging science of race, while the rise of anthropology also made an important contribution to the nineteenth-century crisis of faith. Largely, this concerned the emergence of an anthropology of religion which prompted questions – sometimes formulated obliquely – about the uniqueness, historicity, divinity and cosmic significance of central elements in the Christian story.[1] However, it is easy to overlook the fact that the anthropology of race had its own vexed relationship with Christian orthodoxy. Indeed, monogenesis constituted a staple presence in both the scientific and the theological literatures of the nineteenth century.

To tease out the inner turmoil which seethed beneath the white man's swagger is not in any way to apologise for the latter, but to provide a more rounded picture of a phenomenon which so rarely attracts nuance and shades of grey. Race slavery – as we shall see – would have been much easier for its Southern champions in the United States to defend had they not been so troubled by the heretical implications of polygenesis. Was it worth sacrificing the truths of Christianity to maintain the South's 'peculiar institution'? Southern conservatives – however crude their racism now seems to us – had to navigate their way through a minefield of theological as well as sociological and supposedly scientific issues. Similarly, however much we regret their racialist activities, nineteenth-century ethnologists did not lead one-dimensional lives. Race science was no monolith, and it also incited opposition within the scientific world and from other branches of intellectual life. Nor should we imagine that a

sense of racial superiority occluded deeper fears about the human condition and the prospects for life after death in what several intellectuals
began to conclude was a Godless universe, or at best a universe to which
the Bible was an unreliable guide.

The status of Genesis itself had changed significantly, and not only or
even primarily because of the challenge of science. Biblical scholarship
wrought heavy damage on the authority of Genesis. Nineteenth-century
German Pentateuchal scholarship was underpinned by the assumption
that Genesis was not based on a single source or a unitary Mosaic
authorship. Rather, as the likes of Johann Eichhorn (1752–1827) and
J. C. F. Tuch (1806–67) showed, the narrative had been composed by two
different writers, the Elohistic and the Jehovistic (or Yahwist), so distinguished because of the different names they gave to God – Elohim and
Jehovah. Further scholarship revealed that Genesis was a compilation of
more than these two sources. In 1853 another German Old Testament
scholar, Hermann Hupfeld, claimed that rather than there being a single
source which used the term Elohim for God there were in fact two
separate sources which used the same term for the divine name.[2] As we
shall see later in this chapter, some scriptural anthropologists perverted
this notion (that there were two creation accounts in Genesis) into a quite
different proposition – namely, that there were two separate and
chronologically distant creations of mankind. This strategy was used as a
means of reconciling scripture with the findings of modern science,
though at the cost of separating mankind into two distinct races.

The frictive interaction of Christianity with the sciences of biology and
geology had implications for the established contours of scriptural
knowledge. At bottom it raised the question of whether or not the Bible
was true and, moreover, the reliable Word of God. Asked one English
Christian troubled by the new science: 'Have we in the book called the
Bible a revelation from another world, or merely the coruscations of
human genius?'[3] Bizarre contortions ensued. Over the course of the
nineteenth century, theologians and orthodox scientists came to adopt
various strategies (some of which overlapped or were deployed in concert)
to reconcile Genesis with the potentially destructive findings of geochronology. Numerous apologists for scripture accepted the apparent
incompatibility of Genesis and science, only to explain away such
inconsistencies with the argument that the Bible was not a scientific book.
Why, many asked, should anyone expect a systematic account of
astronomy, geology and biology in a work designed rather to instruct
man in the truths of religion?[4]

A kindred argument involved the suggestion that geological science was as yet in its infancy: what was the point at this stage of trying to reconcile scripture with an immature science?[5] As geologists acquired a surer and more refined body of knowledge, geology would be found to have cast off its juvenile errors and to accord closely with Genesis. It was better, it seemed, to await future developments than to agonise over the current abyss which seemed to divide these two kinds of knowledge. Others recognised that such discrepancies needed to be confronted more directly. One influential solution, pioneered by the Scots evangelical leader and polymath, Thomas Chalmers (1780–1847), was to posit an enormously lengthy 'gap' between an initial divine creation and a subsequent creation of life in six days.[6] A more daring variant of this manoeuvre, as we shall see, was to exploit the Higher Critics' recognition of two distinct creation narratives in Genesis, and to pervert this finding (of two accounts of the same single phenomenon) into a sequence of creations.[7] Another line of interpretation, associated with the Scots geologist and evangelical Free Church propagandist Hugh Miller, was to construe the 'days' of creation recounted in Genesis in allegorical terms as lengthy geological epochs.[8] The text of Genesis appeared to allow for still further contortions which might reconcile scripture and geological knowledge. The Congregation-alist writer John Pye Smith (1774–1851) argued that the creation narrative in Genesis referred not to the whole earth but only to a portion of it in western Asia, thus excluding the longer geological transformation of the whole planet from the week-long history of divinely wrought changes recorded in scripture.[9] In a compelling but bizarre argument, James Sime reconstructed the communication of revelation to Moses, who had indeed been the author of Genesis. However, there was a problem to resolve, for Moses, of course, had not himself been present at the Creation. Yet this apparent weak spot in the authority of Mosaic revelation offered a solution to the puzzle of how nineteenth-century man might reconcile Genesis and a geological timescale. God, according to Sime, had enabled Moses to witness the events of the Creation by way of a divinely inspired 'trance' in which the scenes of Creation passed before the eyes of Moses as if at the rate of a day at a time, though, of course, the geological processes involved had taken much longer in reality.[10]

In the United States, similar sorts of defensive strategies were employed to conserve the authority of Genesis. Moses Stuart (1780–1852), a professor of sacred literature at Andover Seminary in Massachusetts and the leading American interpreter of the new biblical criticism, recognised that Christianity in the New World was now exposed to a more insidious solvent of belief than Enlightenment infidelity: 'Unbelief in the Voltaire and the Thomas Paine style we have coped with, and in a measure gained the victory. But now it comes in the shape of philosophy, literature, criticism, philology, knowledge of antiquity and the like.' In defence of Genesis, Stuart argued that Christ and his apostles had regarded the 'Jewish canon of scripture' to be of divine origin and authority. Therefore, if doubters quibbled with the 'Jewish' Pentateuch as a compendium of trivia and incredible happenings, then this brought them into direct confrontation with the message of Christ. Stuart also denied that the findings of modern geology undermined the credibility of Genesis. Those who argued that the two were incompatible were guilty of a major category error. The Bible had not been composed as a training manual for scientists; that was not its point at all. Therefore, Stuart contended, 'modern science not having been respected in the words of Moses, it cannot be the arbiter of what the words mean which are employed by him'. Genesis presented a philological rather than a geological problem.[11] In this respect, if not in others, most notably a difference over the reading of Genesis 1, Stuart agreed with the geologist Edward Hitchcock (1793–1864), a professor at Amherst College in the same state of Massachusetts where he promoted an optimistic concordance of science and religion. Hitchcock argued that, as science and revelation 'treat of the same subjects only incidentally', we should not expect them to be entirely congruent in their verdicts upon them, while perceived 'discrepancies' were more apparent than real. Indeed, noted Hitchcock, was not the stratigraphic fact that remains of man were found only in the higher strata evidence – in striking confirmation of scripture – of man's recent appearance on the earth?[12]

On the other side of the fence there was some sharp questioning of the status of Genesis itself, as in *History of the conflict between religion and science* (1874), the best-selling work of the American-based rationalist John W. Draper (1811–82), which went through fifty American printings as well as numerous overseas editions and translations. Draper argued that it had been the anthropological precision of the Augustinian doctrine of original sin and its consequences that had generated an inevitable conflict between religion and science, for, in the Augustinian revolution in theology which Draper detected, Genesis had been elevated in status. From a creation narrative which had not in itself been integral to the plan of Christian redemption, Genesis had become since Augustine's time the fundamental basis of Christianity. As a result, Draper argued, 'all the various departments of human knowledge' from anthropology to astronomy had been perverted by religion in order to 'conform' to the legends set out in Genesis.[13]

Yet Genesis could not be jettisoned so lightly. As a result, conventional notions of time and chronology were not only elongated as a means of reconciling the Bible with science, but also bent out of shape. Indeed, the creation of Adam had implications for the way in which the concept of time ought to be understood. In his bizarre and much-ridiculed work *Omphalos* (1857), the devout naturalist Philip Gosse (1810–88), explored the vexed question of Adam's navel. It was not, it transpired, a matter of whether or not Adam had possessed a navel – but of how he had been created, at what stage in his life and at which particular wrinkle in the unfolding fabric of time. Gosse pointed out curious limits in any strict biological interpretations of the origins of man. Adam, it seemed, must have been created as an adult: 'If it were legitimate to suppose that the first individual of the species man was created in the condition answering to that of a new-born infant, there would still be the need of maternal milk for its sustenance, and maternal care for its protection, for a considerable period.' Gosse's imaginative solution to this riddle was a cyclical interpretation of the creation process. Anteriority, it seemed, was implicit in creation, albeit not historically factual. Creation was not a straightforward linear *terminus a quo*, but rather, argued Gosse, 'the sudden bursting into a circle'. Some things, it seemed, were prochronic – that is, antecedent to time – such as Adam's navel, a symbol which acted as a providential testimony to anteriority.[14]

However, it proved much easier on the whole for Christian intellectuals to make concessions in the sphere of chronology than it was to concede the sacred fact of monogenesis. Indeed, sophisticated defenders of the faith recognised that it was imperative to drop certain aspects of the Mosaic narrative in order to preserve its most significant elements. This was the approach taken by the leading British intellectual and politician, George Campbell, 8th Duke of Argyll (1823–1900). As far as Argyll was concerned, the unity of man was a core doctrine of Christianity, but one whose ongoing credibility necessitated the abandonment of more peripheral doctrines, such as the brief chronology of human history from the Creation: 'I know of no one moral or religious truth which depends on a short estimate of man's antiquity. On the contrary, a high estimate of that antiquity is of great value in its bearing upon another question much more important than the question of time can ever be – viz., the question of the unity of the human race.' Argyll conceded that in so far as defenders of the unity of the human race, like himself, depended on a gradualist narrative of 'small and insensible' changes in colour, they had to be 'prepared to accept the high probability if not the certainty, of the very great antiquity of the race'. The aboriginal beginnings of mankind in a single pair lay beyond the hitherto conventional bounds of chronological orthodoxy.[15]

This reluctance to abandon monogenesis meant that the question of mankind's racial origins became a constituent element in the nineteenth-century crisis of faith. Contemporary scientists and theologians recognised the centrality of monogenesis to the logical coherence of the Christian scheme of redemption. In addition, the more scholars worried over the threat posed to monogenesis by new scientific insights, the higher the profile of monogenesis was raised, until it seemed to be the very heart of Christian doctrine. Thomas Smyth, possibly the most influential defender of monogenesis in the nineteenth-century United States, waxed hyperbolic on the subject of monogenesis, arguing that 'momentous interests' were at stake in the 'question of the unity or diversity of the human species'. Indeed, the issue of racial origins, he declared, 'involves the truth or falsity of the Bible', comprehending as it did 'all that is important and essential in the inspiration of the Bible and the scheme of redemption'. Therefore, Smyth concluded, the monogenist–polygenist debate did not revolve around the interpretation of a few passages near the beginning of Genesis. Rather, Smyth insisted that 'the testimony of the Bible to the unity of the races [was] not found in any one, or in any few passages, but in all its doctrinal and practical teaching'.[16] Nor was the importance of monogenesis obvious only to Christianity's most resolute defenders. It featured too in the literature of concordance. James Allin, who insisted that Genesis was 'never intended to teach men astronomy, or even geology', contended that it was meant instead 'to show our accountability and connexion with the first created man'.[17] By the same token, Pye Smith, who attempted to forge some sort of subtle reconciliation between scripture and the new science, claimed that monogenesis was 'a fact which lies at the foundation of revealed religion'.[18]

According to the Scottish Free Churchman Donald Macdonald, the unity of mankind was

the very foundation of the cardinal doctrine of Christianity – the atonement through Christ. It is on the assumption that all men are descended from the first Adam, and involved in his guilt, that the atonement proceeds, and the offer addressed to sinners of the blessings procured by the second Adam . . . The denial of this doctrine, then, involves more than the rejection of so-called Hebrew myths. It is practically a rejection of Christianity, and, in a personal point of view, raises doubts which on this theory are from their nature incapable of solution. For, if there be any tribe not descended from Adam, how can any individual assure himself or those around him of this connexion, and so of any title to participate in the blessings of the gospel?'[19]

Were it not underwritten by monogenesis, it was recognised, Christian hope would dissipate. John Laidlaw (1832–1906), the Free Church Professor of Theology at New College, Edinburgh, contended that without monogenesis the Christian faith became a much darker, indeed an altogether different, creed. 'The universality of sin', he asserted, was 'a corollary and consequent from the unity of the race. The fact of that unity has a most direct theological interest.' Indeed, reasoned Laidlaw, to challenge monogenesis was to open a dark corridor of logic without exits which led inevitably to a bleak 'fatalistic despair'. The polygenist thesis of multiple human origins 'taken in connection with the fact of universal sinfulness, would go to make moral evil something original in man's constitution – a characteristic of the whole genus homo'. Laidlaw insisted the evil was not intrinsic to mankind, but that this whole position depended upon an acceptance of the monogenist narrative found in scripture. The Genesis narrative of monogenesis and Fall was central to the uplifting Christian explanation that evil was neither 'necessary, eternal and irremediable', nor an 'inherent part of man's nature as created'; rather scripture explained how through the actions of one man sin had entered into the world. The Christian doctrine of evil was historical rather than metaphysical, resting upon a story of the biological propagation of sin by sexual 'generation', the universality of sin underwritten by the fact of monogenesis.[20]

Similarly, nineteenth-century Canada's leading intellectual, Sir (John) William Dawson (1820–99), the principal of McGill University and first president of the Royal Society of Canada, saw the devastating potential of polygenesis to wreck the Christian faith:

The Bible, as we have seen, knows but one Adam, and that Adam not a myth or an ethnic name, but a veritable man; but some naturalists and ethnologists think that they have found decisive evidence that man is not of one but of several origins. The religious tendency of this doctrine no Christian can fail to perceive. In whatever way put, or under whatever disguise, it renders the Bible history worthless, reduces us to that isolation of race from race cultivated in ancient times by the various local idolatries, and destroys the brotherhood of man and the universality of that Christian atonement which proclaims that 'as in Adam all die, so in Christ shall all be made alive'.[21]

Not everyone was so convinced of the centrality of monogenesis. Some wondered whether a heightened emphasis on defending monogenesis merely exposed the real truths of Christianity to unwarranted attack. Reginald Poole (1832–95) invoked Reformation principles – the sole authority of scripture and the right of Protestant judgement – to question how monogenesis had come to assume the status of an unquestionable dogma of the Christian faith. Poole regretted the elevation of monogenesis as a defining feature of Christianity. Far from being a central totem of Christianity, monogenesis was a thing indifferent. Monogenesis, he insisted, 'is not to be thus treated as a theological dogma while the evidence of the scriptures is not conclusively in its favour'.[22] By the second half of the nineteenth century, as we shall see, pre-Adamism – the traditional bogey of men before Adam countered by early modern defenders of the faith – was recycled, now as a last-ditch defensive option for the Christian worldview in the face of a new enemy, Darwinism, which stood at a considerable remove from the old polygenist heresy.

Yet Darwinism appeared just when monogenesis had come to assume a new prominence as a test of orthodoxy, at least in some quarters. When the chair of natural history became vacant at the University of Edinburgh on the death after only six months in post of Professor Edward Forbes (1815–54), there was a brouhaha in the press when a member of the Edinburgh corporation, fearing the appointment of a polygenist, or even a quasi-polygenist such as Louis Agassiz (1807–73), insisted upon the 'disqualification for a chair in a Scottish university of any one venturing to entertain a doubt as to the unity of the human race'.[23]

The nineteenth-century crisis of faith generated various different strains of response from the defenders of monogenesis, which belong to two broad categories: on the one hand, a number of sophisticated attempts to accommodate science, anthropology and biblical criticism with a revised version of scripture history which conserved its core truths and, on the other, a set of defences of the sacred history of the Old Testament which appeared at first sight to engage with intellectual developments in these fields, but in fact conceded nothing to them. While the first group might sacrifice, say, Old Testament chronology in order to preserve the doctrine of monogenesis, the second group of responses would involve a parade of learning in order to obfuscate a traditionalist reluctance to shift any ground whatsoever. Although some Christian monogenists were prepared to concede some incidentals of the sacred history found in Genesis in order to preserve the central theological truth of mankind's unitary origins, others defiantly upheld the full narrative of the Noachids.

Historians of ideas have tended to ignore the latter group, whose intellectual anachronism did not always limit their influence in the churches. Variants on the traditional arguments of early modern ethnology persisted, notwithstanding nineteenth-century conditions. Casaubons abounded. The defence of the Old Testament as history prompted an obsessive quest for evidences of serpent worship among the various heathen cultures of the world. In its supposed universality serpent worship seemed to provide compelling support for the fact of the Fall of Man and the subsequent diffusion of the human race from a single centre of origin. John Bathurst Deane (1797–1887), a learned Anglican antiquary, found traces of serpent worship, crucially antecedent to the rise of polytheism, in the cultures of Persia, India, China, Mexico, Asia Minor and Phoenicia as well as in the paganism of ancient Europe. According to Deane, serpent worship had been the first idolatry of post-diluvian mankind and its diffusion was more widespread among the world's religions even than solar worship.[24] Heathenism stood as an ironic and unsuspecting testimony to the truth of the Fall of Man in paradise, and implicitly to the fact of monogenesis. Similarly, Matthew Bridges (1800–94) not only found elements of serpent worship in the rites of the world's pagan religions, but also detected there vestiges of a need for atonement. In addition, Bridges also noticed that the tree – a memory of the events of the Garden of Eden – was the earliest heathen idol.[25]

For some defenders of orthodoxy, the heathen world – if properly decoded – provided a sure and compelling (because apparently non-Christian) vindication of the truths of the Christian worldview. For instance, George Smith (1800–68), a Cornish-born Methodist lay preacher and largely self-taught polymath, drew upon the insights of Sir William Jones in India as well as evidence from various other ancient Asiatic cultures to bolster the claims of Old Testament history. Smith tried to synchronise sacred history, according to the Septuagint version of the Old Testament, with the chronologies of other civilisations and to uncover the corrupt elements of Mosaic tradition which lay concealed beneath heathen polytheisms. The Noachids maintained a central place in Smith's system. Smith accepted Jones's division of the world's languages into three families – the Sanskrit, Arabic and Tartarian – which had spread out from ancient Iran (recognisable to Smith as the plains of

Shinar mentioned in scripture), and he also contended that 'the leading deities of the heathen world', including Osiris, Bacchus, Saturn, Uranus, Deucalion and Janus, 'stood in intimate relation to the persons preserved in the Ark'. The triadic patterns which surfaced in various pagan theologies Smith attributed to the three sons of Noah, though other Christian apologists detected there another code, the relics of mankind's ancient universal adherence to the doctrine of the Trinity.[26]

Indeed, some scholars wondered whether the new sciences had really changed much of importance. Accommodation might not require strenuous efforts. Somewhat optimistically, the Anglican apologist George Rawlinson (1812–1902) argued that the findings of various sciences reinforced the monogenist truth of scripture. Geology, however problematic it appeared in other respects, Rawlinson claimed, 'at least witnesses to the recent creation of man, of whom there is no trace in any but the latest strata'. Physiology, much less ambiguously as far as Rawlinson was concerned, favoured 'the unity of the species, and the probable derivation of the whole human race from a single pair'. He found that comparative philology, in spite of some ambivalent findings, settled on the conclusion that 'languages will ultimately prove to have been all derived from a common basis'. Finally, ethnology had fixed on the plains of Shinar, 'independently of the scriptural record', as the 'common centre, or focus, from which the various lines of migration and the several types of races originally radiated'.[27] In a similar vein, Archdeacon John Pratt (1809–71) of Calcutta found it 'quite conceivable' that in 'primitive and half-civilized times, physiological changes might take place much more rapidly than they have done more recently and among nations of civilized and settled habits'.[28]

Such attitudes survived even at the highest levels of academic and scientific life. Given his eminence in geology, it is perhaps not surprising that the leading Canadian defender of Christian orthodoxy, Sir William Dawson, tried to reconcile Mosaic history with 'the disclosures of the gravels and caves'. The findings of palaeontology and physical anthropology were woven into an apparently updated – but remarkably unchanged – scheme of sacred history. In a similar manner, Dawson also married the findings of Indo-European philology to the scripture ethnology of Genesis 10. Dawson's strategy was to identify 'Palaeocosmic man, or man of the mammoth age', with man in the era before the Flood. According to Dawson, Europe had first been colonised before the Flood, and then only recolonised afterwards. Archaeological discoveries in Europe were of an antediluvian provenance, but not at odds with the timeframe set out in Genesis. Dawson conceded that the biblical Adam would probably have had the racial features of a primitive Turanian. However, he did not depart either from a biblical chronology of 6,000 years or from the core doctrine of monogenesis. Within a single species, racial varieties had emerged at a very early stage and had shown 'a remarkable fixity' in later history.[29]

However, others recognised that accommodation was not so easily achieved, and that some concessions would have to be made to science in order to preserve the core truth of monogenesis. Monogenist strategies dominated the British science of race during the first half of the nineteenth century, with James Cowles Prichard its most significant exponent. Although his primary background was medical, Prichard did not confine his monogenist argument to the realm of physical anthropology. Indeed, he came to the conclusion that physiological and anatomical researches were proving inadequate to pinpoint the exact links between specific peoples. Historical and comparative linguistics held out the promise of a more precise genealogical complement to monogenist anthropology. Thus, during the second decade of the nineteenth century, Prichard became attuned to the insights of the new philology and immersed himself in the Germanic scholarship of language families. However, where German philology confined itself to mapping distinctive language groups, Prichard sought out the ultimate relationship between language groups. Without some sense of the affinities between them, the new philology did nothing to bolster the case for monogenesis, which was Prichard's overriding concern. In *The eastern origin of the Celtic nations* (1831), Prichard identified the Celtic languages as a hitherto unsuspected linkage between the Indo-European and the Semitic language groups. Celtic, Prichard conjectured, was the remnant of a language older than other Indo-European languages and, as such, had a special affiliation with Sanskrit; however, by way of the pronomial suffixes, which Prichard believed to have been present in both ancient Celtic and Semitic languages, Celtic also seemed to suggest a bridge between Indo-European and Semitic languages. While other philologists sniffed at Prichard's hypothesised relationship between Celtic and Semitic languages, it seemed to Prichard, whose pole star was monogenesis, that the aboriginal unity of mankind should, in theory, be recoverable by way of historical linguistics.[30]

Prichard's influence extended beyond ethnology to adjacent branches of knowledge. In the field of archaeology the principal defender of monogenesis was Sir Daniel Wilson (1816–92), coiner of the term 'prehistoric' and a significant contributor to the study of prehistoric antiquity, first in his native Scotland and later in Canada where he was a professor from 1853 at University College, Toronto. A Scots Episcopalian of evangelical leanings, Wilson exhibited a clear debt to Prichard in his early works, not least in his researches on crania. Nevertheless, his career exhibits the marked tensions which scientists felt over the issue of monogenesis. The issue was, after all, of critical scientific importance. Writing in 1855, Wilson took the view that the 'question of the unity and common origin of mankind, with the consequent opinions as to the human race consisting of only one, or of several species, promises, from various causes, to become one of the most prominent scientific problems of our day'. Despite his evangelicalism, Wilson had a canny under-standing of the limits of scriptural authority in an era when the uni-formitarian geology of Lyell had rendered absurd the chronology of the world apparently set out in Genesis. The solution adopted by Wilson was to make a careful distinction between the authority that might justly be claimed for the Bible in the quite different fields of geology and ethnology. The scriptures, Wilson insisted, were 'never designed to furnish' any 'systems of science'. The creation story could be safely abandoned even by loyal defenders of scripture, for it was merely incidental to the overall theme of the Bible, the story of man. Thus the geologist could 'turn aside from the Mosaic record as a book never designed for his aid'; but the ethnologist would be wise to acknowledge the central truths about mankind in a book, after all, which was expressly devoted to that subject. Wilson remained a cautious guardian of the sacred narrative, chastising overzealous partisans of scripture and 'over-sensitive Mosaic geologists' for their incredible defences of biblical authority in contradiction of both the accepted truths of the new sciences and the very words of scripture themselves, if properly and modestly interpreted. Just how watertight were conventional canons of exegesis? Even the most frequently cited verses in defence of monogenesis did not quite say what monogenists insisted they said:

The simple declaration addressed by St Paul to the assembled Athenians, that God has 'made of one blood all nations of men to dwell on the face of the earth', has been produced as conclusive; but a more rigorous criticism compels the Christian student of science to admit that the interpretation of it, as meaning strictly a universal descent of every human being from one common pair of ancestors, is not necessarily the logical deduction from that beautiful and significant passage.

Thus, in lieu of any fantastical hypotheses about extinct species of anthropoids, Wilson preferred to take the straightforward line that the creation of the human race from a single beginning had followed eons of geological and natural change. In *Prehistoric man* (1862), Wilson challenged the polygenist error – and heresy – peddled in the United States by the likes of Samuel Morton, Josiah Nott and George Gliddon. On a visit to Philadelphia, Wilson was appalled at the coexistence of scientific learning and racial bigotry, indeed at their symbiosis given the legitimacy which polygenist science appeared to confer upon white prejudices. From his Canadian vantage point he wondered aloud 'how far the prejudices of cast [sic], and the motives of self-interest, or political bias, leave the American of the United States open to the impartial investigation of this important inquiry'. In particular, Wilson complained that the destructive polygenist certainties of the likes of Gliddon and Nott were somewhat premature, given the fact that ethnology as a discipline was still in its infancy. Who were they to drag 'into the arena of theological controversy' a science that still had 'its data to accumulate'? In response to the polygenist assumptions of the American school of anthropology, he carefully deployed craniometry to undermine racialist assumptions, demonstrating the immense variety of cranial forms within the supposedly distinct native Amerindian race. The New World, Wilson insisted, had been settled by peoples from the Old. Nevertheless, the scrupulous Wilson was prepared to shift his ground in response to scientific data. During the course of the mid-1860s he came to accept the overwhelming evidence of palaeolithic artefacts that the origins of man lay far beyond the conventional parameters of biblical chronology and even that man might have evolved from some higher ape. Yet Wilson in his latter years was no Darwinian, continuing to believe that humans had souls – implanted within them at a specific stage of the process of evolution – and to deploy biblical genealogy as a legitimate source for man's early history. Moreover, to the end of his career Wilson maintained a belief in the unity of humanity and the common potentiality of races.[31]

Similarly, the English Congregationalist lecturer John Pye Smith acknowledged that some concession had to be made from exegetical tradition to the new facts of science. He was keenly aware that the numbers of animals currently known to naturalists in the nineteenth century vastly exceeded the number previously fed into the calculations of generations of biblical commentators who had accounted for the conservation of all the world's species in the Ark. Indeed, a 'universal contemporaneous flood' was somewhat at odds, Pye Smith claimed, with the exact words of scripture. There were elements of scripture, he emphasised, which were 'figurative' and in the peculiar idioms of a primeval age, and these had to be converted into the 'plain diction' familiar to a modern readership to be properly understood. Moreover, Pye Smith also recognised that the distribution of flora and fauna throughout the world seemed to provide compelling evidence in support of polygenesis. The world seemed to be divided into 'several distinct regions, in each of which the indigenous animals and plants are, at least as to species and to a considerable amount as to genera, different from those of other zoological and botanical regions'. Pye Smith conceded the lack here of a 'common ancestry' and admitted that the various botanical and zoological zones of the world indicated the likely fact of there having been 'separate original creations, perhaps at different and respectively distinct epochs'. Nevertheless, Pye Smith could concede no more, insisting that man must be different. The races of men, he argued, constituted 'varieties', but not distinct 'species'. The descent of mankind from a single pair was, Pye Smith asserted, 'confirmed by an accumulation of proof from anatomical structure, from history, from the theory of language, and from the philosophy of intellectual and moral qualities'. Moreover, man and 'a small number of animals peculiarly serviceable to man' had been exempted from the zoological norm of localised ecological limits, but had been 'endowed with a capacity of adaptation' to a wide range of climates. Monogenesis was not something that an accommodationist could concede – at least at this stage in the first half of the nineteenth century.[32]

Clearly, the rise of race science should not be misconstrued. The mainstream version of race science in the British world during the first half of the nineteenth century – as a body of enquiry whose aims were to reconcile the fact of the world's racial diversity with a common humanity and to see off the polygenist heresy – was anti-racist in its motivations. The defence of Christian truth was for many of its defenders inextricably linked to the cause of racial harmony and mutual respect. The historian Sharon Turner argued that a pan-racial philanthropy was intrinsic to the monogenist story of creation found in the Old Testament: 'it has been made an unaltering principle in the divine creation of human nature, that all mankind shall be of one blood and of one descent, with perpetually attaching sympathies thence arising toward each other'.[33]

Nowhere did the nineteenth-century crisis of faith, and the polygenist question in particular, generate such pronounced and agonising tensions as in the United States of America. American polygenesis emerged out of a liberal reading of the Bible which minimised its scientific authority, as opposed to its undoubted religious and moral significance. In his *Thoughts on the original unity of the human race* (1830: 2nd edn, 1852), Dr Charles Caldwell (1772–1853) insisted that the scriptures were 'intended for our creed and direction exclusively in high and heavenly things, and not in matters pertaining merely to earth'. As such, they had 'no actual connection with physical science'. On this basis Caldwell felt able to challenge the prevalent notion that a 'disbelief in the hypothesis of the original unity of man' was tantamount to a 'disbelief of the Christian religion'. Nothing could be further from the truth; for, read in a liberal light, 'the writings of Moses offered no shadow of evidence' in favour of monogenesis. The Bible, according to Caldwell, told the history of the Caucasian race descended of Adam and Eve. Otherwise misguided 'scriptural unitists', as he termed them, would 'charge on the Deity the enforcement of incest between the sons and daughters of Adam'. There was, moreover, the particular problem of Cain, his fears of other humans and his marriage, presumably outside the line of Adam. In a similar vein, William Van Amringe also insisted that the 'Bible was not given for scientific instruction', and indeed that Genesis, in particular, was properly 'open' to 'a wider range of investigation than is generally supposed'. Van Amringe thought it 'no heresy to assert, that all men are not of the same species'. However, he backtracked from a clear enunciation of polygenesis to an ambiguous quasi-polygenist position which appeared to endorse mankind's original unity with God's rapid primeval conversion of Adamic humankind into four distinct 'species': Shemitic (including Israelites and Europeans), Japhethic (including Chinese, Eskimo, Aztecs and Incas), Ishmaelitic (including Tartars, Arabians and some Amerindians) and Canaanitic (including black Africans, Hottentots and Malays). This flagrant attempt to justify both racialism and the basic truths of scripture in an uneasy hybrid of monogenesis and polygenesis was – as we shall see – not untypical of mid-nineteenth-century American ethnology.[34]

Nevertheless, as in Britain, polygenesis and quasi-polygenesis were less central to ethnological opinion than defences of monogenesis, which ranged from straightforward revivals of environmentalist arguments to more original explanations of human unity, such as that proposed by the Presbyterian-turned-Swedenborgian Alexander Kinmont (1799–1838) in his *Twelve lectures on the natural history of man* (1839). Kinmont was a convinced monogenist, but had little truck with unpersuasive climatic theories of racial divergence. On the contrary, he found it more likely that 'the whole human family is actually sprung from a single pair, but that this single pair possessed within them the innate tendency to give rise, in the progress of generations, to several distinct origins of races'. Kinmont perceived that this monogenist theory of an aboriginal 'unity-in-variety' would guard against the irreligious consequences which lurked in the neglected penumbra of environmentalist anthropology: for, he argued, if racial variation were ascribed to environment, then 'so at last not only the modifications of man, but the entire man might be declared the pure creature of circumstances, endowed with the prerogatives of creation'. Environmentalism led logically, Kinmont opined, to a kind of atheistic evolutionism. Furthermore, Kinmont insisted that his theory avoided the prejudiced delusion of white monogenists questing after a single aboriginal 'type' of mankind – white, unsurprisingly – which they selected as the 'pattern card, as it were, after which all other [races] were to be formed'. Aboriginal unity resided, Kinmont believed, in the primeval 'harmony' of extant racial varieties, not in any single racial type.[35] Kinmont, however, stands at the anti-racialist extreme of nineteenth-century American ethnology. More commonly, nineteenth-century Americans found themselves more compromised, or even tied in knots, by the divergent ethnological meanings of scripture.

In the United States during the ante-bellum era there were two principal lines of division in the theological debate over race, and these did not run in parallel. The crisis of faith and in particular the vexed question of scriptural interpretation intersected with the debate over the morality and legitimacy of race slavery. Regardless of one's views, it was impossible to obtain absolute consistency between one's position on scriptural interpretation and one's stance on the subordination of blacks. Inconveniently for all concerned, scripture contained apparent endorsements of both slavery and monogenesis. In other words, the scripture seemed to offer a legitimation of slavery, but also upheld the unity and brotherhood of all races.

This explains why the theological battlelines over race slavery do not conform to modern expectations of sectional division. Of course, on one level, it appears that the denominational schisms – along sectional lines – which affected the Presbyterians, Methodists and Baptists between 1838 and 1845 provided a direct ecclesiastical precedent for the political division of the United States in the Civil War. Although the division of Presbyterians in 1837–8 between Old and New Schools was primarily theological, it was nevertheless exacerbated by the slavery issue which united Northern conservatives with Southern Old Schoolmen, and the secessions of Southern Methodists and Southern Baptists, both in 1845, were explicitly driven by the issue of slaveholding and a rejection of Northern abolitionism.[36] Yet in Northern theological circles matters were far from clear-cut over the issue of slavery. Some Northern theologians, including Moses Stuart, the most sophisticated defender of traditional biblical hermeneutics within the world of higher learning, accepted the legitimacy of slavery on the literal word of the Bible. In his *Critical history and defence of the Old Testament canon* (1845), Stuart tried to outlaw sceptical Christian questioning of the authority of the Old Testament, which some seemed to look upon as a heap of Jewish fables from which permanent truth had to be sifted from contemporary legend. Stuart reminded sceptics that in this respect Christ had most definitely not inaugurated a new dispensation. Christ and the apostles had clearly regarded the Old Testament as of divine origin and authority, which left nineteenth-century Christians little room to question that judgement. Nor did Stuart have much time for those German biblical critics who identified two different authors of Genesis, termed the Elohist and the Jehovist on account of the different names they deployed for the godhead. The most significant element bearing on the authority of Genesis, Stuart claimed, was not its presumed Mosaic authorship, but the fact that, whatever his namesake's authorial or editorial role, Moses had acted 'under Divine influence': 'It matters not to us who wrote these pieces, or when they were written. They have passed, as I believe, through Moses' hands, and are authenticated by him.'[37]

John Henry Hopkins (1792–1868), the Irish-born bishop of Vermont, was another prominent Northern defender of race slavery on the grounds of the inescapable authority of scripture. Hopkins was most alarmed at the impiety of those who challenged the authority of the Bible on the very grounds that it appeared to uphold the legality of slavery. There were some abolitionists, he feared, who would rather have an anti-slavery God and an anti-slavery Bible. In the face of the harsh truths of scripture history, Hopkins sought refuge in theodicy. He noted that in the aftermath of the curse upon Ham's lineage there had ensued the 'total degradation of the posterity of Ham, in the slave region of Africa'. Race slavery became, in effect, the benign stewardship of a lesser people. For those offspring of Ham who had 'lost knowledge of God, and become utterly polluted by the abominations of heathen idolatry', enslavement to the descendants of Shem and Japhet might seem to God, suggested Hopkins, their 'fittest condition'.[38]

There was nothing atypical about Stuart or Hopkins. As Mark Noll has shown, a biblicist acceptance of slavery was the position of 'most southern theologians and a large number of their northern colleagues'.[39] The words of the Bible could not be interpreted away, concluded many Northern traditionalists, without some sleight of hand which threatened the dominant 'Reformed literalist' reception of scripture. Abolitionism was not only considered to be unjustified by scripture but was also identified as a threat to the very authority of scripture. Given the apparent strength of the biblical case for slavery, Southerners were able to denounce abolitionism as a heresy. Abolitionism, claimed the Southern lawyer and politician Howell Cobb (1815–68), 'is not a political question; it is a religious delusion'. To be fair, however, the scrupulous Cobb also recognised that the warrant of scripture should not be abused to justify all kinds of slavery. Non-biblical forms of labour regulation were illegitimate: 'Any system of slavery outside of the Bible system, we regard as of human origin, and therefore an abuse.'[40]

How could Christians appalled at the crime of slavery evade the unwelcome facts of Old Testament history? There were, fortunately, some escape routes available to moderate emancipationists. One involved an acceptance of biblical slavery, but a refusal to accept that the highly regulated system of servitude found in the Old Testament was in any way the equivalent of the modern American form of chattel slavery. Another option was to disaggregate the historical from the moral elements of the Bible in order to point up the sharp contrast between the letter and the spirit of its contents. Although the Bible appeared to endorse slavery, its overwhelming message centred upon the liberation – spiritual as well as practical – associated with Christianity. Did the clear moral code of the gospels not trump the less significant aspect of the Bible as a bare historical record of the doings of the nation of Israel? Moreover, why did defenders of slavery not spring also to the defence of polygamy and Jewish dietary laws, for which the Old Testament also appeared to legislate? The religious debates over slavery raised in an acute form fundamental issues of scriptural interpretation. Did the Bible convey a 'progressive revelation', whereby the New Testament discredited the message of the Old? How were Americans to make sense of a body of scripture about which theologians disagreed so vehemently? Indeed, extreme abolitionists also had the option of rejecting the Bible's message in the greater cause of defeating slavery. This was, of course, not a popular choice, but it did have the merit of clear ethical and exegetical consistency.[41]

The story of Ham, on the other hand, seemed to offer Southerners a divine sanction for race slavery. This was certainly the view of contemporary commentators. The Northern anti-slavery theologian Theodore

Dwight Weld (1803–95) claimed that the 'prophecy of Noah' found in
Genesis 9:25 was 'the vade mecum of slaveholders, and they never venture
abroad without it'. It seemed to Weld that proponents of slavery used the
story of the curse upon Ham's lineage as a 'charm to spell-bind opposition'.[42] Southerners generally subscribed to a less cynical interpretation
of this phenomenon. Indeed, Frederick Ross of Huntsville, Alabama, in a
speech delivered to the General Assembly of the Presbyterian Church,
declared – as a defender of slavery – that the future of the American slave
was 'the last scene in the last act of the great drama of Ham'.[43] In a very
influential pamphlet which went through several editions, *Scriptural and
statistical views in favor of slavery* (1841), Thornton Stringfellow, a Baptist
minister in Culpeper County, Virginia, claimed, on a careful reading of
Genesis, that God himself was the begetter of slavery. The story of the
curse on Ham's lineage in Genesis 9:25–7 not only showed 'the favor
which God would exercise to the posterity of Shem and Japheth' –
identified as the peoples of Europe, America and a great part of Asia –
'while they were holding the posterity of Ham in a state of abject bondage'; its implications for the scriptural debate on race slavery went even
deeper. This was the 'first recorded language which was ever uttered in
relation to slavery', and this led Stringfellow to wonder, indeed, whether
it might 'not be said in truth, that God decreed this institution before it
existed; and has he not connected its existence with prophetic tokens of
special favor, to those who should be slave owners or masters?'[44] Historians have concurred with contemporary assessments. William Sumner
Jenkins in his classic study of Southern defences of slavery argued that,
'throughout the entire controversy', this biblical argument 'was made use
of more often than any other'. More recently, this view finds endorsement
in the work of Thomas Peterson, Stephen Haynes and the Genoveses.[45]

   The curse upon Ham was not simply the easy slogan of stupid racists.
'Clever' racists showed a certain sensitivity to the nuances and implications of the curse upon Ham, in particular its wider bearing upon the
overall coherence of Christian anthropology. The apparent incompatibility of racial subordination and scriptural monogenesis necessitated
some creative extrapolations from the bare words of scripture. These
combined an appalling racial bigotry with a degree of theological
sophistication. For instance, Josiah Priest, a Northerner from New York,
managed to reconcile natural and intrinsic black inferiority with an
ultimate Adamic monogenesis. Priest argued that 'negro' blood had been
created by a special divine providence in the womb of Noah's wife when
she was carrying Ham. This punctured the abolitionist claim that blacks

bore the same Adamic blood as whites. Blacks were, Priest claimed, somehow physiologically different from whites, though they too ultimately traced their descent back to Adam. Monogenesis was not, therefore, incompatible, Priest could boast, with white superiority.[46]

On the other hand, of course, polygenesis had become a respectable *scientific* option in the United States by the middle of the nineteenth century, notwithstanding the unwelcome theological baggage it brought in its wake. Polygenist, or quasi-polygenist, science appeared in the universities and learned societies of the North. This left those scientists who reached polygenist conclusions for purely scientific reasons but abhorred the idea of white supremacy in an awkward position. Most prominent among such equivocal polygenists was Louis Agassiz, the Swiss-born geologist and naturalist who became the doyen of American science during his years at Harvard. Responding to a paper by Nott at the March 1850 meeting of the American Association for the Advancement of Science, Agassiz found himself on a very narrow strand of middle ground between the polygenists and the monogenists. Here he effected an elegant pirouette, sidestepping both the orthodox theory of monogenesis, which in his estimation now lacked scientific credibility, and an offensive white racial supremacy unwarranted by biological theories of polygenesis. Agassiz claimed that all men shared a spiritual and moral unity, but that zoologically they were distinct. Such distinctions were permanent and primeval. Nor did the different races of men spring from a single pair of humans. However, as men possessed a unified moral and spiritual nature, polygenist science did not legitimise slavery, which, regardless of polygenesis, was an immoral abomination. Indeed, Agassiz was not conscious of differing from the Bible. The scriptures, he insisted, described only the origin of the Caucasian race. Genesis said nothing about 'the origin of the inhabitants now found in those parts of the world which were unknown to the ancients'.[47]

In a fuller analysis of the question in the July 1850 number of the *Christian Examiner*, Agassiz detached the issue of 'the unity of mankind' from the separate problem of 'the diversity of origin of the human races'. The result was a benign discord as Agassiz tried to build upon a polygenist account of the races of mankind what seemed like an implausibly monogenist ethic of Christian philanthropy:

We recognize the fact of the unity of mankind. It excites a feeling that raises men to the most elevated sense of their connections with each other. It is but the reflection of that divine nature which pervades their whole being. It is because

men feel thus related to each other, that they acknowledge those obligations of
kindness and moral responsibility which rest upon their mutual relations.

Here Agassiz almost conceded the dependence of good race relations
upon the fact of monogenesis, which he then proceeded to reject, at least
in the terms in which it was then commonly understood. Agassiz was,
however, acutely self-conscious that his sleight of hand had hitherto gone
unappreciated: 'The writer has been in this respect strangely mis-
represented. Because he has at one time said that mankind constitutes one
species, and at another time has said that men did not originate from one
common stock, he has been represented as contradicting himself.' Not so,
protested Agassiz, distinguishing unity of species from unity of origin. A
diversity of origin, he insisted, did not mean automatically that the races
of mankind constituted a 'plurality of species'. His critics, he alleged, had
failed to perceive the human unity in racial diversity.[48]
    Nor did Agassiz concede that his arguments for racial diversity within
the unity of the human species involved any retreat from the truth of
scripture, and in particular from the narrative of the beginnings of
humankind in Adam and Eve. The Bible, Agassiz noted, was severely
circumscribed in its geographical matter: 'Do we find in any part of the
scriptures any reference to the inhabitants of the arctic zone, of Japan, of
China, of New Holland, or of America?' The Bible said nothing about
how these parts of the world were peopled. Therefore, Agassiz claimed,
his investigations of the origins of humanity in these parts of the world
had 'nothing to do with Genesis'. A doubly agonised Agassiz felt obliged
to 'disclaim any connection of these inquiries with the moral principles to
be derived from the holy scriptures, or with the political condition of the
negroes'. He felt keenly the charge that his scheme of polygenesis tended
to support the institution of slavery. Surely, Agassiz pointed out, slavery
had nothing to do with the origins of the races of Asia or the Americas.
Moreover, all races were equal before God, each possessing 'a spark of
that divine light' which rendered man conscious of eternity. Indeed,
Agassiz tried to turn the tables on the strict monogenists, for the environmentalist arguments put forward by monogenists appeared to down-
grade the role of God in the creation of races: 'Unconsciously, they
advocate a greater and more extensive influence in the production of
those peculiarities by physical agencies than by the Deity himself. If their
view were true, God had less to do directly with the production of the
diversity which exists in nature . . . than climatic conditions.' Agassiz, on
the other hand, accorded a more significant role to God in the creation of

the distinct races of the human family. Races, science appeared to confirm, were of divine creation. Yet Agassiz's rhetorical coup scarcely veiled his pronounced anxieties. To us they serve as a reminder that in the intellectual elites of the United States in the nineteenth century the political question of black slavery did not eclipse the equal, if not greater, theological issue of the unity of races.[49]

While the ethnological literature of the 1850s is read – inevitably – in the retrospective light of the Civil War's imminence, it is important to acknowledge that to contemporaries it seemed that the South faced not only the obvious threat posed by Northern abolitionism, but also the equally potent menace of 'infidelity', not least in the all-too-alluring form of polygenesis. Michael O'Brien, the leading authority on intellectual life in the South, has argued that ante-bellum Southern intellectuals were conscious too of participating in an international debate on the relationship of scripture, race and science which transcended the local matter of slavery. For instance, the works of French racial theorists, such as Virey and Gobineau, surfaced in American editions. According to O'Brien, it was the threat posed to scripture by the natural sciences (including the science of race) which 'agitated nerves', while 'the social subjection of Africans to white Southerners' control was almost the least important issue embroiled in these disputes'. Indeed, the defenders of slavery in the South were sharply divided between those who aimed to uphold both slavery and the authority of scripture and those who took issue with traditional Christian ethnology while using polygenist arguments to justify the prevailing system of race slavery. The battle between unitarists and pluralists cut across the more memorable conflict between defenders of slavery and abolitionists.[50]

George Fitzhugh (1806–81), the subtlest and most adept of slavery's defenders, perceived the logical connection between slavery and scriptural authority. As slavery was 'expressly and continually justified by Holy Writ', any concession of its legitimacy signalled not only an abandonment of the Southern 'cause', but also an implied rejection of the authority of Christian revelation: 'if white slavery be morally wrong, be a violation of natural rights, the Bible cannot be true'. On the other hand, Fitzhugh saw immediately the heretical baggage that accompanied polygenist arguments. These, he claimed, were 'at war with scripture, which teaches us that the whole human race descended from a common parentage'. Indeed, 'the argument about races' was, Fitzhugh argued, 'an infidel procedure'. His position in 1857 was resolute, that 'we had better give up the negroes than the Bible'; nevertheless, by 1861, with a heightening of political tensions and under the influence of the racialist arguments of John Van Evrie, the staunchly monogenist Fitzhugh had been won round to the hitherto despised arguments for polygenesis.[51]

Indeed, the siren voices of polygenesis which so distracted the South also sang in a Southern accent, most notoriously in the work of Josiah Nott (1804–73) of Mobile, Alabama, who collaborated on a major polygenist project with George Gliddon, the *Types of mankind*, which went through ten editions by 1871. Nott and Gliddon did not mount an open challenge to the authority of scripture. Rather, they pretended that they were updating scriptural interpretation, bringing it into line with developments in science and ironing out wrinkles within scripture itself. They denied that there was anything 'heretical' in polygenesis, for scripture did not deal with the totality of the human races. Monogenesis was to be rejected as an 'ecclesiastical prejudice' based upon a profound misreading of scripture.[52]

Nott and Gliddon exposed the 'illusion' that any but the white types of mankind are to be found in Genesis: 'The Bible really gives no history of all the races of men, and but a meagre account of one.' Too often, misguided Christians failed to realise that the sacred history, geography and ethnology of Genesis did not present a global picture, but a localised history, geography and ethnology of part of the ancient Middle East. As a body of knowledge about ethnology, Genesis was circumscribed and local. The Negro races, Nott and Gliddon claimed, were not known to the author of Genesis. Thus, it appeared, the Bible uses 'universal' terms loosely without any intention that they be read as literally universal in scope. The Bible is in fact very restricted in its geographical and anthropological coverage. Nor, indeed, was Acts 17:26 – that God 'hath made of one blood all nations of men' – to be read in a universal sense.[53]

Monogenesis, Nott and Gliddon argued, was inconsistent with the findings of science and could be explained away only by a miracle. No causes were currently in operation which could 'transmute' one type or race of man into another. Rather, the existing human races were 'distinct primordial forms of the type of man'. History and archaeology vindicated science. Certain types had been permanent through 'all recorded time'. Nott and Gliddon went on to reject the otherwise persuasive argument for human unity on the basis that males and females of all races could successfully interbreed with one another. Rather, Nott and Gliddon argued that 'those races of men most separated in physical organisation – such as the blacks and the whites – do not amalgamate perfectly, but obey the laws of hybridity'. In other words, the genus *homo* embraced several 'primordial types or species'. Nott and Gliddon divided the globe into distinct zones of creation each with its own particular flora, fauna and races; for 'the human family offers no exception to this general law, but fully conforms to it: Mankind being divided into several groups of races, each of which constitutes a primitive element in the fauna of its peculiar province'.[54]

Together the crisis of faith and the rise of Northern sectional hostility to the race slavery of the South cast a very dark shadow over mid-nineteenth-century Southern ethnological speculation. The two issues were inseparable. Generally, however, slaveholders and their apologists seem to have found greater security in a literal reading of scripture, than in the risky speculations of ultra-racist polygenesis. The clarity of the scripture record on the subject of slavery seemed to drown out most effectively other discordances, while monogenesis offered itself as a proven – albeit wobbly – platform which might be renewed and strengthened in the cause of Christian racialism. Nevertheless, as Peterson noted, Christian racists in the American South 'had to maintain a difficult middle position'.[55] They were compelled by religious obligations to acknowledge that Africans were their brothers in a shared descent from Adam, as well as that their African kindred ought to be converted to Christianity and to receive its benefits. On the other hand, Christian racists had to find some way of explaining why their darker-skinned brothers were inferior and should be subordinated within the slave system to Caucasian Americans without undermining the biblical story of racial unity.

Which posed the greater threat to Southern conservatives, the abolitionist denunciation of slavery or the polygenist subversion of biblical authority? Perceptive Southerners recognised that polygenist racialism – however superficially convenient it might appear – was an even greater threat to their worldview than abolitionism or abolitionist readings of scripture. Ironically, some of the most noted and forthright defenders of monogenesis in the United States in the nineteenth century were based in the South, men such as Thomas Smyth, the Lutheran clergyman-scientist John Bachman (1790–1874) of Charleston, South Carolina, and J. L. Cabell (1813–89), a professor of comparative anatomy and physiology at the University of Virginia.[56] In particular, monogenists identified the polygenist theories of Nott and Gliddon as a polygenist fifth column which threatened to weaken the South's white Christian society from within. Bachman reckoned polygenist heterodoxy more insidious than the more obvious external threat of abolitionism: 'In a political point of view, we regard the effort made by Nott and Gliddon, to establish their theory by a denial of the veracity of the historical scriptures, as more dangerous to our institutions than all the ravings of the abolitionists.' At the heart of Bachman's monogenist analysis of race lay an analogy with the domestication of animals. Had not breeding led to a diversity of colours in cattle? Then, what was so unusual about a diversity of colours within the human species? However, his logic led Bachman to the conclusion – strictly speaking not heretical, but far from palatable in the South – that the earliest humans had not been white. Nor had they been black, but some indeterminate colour between the extremes of European whiteness and African blackness. Although Bachman insisted that blacks were of the same original stock as other humans and that all humans belonged to the same species, he argued that as a result of certain adaptations to climate Africans now constituted 'an inferior variety of our species'. Nevertheless, Christian paternalism of the Southern sort offered a means of the moral and intellectual elevation of the black race. The prudent Bachman wondered whether anti-Christian polygenist arguments might backfire on their champions:

the advocates of a plurality of races should especially be on their guard lest the enemies of our domestic institutions should have room to accuse them of prejudice and selfishness, in desiring to degrade their servants below the level of those creatures of God to whom a revelation has been given, and for whose salvation a Saviour died, as an excuse for retaining them in servitude.[57]

The defence of slavery, it seemed, was more compelling when yoked to the norms of Christian orthodoxy. Similarly Cabell issued a warning that

those who, in the providence of God, have been placed in that part of our common country in which the African race is held in servitude, will not be induced by the weak reasoning of a shallow book [Nott and Gliddon's *Types of mankind*] to put themselves in a false position before the Christian world, and foolishly to seize upon a scientific error, as a mode of asserting rights which have been guaranteed by the Federal Compact.

However, Cabell was equally critical of the 'modern fanaticism' of the abolitionists which he believed to be mistakenly inspired by following a false trail of deductive logic from the basic truth of monogenesis.[58] For Southern monogenists, the basic unity of humanity did not lead inexorably to a Christian critique of slavery.

Indeed, might it not be possible to square the circle of monogenist truth and racial hierarchy? Samuel Davies Baldwin's defence of the fundamental racial distinctions that underpinned Southern slavery declared its primary intent as a prophetic vindication of the truths of Genesis against 'the recent attacks of ethnological infidelity on the credibility of scripture'. Baldwin resolved the Southern dilemma of monogenist obligation and polygenist inclination by asserting both the unity and trinity of race. All men were descended from Adam, and in the antediluvian era there had been an equality of races. In the aftermath of the Flood, however, God had made distinct promises to the lineages of Shem, Japhet and Ham – 'the divine rights of races proclaimed in the law of Noah'. These promises were reflected in the varying modern conditions of the great races of mankind, a fulfilment of prophecy which also happily confirmed the truth of scripture. The accomplishment of racial prophecy was evident, Baldwin contended,

in all quarters of the globe since the flood, but most sublimely in America. It is obvious in a universal and permanent trinity of races; in their political inequality of condition; in the Christianization of all the Japhetic nations, and of no others; in the occupation of the Shemitic wilderness of America by Japheth; and in the service of Ham to Japheth in the Southern States, in the islands, and in South America.[59]

Conservative Southerners commonly charged the abolitionist North with being the source of the heretical poison of polygenesis. James Henley Thornwell (1812–62), one of the South's leading Presbyterian intellectuals and a convinced monogenist, claimed that it was 'as idle to charge the responsibility of the doctrine of separate species upon slaveholders, as to load them with the guilt of questioning the geological accuracy of Moses'. Such 'assaults of infidel science upon the records of our faith' did not stem from the South, but had rather 'found their warmest advocates among the opponents of slavery'. This was, of course, far from true.[60]

While few Southern polygenists were as unequivocal as Nott and Gliddon, others were just as offensive. Consider the bizarre contortions of Dr Samuel Cartwright of New Orleans (1793–1862), an outspoken Southern proponent of the scientific case for slavery. Cartwright flirted with polygenesis while denying it, and aligned himself with the Bible while decrying Southern clergymen for ignoring the racist potential of sacred writ. In his discussion of 'The prognathous species of mankind' (1857), Cartwright protested that he did not intend 'by the use of the term prognathous to call in question the black man's humanity or the unity of the human races as a genus, but to prove that the species of the genus homo are not a unity, but a plurality, each essentially different from the

others'. Within this advertised monogenist framework, however, Cartwright proclaimed the prognathous black race to be 'so unlike the other
two' as to share the prognathism or forward-jutting jaw of the 'brute
creation'. Not that the prognathous Negro was 'a brute', Cartwright half-
retreated, 'or half man and half brute, but a genuine human being,
anatomically constructed, about the head and face, more like the monkey
tribes and the lower order of animals than any other species of the genus
man'. Cartwright was content to describe the 'prognathous race' as
'Canaanites' or 'Cushites', and he wove the biblical account of the origins
of mankind seamlessly into his scientific analysis of racial difference.[61]

Similarly, in his article 'Unity of the human race disproved by the
Hebrew Bible', Cartwright highlighted distortions and errors in the
transmission of the true words of sacred writ in the Hebrew Bible as a way
of conjuring up a biblical sanction for a kind of polygenesis in which
there were two separate creations of races, though both races were
'intellectual creatures with immortal souls'. According to Cartwright, the
Hebrew Bible

positively affirms that there were, at least, two races of intellectual creatures with
immortal souls, created at different times. Thus, in the 24th verse of the 1st
chapter of Genesis, 'The Lord said, Let the earth bring forth intellectual creatures
with immortal souls after their kind; cattle, and creeping thing, and beast of the
earth after his kind, and it was so.' In our English version, instead of 'intellectual
creatures with immortal souls', we have only the words 'living creature', as
representing the Hebrew words, naphesh chaiyah. The last word means living
creature, and the word naphesh, which invests chaiyah, or living creature, with
intellectuality and immortality, is not translated at all, either in the Douay Bible
or that of King James. But there it stands more durable than brass or granite,
inviting us to look at that, and we will understand it.

Cartwright blamed Protestant as well as Catholic translators of the Bible
for ignoring the racial significance of the expression 'naphesh chaiyah'
and thus for missing the full translation of all they purported. Thus
modern renderings of the Bible had at their core a crucial ethnological
absence which misled Christians on the race question: 'Mississippi and
Louisiana are half full of negroes, and so is the Hebrew Bible, but our
English version has not got a negro in it.' Cartwright extrapolated from
this insight to draw an ethnological account of the Fall which firmly
linked the black race with evil purposes. Drawing on some suspicions first
aired by the English biblical critic Adam Clarke (1762?–1832), to the effect
that the creature that had beguiled Eve was endowed with the gifts

of speech and reason, and might be presumed to be a creature more like an orang-outang than a serpent, Cartwright went a whimsical and obnoxious stage further to identify Nachash, the Hebrew term for the tempter of Eve, as Eden's 'negro gardener'. Not that the serpent was dispensed with altogether. Cartwright also drew upon the old early modern identification of Hamites with paganism, to identify blacks as an idolatrous serpent-worshipping race.[62]

This tradition was refurbished in the aftermath of the American Civil War as a justification for continuing white supremacy. Writing in 1867 under the pseudonym of Ariel and a misleading Northern imprint, Buckner H. Payne, a Nashville publisher and clergyman, insisted that all the sons of Noah had been white and that the curse upon Ham had changed neither his own colour nor the colour of his descendants. All the descendants of Noah, it appeared, including those lines which sprang both from Ham and from his son Canaan, had been of the white race. Payne, indeed, set out in some detail the physical features of the entire Hamitic line, which included 'long, straight hair', 'high foreheads', 'high noses' and 'thin lips'. This conclusion, however, led to a further problem. If the Flood had been universal and all the humans on the Ark had been the racially pure white family and daughters-in-law of Noah, then how was it that a black race existed in a world populated from the survivors of the Flood? Payne solved this conundrum by arguing that blacks had been created separately from whites as an inferior species without immortal souls and that they had indeed been present in the Ark – not as humans but as 'beasts'. Indeed, according to Payne, God had decided to destroy the world in a wholly justified act of ethnic cleansing to rid the world of the mixed race which had come about through miscegenation between the white, spiritual offspring of Adam and Eve and the soulless blacks, 'a separate and distinct species of the genus homo from Adam and Eve'. Being racially pure, the clan of Noah had escaped this racial genocide. The racist Payne was convinced of the righteousness of God's actions; indeed, he pointed out that while God saw a number of vile sins committed in the course of Old Testament history – the eating of the forbidden fruit, the murder of Abel, Lot's incest and the selling of Joseph into slavery by his own brothers – it was only the obnoxious inter-racial 'mésalliance' of black and white, a crime which 'could not be, or ever will be, propitiated', that had driven Him to universal genocide. In his creative reinterpretation of scripture, Payne provided an even more compelling biblical justification for race slavery than that found in the story of Ham, and one which also incorporated a divine ban on miscegenation, which provided a chilling message for a threatened white society when his pamphlet was republished in a second edition in the aftermath of the American Civil War. So horrible indeed was the impending threat of miscegenation, the worst of all possible sins, that Payne concluded that the future prosperity of the United States could be obtained only by way of the exportation of its blacks back to Africa or by their immediate re-enslavement.[63]

Payne's outrageous scheme of scriptural ethnology attracted a measure of support from disillusioned Christian racists, notwithstanding its cavalier interpretation of Genesis. In *Nachash: what is it?* (1868), the Reverend D. G. Phillips of Louisville, Georgia, agreed that the Bible identified the blacks as pre-Adamites and insisted that the curse on Nachash was the divine justification of 'slavery', which he interpreted broadly – and conveniently – to include not only the chattel slavery extinguished by the Civil War, but also a more general political subjection consonant with white supremacy.[64] The anonymous author of *The Adamic race* (1868) repudiated the notion that blacks were soulless beasts, but endorsed the view that they (along with five other inferior pre-Adamite races) had been created separately from white Adamites – and not after the image of God.[65] Similarly, the pseudonymous Sister Sallie argued that neither the Amerindian nor the black was of Adam's posterity and that the Flood had been a punishment for miscegenation.[66] In *The pre-Adamite, or who tempted Eve?* (1875), A. Hoyle Lester claimed that there had been five distinct creations of races, of which only the fifth, the Caucasian race, of which Adam was the father, had been 'made in God's own image and likeness'. Nevertheless, Lester identified the serpent not as a black, the first of the pre-Adamite races, but as a slippery Mongolian, of a later pre-Adamite race.[67] By contrast, Charles Carroll (b. 1849) in *The tempter of Eve* (1902) identified Nachash as a Negress, Eve's black maidservant. Nevertheless, in spite of these minor variations in the identification of this curious 'serpent' – which possessed the gifts of speech and reason, and walked upright – with non-white races, these works maintained a consistent interpretation of blacks as an inferior, pre-Adamite race whose members did not have immortal souls. Indeed, the blending of the soulless races with Adamic whites had not only caused an affront to God, spoiling his racial plan of Creation, but had also led, according to Carroll, to the delusive errors of evolution. Miscegenation became in time 'the parent of atheism, with its theory of development [evolution] . . . which attributes the whole phenomenon of the universe to natural causes'.[68]

The Nachash tradition had its critics, not least because it transgressed the conventional racist identification of blacks as the cursed progeny of Ham. Indeed, bizarrely, Payne's controversial publication provoked a war of words between his hyper-racialist followers and, on the other side, diehard racialists of an older stamp, who on this occasion occupied the more 'liberal' position. Whereas the hyper-racialists insisted that blacks were not descended of Ham, old-time Christian racialists continued to defend the Hamitic – by extension, Adamite – descent of blacks. Robert Young, a Nashville divine, aligned himself with a more traditional strain of Christian racialism:

We do not believe in the social equality of the Negro. We do not believe he knows how to handle the vote . . . Still, we believe the Negro is a descendant of Adam and Eve; that he is the progeny of Ham; that he is a human being, and has an immortal soul.[69]

For traditional racists, blacks constituted an inferior race, but their Adamic ancestry nonetheless entitled them to the blessings of eternal life, which Payne and his cohort explicitly denied them.

The theological tensions that bedevilled white intellectuals who participated in debates over American race slavery and its troubled aftermath also surfaced in other contexts of racial subordination. In particular, the issue of race within the nineteenth-century British Empire was also conceived as a theological problem, which constituted part of the wider crisis of faith. The twinned issues of religious orthodoxy and inter-racial philanthropy contributed to a faultline within the British science of race between 'ethnology' and 'anthropology', which was for a time represented by divisions between distinctive Ethnological and Anthropological Societies. Ethnology developed as a science of human unity, but anthropology placed much greater emphasis upon the scientifically irreconcilable differences between physical races. Whereas the Ethnological Society of London embodied monogenist approaches rooted in Christian principle, the Anthropological Society of London was more radical in orientation, free of the shackles of religious scruples and untroubled by the heretical associations of polygenism. Anthropology emerged in good part as a reaction against the religious constraints which circumscribed ethnology. Ethnology, on the other hand, had a clear religious provenance in a milieu dominated by Evangelical and by Quaker influences, the Ethnological Society having emerged out of the Aborigines Protection Society. The Aborigines Protection Society, which was founded in 1837 by the Quaker doctor Thomas Hodgkin (1798–1866), had as its motto *ab uno sanguine* ('from one blood'), and it is clear that its philanthropic attitude to the plight of indigenous peoples was underpinned by monogenist theology. The society was committed both to the furtherance of 'sacred truth' and to a heartfelt acknowledgement of the 'desolation and utter ruin' which the British Empire had caused to native societies. The aim was to bring about a reformation in the nature of colonialism. However, the society was torn between humanitarian and ethnological impulses. In 1843 the Ethnological Society emerged out of the frustrations of the scientific wing of the Aborigines Protection Society, though some members had no trouble maintaining membership of both organisations, including Hodgkin himself. However, the Ethnological Society contained its own divisions, and those of its members who felt trammelled by the dominant monogenist orthodoxy of the society, such as James Hunt (1833–69), formed a rival Anthropological Society of London, whose focus was more intently on the physical differences between races. Nor, as George Stocking has pointed out, would the new discipline of 'Anthropology' be 'hamstrung by biblical dogma'. The anthropologists regarded the idiom of monogenist ethnology inspired by Prichard to be fundamentally unscientific, and there were insinuations that opposition to the science of race was connected to a morbid 'religious mania'. Contemporaries perceived a close linkage between attitudes towards the darker races and one's position on the ever more significant Christian tenet of monogenesis. In a rebuke to the polygenists, the Reverend J. Dingle argued at a meeting of the Anthropological Society in 1864 that polygenist theory had been deployed to 'justify the most outrageous oppression, and to palliate the most disgusting cruelty' towards indigenous peoples.[70]

Christian missionaries in Africa confronted the theological issue of the racial origins of man in its starkest and most vivid form – face to face with a black African race which polygenists suggested might not be descended of Adam, but which missionaries acknowledged as fellow children of God whom they hoped to convert from heathendom. Here one highly unusual figure stands out for his formidable intellectual engagement with the latest developments in the sciences and in biblical criticism which together threatened the reassuring monogenesis upon which the missionary enterprise generally rested. This unconventional standard bearer of Christianity was John William Colenso (1814–83), Anglican bishop of Natal, who came to develop serious doubts about the historical veracity of the Old Testament. Ironically, Colenso's doubts stemmed largely from his missionary enthusiasm to convert the Zulu to the 'truths' of

Christianity. Colenso studied the Zulu language and translated into Zulu first the New Testament, then some of the early portions of the Old Testament, including Genesis and Exodus. He also published a Zulu grammar and dictionary. Colenso's philological labours benefited from the assistance of native amanuenses, and through such close contact he came to appreciate the 'objections and difficulties' which the Bible presented to the Zulu mind:

While translating the story of the Flood, I have had a simple-minded, but intelligent native – one with the docility of a child, but the reasoning powers of mature age – look up, and ask, 'Is all that true? Do you really believe that all this happened thus – that all the beasts, and birds, and creeping things, upon the earth, large and small, from hot countries and cold, came thus by pairs, and entered into the ark with Noah? And did Noah gather food for them all, for the beasts and birds of prey, as well as the rest?'

Such questions posed an agonising dilemma for the scrupulous Colenso, who was himself curiously literal-minded. He acknowledged inwardly that 'on geological grounds' a global deluge of the sort 'the Bible manifestly speaks of, could not possibly have taken place in the way described in the Book of Genesis'. To take but one destructive fact: the volcanic hills of the Auvergne had clearly been formed long before the Flood, yet were covered with a light pumice stone which would have been easily swept away by a universal inundation. Nor was a 'partial' Flood a possibility up to the height of the mountains of Ararat on which the Ark had finally come to rest; for a flood of this depth 'must necessarily become universal'. How was Colenso to answer his truth-seeking Zulu enquirer? Honesty on this occasion prompted a truthful answer which, however, fell short of the whole truth, which would have subverted the very biblical foundations of his missionary enterprise. 'I felt', confessed Colenso, 'that I dared not, as a servant of the God of Truth, urge my brother man to believe that, which I did not myself believe, which I knew to be untrue, as a matter-of-fact, historical narrative.' Nevertheless, Colenso stopped short of openly discrediting 'the general veracity of the Bible history'. Yet this painful encounter prompted a deep engagement with the historical truthfulness of scripture. Ultimately, nothing was too good for Colenso's Zulu flock: if white Europeans were being exposed to the devastating insights of biblical criticism and the revolutionary speculations of biological and geological sciences, then these should not be denied to his potential Zulu converts. Colenso wanted to convert the Zulu to the most authentic, rigorous and compelling version of Christianity which science and biblical criticism would allow.[71]

It so happened that Colenso, as well as being utterly literal-minded, was by training a very able arithmetician and the author of various books on mathematical topics. As a result, his probings of Old Testament history took the form of an absurdly literal attempt to calculate from the evidence casually set out in the first books of the Bible such things as the population of the Israelite nation and the number of livestock required to support the Israelites and their ritual sacrifices. Indeed, no theologian has ever paid such close attention to the number of sheep and cattle in the Bible. Close demographic calculations of both human and livestock populations exposed the Old Testament as a tissue of arithmetic absurdity. Exodus 12:37 indicated that around 600,000 male Israelites aged twenty and upwards had left Egypt under Moses. Extrapolating from this biblical fact, Colenso calculated that over two million Hebrews (including women and children) had participated in the Exodus, as well as two million sheep and 50,000 oxen. The sheep alone would have required twenty-five miles of grazing. Colenso found that the court of the tabernacle, which was supposed to hold the assembled congregation of the nation of Israel, would need to have been twenty miles deep. Moreover, the Israelites would have needed around 200,000 tents, and their encampment would have covered an area of roughly twelve miles by twelve miles. The scale of this encampment would have imposed a particular problem for those who lived far from the perimeter, for, according to the prescribed rules of cleanliness set out in Deuteronomy 23:12, the Israelites were compelled to travel outside the camp to relieve themselves. Indeed, dung – human and animal – was a minor obsession of Colenso's. Not only did Colenso's demographic approach to herme-neutics directly challenge the veracity of scripture; but his fascination with the quantities of excrement produced by the Israelites and their cattle constituted, in the eyes of his critics, an affront to the dignity of scripture. Noah's Ark presented its own problems in this regard. How did Noah and his family manage to clean out the droppings of all the various pairs of animal conserved in the Ark, never mind the excrement of the multitudes of additional sheep required to keep the carnivores fed? The more Colenso thought about the implications of the Ark and its place in the populating of the animal world, the more troubled he was by the narrative set out in Genesis. Selection by pairs surely presented a difficulty for animals such as insects which did not pair up as such but cohabited in other arrangements. How did the surviving animals, such as the flightless dodo of the island of Mauritius, manage to populate those remote parts of the world in which they were now found? It is, perhaps, hard for a modern reader to grasp that there was nothing irreverent in Colenso's tone; if anything Colenso had a straightforward and uncompromising reverence for truth. So simple-minded was Colenso's honesty in the face of sacred history – unlike the sophisticated probings of the Higher Criticism – that his was an argument that the laity found all too easy to follow by way of offensive trivialities to its manifestly heretical conclusions. Colenso had drawn attention to 'the absolute, palpable self-contradictions' of biblical narrative.[72]

Biblical ethnology was also found wanting. Colenso openly rejected monogenist orthodoxy. Who now believes, asked Colenso, 'that all mankind sprung from one single pair of human beings of whom one was made from the rib-bone of the other?' Nor, according to Colenso, was the Noachic story of the peopling of the world any longer tenable. Drawing on the speculations of Nott, Colenso thought it 'probable' that the black races of Africa had not featured in the Table of Nations outlined in Genesis 10, 'possibly, not being known to the Hebrews at the time when the document was written'.[73]

Egyptology seemed to provide compelling evidence against the Mosaic view that the whole world had been peopled in the – relatively – recent past by the family of Noah in the aftermath of the Flood. After all, Colenso argued, 'we know that on the monuments of Egypt, dating shortly after the scriptural date of the flood, if not even before it, there are depicted the same distinctively marked features as characterizing the different races of men and animals just exactly as we see them now', including both the Mongol and the Negro. Ancient Egyptian representations of blacks, for example, showed the same 'thick lips, projecting mouths, and woolly hair' Colenso observed in their modern descendants. Yet such was the brevity of the 'interval' between the Noachic deluge and these depictions that it surely left insufficient time for the development of clear racial demarcations out of the different lineages of Noah. By contrast, Colenso detected 'no perceptible change' in the Negro face in the roughly 4,000 years which had elapsed from Egyptian antiquity to the present. Egyptological evidence seemed to indicate the existence of 'remarkable permanent differences in the shape of the skull, bodily form, colour [and] physiognomy' which were difficult to reconcile with biblical monogenesis.[74]

Colenso was unconvinced by the argument that climate explained racial variation. Why, then, asked Colenso, did Amerindians possess the

'same hue' whether on the northern lakes or in Amazonia? Yet, characteristically, Colenso eschewed dogmatism, even in his conviction that
polygenesis provided a more credible account of human origins than the
traditional narrative found in the book of Genesis. Indeed, there was even
something to be said for Darwinism, which ran against the grain not only
of scripture, but also of the familiar polygenist alternative to the Bible.
Colenso conceded that the Darwinian scheme might allow for the emergence of substantial racial differences from a single aboriginal pair after the
passage of millions of years. On the other hand, absurdly open-minded
and optimistically syncretic in his beliefs, Colenso also recognised that a
more persuasive version of Christian anthropology might be recovered by
way of the curious combination of polygenesis and the new insights of
Darwinism within a broadly providentialist account of creation:

> it seems most probable that the human race, as it now exists, has really sprung
> from more than one pair, whether brought into being by the direct fiat of the
> Almighty, or developed from lower forms of animal life through the power of
> the same Almighty word, by the processes of natural selection, which the same
> Divine wisdom appears to have ordained to play an important part in the
> scheme of this wondrous universe.[75]

Nevertheless Colenso also denied that the likely fact of polygenesis
provided a warrant for racialist attitudes or practices. The only substantial
difference within the polygenist scheme between whites and blacks,
Colenso claimed, was that the black 'has not sprung originally from the
same pair of parents as ourselves'; but the black race was otherwise
'fashioned in all points like ourselves, with reason, intellect, conscience,
speech, and all the affections and attributes of our nature'. Thus Colenso
urged that whites should recognise, the plural origins of races notwithstanding, that there was a 'common brotherhood' between black and
white which was 'higher than that of mere blood'. Polygenesis did not
subvert the notion of a divine creator, and there was no reason to suppose
that whites and blacks did not share a 'common Father'. Colenso pondered the real moral question which ought to shape the response of white
Christians to their encounter with the black race, besides which polygenesis was but an irrelevance: 'if we love God ourselves, can we help
loving this our brother, though not by blood, because of the evidence
which he gives that he, too, has the Divine Seed within him – that he, like
us, is begotten of God?' Colenso firmly believed that all men were made
in God's image, regardless of the debates between the monogenists and
polygenists.[76]

Other missionaries tackled the monogenist–polygenist debate in more conventional ways, drawing on their immediate experiences – or implicit ethnographic fieldwork – of other races to posit some sort of reconciliation between the Mosaic history of the Old Testament and the challenge posed by modern science and biblical criticism. Nevertheless, even missionaries of a much more orthodox bent than Colenso came to realise that the options were now extremely limited for a naturalistic monogenist anthropology which eschewed recourse to divine, miraculous intervention in the sphere of biology. For instance, the Reverend William Holden, a Wesleyan missionary with considerable experience in southern Africa, found traditional explanations of black racial distinctiveness somewhat unconvincing. In his *Past and future of the Kaffir races* (1866), Holden attempted to use his specialist knowledge of the region's ethnology to see off 'modern scientific opponents of the Bible narrative of the human race'; but was 'unable to account for the thick, matted, woolly hair of the Negro, Kaffir and Hottentot, as distinguished from the long fine hair of the European, on the grounds usually assigned to them', such as climate. Moreover, why did these groups, which inhabited the same region of southern Africa, differ so markedly from one another in racial appearance? Environmentalist explanation suggested that shared climate should result in a common southern African racial appearance. But to Holden's consternation this had clearly not happened: 'The Hottentots live in the same country, subsist on the same food, breathe the same air, bask under the same sun, and are the subjects of the same habits; and yet they assimilate no nearer their Kaffir neighbours than they did centuries ago.' Nor was an extended human chronology of 30,000 years – far beyond the permitted limits of biblical orthodoxy – as posited by some scientists sufficient in itself to explain the facts of human racial diversity. Holden took refuge in a creative extrapolation of Genesis, arguing that as it took no greater effort of 'Divine power' to change the colour of a man's skin than it did to change his language, then the solution to the problem of racial diversity was to be found at the post-Babelian confusion of tongues when God had 'added to the confusion of language distinctions of colour, size, and other great family characteristics'.[77]

From the 1850s there was a curious and ironic shift in the defence of Christian 'orthodoxy'. The pre-Adamite heresy, which it had hitherto been the objective of orthodoxy to defeat, was now enlisted into the defence of scripture against the threat of secular evolutionism. Although Darwinism proper was not to arrive until the appearance of *The origin of species* in 1859, other schemes of evolution were already common currency, including the notorious *Vestiges of the natural history of creation* (1844), the anonymous work of Robert Chambers (1802–71).[78] Mid-nineteenth-century monogenists confronted a more onerous task than their late eighteenth-century forebears. Moreover, archaeological evidence from Egypt which depicted the different races of humankind seemed to lend weight to polygenist conjectures. How could Christian monogenists account for Egyptological finds which appeared to indicate the ancient longevity of racial types? Orthodox Christian chronology – already under pressure from other directions – appeared impossible to reconcile with such compelling witness to primeval racial diversity. Alternatively, of course, an extended chronology offered a more plausible framework for the emergence of racial diversification within a unitary mankind. However, another strategy involved a concession of some of the principal features of monogenist argument, if not an outright surrender to an attractively refurbished Christian polygenesis.

Darwinism itself impacted on the monogenist–polygenist debate only at a very oblique angle. Indeed, evolution seemed to hold out not only an obvious threat, but also the possibility of effecting some sort of compromise between monogenist ethnology and polygenist anthropology. Few Darwinists espoused polygenesis, which appeared to run against the central thesis of Darwinian evolution, that of an all-encompassing biological ancestry. The most prominent exception was in the German world where Ernst Haeckel (1834–1919) upheld a scheme of polygenist evolution and Karl Vogt (1817–95) speculated that human races might be descended from different ape ancestors; though Alfred Russel Wallace (1823–1913) had himself wondered at one stage whether monogenesis and polygenesis might be reconciled by way of an evolutionary separation of proto-humankind into distinct races prior to the full endowment of human mental capacities. But Vogt's polytypic theory and Wallace's contemplation of the parallel evolution of races involved crucial divergences from the mainstream of evolutionary thought, which remained detached from the similarly radical heterodoxies of polygenist anthropology. Indeed, Peter Bowler ascribes the decline of polygenesis in late nineteenth-century Britain to the influence of the major evolutionists. Michael Banton has put this another way, arguing that, in a sense, Darwin managed to 'subsume' both the theory of racial diversification from a single ancestral pair and the rival account – not necessarily polygenist – of primeval racial types 'within a new synthesis which explained both change and continuity'. Nevertheless, the 'new synthesis' did away with any imperative for scientists to invoke polygenist hypotheses. Logically, from the perspective of monogenists, mainstream Darwinism did not represent a further accession of scientific strength to the cause of polygenism. Darwinism was itself monogenist in its account of the descent of man, though obviously an insidious fifth column in that it presented a monogenist narrative which dispensed not only with divine providence and sacred history, but also with the distinction between humanity and the animal world which underpinned Christian anthropology, and ultimately soteriology.[79]

Yet there were also other immediate – and deeply insidious – threats with which Christian intellectuals had to contend. Indeed, it seemed as if some of their fellow biblical scholars were intent upon poisoning the wells of Christian truth. The winter of 1859–60 proved an especially troubling time for the orthodox. The publication of Darwin's *Origin of species* in November 1859 was quickly followed by another heretical thunderbolt, the appearance in February 1860 of *Essays and reviews*, a devastating collection of pieces by seven liberal Anglican Broad Churchmen, six of whom were in holy orders. Notwithstanding its innocuous title, *Essays and reviews* seemed to its opponents – who were legion – to subvert the church from within. The essays argued, variously, that the Bible should be read just like any other book, and therefore was subject to free interpretation; queried the currently acceptable 'harmonies' between geology and the supposed 'facts' of Genesis; and challenged the conventional acceptance of miracles and prophecies. Nevertheless, the historian can learn a great deal from the fuss which accompanied this perceived betrayal of the church by some of its leading intellects. *Essays and reviews* provoked around 140 replies, which remind the historian that, the assaults – or rather, it seems, pinpricks – of Enlightenment notwithstanding, the Old Testament remained for an otherwise sophisticated Anglican intelligentsia a compelling compendium of historical and scientific data.[80]

In the face of these intellectual revolutions, however, Christians, clearly, needed to upgrade their weaponry. A corresponding apologetic revolution was required. Yet who would have predicted that this revolution would be so complete; that the idea of pre-Adamites, of men before Adam, once the notorious bugbear of monogenists, would feature in the arsenal of self-proclaimed defenders of Christian orthodoxy? Hitherto, monogenesis had been a crucial pillar of orthodox Christian theology; any suspicion that there were men before Adam had challenged the universal pertinence of the sacred drama of original sin and Christian redemption. Nevertheless, pre-Adamism became a vital ideological prop anonymous。

of Victorian racial science as a result of pre-Adamism's gradual detachment from heterodox polygenesis. Indeed, in the late nineteenth and early twentieth centuries, pre-Adamism was deployed somewhat surprisingly as a conservative strategy to counter the explosive theological consequences of Darwinian evolution. In recent years Professor David Livingstone has shown how pre-Adamism was transformed from an engine of scepticism, heterodoxy and biblical criticism into a – not uncontroversial, but potentially useful – tool of orthodox apologetic. In particular, Livingstone provides compelling evidence that neither science nor religion was a monolith, and that enterprising scientists and theologians were cleverly able to utilise the notion of men before Adam to suggest solutions to the thorny problems of how the creation of the human soul, an Adamic Fall and the transmission of original sin might be aligned with new paradigms in natural history and chronology.[81]

Much hinged on how the two creation narratives which coexisted in Genesis might be related. Did they simply relate different versions of the same narrative, as the insights of Higher Criticism suggested, or did they tell of two separate creations of distinct races of mankind, which offered a way forward for defenders of biblical literalism confronted by the combined challenges of geochronology and Darwinism? This in turn raised another question. Was the Bible itself so clearly committed to the truth of monogenesis? George Harris (1809–90), a barrister and president of the Manchester Anthropological Society, claimed that the dispute over monogenesis highlighted 'exactly one of those cases where the Bible has not been allowed to speak for itself, but its meaning has been explained through the forced and unwarranted interpretations that have been put upon it by writers in ages gone by'. He argued that the second chapter of Genesis was 'never intended to contradict or nullify the first, but only added to give an account of the creation of a particular race of people'. Harris even questioned the supposed reliance of the Christian scheme of redemption on the Adamic unity of the human race. For instance, he engaged in a close reading of Corinthians 15:22, 'For as in Adam all die, so in Christ shall all be made alive', a passage which seemed to 'argue against the plurality of races'. Harris insisted that there was 'no assertion here that all were descended from Adam, but that all died through his transgression; and for this purpose it seems to matter little whether the whole human race was actually descended from him, or whether he was to be regarded as the representative of that race'. Monogenists, he concluded, were 'misguided zealots'. Harris blamed St Augustine for introducing the misleading notion 'that all mankind were descended from Adam, and that all Christians were bound to adopt that view as regards the sacred narrative'. The sacred narrative did not run quite as St Augustine imagined.[82]

Yet 'orthodox' pre-Adamites were playing with fire. Although pre-Adamism promised to relieve the pressure imposed by new scientific developments on the authority of the scriptures, it also threatened to wreak collateral damage on the fabric of Christian theology. The crux of the matter was to find a way of answering the cavils of the evolutionists without sacrificing the universal transmission of original sin and Christ's blood-relationship to all humanity, which were essential ingredients of Christian theology. Could mankind's pre-Adamite origins be reconciled with these core elements of the faith? In his *Genesis of the earth and man* (1856), the Orientalist Edward Lane (1801–76) advanced the solution

that Adam, by creation, received a physical nature specifically the same as that of the Pre-Adamites; that by his fall, he assumed a corrupt moral nature, rendered more guilty than that of these latter by his superior knowledge; that he transmitted this physical and moral nature to his sons and daughters; and that these, by their intermarriages with persons of Pre-Adamite origin, while they transmitted the same physical and moral nature to their descendants, effected also a union of blood between their own progeny and all the Non-Adamites; so that Christ, when He assumed the physical nature of Adam, became related by blood to all mankind.

Lane argued that 'the tenet of the Saviour's blood-relationship to every human being rests upon no such certain scriptural evidence as to demand the rejection of any theory that does not admit the universal con-sanguinity of our species'.[83]

This curious vein of orthodox pre-Adamism held significant implications both for the science of race and, more particularly, for the ethno-logical treatment of scripture. The bizarre Christian invocation of a pre-Adamite mankind allowed defenders of orthodoxy to retreat from the embarrassing though impeccably unheretical notion of a black Adam which had hitherto provided one of the most compelling ways of reconciling the facts of racial diversity with a monogenist account of environmentally induced changes in human colouring. Instead, within the new pre-Adamite scheme, Adam became the father of the Caucasian race.

The appeal of pre-Adamism reached even into evangelical circles, not least because it, besides seeing off the anti-scriptural pretensions of the scientists, also promised to resolve other problems which lurked in the scriptures. In 1860 Isabelle Duncan, the wife of a Presbyterian Free Churchman, published *Pre-Adamite man: or the story of our old planet and its inhabitants as told by scripture and science.* Given the work's near-coincidental appearance with the *Origin of species*, it enjoyed an immediate impact. By 1866 *Pre-Adamite man* had gone through six printings. Duncan was a theological conservative, who subscribed to the plenary inspiration of scripture. At the core of her analysis was an interpretation of Genesis 2:3–4 as marking a major and lengthy gap between a first creation of mankind and a wholly distinct second Adamic creation. Duncan denied any biological continuity between the pre-Adamite creation and the Adamites. This caesura amounted to a water-tight seal between totally distinct creations, which protected Duncan's reading of Genesis from any allegations that it might undermine an orthodox reading of original sin and its transmission. The creatures of the first dispensation, recorded in Genesis 1, it transpired, were angels. Here Duncan answered a pressing theological need, as she saw it; for the scriptures otherwise appeared to say nothing about the origin or creation of angels – an unaccountable omission. Duncan's version of pre-Adamism thus met a serious problem in the more obscure field of angelology as well as providing a solution to the more immediate challenges posed by scientific and palaeontological discoveries.[84]

The Irish barrister and religious writer Dominick McCausland proposed an ingenious solution to the 'ethnological difficulties' of scripture. To McCausland the choice confronting scriptural ethnologists appeared stark:

If the Mongol was a Mongol, and the Negro was a Negro, before Adam became a living soul, the Mosaic record harmonizes with, and is confirmed by, all that science and philosophy have discovered and proclaimed to have been the course of nature . . . if, on the other hand, the Mongol and Negro are to be considered descendants of Adam, the facts of science and the words of scripture are irreconcilably at variance.

Subtly, McCausland argued that 'the unity of mankind' and 'the unity of mankind in Adam' were 'two different propositions'. In the light of this distinction, Genesis was to be read 'as a description of the creation of a human being of a superior race among pre-existing inferior races of mankind'. But did this mean that the scope of Christ's work of redemption was then narrowly limited to the race of Adam? McCausland denied this implication. Redemption, he insisted, did not depend on lineal, biological descent from Adam.[85]

McCausland cynically exposed the practical limitations of the supposedly philanthropic doctrine of monogenesis which had hitherto prevailed:

Brotherhood after the flesh is a bond of union; but the true spirit of Christianity reveals to us, that the only brotherhood of all the races of mankind which can bear fruit, either here or hereafter, is the brotherhood in Christ; and the false and bare acknowledgement of a blood relationship with which the inferior races have been so cruelly mocked, and which has failed to save them from despiteful usage at the hands of the most civilized communities of the earth, must yield to the better title which has been purchased and laid up for them by the death and resurrection of the Saviour.

The pre-Adamite conjecture offered the only obvious solution to the vexed problem of reconciling nineteenth-century scientific developments with the basic features of the Mosaic story found in Genesis. Where once scripture was interpreted for its anti-racist sentiment, now apparent contradictions within scripture and between scripture and science were being resolved at the cost of injecting a novel racialist hermeneutic into readings of Genesis. The Bible had been conserved – but as a saga of racial superiority.[86]

The American geologist Alexander Winchell deliberately distanced himself from 'ecclesiastical polygenists' like McCausland, while adopting a not dissimilar overall strategy. Winchell proclaimed his orthodoxy, denying that he had 'disputed the divine creation of Adam, even in maintaining that he had a human father and mother'. Nor had he undermined the Christian shibboleth of the underlying unity of mankind; rather, Winchell boasted, he had 'removed the incredibility of that doctrine as grounded in the descent of Negroes and Australians from Noah and Adam'. Indeed, Winchell's principal claim to orthodoxy lay in an ostensibly less polygenist interpretation of the pre-Adamite races. Winchell maintained that his system of exegesis endowed the scriptures with a degree of credibility which they had hitherto lacked in the hands of less sophisticated interpreters.[87]

Conventional readings of Genesis, as in the problematic narrative of Cain and his wife, were dismissed as the 'current pseudo-orthodox interpretation' of scripture. Winchell's was the authentic orthodox account, the only one which could reconcile the true sense of some treacherous passages whose conventional exegesis flew in the face not only of the sciences – and, above all, chronology – but also morality. Winchell reintroduced exogamy and with it nineteenth-century bourgeois respectability into the marital history of the early Adamites. No longer need Victorian womanhood – mildly discomfited, no doubt, at Cain's murder of his brother Abel – swoon with the profoundest shock as recognition dawned that Cain must have procreated with his sister.[88]

Similarly, Winchell put paid to the qualms of the orthodox that pre-Adamite theories inevitably undermined the Christian scheme of redemption. After all, Winchell noted, even the most ultra-orthodox versions of Christ's atonement hold that it was 'retroactive' for 'at least four thousand and four years'. If so, then, he wondered, 'why not a few thousand years further?' Surely, if the effects of the atonement could reach back to Adam, then it would not be absurd to assume that it also had the potential to reach 'the little-divergent ancestry to whom Adam was probably able to trace his lineage'.[89]

Winchell declared that scripture itself 'clearly implies the existence of nonadamites'. According to Winchell, the biblical Adam was a member of the Mediterranean race and 'simply the remotest ancestor to whom the Jews could trace their descent'. The Adamites indeed were an 'offshoot from the Dravidians'. Nevertheless Winchell, unlike McCausland, tried to play down the degree of racial differentiation between the Adamite and non-Adamite races. Hence intermarriage had been possible and the taboo of incest survived: 'no such racial contrast existed between the family of Adam and the nonadamites as to originate a racial repugnance. Adam, probably, bore a close physiological resemblance to the nonadamites.' Winchell estimated that Adam had been 'ruddy-complexioned'.[90]

Winchell's theories held out the prospect of a refurbished pre-Adamite scheme of monogenesis. Moreover, it was presented as one in which the inter-racial philanthropy underpinned by conventional readings of Genesis was substantially reaffirmed:

Preadamitism means simply that Adam is descended from a black race, not the black races from Adam. This leaves the blood connection between the white and black races undisturbed. It affirms their consanguinity. It accounts for their brotherhood. It is consistent with their common nature and common destiny.

However, pre-Adamite monogenesis was drawn ineluctably into the orbit of an untrammelled polygenist racialism.[91]

Like McCausland, whose flagrant polygenist errors he had consciously tried to avoid, Winchell – however well-intentioned – lapsed into an obnoxious racialist travesty of Christianity, at least where the black (though not the brown) races were concerned. Winchell argued that the pre-Noachite black races had been 'strongly isolated from the rest of mankind'. Indeed, he railed against the 'untenability of the theories which trace the black races to Noah or even to Adam'. This was not simply a matter of colour: while descendants of Noah had generally had round-headed skulls, Negroes, he believed – somewhat against the run of conventional craniology – had tended to be dolichocephalic (long-headed). Somehow, it seemed to Winchell, blacks had become vastly different from the rest of mankind: 'In their anatomical, physiological and psychic characteristics, we can barely say that a deep-laid basis of human sympathy and likeness exists between them and us.' An 'ethnic chasm' gaped between the black race and the 'mass of Noachite humanity'. Despite his protestations to the contrary, Winchell appeared to excuse racism. Far from being the exclusive property of polygenist secularists, racialism was also a by-product of the pre-Adamite refurbishment of Christian anthropology.[92]

By the early twentieth century the old pre-Adamite heresy had attained a degree of respectability on both sides of the Atlantic. One of the pre-eminent founders of the American fundamentalist tradition, the evangelist and biblical scholar Reuben Archer Torrey (1856–1928), flirted with pre-Adamism as a solution to knotty problems in scripture. Torrey subscribed to the divine origin and absolute inerrancy of scripture; but this did not preclude distancing himself from conventionally orthodox interpretations of scripture when these seemed to threaten the veracity of the Word. In his seminal guide to scriptural cruxes, *Difficulties and alleged errors and contradictions in the Bible* (1908), Torrey appeared to endorse pre-Adamite solutions to the interpretation of the early parts of Genesis, and to distinguish the longer chronology of the pre-Adamite peoples from the history of the Adamic race, though he was untroubled by the notion that Cain might have married one of his sisters, as incest had only become a sin after the divine commandment to that effect.[93] On the other side of the Atlantic, the Scottish millennialist George Dickison also used the pre-Adamite thesis to bring about a creative reconciliation of science with a revised – indeed scientifically enhanced – reading of Genesis. Traditionally theologians had read the two Creation narratives of Genesis 1 and Genesis 2 as different versions of the same single Creation of the Adamic world. But now scientific developments rendered this assumption improbable; for geological discoveries made 'it certain that the earth was full of both plant and animal life, including man himself, which must have existed for long ages before the time at which Adam was created'. The world was clearly much older than the 6,000-year span of Adamic man, and so too, according to the palaeontological record, was the rest of 'prehistoric' mankind. Rather than bemoan, dismiss or evade the findings of modern science, Dickison's *The Mosaic account of Creation, as unfolded in Genesis, verified by science* (1902?) welcomed scientific discoveries as providing a firmer foundation for the interpretation of Genesis 1 and 2 than had hitherto been available to theologians:

If it had not been for the discoveries of modern science, it is not likely that such beings as prehistoric men would ever have been thought of, either by theologians or scientists. The belief that the two accounts referred solely to the creation of the Adamic world was established all along the ages, previous to the discoveries of man's implemental remains in surface strata, in association with those of extinct animals. These are discovered facts that cannot be gainsayed: nor is there any need that they should be disputed from a Bible point of view.

Now theologians, their eyes opened by the findings of geology, were able to read Genesis 1 and 2 as two quite separate accounts of chronologically distinct phases of Creation. Primitive man had been created in the first phase of Creation set out in Genesis 1 which had preceded by many thousands of years the second, more recent Creation of Genesis 2, when Adam and Eve had been created, along with some additional plants and animals, which supplemented those created in the first phase of life on earth. Indeed, not only could theologians read Genesis 1 and 2 in a straightforward way; but they could now solve the conundrum of Cain's marriage and his awareness that there were other people besides himself and his parents in the world. Dickison could now proclaim the obvious, which previous generations of theologians had tied themselves in knots trying to avoid, that it would have been a sin for Cain to marry his sister. They could safely acknowledge what was 'clearly admitted in the second Mosaic account that there were other people in existence before Adam and Eve were created'. What were the differences between the 'palaeolithic men' created on the sixth day of the first Creation and the Adamic men of the second Creation? Dickison insisted that both were made in the image of God 'of the same bone, flesh, and blood, and mental endowments'. Moreover, primitive man, just as much as Adamic man, was capable of religious sentiments and the enjoyment of 'spiritual fellowship'. Nevertheless, the cold of the Ice Age had been a punishment of primitive man for his religious declension and alienation from God. The post-Adamic Flood, however, had been a regional incident, and had not involved the destruction of the pre-Adamite 'aboriginal races' across the globe. Thus, although striving to avoid the racialist implications of pre-Adamism, Dickison appeared to hold the view that the white peoples of the world were descended from the Adam of Genesis 2, while the 'present aboriginal races of mankind' were the 'lineal descendants of the people who were created in the image of God' in the first book of Genesis.[94]

It tends to be forgotten that the crisis of faith did as much to shape nineteenth-century views of race as white assumptions of racial super-iority, powerful though these were. The mere fact that the intellectual elites of the nineteenth-century white Atlantic were racist does not mean that they always – or even usually – succumbed to the temptations of arguments that might justify their own racial superiority; or at least they rarely did so without being acutely conscious of the wider theological implications. In a sense, theology trumped race. Yet, equally, the defence of sacred history was rarely constrained, alas, by anxieties that racialism might be at odds with the deepest truths of the Christian message. Just as during their defence of slavery the South's Christian racists eschewed the opportunity provided by heretical polygenist arguments to provide a resounding case for slaveholding, so, when Christianity was threatened by new scientific approaches, Christian ethnologists did not scruple to use racist arguments which might help to shore up the authority of scripture against its critics. Any fears about lapsing into racism did not provide insuperable obstacles to pre-Adamite revisionists. There were, it should now be clear, many different ways of being a Christian racialist. The pre-Adamite revisionists had rejected the association of blackness with the curse of Ham; however, their own theories were fully as obnoxious, if not more so, than the story of Ham which they disowned. Ironically, how-ever, the very ubiquity of racialism in nineteenth-century culture also began to weaken the foundations of monogenesis. Although the psychic unity of mankind – reflected, it was argued, in a commonality of morals, myths and linguistic structures – was one of the principal props of monogenesis,[95] some nineteenth-century ethnologists, oblivious of the ultimate consequences of this dangerous chain of argument, began to offer racial explanations for the world's religious diversity.

CHAPTER 6

The Aryan Moment: Racialising Religion in the Nineteenth Century

Racialism was an omnipresent factor in nineteenth-century intellectual life, and the study of religion proved no exception to the trend towards racialised explanation. Indeed, the Bible was grist to the racialist mill, a source book of evidence for the dispersion of races and the beginnings of racial divisions and patterns. The Old Testament, in particular, was plundered for insights into the problems of ethnology, with especial attention devoted to the racial significance of chapters 10 and 11 of Genesis. However, the impact of racialist analysis on biblical scholarship was even more profound. Ethnology was added to the subjects on which a thorough biblical scholar needed to be expert, alongside a knowledge of the geography, flora and fauna of the Middle East. Race began to assume a place in encyclopedias of biblical studies, without any suggestion of impropriety or incongruence.[1]

The Holy Land, moreover, became a scene of racialist anthropology. In *The races of the Old Testament* (1891), the distinguished British Orientalist Archibald Sayce (1845–1933) set out to promote the infant science of 'biblical ethnology'. Sayce, who was an ordained Anglican cleric as well as the holder of the Oxford professorship in Assyriology from 1891, had no doubts about the importance of applying ethnological methods to the study of the Old Testament:

especially does it concern us to know what were the affinities and characteristics, the natural tendencies and mental qualifications of the people to whom were committed the oracles of the Old Testament. Theirs was the race from which the Messiah sprang, and in whose midst the Christian church was first established.

Despite his concentration upon the physiology of race and his warning not to confuse race and language, which were not necessarily synonymous, Sayce nevertheless took the view that race had a psychological, if not cultural, dimension: for racial traits, he contended, 'include not only physical characteristics but mental and moral qualities as well'. Sayce identified skull shape as 'one of the most marked and permanent characteristics of race'. Prognathism – the projection of the jaw from the rest of the face – Sayce pronounced a 'characteristic of the lower races'. A high forehead was a sound benchmark of 'intellectual capacity'. Teeth provided another reliable test of racial status. While in the so-called higher races, Sayce argued, the wisdom teeth 'remain embryonic', in the black races the wisdom teeth became fanged. Nevertheless, in spite of his conventional racism, Sayce appeared to identify the black race as the original type of mankind. He could find a way of explaining how black pigmentation might have been lost, by analogy with albinism, but could find no correspondingly satisfactory explanation for the acquisition of dark pigment. Indeed, the presence of freckles on some Europeans struck Sayce as a clue to the darker provenance of the white race.[2]

Ancient Palestine, Sayce argued, had been populated by three distinct racial groups: the Amorites; the Canaanites, who were a Semitic people that had separated at an early stage from the main Semitic stock; and, third, a later wave of Semitic invaders, including the Edomites, Ammonites, Moabites and Israelites. The Amorites particularly intrigued Sayce, for they, who had lived in Palestine before the days of Exodus, had, he claimed, been blond, blue-eyed and dolichocephalic and possibly related to the cromlech-building people of European antiquity. Sayce, indeed, celebrated the Amorites in a separate essay as 'the white race of ancient Palestine'. Long after the admixture of the other two racial groupings in Palestinian ethnology, the population of southern Judah remained 'Amorite in race, though not in name'. Crucially, King David, as it appeared from I Samuel 17:42 where he is described as 'ruddy, and of a fair countenance', had been blond or red-haired, and presumably of Amorite blood. Jesus Christ had, of course, come from the lineage of David.[3]

A sharply contrasting view of the Amorites appeared in Claude Regnier Conder's *Bible accuracy as shown by monuments* (1903). Relying on representations of peoples in archaeological evidence, Colonel Conder (1848–1910), a Royal Engineer, explorer and antiquary, took the view that the Amorites had been a 'brown race, with black hair', who spoke the language of the Semitic Babylonians. The identity of the Amorites – fascinating as it is in its own right – is not, of course, what interests us at this juncture; rather it is the fact that Conder, like Sayce, was fascinated with the racial characteristics of the peoples of Old Testament antiquity. The Hittites, according to Conder, had been 'Tartar-like, with slanting eyes, light complexion, and black hair worn in a long pigtail', while the tribes of Asia Minor who 'appear to have been Aryans' were 'fair people, with blue eyes, and light-coloured hair', and the Egyptians were racially distinct from both those races and from the black Nubians. Conder also considered the relationship of these races to the Table of Nations set out in Genesis 10; for instance, the 'fair Aryans of the monuments' were, in his reckoning, the descendants of Japhet.[4]

Theologians responded creatively to the emergence of racial science. For instance, Shawn Kelley has argued most persuasively that the emergence of modern biblical criticism in nineteenth-century Germany was tightly interwoven with the science of race. F. C. Baur (1792–1860) and the Tübingen school identified a critical divide in the early Christian world between Jewish Christians, who belonged racially and culturally to the static and despotic Orient, and Hellenistic Christians who embodied the values of the Occident, in particular freedom and dynamism. Christianity united these ethnic antitheses. However, the Romans provided a further complicating factor in the analysis of the Tübingen school, for they tended to be more authoritarian in outlook and as a result qualified some of the liberalism inherent in the Hellenistic conception of Christianity. In this way these Protestant critics constructed an interpretation of primitive Christianity in which dynamic Hellenistic elements liberated Christianity from its oppressive Oriental roots in Judaism, but were then for a time circumscribed by the Roman Catholic Church which reimposed an Oriental tyranny over Christianity. However, the story had a happy ending, for the coming of Protestantism represented a dynamic revival of the Hellenistic instinct.[5]

Other developments in theology were openly indebted to developments in ethnology. If Indo-European philology had transformed the study of language and yielded new insights into the early history of human populations and their movements, it seemed, might not the new philological paradigm have something to contribute to the study of religion? The liberal American Unitarian James Freeman Clarke (1810–88) promoted the discipline of 'comparative theology' as a logical offshoot of the new sciences of race, which he termed 'comparative anatomy' and 'comparative philology'. Clarke nevertheless exhibited a clear preference for the insights of Aryan philology over the crude taxonomy of races generated by the study of race exclusively in its physical manifestations. Although Clarke recognised the importance of physiology in revealing the 'anatomical differences between races', which were 'marked and real', he applauded recent philological developments in this formative area of enquiry: 'The science of ethnology . . . has forever set aside Blumenbach's old classification of mankind into the Caucasian and four other varieties, and has given us, instead, a division of the largest part of mankind into Indo-European, Semitic, and Turanian families.' Clarke assigned particular importance to pioneers in the fields of Aryan mythography, for the stimulus they had given to the field of 'comparative theology'.[6]

It was but a short step from the study of race through language to the contemplation of religion as an aspect of race. Just as racialists ascribed distinctive intellectual qualities (or failings) to particular races, so they also associated particular racial groups with certain spiritual characteristics. Nineteenth-century writers on non-European religious cultures came to focus less on issues of idolatry and paganism and more on race. Where once Christian theologians during the early modern era had explained the religious diversity of mankind in terms of the corruption and distortion of an ancient patriarchal religion, now nineteenth-century anthropologists began to explain religious phenomena as manifestations of racial mentalities. Race was not simply a matter of external physical differences but of deep psychic differences, which manifested themselves in the varieties of religion found throughout the world. As a result, religion began to be treated by some commentators as an epiphenomenon of race: race was the ultimate reality in human affairs, religious diversity an expression of the deeper underlying truth of racial differences. As Chris Bayly notes, during the nineteenth century loose ensembles of indigenous beliefs and rituals became reified – by colonial interpreters and native reformers alike – as 'homogeneous religions' which reflected underlying 'national or racial essences', such as the supposed Hindu religion of Indians or the 'Confucianism' of China. By extension, religion came to be seen as an expression of the instincts of the race, a manifestation of racial characteristics.[7]

Religious differences were attributed to the apparent contrast between the mental worlds of the white races and their supposed savage inferiors. In lectures delivered at Boston in 1865–6, John Lesley contemplated

how the tropical black races, and the hyperborean stunted races, seem never to have had the ability to lift their spiritual life out of the bogs and swamps of fetichism upon the firm land of theism, but have been a prey in all ages to the cruelties of demon worship and the low trickery of shamans or sorcerers . . .

Lesley claimed that it was 'the central white races alone' who had enjoyed first of all the 'powers of imagination to devise symbols to represent abstract thoughts'.[8] Similarly, the American scientist Alexander Winchell reckoned that there was a significant gulf between the pre-Adamite black and Noachite white races which took the form not only of 'anatomical' and 'physiological' features, but also 'psychic characteristics'. Indeed Winchell attributed a psychic weakness to the black races: their religion, consisting of the worship of idols and fetishes, amounted to no more than 'a brainless voluptuousness of religious emotion'.[9]

To many nineteenth-century eyes, variations in mental capacities between races were not simply a matter of differences in intelligence, but concerned the aptitude of races for spirituality, for the appreciation of theological concepts and for religious and moral development. Religion was often treated as an authentic reflection of the spiritual aptitudes of a racial group. Some races, so it was argued, had an inferior grasp of the truths of religion which inhibited a full understanding or appreciation of Christianity. On the other hand, it was claimed that certain races – most notably the Aryans – had shaped Christianity, itself originally of Semitic origin, in beneficial ways which, it was claimed, would have been beyond the comprehension of the Semitic mind.

For some commentators, spirituality was an epiphenomenon of biology, which might be traced in the conformation of the skull; for others, the new science of linguistics held the key to unlocking the ways in which patterns of speech and in particular their grammatical underpinnings influenced the sense of the numinous found in different language groups. Craniology and phrenology helped to establish linkages between racial anatomy and the mental life of races. Few racialist interpretations of religion were more crudely reductive and materialist than that advanced by phrenologists. In their maps of the cranium, phrenologists located organs of 'veneration' and 'spirituality' near the crown of the skull, to which organs they traced the religious impulse. This opened the way to the claim that these organs – and by extension religious capacities – were more highly developed in some races than in others. For some commentators – as we shall see – the type of religion to which an ethnic group adhered was deducible from its cranial formation, with Protestantism bearing a strong correlation to dolichocephaly (long-headedness), Catholicism to brachycephaly (wide-headedness). But the linkage did not have to be quite so crudely physical. By contrast with anatomy, linguistics seemed to offer an 'open sesame' into a deeper and richer realm of knowledge about the races of humanity and their relationships. The racial science of philology considered the mental life of racial groups – what went on inside the head, not merely the outer phenomena of skull shape or measurable phenomena such as cranial capacity. The distinctive grammatical characteristics of different language groupings provided a more sophisticated and apparently plausible pathway by which ethnic origins might be connected to religious preferences.

The science of language groups dictated a new approach to the study of religion and mythography. Language groups were treated not only as races but as families which shared certain religious characteristics. Whereas during the early modern era Christian scholars attempted to explain the global variety of non-Christian religions in terms of the polytheistic distortions of a universal patriarchal religion, and Deistic Enlightenment critics also roved cavalierly across pagan civilisations in an attempt to trace the rather different corruptions of a primitive natural religion, now such broad cross-cultural analysis was much harder to sustain. The basic starting point for the study of mythologies and religions was now the language family, such as the Aryan group or the Semitic. For many scholars, no longer was the primary division in the study of religions that between revealed and natural religion; now religions were reclassified according to their provenance in the major linguistic groups, Turanian, Aryan and Semitic. It was only a short step from locating religion in the paradigm of language groups to explaining religion as a manifestation of race. In particular, philology seemed to offer a compelling insight into the origins of monotheism. After all, the three great monotheistic religions – Judaism, Christianity and Islam – had all arisen in the Semitic world. Was monotheism a direct and racially unique expression of the Semitic mind? Did the new sciences of race and philology offer an insight into the secret ethnic underpinnings of religious doctrine? Might a new understanding of religion be built on ethnological foundations?

Ironically, nineteenth-century champions of the Aryan race did not congratulate their ancient Aryan forebears as the leading communicators of the monotheistic ideal of modern Christianity which nineteenth-century Aryans were exporting across the globe. Rather polytheism and mythology were celebrated as the manifestations of the glories of Aryan language. One could, it seemed, have an excess of monotheism. This was the surprising problem faced, some nineteenth-century commentators believed, by the Semites of old. On the other hand, a language fertile in nuance and rich in verb forms, such as the Aryans had possessed, begat mythology; mythology in turn, by way of the intermediate deities which stood between the supreme deity and nature, begat scientific and philosophical reasoning. By the lights of a racialist interpretation of religion, Christianity was an unstable hybrid.

The application of racial insights to religious issues did not predetermine commentators to any particular line on the great religious questions of the day. The connections between race and religion were obvious to defenders of Christian orthodoxy and to its critics alike. Racialist readings of religion surfaced in a variety of settings throughout the nineteenth century, sometimes reinforcing traditional tellings of sacred history, sometimes twisted into an ethnological or philological challenge to traditional understandings of the Christian religion. Curiously, the thesis that different races generated their own distinctive religions proved compatible in many cases with mainstream Christianity, despite its dangerous proximity to the devastating idea that religion was but a man-made race creation. Some Christian ethnologists believed that race operated instrumentally, indeed providentially, in the filtration of an ultimately indivisible religious truth among peoples who were capable of appreciating – and expressing their appreciation of – different aspects of that truth. At the secular extreme of nineteenth-century culture, there emerged a naturalistic and free-thinking science of religion which unmasked the supernatural pretensions of religion – to reveal instead the deeper truths of biology, linguistics or sociology. Radicalism was sometimes tinged with racial irony. By what absurd twist of fate had the Aryan peoples of Europe come to venerate the Semitic Bible as their holy book? The logic of race dictated that Europeans would have been better off with the *Vedas*, the ancient sacred books of the Hindus. Was Christianity, indeed, an appropriate form of religion for an Aryan people? This subversive strain of religious ethnology was stronger in France than in Britain or North America, but the impact of the French science of religion was felt throughout the Atlantic world.

There were, however, within the Protestant mainstream conventional limits to this line of analysis: the racialist interpretation of religious diversity was constrained, in most cases, by an acknowledgement of the psychic unity of mankind. Racialism nibbled – delicately – at the edges of monogenist orthodoxy. Alongside orthodox arguments that invoked the psychic unity of mankind as one of the best proofs of monogenesis, there grew up another line of analysis that religion was an expression of mental and linguistic differences between races. Just as monogenist anthropology did not preclude a wide measure of racialist speculation, neither did an adherence to the ultimate psychic unity of humanity inhibit a considerable degree of speculation about the ways in which racial groups manifested characteristic differences in intelligence and spirituality.

James Cowles Prichard, noted earlier as the leading ethnologist in Britain during the first half of the nineteenth century, staked out a careful position on the relationship between race and religion. He contrasted the different forms of religion which had arisen in the major racial groups. Whereas the Indo-Europeans had worshipped 'unseen powers in the darkness of sacred groves', with religious principles taking 'deep root' in the 'mind and character' of the race, the Allophylian races, by contrast, had been 'nearly destitute of any traditionary creed or doctrine', living instead 'under a sort of instinctive religion'. Prichard also highlighted the major 'psychological' differences between the 'Japetic' Indo-Europeans and the Semites. These two races had sharply differing conceptions of the nature and attributes of the godhead. Mythology had arisen as a characteristically Indo-European approach to the portrayal of the numinous realm. In countries such as Greece and India, the 'Japetic' nations managed to 'clothe the few original principles or elements of human belief with a splendid garb of imagery'. On the other hand, the Semites had alone fathered all three of the 'great systems of theism' – Judaism, Christianity and Islam – because of the peculiar intensity and abstraction of their conceptions of the divine. The Semitic peoples 'alone' appear to have possessed of old sufficient power of abstraction 'to conceive the idea of a pure and immaterial nature' distinct from the physical universe. Language provided a persuasive explanation of why the Semitic race held to such distinctive conceptions of divinity. Prichard speculated that, whereas in most language groups idiom had developed by way of 'the gradual superimposition of supplementary syllables upon monosyllabic elements' leading to agglutinative, polysyllabic words, among the Semites language consisted of 'disyllabic roots, of which the three consonants express the abstract meaning', with changes of time, agency and the like 'denoted by changes in the interior vowels', a distinctive patterning which underpinned the 'reflective' character of Semitic religiosity. Language offered a plausible mechanism by which significant differences between races might be realised. Indeed, Prichard was reluctant to press any argument about the religious psychology of racial groups too far. Committed as he was to monogenesis, Prichard stressed the underlying unity of the human mind. The races of mankind had experienced differing degrees of 'mental culture', but there was no impassable gulf between the race-religions. Prichard considered that, despite the wide variation found among the different branches of the 'human family' in the 'conceptions' formed of 'the nature and attributes of the divine rulers of the world', one could also detect a deeper 'harmony' if one examined the basic 'moral sentiments and impressions which have exercised so extensive an influence on their imaginations'. Throughout the nineteenth century, some of the major theorists of the links between race and religion were careful to maintain something of this reticence and caution. Nevertheless, such hesitations and equivocations made less impression than the wider argument about deep religious differences between races.[10]

Indeed, the racialist understanding of religion was neither hegemonic nor unchallenged. Many commentators on religion, for example, took the view that religions bore the hallmarks of the stage of cultural development reached by the civilisations from which they sprang and which supported them. Culture, including religion, was grist to a civilisational interpretation of the progress of mankind. Alongside this commonplace attempt to link religion to a kind of social evolution, there were other interpretations of religion which used sociological and evolutionary theories, in the latter category often fused with a psychological interpretation. Social evolutionists regarded fetishism, animism, shamanism and totemism as lower forms of religion found across humanity and in all races and cultures at early stages of social development.[11] Sociological, evolutionary and psychological interpretations of religion tended to assume a unitary human nature. Nevertheless, these could be, and sometimes were, combined with racialist perspectives. Moreover, there was a marked difference between eighteenth- and nineteenth-century interpretations of religion. Whereas in the eighteenth century the civilisational model of the progress of a unitary mankind went largely unchallenged in the sphere of social theory, in the nineteenth century race (or, at the very least, language groups) provided a telling counterpoint. Just as philologists now reckoned languages to be expressive of the mental state of a people, so by extension, a substantial proportion of religious observers now took the view that religion expressed underlying truths about the particular features either of a language family or of the character of a race.

The ethnological approach to religion which became commonplace in the nineteenth century was far from monolithic either in its methods or in its findings. Some anthropologists, while working in the idiom of racial religion, questioned the absoluteness of the distinctions between ethnoreligious phenomena posited by their fellow scholars. A case in point is the pioneering work of William Robertson Smith (1846–94), a pious Scots Presbyterian of the Free Church whose biblical researches brought upon himself a successful prosecution for heresy. Robertson Smith's major work, *The religion of the Semites*, established the deep ethnic provenance of the Judaeo-Christian tradition in the culture and sociology of Semitic tribal life. Yet Robertson Smith denied that the gulf between the

Aryan and Semitic races was as 'primitive or fundamental' as some commentators maintained. Far from being 'an affair of race and innate tendency', the pronounced differences between Aryan and Semitic religion and social organisation were more properly assigned, he believed, to the 'operation of special local and historical causes'.[12]

The Aryan idea is, moreover, a treacherous and slippery concept, which has bequeathed particularly acute problems for those scholars hoping to parse it. The leading Aryan philologist of the Victorian era, Friedrich Max Müller, a German émigré who attained the summits of English academic life, came to repudiate the notion that there was an Aryan race in any biological sense. Rather, Max Müller insisted upon the incommensurability of linguistic and physiological categories.[13] However, although Max Müller himself was not a racialist, his ascription of particular religious dispositions to language families contributed, albeit indirectly, to a racialised interpretation of religious phenomena. Aryan philology and mythography, notwithstanding their own sensitivity to the distinction between language families and races proper, furthered the discernible nineteenth-century trend towards treating religions as expressions of ethnicity.

The Aryan idea broke free from its philological moorings. Most commentators regarded 'Aryan' as a racial term, despite the warnings of Max Müller. In the prevailing confusion over the relationship between race and language, subtle arguments that religion was a by-product of differences in grammatical, syntactical and naming practices found in the leading language groups became vulgarised into arguments that religion was an expression of racial character. In the course of the nineteenth century the notion of race shifted significantly, with biology displacing philology as the dominant determinant of racial classification. The Aryan idea which, logically speaking, did not admit of a physical dimension, was distorted along these lines. By the late nineteenth century some commentators, such as the Anglican cleric Isaac Taylor (1829–1901), author of *The origin of the Aryans* (1889), had imported an anatomical dimension into the Aryan concept. The idea of an Aryan language group yielded ground to notions of Aryan physiology and craniology.[14]

An influential lead in this direction came from the radical French science of religion, whose dominant figure was Ernest Renan, author of the controversial *Vie de Jésus*. Renan found the Indo-European peoples 'une race curieuse et vivement préoccupée du secret des choses'; the Semites, by contrast, were 'la race théocratique'. Semitic culture Renan pronounced to be monolithic, stiflingly so: 'Ainsi la race sémitique se reconnaît presque uniquement à des caractères négatifs: elle n'a ni mythologie, ni épopée, ni science, ni philosophie, ni fiction, ni arts plastiques, ni vie civile; en tout, absence de complexité, de nuances, sentiment exclusif de l'unité.' Why were these peoples so different in culture and religion? The answer, Renan believed, was to be found in their languages, for language constituted the essential mould – 'le moule nécessaire' – of a people's mental operations. Semitic language – even in the building blocks of syntax – appeared to lack the complexity necessary for profound thought: 'Il leur manque un des degrés de combinaison que nous jugeons nécessaires pour l'expression complète de la pensée.' According to Renan, the Indo-European 'conjugation of verbs' contained 'in the germ all the metaphysics which were afterwards to be developed through the Hindu genius, the Greek genius, the German genius'. In the Semitic languages, on the other hand, Renan found the expression of tenses and moods of the verb to be 'imperfect and cumbersome'. How-ever, the linguistic differences extended beyond the tense and mood of the verb to the way in which these different language groups rendered the facts of nature. In Semitic descriptions of the natural world God loomed large as the mover of all things. In Aryan phraseology a quite distinct set of possibilities opened up. In phrases such as 'death struck him down' or 'a malady carried him off' there seemed to be 'a being doing in reality the deed expressed by the verb'. Thus, Renan argued, 'each word' was 'to the primitive Aryan, pregnant . . . and comprised within itself a potent myth'. Whereas Aryan words 'contained the germ of individualities' and lent themselves to personification, Semitic roots were crude and one-dimen-sional. Among the Semites both expression and the accompanying train of thought were 'profoundly monotheistic'. 'Realistic and non-transpar-ent', Semitic words were blandly superficial, tending to inhibit abstract deduction and to prevent 'anything like a delicate background in speech'. Without the verbal resources and flexibility of the Aryans, the Semites were incapable of developing a system of mythology, seen as the basic building block of philosophy. After all, mythology was, at root, 'the investing of words with life'; the Semitic languages were, in this respect, dry, inorganic and infertile.[15]

Race was also the key to the new 'science of religions' inaugurated by Renan's countryman Emile Burnouf. Burnouf's work *La science des religions* was first published as a series of articles in the *Revue des Deux Mondes* between 1864 and 1869, appearing as a book in 1872, and then translated into English in 1888, though its influence had been felt in England long before. Burnouf moved beyond the cautiously philological analysis adopted by Renan. Rather Burnouf claimed that the proper study of religion involved a close analysis of the 'aptitude of races'. Far from keeping discussions of psychical and physical characteristics discreetly apart in separate strands of his overall argument, Burnouf explained the mental distinction between the races craniologically. By way of the developmental anatomy of the Semitic skull, he pointed up limitations which, he believed, severely circumscribed the intellectual potential of the race:

A real Semite has smooth hair, with curly ends, a strongly hooked nose, fleshy, projecting lips, massive extremities, thin calves and flat feet. And what is more, he belongs to the occipital races; that is to say, those whose hinder part of the head is more developed than the front. His growth is very rapid, and at fifteen or sixteen it is over. At that age the divisions of his skull which contain the organs of intelligence are already joined, and in some cases even perfectly welded together. From that period the growth of the brain is arrested. In the Aryan races this phenomenon, or anything like it, never occurs, at any time of life, certainly not with people of normal development. The internal organ is permitted to continue its evolution and transformations up till the very last day of life by means of the never-changing flexibility of the skull bones.

Of course, Aryans did experience some cerebral dysfunction in later life, Burnouf conceded, but he noted that this was not in any way owing to 'the external conformation of the head'; rather he attributed such problems to the 'ossification of the arteries'. He also pointed out that a teenage Semite's cerebral development ground to a halt before the onset of adult intellectual maturity at which age a person might be able to grasp the 'transcendent speculations' available only to full-grown Aryans.[16]

Despite their differing approaches to the respective roles played by philological and craniological factors in the racial formation of the great religions, Renan and Burnouf agreed in their assessment of the religious capacities of the Aryans and Semites. Burnouf distinguished the remote and arid monotheism of the Semites from an Aryan metaphysic, which Christianity shared with the Aryan religions of Persia and India, which 'assimilates Christ with the common principle of life'. Essentially, the Aryan idiom was pantheistic. The core doctrines of Christianity were Aryan and close metaphysical counterparts could be found, so Burnouf believed, in the Persian *Zend-Avesta*. Burnouf claimed that the *Zend-Avesta* of the Zoroastrians contained in essence 'the whole metaphysical doctrine of the Christians'. Burnouf argued that the doctrine of Christ's incarnation had its roots in Aryan pantheism and was fundamentally un-Semitic. Such was the monotheistic rigidity of the Semitic mind that it could not abide the notion of an incarnate deity. Properly Semitic religions such as Judaism and Islam accept only that their prophets are inspired, never countenancing the possibility of divine incarnation in human form, which would constitute a heretical affront to the narrowly unitarian conceptions of the Semitic race.[17]

Burnouf also identified an Aryanising process in the development of the gospel from its earliest telling through its different renderings from Matthew to John by way of Luke, though Mark, he felt, had added little to the racial transformation of the narrative. In the first gospel, that of Matthew, Burnouf perceived a predominantly Semitic story of Christ's Jewish genealogy; but in Luke 'Joseph the Jew disappears from the scene, and in his place rises upon the foreground Mary the Galilean, of a race probably apart from Israel'. Indeed, Burnouf even claimed to detect 'Vedic elements' in Luke, not least in the attendance of angels at Christ's birth, while the culminating gospel of John, with its various metaphysical elaborations which he thought bore close affinity with the *Zend-Avesta* of the Zoroastrians, was more Aryan still. Ultimately, indeed, Burnouf found the *Vedas* a more authentic part of the Aryan racial 'heritage' than the Bible, corrupted as it was in part by the legacy of an alien Semitic people.[18]

Indeed, Burnouf perceived 'a duality of origin visible in Christian dogmas', and argued that this racial hybridity led to religious instability. With striking confidence, he attributed the various divisions, deviations and heresies which had beset Christianity over the centuries to the problem of combining elements drawn from two incompatible racial mentalities in a single religious system. Aryanism and Semitism were like oil and water. An irreconcilable clash of racial idioms – one rigidly monotheistic, the other expansively pantheistic – produced a dangerous instability in Christian doctrine. Alexandrian Trinitarianism, for example, was 'exclusively Aryan', its theory of hypostasis drawing heavily on the Aryan metaphysic of the Platonists. Burnouf went on to present a racialised picture of Western Christendom with its 'peoples of Aryan origin in some sort semitised in Christianity'. Indeed, he identified Roman Catholicism as the branch of Christianity most definitively marked by the legacy of Semitism, both being based 'on the absolute personality of a god separate from the world'.[19]

This emphasis upon the role of race in religion persisted in the emergent and internationally influential French science of religions. In his *Prolégomènes de l'histoire des religions* (1881), the French Protestant theologian Albert Réville (1826–1906) identified 'le génie des races' as one of the principal 'causes motrices du développement religieux', alongside knowledge of the natural world, the progress both of reason and morality, and the social and political context, as well as internal religious factors. Historically, the spirit of the racial group became a decisive factor in the formation of a religious worldview, contended Réville, at the point where a race began to import a sense of drama into the natural world. Evidence drawn from the ancient cultures of various peoples provided examples of how racial mentalities shaped mythology. Réville argued that races whose sense of imagination was stunted tended to generate a very impoverished mythology. The Semites were in a somewhat different category, for their lack of a dramaturgical inclination meant that within their religion there would be a somewhat restrained mythological dramatisation of nature. The religion of the Chinese was of a monotonous regularity and highly ritualistic. On the other hand, the Celts generated a dreamlike mythology of alternating passion and tenderness, while the Germanic races produced an ancient religion which combined idealism, vigour and brutality.[20]

However, the insights of the French school on the British ethnology of religion were substantially qualified by a less radical German tradition of philology which established its home in England in the mid-nineteenth century. A crucial figure in this transplantation was the London-based Prussian diplomat, Baron Christian Bunsen (1791–1860). The new insights of Indo-European linguistics underpinned Bunsen's *Philosophy of universal history* (1854). The metanarrative of history, Bunsen proclaimed, was a grand racial dialectic, out of which Christianity had emerged as the – somewhat ironic – synthesis. In the scheme of universal history outlined by Bunsen, the Semitic and Japhetic or Iranian (by which he meant Aryan) races had played central roles in the unfolding of the human spirit. Human consciousness of God was innate; however, different races had channelled this intuition in different ways. Bunsen argued that the Semitic and Aryan races had played complementary roles in the progressive unfolding of human consciousness, not least in a racially hybridised Christianity. However, the work of providence had been far from straightforward. Complications arose from the fact that Christianity had no sooner arisen from Semitic foundations than it became primarily the religion of 'Iranian' (meaning Aryan) nations, whose culture was antagonistic to the values of Semitism. Nevertheless, the cunning of history had brought about a resolution of these jarring race elements. Hellenic Aryanism had 'universalized the Semitic elements in Christianity', while Semitism had given to Hellenism 'its ethical earnestness, and raised it from the idolatry of Hellenic nationality to a purer feeling of brotherhood'.[21]

Bunsen played a part in introducing the German philologist Friedrich Max Müller into English intellectual life. Max Müller's account of religious differences between the Aryans and Semites stood in a somewhat ambivalent relationship to the not entirely dissimilar views of Renan. Max Müller agreed – up to a point – with Renan that there had been from ancient times a basic difference between the 'mythological phraseology' of the Aryans and the 'theological phraseology' of the Semites. However, Max Müller could find no evidence for Renan's supposition of 'the monotheistic instinct of the whole Semitic race'. Quite the reverse, if anything, suggested Max Müller, for polytheism seemed generally to have prevailed among the ancient peoples of Babylon, Nineveh and Arabia.[22]

Such basic differences notwithstanding, Max Müller did appear to be endorsing a subtler version of the race-character theory of religion. In Max Müller's case the structures of language supplied a persuasive mechanism for explaining the religious and mythological divergences found between different peoples. Semitic language was simple and plain in meaning and its word roots were so obvious as to leave little room for ambiguity. This linguistic environment encouraged the development of a straightforward monotheistic religion among the Semitic peoples. By the same token, mythology was the distinctive racial inheritance of the Aryan peoples, though at bottom it was 'only a dialect, an ancient form of language'. It was not so much the case that Semites were racially programmed for monotheism as that the fundamental patterning of their language did not encourage the emergence of a polytheistic mythology. 'The Semitic man', noted Max Müller, 'had hardly even to resist the allurements of mythology. The names with which he invoked the Deity did not trick him by their equivocal character.' The 'pellucid' quality of Semitic vocabulary rendered it immune to the 'mythological refraction' experienced by the speech of the ancient Aryans.[23]

Max Müller's famous observation that religion was a 'disease of language' was underpinned by a sophisticated theory of how different language families conceptualised deity. All mankind, Max Müller contended, had been endowed with an instinct for religion which had manifested itself, universally in the primitive stage of society, in what he termed 'henotheism'. This was a kind of religion where 'each god, while he is being invoked, shares in all the attributes of a supreme being'. A 'feeling of sonship', of being the offspring of a divine Creator, was a universal attribute of primitive humanity. However, this primitive sense of deity was neither properly monotheistic nor polytheistic. It could not have been polytheistic, for surely, argued Max Müller, nobody could have conceived of the idea of a plurality of gods without first conceptualising the idea of a god. Yet neither was henotheism monotheistic in the sense of involving a negation of other gods. Over time fundamental linguistic differences between peoples served to bring about significant reformulations of henotheistic divinity in subsequent phases of cultural development. Nevertheless Max Müller did not hold to a hard-and-fast distinction between Aryan polytheism and Semitic monotheism.[24]

Max Müller conjectured three distinct phases of development in the early history of the great language families. In the initial 'Rhematic' period the languages of the race ancestors of the Turanians, Semites and Aryans had acquired a basic vocabulary with pronouns, prepositions and numerals, as well as a simple agglutinative grammar. In the second phase, the 'Dialectical' period, the Aryans and Semites, though not the Turanians who remained stuck with an agglutinative grammar, had developed a systematic grammar. Then, in the third, the 'Mythical' period, the distinctive structures of an as yet undivided Aryan language – in an age 'when Sanskrit was not yet Sanskrit, Greek not yet Greek' – had given birth to the mythology which would flourish in various forms as the common ethnic heritage of the Indians, Persians, Greeks, Italians, Slavs and Teutons.[25]

It was not only numerals, pronouns, household words, prepositions and grammatical terminations which the Aryan peoples shared; they also 'possessed the elements of a mythological phraseology, displaying the palpable traces of a common origin'. Just as it was no longer possible in the wake of the discoveries of Indo-European philology to treat languages by themselves without reference to the broader group, so in the science of mythology it was now necessary to study religious and mythological developments within the Aryan language family; for the various nations which comprised the Aryan family shared a basic vocabulary of godhead.[26]

Here Max Müller's principal target was the old tradition of Christian mythography which tended to 'confound the religion and mythology of the ancient nations of the world'. In particular, he rejected the old school of euhemerist mythography which read pagan deities as posthumously deified leaders, kings and generals; nor did he follow the traditional attempts of Christian theologians to explain pagan religions as corruptions of the ancient patriarchal religion of Noah. 'Race' – by which he meant language groups – provided for Max Müller a compelling new tool into the study of myth. Comparative philology functioned as a reliable 'telescope' into a distant past.[27]

Max Müller deduced that the 'ancestors' of the Aryan and Semitic races 'had long become unintelligible to each other in their conversations on the most ordinary topics, when they each in their own way began to look for a proper name for God'. The multiplication of names for deity – and then of deities – in Aryan religion Max Müller traced to the way in which the roots of Aryan words were liable to be obscured in complex words. On the other hand, Semitic words were not liable, argued Max Müller, to phonetic corruption in the same way. Semitic appellatives 'could never be thought of as proper names' whether of different deities or as different names of the deity:

In the Semitic languages the roots expressive of the predicates which were to serve as the proper names of any subjects, remained so distinct within the body of a word, that those who used the word were unable to forget its predicative meaning, and retained in most cases a distinct consciousness of its appellative power. In the Aryan languages, on the contrary, the significative element, or the root of a word, was apt to become so completely absorbed by the derivative elements, whether prefixes or suffixes, that most substantives ceased to be appellatives, and were changed into mere names or proper names.

This 'peculiarity' of the Aryan and Semitic languages, Max Müller conjectured, had exercised a strong influence on 'the formation of their religious phraseology'. Whereas 'the Semitic man would call on God in adjectives only, or in words which always conveyed a predicative meaning', the Aryan was not so restricted. Among the Aryan peoples, Max Müller argued, such was the metaphorical richness of language – where, for example, the roots of words disappeared from view under prefixes and suffixes – that the sense of a word could become blurred. A characteristic example of this blurring involved the ways in which the names for natural phenomena became in effect proper names. Terms used to describe the surrounding natural world became 'obscured, personified and deified'. In this way the fertile ambiguities of the Aryan languages gave birth to polytheistic mythologies of the sort found in Sanskrit India or among the ancient Greeks.[28]

Nevertheless, the 'history of religion [was] in one sense a history of language'. The name for the supreme deity among the Aryan peoples 'was framed once, and once only': the Greek 'Zeus' was the 'Dyaus' of Sanskrit, the 'Jovis' of Latin, the 'Zio' of Old High German and the 'Tiw' of Anglo-Saxon. The Aryan language family had its own distinctive history of 'expressing the Inexpressible'. Dyaus had originally meant bright and had come to mean sky. Later the expression 'Dyaus thunders' had come to be understood in the verbal formula 'He thunders'. Dyaus became 'He' by 'habit of speech', whereby Dyaus became a name for the deity by way of an ambiguous verbal construction. Similarly, the deity 'Agni' had derived from ambiguities in the expression 'fire burns'. From a variety of such verbal ambiguities involving names for natural phenomena the names of 'god' had multiplied. According to Max Müller, the road to mythology ran through the metaphorical use of language. Hence, religion – or, more properly, mythology – was a 'disease of language'.[29]

Such ideas – however subversive in some of their implications for religious orthodoxy – became the stock in trade of British and American anthropologists and mythographers. The Anglican mythographer, the Reverend George Cox (1827–1902), contended in *The mythology of the Aryan nations* (1870) that primitive man had responded in three different ways to the sense of a superior being lurking behind natural phenomena. The less creative races, oppressed by the harsh realities of nature, had resorted to a crude fetishism. The Hebrews had been led by their observations of nature to the conclusion that they were 'simply passive instruments in the hands of an almighty and righteous God'. The Aryans, however, amidst the subtle distortion of their original language, came to populate the world with anthropomorphised deities.[30]

In his *Outlines of primitive belief among the Indo-European races* (1882), the antiquary Charles Francis Keary (1848–1917) rejected comparative mythology for the study of the progress of religious belief within a single race. In addition, the history of religion was calibrated against a theoretical model of religious evolution. However, Keary recognised the different potentialities of the Aryans and other peoples within the scheme of religious evolution. From distant antiquity Indo-European religion had possessed a distinctive flavour: according to Keary, the 'primitive Aryan creed rested upon a worship of external phenomena, such as the sky, the earth, the sea, the storm, the wind, the sun – that is to say, of phenomena which are appreciable by the senses, but were at the same time in a large proportion either abstractions or generalisations'. However, this was not necessarily a matter of race instinct. Given the place of natural phenomena within the mythology of the Aryans, Keary stressed the influence of the climate and natural environment of the Aryan Ur-homeland in the shaping of the Indo-European religious tradition. Moreover, this milieu of innumerable streams and valleys (sharply contrasted with the less differentiated landscape which produced Asiatic despotism) also gave rise to the village – the characteristic form of Aryan community, whether in the form of the Indian village, the Russian mir or the Swiss canton. The village was a form of republican community, to which corresponded the 'republican and . . . manysided' qualities of Aryan religion.[31]

Aryanism had many mansions. The self-described 'Aryo-Semitic' school, whose members included Canon Isaac Taylor, Sayce and a repentant Cox, qualified the judgements of Max Müller's Aryan mythography. Robert Brown (b. 1844), the leader of Aryo-Semitic scholarship, claimed that Max Müller had partially misinterpreted the ethnic underpinnings of ancient Greek religion. Although Greek culture descended from an Aryan lineage, the Greeks had been receptive to religious influences from the non-Aryan East. Thus, while Brown accepted that some Greek divinities, such as Zeus, Apollo and Athena, were clearly Aryan, others, including Poseidon, Kronos, Dionysos and Aphrodite, betrayed evidence of a Semitic provenance. Against the exaggerated purism of the Aryanists, Brown reckoned that the Greek pantheon represented a blend of ethnic elements.[32]

Racialism itself constituted another major divergence from the purity of Max Müller's interpretation of Aryan religion. Of course, for Max Müller religion was not a manifestation of race as such. Rather, it was a manifestation of the deeper philological structures of language families such as the Aryans and the Semites whose names were themselves all too easily confounded in nineteenth-century culture with racial terminology. Max Müller insisted that language and race were not equivalent. But the genie was out of the bottle. Even today the term 'Aryan', which retains colloquial currency, makes most otherwise educated westerners think of tall, blond Nordics rather than Indo-European languages, including those spoken by darker-hued Indians and Persians. For Max Müller, Aryan religion was an expression of the traits of Indo-European language; for some of Max Müller's wider readership, Aryanism (not least given the looseness of Renan's terminology and the unequivocal racialism of Burnouf) was a matter of race, and Aryan religion a manifestation of Aryan racial characteristics.

The intellectual borders between philology and race were porous. According to Dominick McCausland, the two principal branches of the Caucasian race – the Aryans and the Semites – were 'distinguishable from each other, not only by their languages, but by moral and intellectual qualities which have never been known to change throughout all the generations'. McCausland emphasised the 'devotional tendency' of the Semites as the principal explanation of what differentiated them from

Aryans: 'The simplicity of their idea of a supreme being, separate and distinct from the works of the Creation, has been instrumental in preserving them from the mythological fantasies that prevailed among the Japhetites, whose rationalistic imaginations effaced the boundaries between divinity, humanity, and the universe – mingling gods and men in the mazes of polytheism.' Yet Aryan polytheism, it seemed, had been the cradle of science and philosophy: 'The intellectual qualities predominate in the Japhetite, and the moral in the Semite. Philosophy is the vocation of the one, and religion is the mission of the other.' Nevertheless, it had been language, McCausland believed, which had provided a catalyst for Aryan philosophising. The Aryan tongues, McCausland claimed, had been prone to 'phonetic corruption', whereby Aryans came to attribute personal characteristics to natural phenomena. Fire was the being that burned, thunder the being that thundered. On the other hand, natural phenomena in the Semitic languages had not become 'personages', which 'shielded' Semites 'from the confusion of words and names that gave birth to the multitude of legendary myths that constituted the life of the Aryan, both in Greece and India'.[33]

The Aryan–Semitic distinction was an influential factor both upon defenders of traditional religion, who recognised in race a new factor that might assist in understanding the truths of religion, and upon those who adopted a critical, if not hostile, approach to Christianity. The philological interpretation of religion found its way to the heart of Anglicanism. The Reverend Frederic W. Farrar (1831–1903), an academic philologist and royal chaplain, dealt with the two great culture-races – the Aryans and the Semites – in his lectures on *Families of speech* (1870), the publication of which was dedicated to Max Müller. Farrar drew attention to those very aspects of the Semitic race-character which ethnologists found unattractive as the obverse of the gift for spiritual immediacy which was exclusive to the Semites:

Yet while we dwell on these intellectual deficiencies, while we admit that there was in the Semite but little of that science, or philosophy, or courageous love of truth which are the glory of the Aryan – while we acknowledge him to have been utterly deficient in the spirit of liberty which solved the problem of rendering individual development compatible with imperial and military organisation – while we point out the onesidedness of his intellect, the sameness of his passions, the monotony of his history, the uniformity of his literature, the deficiency in him of the social instincts and of large humanitarian conceptions, the religious absorption which deadened in him all interest for science, and the iconoclastic zeal which destroyed for him the possibility of art – let us never forget the truly immeasurable work which he effected for the world. The very intensity and subjectivity of his religious conceptions were his weakness no less than his strength. They were his weakness, because a noble and fertile spirit of inquiry is impossible for one whose capacity of wonder is swallowed up in his awe for the Infinite and the Unseen . . . No philosophic conception of great demiurgic laws, and no modification or adaptation of those laws to human purposes, was possible in a nation which regarded everything as the direct, immediate, unconditioned exercise of divine power.

However, to the energetic Aryans had fallen the role of spreading Semitic religion to the world. In welcoming the insights of modern Indo-European philology, Farrar, like so many of his contemporaries, wove this modern philological paradigm seamlessly into the inherited scheme of ethnology found in Genesis. Farrar described Japhet as 'the ancestor of the Aryans'. Indeed, the variety of the world's races and language families (which seem to have been equivalent categories in Farrar's work) formed part of a providential pattern in human history. Different races had contributed, by way of their particular aptitudes and mentalities, to the unfolding of civilisation, religion and progress. The Aryan alone could not supply man's deeper spiritual wants. The Semite, while ennobling man in his 'moral bearings', was incapable of bringing about wider intellectual and scientific changes. The Chinese and Negritic peoples had their own particular characters and aptitudes, but would, Farrar argued, have raised only a low level of civilisation without the beneficial leavening of Semitic and Aryan race influences. A mixture of quite different racial cultures supported the elevation of humanity.[34]

Aryan philology, it seemed, possessed the capacity to invigorate a science of religion consonant with the canons of Christian orthodoxy. This was apparent in the work of Sir (John) William Dawson, who was also the principal Canadian opponent of Darwinian and polygenist assaults on Christian ethnology. Dawson argued that there had been a racially based religious division in mankind from the earliest antediluvian times, in the era when humanity was divided into the Cainite and Sethite races. Whereas the Cainites subscribed to belief in a Creator-God, they had lacked the doctrine of a redeemer. Therefore, their religion held the potential for future degeneration into polytheistic nature worship. The Sethites, on the other hand, acknowledged the promise of a Saviour who would provide deliverance from man's Fall, a doctrine which inoculated their religion from the corruptions to which the religion of the Cainite race was liable.[35]

Did Aryan philology, Dawson wondered, provide a telling confirmation of Old Testament prophecy? Genesis 9:27 anticipated the evolutionary cul-de-sac encountered by an Aryan mythology which, lacking the vital elements of monotheism and a clear ethical vision, was to be displaced by Semitism: 'Hence they have given way before other and higher faiths; and at this day the more advanced nations of the Aryan, or in scriptural language the Japhetic stock, have adopted the Semitic faith; and, as Noah long ago predicted, "dwell in the tents of Shem".' After the Flood, another process of differentiation had occurred. Dawson stressed the aboriginal unity – of a common Turanian stock – which had preceded the development of races and language groups. The Semitic and Aryan languages had emerged as offshoots of a common Turanian culture, which had failed to develop in creative ways and remained sunk in a fossilised linguistic culture devoid of 'grammatical structure'. Parallel to this story, Dawson argued that divine revelation was a continuous process which had begun in the earliest patriarchal period, before the development of Aryan or Semitic offshoots from the old Turanian stock. Therefore, Dawson conjectured, if Semitic religion were 'as old as it professes to be', then 'it must include a substratum common to it with the religions of the Turanians and Aryans', as well as the later special spiritual revelations which God had communicated to the Semitic race. In his book *Fossil men and their modern representatives* (1880), Dawson reconciled current ethnographic knowledge of Amerindian religions with both the new philology and the traditional contours of scriptural ethnology. Amerindian religion contained 'remnants of a higher and purer faith', including the ideas of a supreme creator, a fallen human race and a diluvial catastrophe. Dawson concluded that the Amerindian races had diverged from the general mass 'so early that the peculiar features of the Hebrew and Aryan religions had not yet developed themselves out of the primitive patriarchal faith', but that rudiments of the patriarchal religion had been brought to the American continent.[36]

On the other hand, the racialist insights of the new science of religions acquired some purchase on the arch-champion of Darwinian evolution, T. H. Huxley (1825–95), who favoured an anthropological approach to the study of religion. Huxley regarded theology 'as a natural product of the operations of the human mind, under the conditions of its existence', like any other branch of human culture. The progress of mankind as a whole from primitive societies played the dominant role in explaining changes in theology. Huxley identified religious phenomena which were common to different religious cultures at the same stage of their development, in particular a universal 'sciotheism' or a theology of ghosts which could even be found in the religion of the early Israelites. Sciotheist

religious forms, argued Huxley, had preceded the emergence of ethical
components in the world's religions. Race too had a part to play in the
unfolding of religion. Huxley traced the provenance of European moral
and intellectual life to the 'profitable interchange' of Semitic and Aryan
cultures. Whereas art and science were the bequest of the Aryan, 'the
essence of our religion', Huxley claimed, was 'derived from the Semite'.
However, Christianity also carried a load of Aryan baggage which Huxley
was happy to jettison in the name of science: 'What we are usually pleased
to call religion nowadays is, for the most part, Hellenised Judaism; and,
not unfrequently, the Hellenic element carries with it a mighty remnant
of old-world paganism and a great infusion of the worst and weakest
products of Greek scientific speculation.'[37]

Christianity presented a particular problem to a culture which obsessed
over the new insights and higher truths of the emergent human sciences;
it appeared to be a religion of Semitic provenance which had, however,
gained an ascendancy not over Semites but over the Aryan population of
Europe. Was Christianity then a Semitic perversion and distortion of the
Aryan race-soul; or did Christianity rather involve the fruitful Aryanising
of a lesser Semitic form of religious worship? More crudely, was Christianity – properly speaking – Aryan or Semitic?

The American Congregationalist Charles Loring Brace (1826–90)
claimed that through the Semitic race had 'come forth the most sensual
and debased conceptions in mythology which have ever cursed mankind;
while from its deep sense of divinity have sprung all the religions of the
civilized world'. From one branch of the Semitic race had come Islam,
but from another 'the spiritual and inspired conceptions of Judaism and
the divine revelation in Christianity'. Brace saw the Aryan race simply as
the vehicle for the spread of Semitic religion, the Aryans being 'instruments through which the Semitic conceptions of deity, and the Semitic
inspirations of Christianity, have been spread through all nations'. Others
accorded a more dominant role to the Aryan race in the formation of
Christianity.[38]

In 1867 the *Anthropological Review* published an article by the heterodox Anglican cleric-turned-anthropologist Dunbar Heath (1816–88)
which was entitled 'On the great race-elements in Christianity'. Heath
was unambiguous in his answer to the question whether 'the moral, social
and intellectual principles of Christianity are Semitic or Aryan'. The
Christian incarnation, he argued, was an idea of Aryan provenance.
Heath noted that 'all Aryan mythologies delight in depicting the descent
of gods upon the earth to combat evil'. Aryan legends told of numerous

gods in human form and their struggles against evil. On the other hand, within Semitic religions, there appeared to be no example of a god appearing on earth to 'combat moral evil, succumbing to it for a while, and finally triumphing'. Heath took the view that Aryans and Semites differed fundamentally in their attitudes towards the law, not least upon the question of how far the law bound the individual conscience: 'the true Aryan spirit considers law to be an evil, and supports the rights of con-science, not only as the Jew did, against the heathen foreigner, but, as no true Semite would do, against his own government and his own priest'. Moreover, the 'failure' of the Semite apostles – Peter, James and John – 'to originate a Semitic church' provided 'proof' that 'Christianity never was Semitic':

It is admitted that at the time of the origin of Christianity large Semite and Aryan populations were in existence, each of them highly civilised, each of them so circumstanced as to be ready as an audience to hear, to receive, or to reject the new religion. Had the religion been a Semitic one, both its geographical origin and the nationality of its earliest preachers would have favoured its reception by that race, but the stubborn fact is that the new religion depreciated law, depreciated constituted authorities, recognised an incarnation, recognised a God becoming, in strong Aryan language, 'a slave to sin', recognised that the recognised law courts could be wrong, and the crucified defendant could be right. The historical success of Christianity is undoubtedly due to the historical sympathy with Christ, and the sympathy with Christ was an Aryan sympathy with the defendant.

Christianity, in Heath's estimate, was based ultimately upon the Aryan theme of 'moral contest'. The fact that Semites were polygamous and Aryans monogamous seemed to Heath to offer a fascinating insight into the roots of these radically different approaches to constituted authority. Polygamy required a greater emphasis upon law and order than a system of monogamy, which was capable of greater looseness in the ordering of families. Indeed, Heath regarded Aryan ethics as superior in their moral content to the rule-bound system of the Semites: 'Christianity being a religion recognising that the principle of faith or mutual trust is far preferable to the dead hard power of law for the purpose of sustaining justice or order in the human race, is a religion acceptable to Aryans.'[39]

Alexander Lindsay (1812–80), the 25th Earl of Crawford and 8th Earl of Balcarres, took a quite different line. In his posthumously published book *The creed of Japhet* (1891), Lindsay argued that God had revealed his truth to the three branches of the Noachids. Semites, Hamites and

Japhetites – the last identified by Lindsay as the Aryan race – had all received the message. However, the divine message had become more seriously corrupted among the Hamites and Semites. This had necessitated a re-revelation to the Semites with the coming of Christ. On the other hand, the Japhetites had preserved their ancient religious truth including the bi-fold nature of Christ and the Trinity. According to Lindsay, Christianity was a union of ancient Aryan–Japhetic truth with the re-revealed gospel of Jesus as delivered to the Semites.[40]

Some ethnologists also perceived crucial religious differences between races within the Aryan group, such as between Teutons, Celts and Latins. Indeed, nineteenth-century anti-Catholicism became tinged with racialism, which rendered it even more potent, for race lent a pseudo-scientific justification to Protestant bigotry, deepening and hardening traditional confessional prejudices. Why, nineteenth-century commentators asked, were Teutonic peoples more susceptible to Protestantism, and Latin and Celtic peoples so reluctant to abandon the old superstitions of Catholicism? Was this no more than a historical accident or did it reveal a deeper truth of race? The controversial Scots anatomist Robert Knox (1791–1862) argued that race, rather than religion, was the fundamental determinant of culture and civilisation. The protean forms assumed by Christianity struck Knox as manifestations of deeper and more basic racial types. Christianity, he argued, 'presents also a variety of forms essentially distinct: with each race its character is altered'. Races such as the Saxons and the Celts expressed their Christian beliefs in different forms of worship and doctrine. Moreover, one had only to look at a map and one would see that 'with a slight exception, if it really be one, the Celtic race universally rejected the Reformation of Luther; the Saxon race as certainly adopted it'. For Knox, Christianity was an 'elastic robe' which 'adapts itself with wonderful facility to all races and nations'.[41]

Racialised confessionalism – albeit of a milder sort – surfaced within the mainstream of Christian thought. Henry Milman (1791–1868), who rose within the Church of England to become dean of St Paul's, discerned a distinctive racial pattern beneath the vicissitudes of Europe's Christian past. Without questioning the core spiritual truths of Christianity, Milman perceived that the *human* expression of Christian worship, theology and churchmanship had been racially inflected. In his *History of Latin Christianity* (1855; 3rd edition, 1872), Milman contrasted the dominant Latin strain in the history of Christendom with a long suppressed Teutonic spirituality which had eventually burst forth in the Reformation of England and the Germanic world. The Reformation, declared Milman, was an assertion of 'independence' by 'Teutonic Christianity'. Indeed, the division between Latin and Germanic peoples constituted the frontiers between the Catholic and Reformed faiths: 'Throughout the world, wherever the Teutonic is the groundwork of the language, the Reformation either is, or, as in Southern Germany, has been dominant; wherever Latin, Latin Christianity has retained its ascendancy.' Papalism marked the fullest expression of Latin Christianity, a form of religion grounded in a 'rigid objectiveness', with a tendency to promote 'materialism', 'servility' and 'blind obedience'. Teutonism, on the other hand, was a more 'subjective' form of spirituality, which, in addition, 'exercised a more profound moral control, through the sense of strictly personal responsibility'. The Reformation did away with the divine intermediaries – saints, martyrs and the virgin – who led the Latin mind up a scale of spiritual gradation towards heaven. But this aspect of Catholicism was anathema to the 'contemplative Teuton', for whom, according to Milman, it 'obscures and intercepts his awful intuitive sense of the Godhead, unspiritualises his Deity, whom he can no longer worship as pure Spirit'.[42]

This division had deep roots in European history. Even before their conversion to Christianity the Germanic peoples of antiquity had a distinctive 'religious character' which facilitated their reception of the gospel. In particular, they possessed a 'conception of an illimitable Deity' whom they regarded with 'solemn and reverential awe'. Milman insisted on the shared ethnic provenance of the pagan cults of the various Germanic tribes and peoples: 'Certain religious forms and words are common to all the races of Teutonic descent. In every dialect appear kindred or derivative terms for the deity, for sacrifice, for temples and for the priesthood.' Teutonism was not simply a matter of language, though the contrast between the religious vocabulary of German and Latin did play a crucial part in the narrative. Teutonic religion was also deeply rooted in the mental equipment of the race. Although the Germanic peoples found themselves, once converted to Christianity, exposed to the practices and ethos of an authoritarian and despotic 'Latin Christianity'; yet 'Teutonism only slumbered, it was not extinguished.' Despite its apparent subservience to Latin norms, the 'Teutonic mind never entirely threw off its innate independence'. In England, for example, the Anglo-Saxons had only been 'partially Romanised' by the Norman Conquest, which ushered in, for a while, a 'period of suspended Teutonic life'. However, the gradual eclipse of the Norman aspect of the monarchy and the language led to the reawakening during the later Middle Ages of an Englishness which, ultimately, paved the way for the Reformation. The common law revived, the English constitution recovered its balance and the English language emerged as the vehicle of a great literature in Langland and Chaucer. John Wycliffe, the guru of the Lollards, stood at the heart of this reinvigorated racial life, his biblical translations epitomising the 'prevailing and dominant Teutonism'. There were parallel developments in Germany during this 'intermediate state of slowly dawning Teutonism.' At the epoch when 'English Teutonism was resolutely bracing itself' for 'religious independence', in Germany 'a silent rebellious mysticism was growing up even in her cloisters, and working into the depths of men's hearts and minds', of which the Dominican mystic Johann Tauler was a leading exponent.[43]

Canon Isaac Taylor, one of the leading English Aryan ethnologists of the late nineteenth century, argued that religion depended 'intimately' upon 'the fundamental ethical character of the race'. According to Taylor, the line of division between Catholic and Protestant Europe coincided 'very closely with the line which separates the two great races of Aryan speech. The dolichocephalic Teutonic race is Protestant, the brachycephalic Celto-Slavic race is either Roman Catholic or Greek Orthodox.' Craniology also provided a key to understanding the distribution of religion across the continent. Dolichocephalic Teutonic Europe was Protestant Europe:

Scandinavia is more purely Teutonic than Germany, and Scandinavia is Protestant to the backbone. The Lowland Scotch, who are more purely Teutonic than the English, have given the freest development to the genius of Protestantism. Those Scotch clans which have clung to the old faith have the smallest admixture of Teutonic blood. Ulster, the most Teutonic province of Ireland, is the most firmly Protestant. The case of the Belgians and the Dutch is very striking. The line of religious division became the line of political separation, and is coterminous with the two racial provinces. The mean cephalic index of the Dutch is 75.3, which is nearly that of the Swedes and the North Germans; the mean index of the Belgians is 79, which is that of the Parisians. The Burgundian cantons of Switzerland, which possess the largest proportion of Teutonic blood, are Protestant, while the brachycephalic cantons in the east and south are the stronghold of Catholicism. South Germany, which is brachycephalic, is Catholic; North Germany, which is dolichocephalic, is Protestant.

Anglicans, who followed a *via media* between Catholicism and the Calvinist extremes of Protestantism turned out, as one might expect, to be 'orthocephalic', in other words, intermediate between brachycephalic and dolichocephalic, with the breadth of the skull being about three-quarters or four-fifths of the length. Nevertheless, Taylor warned against any crude equation of religion with craniology: it was 'not to be supposed . . . that religious belief is a function of the shape of the skull, but that the shape of the skull is one of the surest indicators of race'. Yet race provided a key to a deeper understanding of European history. Protestantism was not an ephemeral attachment of the Germanic peoples. The Teutonic race had ever been 'averse to sacerdotalism'. Taylor thought he discerned the deep roots of Protestant dissent from authority in the Dark Age Teutonic fascination with the heresy of Arianism, an intensely 'rationalistic form of Christianity'. In more recent history, the Thirty Years' War, claimed Taylor, had been 'a war of race as well as of religion'.[44]

The racial underpinnings of religious change became a staple of historical interpretation. This theme surfaced in lectures – subsequently published as *The Roman and the Teuton* (1864) – which the novelist Charles Kingsley (1819–75) gave as Professor of Modern History at the University of Cambridge. Kingsley traced the vicissitudes of Teutonic history, in both its pagan and Christian periods. Yet even the pagan Teutons, he argued, had upheld a 'creed concerning the unseen world, and divine beings' which had been of a 'loftiness and purity' well beyond the 'silly legends', say, of the indigenous religions of North America. Even in their untutored paganism, the Teutonic race signalled its receptivity to its glorious destiny of Christian nationhood. Yet Kingsley was decidedly anti-Catholic, and he took the line that popery was inimical to Anglo-Saxon values. By contrast, he noted in a letter of 1851 to his wife that 'the Church of England [was] wonderfully and mysteriously fitted for the souls of a free Norse–Saxon race'.[45]

A. G. Richey (1830–83), the prominent Irish historian and Deputy Regius Professor of Feudal and English Law in the University of Dublin, took the view that Ireland's lack of receptiveness to the message of the Reformation was essentially caused by its Celtic racial distinctiveness. The Reformation, Richey argued, was an exclusively Teutonic Germanic phenomenon and, as such, 'wholly repugnant to the Celtic mind'. Richey claimed that 'the entire religious movement' had been 'influenced by that characteristic of the German nature in which it differs most from the Celtic – self-completeness, self-confidence and individualism'. Whereas to the 'Teutonic mind' society was 'an aggregate of individuals', to the Celt society was a matter of tribal solidarity, the spiritual counterpart of which was adherence to the community of the church.[46]

According to the Celticist John Rhys (1840–1915), the 'antithesis between the Aryan and the Anaryan elements in the composition of all the great nations of Europe' lay behind the vigour and social diversity of Europe, a situation in sharp contrast with the monochrome stasis of Asiatic life. Moreover, this same antithetical relationship underpinned the religious divisions of Europe. The 'pure Aryan' possessed 'great independence of mind', yet lacked imagination. As a result, 'no priesthood could wholly subdue him': in effect, his characteristics made the 'pure Aryan' highly receptive to Protestantism. Protestantism, insisted Rhys, 'now prevails in all the countries where the Aryan blood is most copious'. By contrast, the conquered non-Aryan peoples of central and western Europe were not only small in stature, but they also had nervous systems which were 'highly strung'. In consequence, the natural world held more terrors for them, and their imaginations 'peopled the dusk of the forest and the darkness of the night with all kinds of horrors', whose suppression, in turn, called forth the solidarity of the group and the intercession of a priesthood. England was a mixture of ethnic elements, including both the 'tall, muscular and light-haired' Aryan as well as a shorter and darker racial stock. Racial hybridity took a predictable turn in the religious sphere, the Church of England representing an equilibrium of Aryan and Anaryan elements in the English people. According to Rhys, 'the mixture of races in England' had 'curiously stamped its duality on the history of the English church, which is such that it can neither be called a Roman church, nor altogether ranked with the Protestant ones'.[47]

Other commentators stressed the racial individuality of English Protestantism. In *The origins and destiny of imperial Britain* (1915), John Cramb (1862–1913), Professor of Modern History at Queen's College, London, traced the glorious history of an expansive English nation back to its ultimate provenance in a Teutonic proto-Protestantism. Cramb took the view that religion 'incarnates' the mentality of a race, discovering 'the remoter origins and causes' of the English Reformation 'in the character of the race itself'. He perceived the 'same bright energy of the soul, the same awe, rooted in the blood of our race' not only in the Reformation but in the medieval history of the Anglo-Saxons. A 'common impulse of the race', Cramb speculated, had bound 'the whole English Reformation, the whole movement of English religious thought from Wyclif to Cromwell and Milton', and now underpinned England's imperial world mission.[48]

This strain of Saxonist nativism was transatlantic in its appeal. Saxonist religiosity was also a staple of mid- and late nineteenth-century American Protestant culture. While some preachers hailed the United States as the providentially ordained land of the Protestant Saxon race, a less hyperbolic version of such sentiments also circulated in the higher levels of American intellectual life. In his masterwork, *The rise of the Dutch republic* (1855), the celebrated American historian John Lothrop Motley (1814–77) identified two distinct racial elements in the people of the Netherlands which would never properly fuse. In antiquity the Netherlands had constituted a borderland of sorts between Celtic Gauls to the south (the forerunners of the Walloons) and the Germanic ancestors of the Flemish peoples. In antiquity these racial groups had differed not only in their manners and political institutions, but also in their religion. Fundamental racial differences, it appeared, had shaped the emergence of distinct types of paganism whose characteristics foreshadowed later differences between Catholicism and Protestantism. Whereas the Celtic Gauls were 'priest-ridden', ruled over by a 'despotic' caste of Druids who compelled the observance of superstitious and bloody rites of human sacrifice, the Germanic tribes – long before the coming of Christianity – manifested a type of laudable Puritan restraint even in their paganism. According to Motley, the Germans held a 'lofty conception' of the deity far removed from the crude paganism of other ancient peoples. 'The German, in his simplicity', he wrote, 'had raised himself to a purer belief than that of the sensuous Roman or the superstitious Gaul.' The Germans, Motley went on, 'believed in a single, supreme almighty God, All-Vater or All-Father', a monotheistic godhead 'too sublime to be incarnated or imaged, too infinite to be enclosed in temples'. The deity of the Germans was worshipped instead in sacred groves by a community of believers, without the aid of a priestly caste. The 'elevated but dimly groping creed' of the pagan German stood representative of the psychic characteristics of the race and revealed an instinctive racial longing for a pure, simple, unmediated kind of religion. Proto-Protestantism was in the blood, it seemed. Indeed, Motley argued that centuries of history had 'rather hardened than effaced' the racial characteristics of the Germanic and Celtic races in the Netherlands. The Celtic Walloons, Motley noted, had at the Reformation been the first of the Netherlandish peoples to reconcile themselves to Rome.[49]

The transcendentalist James Freeman Clarke described Protestantism as a religion of blood and race. The differences between Protestant and Catholic zones of Europe he identified as primarily racial, relating to the differing ways in which the Teutonic and Latin races of Europe assimilated Christianity:

The southern races of Europe received Christianity as a religion of order; the northern races, as a religion of freedom. In the south of Europe the Catholic church, by its ingenious organization and its complex arrangements, introduced into life discipline and culture. In the north of Europe Protestant Christianity, by its appeals to the individual soul, awakens conscience and stimulates to individual and national progress. The nations of southern Europe accepted Christianity mainly as a religion of sentiment and feeling; the nations of northern Europe, as a religion of truth and principle.

Providence worked through both religion and race. 'God adapted Christianity to the needs of these northern races; but he also adapted these races, with their original instincts and their primitive religion, to the needs of Christianity.' According to Clarke, the Teutonic race character was an indispensable element of Protestantism: 'It was no accident which made the founder of the Reformation a Saxon monk, and the cradle of the Reformation Germany.' Nor was it any accident that the Protestant nations of the world were largely the Scandinavian nations, Dutch and North Germans, the British and Americans: 'The old instincts still run in the blood, and cause these races to ask of their religion, not so much the luxury of emotion or the satisfaction of repose, in having all opinions settled for them and all actions prescribed, as, much rather, light, freedom, and progress.'[50]

The Reverend Josiah Strong (1847–1916), a leading American social reformer and anti-Catholic propagandist of the late nineteenth century, was a convinced Saxonist. Saxonism featured prominently as a potential racial panacea in his Protestant jeremiad *Our country* (1885), which sold more than 175,000 copies in various American editions, as well as being translated into a number of other languages. In *Our country*, Strong, a militant if liberal Protestant who was active in the Congregational Home Missionary Society and would go on to hold the position of general secretary of the Evangelical Alliance for the United States, warned his countrymen that the perils of Romanism threatened the American social fabric. The best hope for American renewal lay in its Anglo-Saxon character. The Anglo-Saxon race, Strong claimed, had been the exponent of two great ideas. In the sphere of politics, law and institutions, the Saxons had upheld the ideals of civil liberty. Balancing this achievement in the realm of religion, the Saxons had promoted a purer and more spiritual type of Christianity than other peoples:

The other great idea of which the Anglo-Saxon is the exponent is that of a pure spiritual Christianity. It was no accident that the great reformation of the sixteenth century originated among a Teutonic, rather than a Latin people. It was the fire of liberty burning in the Saxon heart that flamed up against the absolutism of the Pope. Speaking roughly, the peoples of Europe which are Celtic are Roman Catholic, and those which are Teutonic are Protestant; and where the Teutonic race was purest, there Protestantism spread with the greatest rapidity.

The Anglo-Saxons, boasted Strong, were 'the great missionary race'.[51]

Saxonist racialism remained powerful in the early decades of the twentieth century, most notoriously in Madison Grant's racialist 'classic', *The passing of the great race*. Published to no great fanfare in 1916, the book was taken up during the 1920s by champions of immigration restrictions. Grant believed that the great race – the Protestant Nordics (or Saxons) – constituted the highest point of evolution. Yet this great race of Nordics now appeared to be threatened by an influx of lesser breeds and racial mongrels. The solutions advocated by Grant included sterilisation and controlled breeding as well as a bar on the immigration to the United States of racial undesirables. Religion played a part in Grant's racism. Grant believed that Jesus Christ had been a Nordic, and he interpreted the history of Europe as a story of racial interaction, with rival forms of Christianity operating as fronts for the expression of deeper racial realities.[52]

So influential – indeed hackneyed – was the received idea of the linkage between race and religion that it provoked robust criticism from those who disdained the unwarranted sway of racialist interpretations in the human sciences. Foremost among these was the British freethinker and Liberal politician John Mackinnon Robertson (1856–1933). In his book *The Saxon and the Celt: a study in sociology* (1897), Robertson decisively rejected the assumption that the cultural and political differences of the British Isles, and foremost among these the problem of settling Ireland's place in the United Kingdom, were ultimately predicated upon the basic racial division of Celt and Saxon. Among Robertson's targets was the thesis advanced by Isaac Taylor concerning the fundamental ethno-religious split between individualistic and Protestant dolichocephalic Teutonic peoples and superstitious, Catholic brachycephalic Celts. Robertson contended that, even on its own terms, this racialist argument of Taylor's was self-contradictory. Ethnologically Calvin was a Celt, not a Teuton, and so too was Luther, surely, 'being brachycephalic'. Furthermore, were not the Swiss, including the Calvinist Genevans, brachycephalic?[53]

In his mammoth *Short history of freethought* (1914), which was a universal history of religion and civilisation, Robertson directly challenged the prevailing racialism in biblical scholarship, in ecclesiastical history and in the wider science of comparative religion. Robertson complained of a 'tenacious psychological prejudice as to race-characters and racial "genius"' and the emergence of 'a theory of racial tendency in religion'. For instance, Robertson queried Sayce's use of 'Semitic race elements' to explain ancient ethical systems, and the widely accepted assumption that Semites possessed a 'primordial religious gift' distinct from the Turanian race. There was 'no good ground', Robertson insisted, 'for the oft-repeated formula about the special monotheistic and other religious proclivities of the Semite; Semites being subject to religious influences like other peoples, in terms of culture and environment'. Social and cultural context, as well as historical contingencies, displaced racial factors in the study of religious variations. Furthermore, Robertson reiterated and amplified his rejection of the racialist interpretation of the Reformation. He denounced as an 'inveterate fallacy' the notion that the Reformation was 'a product of the "Teutonic conscience"': it was not by any 'predilection or faculty of race that the Reformation so-called came to be associated historically with the northern or Teutonic nations. They simply succeeded in making permanent, by reason of more propitious political circumstances, a species of ecclesiastical revolution in which other races led the way.' Robertson had no truck with the received opinion that the Latin nations of southern Europe were less equipped, racially, for Protestantism than their Teutonic neighbours to the north.[54]

The racial interpretation of religion gave rise to some unusual by-products. For some Christians, their own religion was the sole globally relevant exception to a world of racially specific religions. Here the racialist interpretation of religion seemed to bolster the truth-claims of Christianity. Christianity alone had an inter-racial missionary appeal which suggested that – unlike other religions – it was not reducible to a narrow, localised manifestation of ethnicity. In *Gospel ethnology*, published in 1887 by the Religious Tract Society, Samuel Rowles Pattison (1809–1901), the Christian geologist, examined 'the place which the gospel holds in relation to ethnology'. Somewhat indelicately, Pattison welcomed the fact that missionaries had 'found no individual heathen so dark, brutish, stolid, and degraded, as to be incapable of being made a new creature in Christ Jesus'. On the other hand, this was not true of other religions. 'No heathen religion can claim for itself what we have shown to be a characteristic of the religion of Christ, for no pagan utterance or provision has successfully appealed to people of every kind.'

Christianity alone was capable of bridging the major psychological and cultural divisions among the world's races.[55]

More dispassionately in *Ten great religions: an essay in comparative theology* (1871), the American transcendentalist James Freeman Clarke used the science of race to produce an academic and dispassionate case for the ultimate truth of Christianity. At the heart of Clarke's sophisticated apologetic was the widely accepted notion that religion was a manifestation of racial character: 'Now we find that each race, beside its special moral qualities, seems also to have special religious qualities, which cause it to tend toward some one kind of religion more than to another kind. These religions are the flower of the race; they come forth from it as its best aroma.' Clarke then proceeded to classify belief systems into the categories of ethnic and universal religions. Hinduism, for example, was a 'strictly ethnic religion', for it had 'never communicated itself to any race of men outside of the peninsula of India'. Buddhism, too, 'though it includes a variety of nationalities, it is doubtful if it includes any variety of races'. Ethnic religions, Clarke reckoned, tended to be lopsided in their doctrines. This imbalance arose, he claimed, from the fact that ethnic religions expressed particular racial characteristics, rather than the roundedness of humanity as a whole. Every ethnic religion had both a 'positive and negative side'. 'Its positive side,' according to Clarke, 'is that which holds some vital truth; its negative side is the absence of some essential truth.' Every ethnic religion, Clarke concluded, was 'true and providential', but was also 'limited and imperfect'. In other words, ethnic religions were not in themselves false, but their truths were limited and circumscribed by racial peculiarities. Universal tendencies, by contrast, were apparent in Judaism, Islam and – above all – Christianity. Judaism and Islam, it transpired, while they had undoubted pretensions to universality, were but particular variants of the truly universal religion: 'All the great religions of the world, except Christianity and Mohammedanism, are ethnic religions, or religions limited to a single nation or race. Christianity alone (including Mohammedanism and Judaism, which are its temporary and local forms) is the religion of all races.' Christianity, 'from the first, showed itself capable of taking possession of the convictions of the most different races of mankind.' It had proved itself 'capable of adapting itself to every variety of the human race'. Other religions involved partial truths, but Christianity alone embodied the 'fulness of truth', being a 'fulfilment of previous religions'.[56]

Indeed, Aryanism was at the heart of what became known as 'fulfilment theology'. Here a global religion of humanity was disaggregated into its various ethnoreligious components. The classic illustration of this phenomenon was the subtle reconciliation of Hinduism and Christianity found in the work of the Scots missionary and Orientalist John Nicol Farquhar (1861–1929). In *The crown of Hinduism* (1913), Farquhar identified 'the religion of Christ' as 'the spiritual crown of the religion of the *Rig Veda*'. Farquhar envisaged a more sophisticated and ethnologically informed strain of evangelicalism which would circumvent the horrors of cruder missionary efforts. Bemoaning the destructiveness of traditional missions which rejected root-and-branch the errors of heathen religions, Farquhar argued that such approaches served only to hamper the real work of the missionary: 'Total loss of faith does not make a Hindu a Christian.'[57]

Nor indeed was there any basic incompatibility between the Ur-religion of the Hindus and Christianity. The ancient religion of the Aryan race revealed its potentiality for the highest truths of Christianity. Both in the *Zend-Avesta* of the western Aryans in Persia and in the *Rig Veda* of the eastern Aryans in India, Farquhar detected the seeds of 'ethical theism'. A monotheistic element was present in both cosmogonies. Indeed, although the ancient Aryans of India were 'polytheists', they were nevertheless 'far enough advanced in thought and religious feeling to be frequently led by their higher instincts to ideas and expressions which are scarcely consistent with a belief in many gods'. But Farquhar went even further in his analysis of the ancient Aryan religion of the *Rig Veda*. He suggested that it was a category mistake to assume that the *Rig Veda* was simply the forerunner of later forms of Hinduism. Rather, the ancient faith of the Indo-Aryans in Farquhar's estimation stood 'much nearer to Christianity than it does to Hinduism'. There was nothing inevitable about a trajectory from the *Rig Veda* direct to caste, sati, child marriage and the other 'offensive' accretions of modern Hinduism: a transition to Christianity would have been more natural and straightforward. Beyond the superficial differences between Hinduism and Christianity there were deep resemblances, including a fundamental doctrine of incarnation. Christianity – in a sense the fulfilment of an ancient Aryan possibility – now provided an opportunity for the full realisation of the 'highest aspirations' of the Indian religious tradition.[58]

CHAPTER 7

Forms of Racialised Religion

Religious movements and churches that originated in the nineteenth or early twentieth century often bore traces of that era's obsession with race. The science of race, after all, seemed, like these new religious formations, to offer new insights into human nature, history and society, of which previous centuries had been unaware. This is not to suggest that there is something unambiguously racist about the religious groupings discussed in this chapter; indeed some of them articulate explicitly anti-racist doctrines. The objective here is not to denigrate organisations 'tainted' with racialist assumptions, but to explore racial-theological connections in the milieu from which they emerged. Religious movements arising in the nineteenth or early twentieth centuries bore the imprint, sometimes perhaps unconsciously, of that era's peculiar concerns and fascinations, among which racialism ranked prominently. Moreover, it should also be remembered that racialism was at that time as often as not a supposedly neutral or disinterested line of analysis in history and the human sciences, and it did not always take the form of an overt prejudice. During the nineteenth century the application of ethnology and philology to the truths of scripture seemed likely to yield dividends for modern and sophisticated biblical interpreters. The 'science' of biblical criticism was itself inflected with contemporary racialist assumptions. Christians recognised that, although the truths of Christianity were timeless, the human understanding of scripture belonged to the realm of history and might be enhanced with the latest aids which the progress of knowledge had made available, the science of race included. In one particular field of scriptural enquiry, racial science seemed eminently suited to provide assistance to scholars and theologians: namely the search for the modern ethnic groups descended from the Lost Tribes of Israel.

BRITISH ISRAELISM AND ITS OFFSHOOTS

The nineteenth century threw up two quite distinctive ways of defining races. The first and more familiar approach, which I have already examined, involved the empirical study of 'visible' races, whether by way of anatomy, physiology, craniology or linguistics. However, the fascination with race which manifested itself in a range of new scientific approaches also found expression in a dramatically different method of identifying 'invisible' races. This second method involved the identification of invisible Israelites, the heirs of spiritual blessings, promises and prophecies conferred upon the people of Israel in the Old Testament, by way of unmasking certain non-Judaic and non-Semitic groups as cryptic Israelites.

In the hands of British Israelite interpreters, the message of the Bible seemed to be reducible to a kind of ethnology. The scriptures appeared to be littered with clues identifying the recipients of the promises offered to the lost tribe of Ephraim; but only modern race science, in conjunction with a new scheme of scriptural interpretation, had made ethnological sense of the mysteries encoded in the text. At the core of British Israelism the incongruous categories of racial science and sacred history overlapped. Here too lay the principal novelty of British Israelite belief. Its defining tenet was the identification of the Anglo-Saxon peoples of Britain and North America as a race of Israelitish origin, indeed whose descent could, in fact, be traced quite specifically to the tribe of Ephraim. In the course of the nineteenth century, British Israelism came to function as the spiritual counterpart of Anglo-Saxon racialism. While racial characteristics, institutions and the Saxons' peculiar aptitude for freedom provided a secular rationale for Anglo-Saxon superiority, the Anglo-Saxons, as it turned out, also happened to be the biological heirs of certain spiritual promises and blessings set out in the Old Testament. The theological system of the British Israelites was a quasi-heresy. It did not directly confront Christian orthodoxy, but approached it at an unusual tangent; nor did it threaten the central tenets of Christianity. Nevertheless, its ethnocentric reading of Old Testament prophecies and promises served to blunt the universalist message apparent in the New Testament.[1]

The British Israelite movement developed out of the long, ongoing fascination with the mystery of the Ten Lost Tribes. By the late eighteenth and early nineteenth centuries, there had been considerable anthropological speculation that the 'strange' Amerindian peoples of the New World might well be the Lost Tribes. In particular, James Adair's *History of the American Indians* (1775) argued that native American tribalism and the Indians' name for the deity – 'Yo-he-wah' (Yahweh?) – indicated their Israelite origins. Adair's theories enjoyed plenty of support, including the endorsement of Charles Crawford and Elias

Boudinot, the head of the American Bible Society. Nevertheless, an alternative line of investigation focused its enquiries with more apparent plausibility on the Near East. Remote parts of the Near East such as Kurdistan or Afghanistan provided a promisingly difficult terrain in which the Ten Tribes might have become lost from the rest of the world and their co-religionists. Unusual peoples and religious groups in the Middle East also attracted attention. Asahel Grant (1807–44), who had been appointed by the American Board of Foreign Missions to work as a medical missionary among the Nestorians of Mesopotamia, came to the conclusion that he had traced the lost Israelites, a discovery unveiled in *The Nestorians: or the Lost Tribes* (1841).[2]

In the late eighteenth century, the notion that the Anglo-Saxon forebears of the English nation might be the descendants of the Ten Lost Tribes surfaced in the prophecies and theological speculations of Richard Brothers (1757–1824). Born in Newfoundland, Brothers had risen through the ranks of the Royal Navy to become a lieutenant, leaving on half-pay at the conclusion of the American War of Independence. Thereafter he became drawn to the radical fringes of religious culture, worshipping with Baptists and adopting a vegetarian lifestyle. His radicalism may have been accentuated by the trauma of discovering his wife's relationship with another man, conducted while he had been absent at sea, now in the merchant marine. At any rate, Brothers became increasingly unconventional in his beliefs, and in 1791 he began to experience visions of God's judgement on London, where he was now living. The early years of the French Revolution witnessed a vogue for millennial ideas. How were the momentous events in France to be interpreted? What was their cosmic significance? Indeed, might they presage the end times? Radical and conservative interpreters of the prophetic books of scripture divided over the issue of whether revolutionary France or the Protestant monarchy of Britain would play the central role in the restoration of the Jewish people to their ancestral homeland in Palestine, an event which would mark the beginning of the end days and the imminence of the millennium. In the following years Brothers became preoccupied with the future in-gathering of the Jews, imagining himself the divine instrument called to bring about the restoration of the Jews. He now styled 'Himself' the Prince and Prophet of the Hebrews and Nephew of the Almighty, and claimed to be descended from King David through James, the brother of Christ. From this fantastic boast of an Israelite genealogy, it was but a small step to the otherwise grandiose claim that the English nation could vaunt a collective descent from the Ten Lost Tribes of the nation of Israel. Brothers predicted that in the midst of the tribulations of revolutionary war-torn Europe, in 1795, he himself would assume the British throne and begin the project to restore the Jews to Israel. Brothers's *annus mirabilis* did not end up as the self-proclaimed prophet had envisaged: he was arrested, interviewed, declared insane and confined to an asylum. Nevertheless, his *Revealed knowledge of the prophecies and times* (1794) proved remarkably influential, prompting several London editions and eighteen in the United States before the year was out.[3]

Brothers also attracted a few powerful and wealthy supporters, most notably a Scottish lawyer, John Finleyson (1770–1854), who abandoned his practice and devoted himself to looking after the personal interests of Brothers and his cause. Finleyson lobbied for Brothers's release, which he obtained in 1806, and also arranged for the publication of Brothers's numerous writings. Brothers set out the Israelite provenance of the English nation in various works, including his *Correct account of the invasion of England by the Saxons, showing the English nation to be descendants of the Lost Ten Tribes* (1822). His disciple Finleyson published similar ideas under his own name. Finleyson asserted the crucial distinction between the 'visible and invisible Hebrews', identifying various groups that belonged in the latter category. As a Scot, Finleyson appeared keen to widen the identification of the modern descendants of the Lost Tribes beyond the Anglo-Saxons, claiming that 'nearly all the Germans, English, lowlanders of Scotland, and Easterlings of Ireland, are the descendants of the Hebrews', along with some other European peoples.[4] However, it took the intervention of John Wilson (1799–1870) to transform this loose strain of speculation into a more disciplined school of biblical interpretation.

Wilson has a better claim than Brothers to be the principal begetter of British Israelism. An autodidact from a radical weaving background, Wilson came to attention through his public lectures in Ireland and Britain.[5] The ideas which Wilson had promoted on the lecture circuit were then published in book form in 1840 in his *Lectures on our Israelitish origin*, which went through five editions by 1876. This mingled a Brothersite strain of biblical exegesis with a more explicit strain of scientific racialism. In particular, an early fascination with Christian phrenology helped to form Wilson's outlook, the dominant feature of which was an obsession with the ethnological aspects of scriptural prophecy. Read properly – and with serious ethnological attention paid not only to its lists of genealogies and accounts of ancient peoples but also to matters of prophecy – scripture provided answers to the search for the Lost Tribes.

In *Lectures on our Israelitish origin*, Wilson claimed that the peoples of northern Europe were the offspring of the Lost Tribes of Israel, the British Isles themselves being the province of the tribe of Ephraim. Moreover, these peoples also inherited from their ancient Israelite ancestors the divine promises which God had given to the northern tribes, and had a central starring role in the fulfilment of prophecy. Wilson read scripture literally. The prophecies, he ventured, did not refer to 'the spiritual, or surrogate, Israel', but to a 'literal' Israel. Thus, the Saxons, who, according to Wilson, possessed the 'physical, moral, and intellectual marks' given to Israel, were 'truly the seed of Abraham according to the flesh'.[6]

Various forms of evidence were deployed to reinforce Wilson's case. Some of these were historical, dealing with similarities in the laws and customs of the Hebrews and the Anglo-Saxons. In addition, Wilson boasted that 'Israel's grave was the Saxon's birthplace.' The lost Israelites, he believed, had disappeared from history in the same location and at the same time that the forefathers of the Saxons had first made their mark on the historical record.[7] However, racial insights garnered from the new ethnological sciences could also help resolve the long-standing puzzle of the Lost Tribes. Wilson read racial differences into the Bible, weaving together traditional understandings of the tripartite division of races which followed the Flood with modern ethnological categories. The three 'grand races of mankind', pronounced Wilson, were the Calmuc-Tartar, Caucasian and Negro, which descended, respectively, from Noah's sons Japhet, Shem and Ham. These races, he argued, were distinguished by 'form of head and other physical marks, as well as by intellectual and moral character'. Of course, for all its apparent ethnological modishness, Wilson's conflation of the Saxons and the Semitic Israelites was at odds with the insights of Aryan, or Indo-European, linguistics. The Indo-European thesis posited the existence of an Indo-European family of languages from which the Semitic tongues were excluded. Wilson, on the contrary, claimed an intimate philological connection between Hebrew and the Gothic languages.[8]

Nevertheless, traces of an odd kind of anti-Semitism lurked in Wilson's Saxonist Hebraism, for he did not acknowledge modern contemporary Jews in the terms in which they saw themselves. Rather he went out of his way to deny the racial purity of their descent from the ancient Israelites, and in particular the integrity of their genealogy in the line of Shem. Wilson noted that 'many of the modern Jews' were 'very dark complexioned', the result of 'having become so intimately blended with the

children of Ham'. Pointedly, he reminded his readers that 'much is said
of the fairness of ancient Israel'. Indeed, some of the Jews, Wilson
believed, had 'become mingled' with 'the worst of the Gentiles – the
Canaanites and Edomites, children emphatically of the curse'. Incorporation with the Canaanites and Edomites had rendered the Jews 'guilty
of the sins of both'. The Jews' only hope for the future, Wilson claimed,
was to associate with 'the One Seed Christ, and as being joined to the
multitudinous seed to come, especially of Ephraim'. Thus, at best, British
Israelism excluded modern Jews from the promises made to the northern
tribes of Israel or, worse, treated modern Jews as sham Israelites, certainly
by contrast with the supposedly authentic claims of the white Anglo-
Saxon Protestant peoples to the status occupied in sacred providential
history by their supposed Old Testament ancestors.[9]

His exposure to phrenology helped to shape Wilson's racialist
anthropology of religion. Wilson attributed variations in the spiritual and
religious capacities of different races to ethnic differences in the conformation of the skull. The descendants of Ham, Wilson claimed, had
possessed longer heads than the offspring of Japhet, who had had wider
heads. In the Caucasian Shemites, on the other hand, the 'reflective
region' of the brain was 'especially well developed' as was the 'imaginative'. The Shemites had, according to Wilson, 'the largest proportion
of those powers which regard the spiritual world, and which tend to
give an elevated and refined exercise to the intellect'. Religion, in other
words, was a racial phenomenon. Such was the strong racial aptitude for
religious knowledge among the Semites, that 'not only [had] the true
religion been more abundant with the Semitic race, but false religions
[had] also abounded'. In sharp contrast, matters were very different
among the black race. Phrenology demonstrated quite clearly that the
black descendants of Ham lacked the mental equipment for higher
religious concepts:

The upper and middle part of the head, where is the organ of veneration, is
generally high; but there is a deficiency in that which gives a tendency to form
ideas respecting the spiritual world, and to hold communion therewith.
Consequently, the mind is left more to the sensible creature rather than to the
unseen Creator.

Nevertheless, in spite of its obvious debt to phrenology and other aspects
of the contemporary fascination with race, Anglo-Israelism, as we shall see
below, redrew some of the central categories of nineteenth-century racial
discourse.[10]

Although Wilson laid the intellectual groundwork for British Israelism, the movement took off in a significant way only around the time of his death. The key figure in the wider transmission of Anglo-Israelism was Edward Hine (1825–91), who took a sharper line on certain racial issues than Wilson. A struggle developed within the ranks of Anglo-Israelism between those who took a Teutonist line on the identification of the Israelites and those who favoured a more Anglo-Saxonist line. The Teutonists, following Wilson, argued that all the Gothic peoples of western Europe were Israelites, whereas the followers of Hine, who eventually prevailed in the dispute, restricted the identity to the peoples of the British Isles. Hine and another influential supporter, Edward Wheler Bird, challenged the Teutonism of the Anglo-Ephraim Association of London, the principal institutional embodiment of Wilson's ideas. In 1874 Bird helped to found the London Anglo-Israel Association which was run on anti-Teutonist lines. In 1878 the Anglo-Ephraim Association was absorbed within a new Metropolitan Anglo-Israel association with the anti-Teutonist Bird as its president. During the 1870s and 1880s British Israelism achieved a measure of doctrinal coherence, largely by way of seeing off the alternative ethnological definition of the Israelites proffered by the Teutonists.[11]

By the early twentieth century, Anglo-Israelism was reputed – optimistically in the light of the active memberships in Anglo-Israelite societies and subscriptions to British Israelite periodicals – to have two million adherents in Britain and the United States.[12] Notwithstanding the unreliability of this figure, it is nonetheless almost impossible to gauge the influence among more passive sympathisers throughout the Protestant world of an approach to scripture that was neither systematised into a distinctive doctrine nor embodied in a separate denomination, and thus not intrinsically divisive. As one of its exponents, Herbert Pain, explained, Anglo-Israelism involved 'a question not of doctrine but interpretation. It is therefore a subject on which men of all shades of religious opinion may meet on the common ground of belief in the Bible'.[13] British Israelism constituted more properly 'an interdenominational fellowship'.[14] Its recruitment base embraced a wide range of churches, with the Church of England at one extreme and, as we shall see, the Pentecostalist churches at the other. Thus British Israelism enjoyed a multi-denominational appeal, and its attractiveness was not limited to any particular type of Protestantism. Nor was British Israelism seen as a dangerous threat to the establishment either in church or in state. On the contrary, it was regarded as a pillar of the British Empire. The list of officers of the British-Israel Association in 1896 included, besides its patron the Earl of Radnor, nineteen clergymen-vicepresidents and ten soldiers of the rank of colonel or above, of whom five were generals. In 1929 the British Israel World Federation – which had over 230 branches – managed to fill the Albert Hall in London, and in 1931 to attract more than 20,000 people to its annual congress.[15]

Clearly, the consolidation of British Israelism into a religious organisation had coincided with the wider popularisation of racial science. Nevertheless, British Israelism enjoyed an ambivalent but intense set of relations with the racialisms prevalent in nineteenth-century culture. Nineteenth-century racialism was, of course, no monolith, but a fiercely contested terrain in which a variety of racialisms found themselves in competition with one another. Phrenology, of course, had exercised a strong influence on Wilson and on the formation of British Israelite race theory. Major-General Rainey claimed that the brain capacity of the skull was a 'sure index of the mental capacity of races'.[16] British Israelism also enjoyed a peculiarly tortured and ambivalent relationship with anti-Semitic prejudice. The British Israelites denied that the Jewish communities of the nineteenth century were the authentic descendants of the Israelites of the Old Testament. Though notionally philo-Semitic – on their own terms – British Israelites denied the authentic Judaism of modern Jewry, unmasking Jews as un-Semitic impostors who had usurped the status which truly belonged to the Saxon peoples of Britain and North America. Hine was adamant that 'the people of the Tribes were never Jews'.[17] The author of *The Ten Tribes* (1882) denied that because Saxons were uncircumcised they were not of Israelite origin.[18] According to T. K. de Verdon, race and phrenology pointed up the sharp contrast between the true Saxon Israelites and the Jews who threatened to usurp that identity:

The central and northern nations of Europe are for the most part of Israelitish origin, as are the Anglo-Saxons wherever they are found. They are easily distinguished from other races of mankind, who are not of the same origin; their complexion, expression of face, and phrenological developments are different... They are fair, clear skinned and at times ruddy: These are of the Ten Tribes of Israel, and quite unlike the Jews, who are dark complexioned, having an evident admixture of the Edomites, with whom they intermarried.[19]

The logic of British Israelism was manifestly incompatible with the logic of Aryan philology. There were blatant inconsistencies between the philological categories of Aryan, Semitic and Turanian and the British

Israelites' own tripartite division of races into Caucasians, Tartars and Negroes. Moreover, the identification of Saxons and Israelites made nonsense of the gulf between Aryans and Semites. Far from identifying white Caucasians as Aryan Japhetites, British Israelite ethnology identified white Caucasians as Semites. Rainey rejected the findings of an Aryan philology which distinguished between Indo-Europeans and Semites.[20] This faulty analysis, as he saw it, undermined the central truth of British Israelism, namely that the Saxon peoples were the true descendants of the ancient Semite Israelites. The author of *Israel in Britain* (1876) demonstrated why the mistaken findings of Aryan philology should be disregarded. The Indo-European appearance of the English tongue, he argued, was only superficial. Deeper analysis penetrated beneath Indo-European borrowings to reveal the authentic structures of a Semitic language: 'the general aspect of the English language, to my mind, is that of a Shemetic tongue which had been for a long period in contact with Aryan tongues, and suffered a large transfusion of verbal roots and dialectic forms, whilst it had preserved with tenacity the primitive basis of its grammatic and idiomatic structure'. Consider, for example, the location of the verb in English sentence structure. English was 'not of that marked Aryan type in which the verb is relegated to a dim perspective at the end of subject and predicate'. Such unconventional philological reasoning was underpinned by theological anxieties about the implications of Aryanism. If it transpired that the English were of 'Yaphetic' – that is Aryan – descent, then 'there is at once an end of our Shemitic–Hebrew origin – prophecy, history, and all else notwithstanding'.[21] British Israelites could also draw comfort from John Pym Yeatman's assault in *The Shemetic origin of the nations of western Europe* (1879) on the alleged 'fallacies' of Aryanism. To Yeatman (b. 1830), Indo-European philology amounted to a plain 'rejection of the Mosaic account of the early history of mankind' and its leading proponent, Max Müller, was an antagonist of sacred history who had deliberately set out to 'heathenise our ancient history'. In particular, Yeatman insisted that the Keltic aboriginals of western Europe had been of Shemitic origin.[22]

Furthermore, British Israelism also relaxed another of the principal racial classifications operating in nineteenth-century culture, by conflating the Anglo-Saxon and Celtic peoples of the British Isles as Israelites. Generally speaking, British Israelites tended to be comprehensively 'British' in their ethnological scheme of prophecy. According to Colonel J. Muspratt Williams, both the Welsh and the English were descended of the Lost Tribes by way of the Gimiri–Sakai peoples, the remote ancestors of both the Cymry (Welsh) and the Saxons.[23] A similar line can also be found in the work of H. W. J. Senior, a lieutenant colonel in the First Bengal Infantry, who argued that the Kymri (Celts) and the Sakai (Saxons) had both been of the house of Israel.[24] Moreover, the Scots were associated – by way of a superficial etymological resemblance – with the Scythians, another group which featured in the British Israelite genealogy. Spurious etymology also brought the Irish within the fold of British Israelism by way of a presumed identification of the ancient conquerors of Ireland, the Tuatha-De-Danaan, with the tribe of Dan.[25]

Though less integral to Anglo-Israelite exegesis than the identification of the Saxon race as the 'true' descendants of ancient Israel, anti-black racism was a further part of the curious compound of ethnological notions which made up British Israelite beliefs. Indeed, British Israelism propagated a religious justification for white superiority. In particular, British Israelite exegesis served to sanctify the British imperialist enterprise as the providential unfolding of ancient biblical promises to the tribe of Ephraim. The British Empire, it seemed, was divinely foretold. British Israelism seemed to legitimise the rule of the white Saxon race over other races. The Bible provided a warrant for the expansion of 'Israel', as in the prophecies of Isaiah 49:19–20 and 54:3. In addition, scripture appeared to endorse specific territorial acquisitions. British control of Gibraltar, Aden and Singapore seemed to be preordained in particular passages of Genesis which explicitly associated the 'seed' of Israel with the possession of the gate of its enemies: according to Genesis 22:17 ' . . . thy seed shall possess the gate of his enemies', while Genesis 24:60 sent up the appeal ' . . . let thy seed possess the gate of those which hate them'. The movement was described by one commentator as 'Jingoism with a Biblical sanction'.[26]

Certainly, British Israelism elevated the white man's burden on to a theological plane. The Teutonic family, it appeared, had a special responsibility in the propagation of the gospel. British Israelites reckoned that no other race was up to the task. The author of *Where are the Ten Tribes?* noticed 'on looking round the world for new races equally capable of taking in higher elements, equally susceptible of religious impressions, and able to perpetuate them and to communicate them to others', that 'no such new and vigorous races seem to exist'.[27] John Gilder Shaw contended that missionary work could not 'succeed until we, as a nation, perceive the truth of our origin – until the British race open their eyes to the glorious truth that we are in the possession of all the blessings promised to Abraham and his posterity, and possessing them in their entirety'.[28]

Nevertheless, some British Israelite commentators took this sanctified imperialism a sinister step further. Edward Hine appeared to condone genocide on Anglo-Israelite grounds. Hine boasted that 'we prove ourselves Israel by the display of our unicorn's horn'. Beneath the metaphorical language what this meant was a programme of ethnic clearance which did not stop far short of genocide. Ethnic extinction, according to Hine, was part of God's plan for humanity:

We have literally fulfilled Israel's mission by pushing the aborigines of our colonies to the ends of what was once their own country, as we require more room, so do we push, drive them into corners. This we have done to the Caffres, the Maoris, the Bushmen of Australia, and notably by our kindred, who are pushing the American Indians to the backwoods...All our aborigines are positively dying out, gradually but surely, before us. Forty years is computed to be enough to thoroughly exterminate the Indians of America. Twenty years will do the same for the Maoris of New Zealand. The last aborigine is said to have died in Newfoundland in 1858. In many more of our smaller settlements they are already totally extinct. Even in India the process is in operation, and two large tribes have positively disappeared from Tasmania.

The fact that ethnic extinction was taking place under the expansion of the Saxon race was not merely a matter of complacency, but to Hine a proof that the Anglo-Saxons were the true heirs of biblical promises, the true Israelites. In these circumstances, ethnic cleansing was not a matter of regret but of celebration. The aborigines of 'Israel's' (i.e. Britain's) colonies appeared to be dying out not because of western invasion but as the result of an act of God: 'When we find that the two large tribes have already disappeared from Tasmania, that at the present death-rate, twenty years will exterminate the Maoris of New Zealand, that forty years will render the Indians of Manasseh [America] extinct...we must submit to the will of God.'[29]

Anglo-Israelism not only provided a justification for the wide-reaching claims of British imperialism; it also provided prophetic sustenance for the manifest destiny and global responsibilities of the United States. Did not Genesis 48:19 promise the independence and glory of Ephraim's junior sibling, Manasseh – that is, in British Israelite exegesis, the United States? In the late nineteenth century, Anglo-Israelite societies sprang up in different parts of the United States, such as the Lost Israel Identification Society of Brooklyn set up by the Congregationalist pastor Joseph Wild (b. 1834). Wild claimed to have given 130 sermons on Anglo-Israelite themes between 1876 and 1879. However, the central figure in the

American reception of British Israelism was Lieutenant Charles Totten (1851–1908), who taught military science at Yale. Totten proclaimed the Anglo-Saxon race to be 'the literal, lineal and blood descendant of the Ten Tribes of Israel'. Through the influence of Totten, British Israelism became a stock feature of American Protestant culture, not least on its vibrant and creative fringes where it combined with a variety of theological positions.[30]

An expansive Anglo-Israelism surfaced in the theology of Charles Fox Parham (1873–1929), the principal founder of the modern Pentecostalist movement. At the core of Pentecostalism is the possibility – indeed the spiritual imperative – of achieving a higher state of Christian attainment by way of the in-dwelling presence of the Holy Spirit, as described in Acts 2:1–47. Pentecostals urge Christians to strive for a post-conversion religious experience known as Baptism with the Holy Spirit. A spirit-baptised Christian, according to Pentecostalist doctrine, ought to receive one or more of the supernatural gifts which the Holy Spirit conferred upon the first Christians in the early church. These include instantaneous sanctification; an ability to prophesy; the capacity to practise divine healing; and the ability to speak in tongues or to interpret other tongues. According to a Gallup Poll conducted in 1980 17 per cent of all Pentecostal-Charismatics in the United States had at one time or another spoken in tongues, while almost 50 per cent of traditional denominational Pentecostals claimed to have experienced this divine gift. Pentecostalist-inspired religion comes in three distinctive types, namely traditional Pentecostals who adhere to separate Pentecostal denominations; neo-Pentecostals, a post-1960 phenomenon, who adhere to their own Protestant denominations while practising Pentecostal worship; and Roman Catholic Charismatics who uphold a Pentecostalist style of worship within the confines of Catholicism. Pentecostalism enjoyed tremendous growth in the late twentieth-century United States. In 1980 Pentecostals and kindred Charismatics constituted 19 per cent of the adult US population, with adherents of traditional Pentecostalist denominations amounting to about ten million Americans in the 1980s.[31]

Most historians of the movement tend to agree that modern Pentecostalism proper began in 1901 with the revival in Topeka, Kansas, led by Parham. This originated out of the practice of divine healing which Parham had begun at the Beth-el Healing Home which he set up in Topeka in 1898.[32] Parham's commitment to spiritual healing was only one of his many idiosyncratic beliefs. In 1902 Parham produced his spiritual manifesto *A voice crying in the wilderness*, which included passages clearly indebted both to Anglo-Israelism and to pre-Adamite racialism. Parham was not a narrow Anglo-Israelite and considered other groups including non-Europeans among the descendants of the Ten Tribes; nevertheless he still took a somewhat dim view of those inferior ethnic groups who did not enjoy the profound capacity for religion of the Israelites. Parham claimed that the Anglo-Saxons and other Israelites were more attuned to deeper spiritual truths than were other racial groups, some of which found themselves limited through racial incapacity only to the half-truths of Catholicism, or worse:

Today the descendants of Abraham are the Hindus, the Japanese, the high Germans, the Danes (the tribe of Dan), the Scandinavians, the Anglo-Saxons and their descendants in all parts of the world. These are the nations who have acquired and retained experimental salvation and deep spiritual truths; while Gentiles – the Russians, the Greeks, the Italians, the Low German, the French, the Spanish and their descendants in all parts are formalists, scarce ever obtaining the knowledge and truth discovered by Luther – that of justification by faith or the truth taught by Wesley, sanctification by faith; while the heathen – the black race, the brown race, the red race, the yellow race, in spite of missionary zeal and effort are nearly all heathen still; but will in the dawning of the coming age be given to Jesus for an inheritance.

Parham subscribed to the view that there had been two creations of human races, pre-Adamite and Adamite, and that the Flood had been a punishment for 'the woeful intermarriage of races' begun by Cain. By contrast, Noah – 'perfect in his generation, a pedigree without mixed blood in it, a lineal descendant of Adam' – had been saved because of the unmixed racial purity of his pedigree. Parham also showed some interest in the global dispersal of the tribes of Israel, some to India and Japan as well as to the Germanic homelands of the Anglo-Saxons.[33] Such views enjoyed some currency in early American Pentecostalism.

   W. F. Carothers, an attorney closely involved in the formative phase of Pentecostalism in Texas, argued that God's plan for mankind included the permanent separation of races. For most of human history, God's plan had worked smoothly, with races settling in different regions of the world. However, whites in the United States had subverted God's plan. Slavery was the culprit. As a result of slavery blacks had been forced into the United States, which threatened the unwelcome mingling of races. The evils of miscegenation seemed to be imminent; but Carothers claimed that the Holy Spirit had retrieved the situation by intensifying the impulse to racialist preferences and prejudices, a providential substitute for the geographical separation of races. Racial bigotry, as far as Carothers was concerned, was not, as others claimed, a work of the devil, but had a divine warrant as an extraordinary measure required to inhibit the impending sins of miscegenation. Parham too had been an opponent of miscegenation – a typical enough position in the early twentieth-century United States – but his attitudes towards race stood at a very considerable remove from the hysterical racialism of his colleague Carothers.[34]

From the outset Parham was a racial paternalist, using racial theories to explain the pattern of global progress. On the other hand, he did not confine the benefits of God's grace to any single racial or national group. Nevertheless, this streak of racialism became more intense as a result of Parham's breach with William Seymour, his ultra-charismatic black protégé. Parham found the Pentecostalism of Seymour to be distorted by what he saw as an excessive black-inspired emotionalism. At any rate, it seems likely that the architect of modern Pentecostalism found himself increasingly embittered, for in 1907 Parham was arrested in San Antonio on somewhat vague charges of sodomy. The charges were dropped, but Parham's rivals within the movement did not pass up this providential opportunity to subvert his standing among Pentecostals. Parham's more pronounced racialism belongs to the less influential decades which followed. In 1927 Parham openly praised the latest incarnation of the Ku Klux Klan, though urging it to hold fast to religious truths. The Pentecostal movement did not escape the pervasive racialism and xenophobia of the United States in the 1920s, though it was by no means a creature or supporter of the Klan. Some Pentecostalist periodicals criticised the Klan, though not for its violent bigotry; rather, they thought an oath-bound secret society an unsuitable milieu for Christians.[35]

Furthermore, British Israelism obsessed only a minority of white Pentecostals, and some Pentecostals rejected British Israelite teaching altogether. Nevertheless, there were various links between the emergence of Pentecostalism in the early years of the twentieth century and Anglo-Israelite ideas. J. H. Allen (1847–1930), who founded a 'Holiness' church in Missouri and later moved to California, was the author of a popular Israelite work, *Judah's sceptre and Joseph's birthright* (1902). Pentecostalism was also associated with the gradual transition from conventional Protestant Anglo-Israelism towards the eccentric theological combination known as Christian Identity (which will be discussed in the next section of this chapter). A combination of Anglo-Israelism, pre-Adamite doctrine and a background racialism absorbed from the surrounding culture indicate that the early stages of white Pentecostalism were indebted in some measure to the highly racialised theories of religion which gained currency in the later nineteenth century.[36]

Whereas racialist and British Israelite ideas were contingent elements attending the birth of Pentecostalism, Anglo-Israelism was, on the other hand, integral to the doctrine of the Worldwide Church of God. This body was founded by Herbert W. Armstrong (1892–1986) in 1933 and known at first as the Radio Church of God. Though a British Israelite exegesis of scripture sits at the core of its doctrine, the origins of the Worldwide Church of God lie in the Adventist movement, from which it also draws inspiration. Indeed, Armstrong's church is an eclectic blend of Seventh-Day Adventism, British Israelism and Judaic observance (including Old Testament dietary practices and sabbatarianism), as well as influences derived from the Mormons and the Jehovah's Witnesses. Initially, the church distanced itself – as an Israelite body – from elements of Christianity which lacked a Judaeo-Christian pedigree, including the Trinity and certain Christian holidays, but some of these have recently been modified and the Worldwide Church of God has become more overtly 'Christian'.[37]

Armstrong's background was in advertising and he displayed a decided flair in the packaging and marketing of religion. In particular, he spread the word by way of radio broadcasts (enhanced from the 1960s by a television ministry) and the publication of a lively, popular magazine, *The Plain Truth*, which blended British Israelite themes with topical stories. Armstrong also founded colleges to propagate the Word and his church enjoyed considerable growth after the Second World War.

In *The United States and British Commonwealth in prophecy* (1967), Armstrong provided an interpretation of both scripture and – by way of the fulfilment of the Bible's divine prophecies – the history, politics and economics of the modern world. Indeed, Armstrong castigated the leaders of the western world for their ignorance of biblical prophecy – the master key to an understanding of international politics. Armstrong believed the Bible to be a much misunderstood book, not least within the mainstream of Christianity. Most Christians extracted a spiritual message from the scriptures while neglecting the Bible's other vital concerns 'with the material, the fleshly, the literal, racial and national'. Moreover, the Bible, it should be remembered, was 'an Israelitish book, preeminently of and for the Israelitish nationality'.[38]

There was also the matter of how the Bible ought to be read. A recurrent leitmotif of Armstrong's thesis was the need to substitute 'race'

for 'grace' in scriptural interpretation. This is what distinguished the
Worldwide Church of God from the rest of Christianity. Armstrong
believed that biblical interpretation needed to address the 'national' as
well as the 'spiritual'. The Bible was a book which dealt as much with
ethnicity – the real Israel – as it did with the emergence of a church. Too
many Christians ignored the 'physical' dimension of the Bible, whether
in terms of material, worldly blessings or the fact, as it appeared to
Armstrong, that such blessings were directed at flesh-and-blood racial
groups. Most Christians, Armstrong contended, 'miss the fact that God
gave Abraham promises of physical race as well as spiritual grace'. Such
promises were not fulfilled in the Jews, nor should they be 'spiritualized
away' by reading them as the inheritance of the Christian church.
Armstrong insisted that the promises pertained not to a church, but to
particular nations. Nor were the blessings spiritual rather than material.[39]

At the core of Armstrong's creed was an interpretation of the promises
made by God to Abraham. These were found in Genesis 12:1–3 and
Genesis 17:1–6. God had pledged that 'Abraham's literal, human flesh-
and-blood descendants' should become great nations. In Genesis 17:6,
God had promised to Abraham, 'I will make nations of thee.' However,
the Jews constituted only a singular nation. Which modern nations
matched the picture outlined in Old Testament prophecy? Which peoples of today, asked Armstrong, are the lineal descendants of the tribes of
Ephraim and Manasseh, the principal recipients of the promises made to
Israel? Unsurprisingly, the 'white, English-speaking peoples' of Britain
and the United States were, respectively, 'the birthright tribes of Ephraim
and Manasseh of the "lost" House of Israel'. Ephraim (Anglo-Saxon
Britain) and Manasseh (the Anglo-Saxon United States) constituted 'the
real Israel (racially and nationally) of today'.[40]

CHRISTIAN IDENTITY AND THE RELIGION OF RACE HATRED

The Christian Identity movement grew out of Anglo-Israelism (indeed,
the lines are blurred and far from discontinuous); but this new religious
entity added to Anglo-Israelism a supplementary strain of racialist theory
which – from the perspective of this study at least – makes Christian
Identity a distinct brand of racialised religion. This is because Christian
Identity blends British Israelism with a racialist version of pre-Adamite
polygenesis, on which is grounded Identity's anthropology of race hatred
and separation. The Bible, viewed from the vantage point of Christian
Identity, tells the Manichaean story of two distinct racial seedlines, one

good, descending from Adam, the father of the white race, the other evil, descending from Satan via Cain (who intermarried with the black pre-Adamites). In Christian Identity genealogy, Cain and Abel are only half-brothers, sharing the same mother – Eve – and two different fathers, respectively, Satan and Adam. Original sin, as understood within Identity theology, is the Satanic seduction of Eve; though Cain's sin of race-mixing was almost as heinous an offence.[41]

Christian Identity, as Michael Barkun has shown, is a modern phe-nomenon, which achieved full realisation only in the aftermath of the Second World War. It emerged as a synthesis of a number of different theological positions, some of much older lineage. This synthesis was not one which can be easily reconstructed in the theology of a single church, for Christian Identity is not a denomination as such but a loose ensemble of autonomous congregations sharing broadly similar beliefs. There are also, as we shall see, non-Identity churches which subscribe to Identitist, or quasi-Identitist, positions. Nevertheless, their various theologies share a common recipe of ingredients. Among the heterogeneous materials out of which Christian Identity was composed, the most obvious are Anglo-Israelism, as received into twentieth-century American culture, where it was given a more overtly anti-Semitic slant; the nineteenth-century pre-Adamite solution to the problem of human origins; the dispensationalist theology formulated in nineteenth-century England by John Nelson Darby (1800–82) of the Plymouth Brethren; and an esoteric tradition of seedline theology. Christian Identity favours biblical literalism and draws not only upon the accepted canon of scripture found in the King James Bible, but also upon parts of the Apocrypha which prove useful to its seedline theology, including the books of Enoch and II Esdras.[42]

The idea of two seedlines has been around in the United States since the early nineteenth century in the work of Daniel Parker (1781–1844), a predestinarian Illinois Baptist, and his followers. In a pamphlet of 1826 entitled *Views of the two seeds*, Parker claimed that Eve had been implanted with two different kinds of seed, good and bad, by, respec-tively, God and Satan (in the guise of the serpent). Thus Parker produced a coherent biological account, analogous to traditional renderings of the transmission of original sin, which explained the gulf between the elect – those who were of the good seedline – and the damned, in Parker's predestinarian anthropology literally the spawn of Satan. Parker's theol-ogy was enshrined in a small sect known as the Old Two-Seed-in-the-Spirit Predestinarian Baptists, which ran to 13,000 followers in 1890, but shrivelled away to a tiny rump during the first half of the twentieth century. Nevertheless, the idea of the two seedlines was popularised beyond the ranks of this Baptist sect, and endowed with a racial meaning which had not been present in the strictly predestinarian logic of Parker's original coining.[43]

Anglo-Israelism was easily syncretised with a variety of Christian or Christian-derived belief systems, for British Israelite exegesis merely identified the descent of the Lost Tribes of Israel, but did not prescribe answers to other areas of exegesis or doctrine. The seedliners' obsession with Cain's lineage surfaced, for example, in Anglo-Israelite literature in the writings of David Davidson, a Scots engineer and pyramidologist, and an English writer, Mrs Sidney Bristowe. Moreover, during the inter-war period Anglo-Israelism in North America was combined with a virulent strain of anti-Semitism, imported largely by William J. Cameron (1878–1955), a close colleague of the automobile manufacturer, Henry Ford, and editor of Ford's Michigan newspaper, the *Dearborn Independent*. British Israelism was, at bottom, ambivalent on the question of how contemporary Jews related to the biblical nation of Israel; but its patent challenge to Judaism's monopoly of the Israelite heritage rendered it ripe for appropriation by committed anti-Semites such as Cameron. Thus American Anglo-Israelism was progressively reoriented towards the shrill anti-Semitism which dominates the Christian Identity movement.[44]

Another key figure in the transformation of British Israelism into Christian Identity was Wesley Swift (1913–70). The son of a Methodist minister brought up in New Jersey, Swift joined the Pentecostalist sect set up by Aimee Semple Macpherson (1890–1944), the International Church of the Four Square Gospel, and then became an independent evangelical minister in California in the 1930s. Unsurprisingly, he was exposed to Anglo-Israelite ideas, which were part of the common currency of evangelical Protestantism in this era. In the late 1940s Swift set up his own British Israelite church in California, the Anglo-Saxon Christian Congregation, which later became the Church of Jesus Christ Christian, sharing the same name with one of the principal Identity sects, which was separately founded by one of Swift's acolytes, Richard Butler, in Idaho in 1973. In the case of these sects, the epithet 'Christian' has become a racial rather than doctrinal label, describing churches which assert the non-Jewish identity of Christ.[45]

As well as adapting British Israelite and pre-Adamite schemes of exegesis, proponents of Christian Identity have also blended these with dispensationalist theology. Darbyite dispensationalism made a profound impact on twentieth-century theology, shaping the dominant prophetic tradition in American evangelicalism. Darby had divided human history into various phases, or 'dispensations'. The final dispensation would be a seven-year period of tribulation which would culminate in the Second Coming of Christ and the re-connection of human and divine history. However, the elect would be spared the terrors of the last days. Instead they would be 'raptured', elevated to heaven until the trauma was over, and then returned to earth with Jesus. Among the events of the last days before the millennium would be the restoration of the Jews to the Holy Land. However, some dispensationalists – turning away from their traditional philo-Semitic roots – blamed the Jews for having rejected Christ during his first appearance among humankind. Christian Identity exploits this negative reading of the Jews' place in the drama of sacred history and, moreover, yokes racialist seedline theory to a millennialist scheme of tribulation and conflict which will usher in a war of Armageddon. Racial holy war is linked to a messianic vision of the last times.[46]

Christian Identity exploits the notion that there were two Creation accounts in Genesis to construct a dualistic theology of racialism. Eve's original sin, in Christian Identity theology, was copulation with Satan (or his proxy, in the form of a dark, satanic pre-Adamite). Moreover, the racial folklore surrounding Cain and Ham is woven into this frightening racialist theology. Cain, it transpires, is only the half-brother of the Adamic Abel; for Cain is the spawn of Satan. Christian Identity exegesis stresses that when in Genesis 4 Cain takes a wife in the land of Nod his spouse is from the pre-Adamite race whose origin is described in Genesis 1:26–7. Moreover, Ham married into Cain's Satanic seedline. The biblical seedlines manifest themselves today in racial differences. Whites – excluding Jews – are the descendants of Adam and are not meant to mix their seed with other races. Jews, claim advocates of Christian Identity, are, like blacks, in a direct seedline from Satan. It therefore becomes vital to establish that Christ was Adamic and not a Jew. Thus Christ becomes a sort of 'race-god' in Christian Identity doctrine. Racial mixing is theologically – not only sociologically or biologically – abhorrent to Christian Identity racists, for to them it constitutes a Satanic attempt to corrupt the chosen seedline.[47]

Beyond the superficial racial differences between Adamic and Cainite seedlines are deeper spiritual incompatibilities. Adamic man, according to Christian Identity, is 'trichotomous', composed of body, soul and an 'implanted spirit' which distinguishes him from the other races of the world. Other races are composed only of body and soul, and are spiritually inferior to the white race. Moreover, eternal life is available only to

those in possession of trichotomous characteristics. Thus, in effect, salvation is restricted by race to the trichotomous white race.[48]

However, there are variations in the racial positions of the different
versions of Christian Identity, though the same underlying pattern can be
discerned all too easily within the core doctrine of each grouping.
Nevertheless James Aho makes a crucial distinction between racist and
non-racist Christian Identity organisations. The most racist form of
Identity is Seedline Identity which emphasises that the Jews are a 'demon-
seed', literally descended from Satan. According to Kingdom Identity
Seedline doctrine, the 'true literal children of Israel' are 'the white, Anglo-
Saxon, Germanic and kindred people'. This grouping further believes
that Adam was 'the father of the white race only'. Yahweh Believers
consider themselves to be authentic Jews. Unlike some other Christian
Identity groupings, they do not proclaim hatred of Jews, but are suspi-
cious of 'pseudo-Jews'. To the Church of Jesus Christ Christian, a 'Jew' is
not specifically an adherent of Judaism, but properly a racial descendant
of Cain, the offspring of Satan.[49]

Some Identity churches are affiliated with overtly racist political
organisations. The Reformed Church of Christ–Society of Saints operates
as a spiritual front for the Social Nationalist Aryan Peoples Party.
Similarly, Aryan Nations is the political wing of Butler's Church of Jesus
Christ Christian. In spite of these appropriations of an 'Aryan' identity,
the 'Aryan' wing of Christian Identity subscribes to an ethnology which
contradicts the findings of Indo-European philology. Rather, Christian
Identity 'Aryans' stress pseudo-linkages between the ancient Hebrew
language and the Germanic tongues spoken by the modern descendants
of the Israelites. According to the Church of Jesus Christ Christian, the
Bible is 'the family history of the white race, the children of Yahweh
placed on earth through the seedline of Adam'. The maintenance of white
racial purity lies at the doctrinal core of the Church of Jesus Christ
Christian: 'We believe in the preservation of our race, individually and
collectively, as a people, as demanded and directed by Yahweh. We
believe our racial nation has a right and is under obligation to preserve
itself and its members.'[50]

The Identity movement has amplified the implicit (though ambivalent)
anti-Semitism of the nineteenth-century British Israelites into an anti-
Semitism which is loud, shrill and offensive. Jarah Crawford, one of the
most influential proponents of Christian Identity exegesis, links Christ's
criticisms of Jews found in chapters 8 and 10 of John's gospel with the
different Creations uncovered by a close reading of Genesis 1 and 2.

For example, John 8:44 – where Christ rebukes the Pharisees – is deployed to lend scriptural credibility to the Christian Identity doctrine that Jews are the offspring of Satan: 'Ye are of your father, the devil.' Similarly, Crawford treats the parable of the good and bad seed in Matthew 13:24–30 as a literal reference to the good and evil racial seed-lines supposedly revealed in Genesis 1 and 2.[51]

Technically outside the family of Identity churches, the Church of Israel nevertheless shares pronounced doctrinal affinities with the Identity movement with a strong emphasis upon the racial dimensions and significance of its version of Christianity. Strictly speaking, the Church of Israel began not as an Anglo-Israelite or Identity body but as a splinter grouping from a schismatic branch of Mormonism, the Church of Christ (Temple Lot). Dan Gayman (b. 1937), the pastor of the Church of Israel, gradually distanced himself from his family roots in dissident Mormonism as his Church of Israel appropriated British Israelite positions. The church abandoned the Book of Mormon and transformed itself into an entity which was doctrinally closer to Anglo-Israelism and Identity teachings than to any residual Mormonism which survived this bizarre denominational change.[52]

Gayman advances a narrowly ethnocentric interpretation of the Bible's meaning, arguing that the Old Testament focuses exclusively on the nation of Israel and that the significance of the New Testament resides in its confirmation of the pledges and promises made to the Old Testament Israelites. These promises, moreover, he insists, were 'made to the ethnic, physical, racial Israel of the Old Testament', and should be interpreted as such. Gayman indicts what he terms 'establishment Christianity' for the fundamental errors committed in its exegesis of scripture. In particular, he denounces the ways in which conventional mainstream Christians wrench the Bible out of its 'ethnic perimeters and boundaries'; they then compound this mistake by transferring to the church all the covenants and promises God had made to the Israelites. Thus conventional theology substitutes 'an international, multiracial body . . . made up of whoever professes a belief in Jesus Christ' for the true church identified in the Bible, which is 'ethnic, racial Israel'. Similarly, the Church of Israel believes that Adam was the father only of the Caucasian race, and that the non-Caucasian races have a pre-Adamite origin. References in scripture to seedlines are not to be interpreted in spiritual or symbolic terms, but in terms of literal genealogies. There is also the important – and offensive – business of defining authentic Jewry. Unlike some Christian Identity hardliners, Gayman concedes that some Jews are properly Israelites,

namely those from the tribes of Judah, Benjamin and Levi, who hailed
from the southern kingdom of Judah. Other supposed Jews, however, are
mere pretenders to an Israelite inheritance.[53]

Such blatant racialism notwithstanding, Gayman insists upon distinguishing the doctrines of the Church of Israel from the crude racist
prejudice of Christian Identity. Gayman denies that the Church of Israel
subscribes to a straightforward bigotry grounded in white Anglo-Saxon
racial superiority or that the church stands for white supremacy. Gayman
also denies that the Church of Israel believes the Anglo-Saxon people to
be 'necessarily superior to any other ethnic group', but argues rather that
the Anglo-Saxon world is 'blessed' as a result of its 'special calling and
election'. All races are God's children, claims Gayman: 'We believe that
all of the nations, all of the separate and distinct races of the earth, are the
creation of God.' However, Gayman believes that each race has
been endowed by God with a different racial potentiality for spirituality
and worship. According to Gayman, 'all of the distinctive races have
their unique way of connecting to God'. This is a clear reiteration of
nineteenth-century racialist understandings of religious variety:

There is a stark contrast between the way that the Anglo-Saxon world has related
historically to Jesus Christ and the way of these other nations. We might
summarize all of this by simply saying that all of the distinctive races have their
unique way of connecting to God, and we believe it is an erroneous assumption
that all of the distinctive created races are going to be able to connect to God in
the very same way.

Gayman contends that the Church of Israel preaches race separatism, not
race hatred. Racial segregation, in his view, is an integral component of
God's plan for humanity.[54]

Christian Identity churches consider themselves to be engaged in a racial
holy war of which mainstream Christianity is oblivious. A few other
churches and religious groupings on the fringes of white American culture
are, however, alert to the same issues and recapitulate some of the same
values and terminology, such as Anglo-Saxonism and hatred of 'mud'
races. Nevertheless, it should be stressed that, although these sects subscribe to a similar vision of racial conflict and share some *superficial*
similarities they do not enjoy any *theological* connection with Christian
Identity. Indeed, some of these churches are explicitly anti-Christian.
Despite its name, the Church of the Creator, founded by Ben Klassen

(1918–93) and subsequently refounded by Klassen's successor Matt Hale (b. 1971) as the World Church of the Creator, has never been a Christian organisation. Creativity is a non-Christian religion of race hatred whose inspiration is Darwinian.[55]

White racial anxieties have also found expression in some forms of Odinist pagan religion. Within the early twentieth-century British Empire, the Australian pagan apologist and Nazi fellow-traveller Alexander Rud Mills founded the Anglecyn Church of Odin as part of a return to Anglo-Saxonist racial purity. As the original pagan religion of the Saxons had long preceded the in-grafting of Christianity on to Saxon life, so Mills recommended that an authentic racial religion replace the alien and outworn Christianity of Protestant Anglicanism. In the 1950s Mills founded the First Church of Odin.[56]

During the 1960s and 1970s some white North Americans of a counter-cultural disposition, disillusioned with conventional Christian worship and morality, tried to recover the pre-Christian roots of European culture in a revived Norse paganism. This fringe movement took a variety of forms, sometimes labelling itself as Odinism, sometimes as the neo-Norse cult of Asatrú. Within the loosely organised neo-pagan cults of Asatrú and Odinism, it appears that non-racist pagans outnumber racist pagans, and indeed that non-racist Asatruers openly denounce their racist co-religionists for bringing the Norse revival into disrepute. This is unsurprising, given the radical, New Age associations of the wider pagan movement. Nevertheless, a significant element of Odinists and Asatruers do consider Norse heathenism to be an expression of the Aryan race soul, and align their religiosity with a white racialist position. Indeed, upholders of an explicitly racial paganism argue that races differ spiritually as well as intellectually and biologically, and that for this reason the syncretism found commonly elsewhere in New Age cults is to import into a religion spiritual elements which properly belong to another racial group. For strict Odinists, spiritual eclecticism leads not only to religious incoherence, but also amounts to racial defilement. Heathen racialists, it should be repeated, do not have any direct theological connection with Christian Identity, but they share a common rhetoric of race war, white supremacy and anti-Semitism, and it seems probable that the pagans have been exposed to the Identity-inspired racism common among disaffected groups on the fringes of white American society. Indeed, the very experience of trawling for supporters within the same waters has led some Identity ministers – incredibly, given the obvious theological incompatibility – to appropriate elements of Asatrú and Odinism for themselves.

While some Identity leaders denounce Odinism as a kind of demonic idolatry, Norse divinities such as Odin and Freya have been reinterpreted by more opportunistic proponents of Christian Identity as mistakenly deified Israelite descendants of Jacob, in the hope of wooing racist youth away from the lures of racial heathenism.[57]

Mormonism, or more precisely, the Church of Jesus Christ of Latter-Day Saints, is the American religion *par excellence*. Indeed, it is a religion whose holy scriptures sacralised the American landscape: for the American continent had seemed irrelevant to sacred history, until a special revelation vouchsafed to Joseph Smith (1805–44), Mormonism's founder. This revelation served to answer some of the problems which American Christians encountered in the Bible, to which Smith's discoveries constituted a necessary supplement. Why did the Bible say nothing about America? Why did Christ confine His mission to the Old World? How did America fit into the grand scheme of – otherwise universal – sacred history outlined in the Old Testament? Furthermore, as we have seen, Christian theologians had also struggled to explain how the native peoples of America related to the rest of humanity. Late eighteenth- and early nineteenth-century America was awash with theories about the provenance of the Amerindian peoples of the New World. The most common explanation offered was the notion that the Amerindians were some remnant of the Lost Tribes of Israel. Were they? Smith's revelation provided solutions to all these questions and stilled troubling doubts about the divine insignificance of America.

With the advent of Mormonism, Americans could rest assured that their land had been the scene of a hitherto unknown biblical past. Mormonism was founded in New York state in 1830 by Smith once he had completed the translation – with the aid of divinely crafted spectacles – of certain golden plates which he had discovered in 1823. These plates, which constituted the principal Mormon scripture, the Book of Mormon, told of migrations to America in the Old Testament era, and the subsequent sacred history of these peoples in the American continent. To begin with Smith's new brand of Christianity, which first emerged as a bizarre restorationist offshoot of an evangelical revival which swept New York state in the early nineteenth century, was known as the Church of Christ. In 1834 it became the Church of the Latter-Day Saints. Smith led his followers first to Missouri, then to Nauvoo in Illinois. The eccentricity of Mormon deviations from conventional Christianity aroused considerable hostility. In 1844 Smith was killed by a mob, and his successor as Mormon leader, Brigham Young (1801–77), led the church in 1847 to the remoteness of the Great Salt Lake in Utah, where it was able to flourish in peace as a *de facto* theocracy. Today the church has around eleven million members worldwide.

The rest of the Christian world knows the Mormons primarily by way of certain peculiarities of doctrine which mark out the Latter-Day Saints from their fellow Christians, and indeed which compel many Christians to reject outright the notion that the Mormons might be a Christian denomination. These alien characteristics include some unusual approaches to marriage, most obviously the practice of polygamy (which the principal Mormon church formally abolished in 1890, but persists among schismatic Mormons) as well as the sealing of marriages for eternity – not merely until death do us part – which entails a more cosily domestic conception of the afterlife than that afforded by mainstream Christianity. In addition, Mormons also stand out from Christians on account of certain other oddities, including their doctrine of the soul's pre-mortal existence; an obsession with genealogy, which provides the factual record upon which living Mormons carry out vicarious retrospective baptismal rites on behalf of the non-Mormon dead; and the belief that the resurrected Messiah appeared in America after his appearance to his disciples in Palestine.[58]

Alongside these exotic beliefs and practices, Mormonism's curious ethnological profile tends to attract less popular attention. Ethnology, however, is inextricably woven into the fabric of the Mormon faith. The Mormon religion is grounded in history, and at the heart of its sacred history is the peopling of the Americas. Nor, given that Mormonism is the leading indigenous religion of white America, should it prove surprising that it has borne some of white America's racial anxieties. Mormonism, moreover, had its origins and significant formative development in the era of scientific racialism. However, the connection here is far from straightforward. For example, Joseph Smith responded to phrenology with a mixture of enthusiasm and downright scepticism, yet continued to be fascinated by it. His successors in the Mormon leadership were also interested in phrenology, which remained a part of Mormonism's wider cultural hinterland until the 1940s.[59] Nor, of course, is Mormon ethnology reducible to such external influences. Mormonism, like Christianity, has at its heart a universalist ideal of common brotherhood which qualifies the ethnological elements in the faith. In the Mormon scripture II Nephi 26:33 is unequivocal: 'and he denieth none that come unto him, black and white, bond and free, male and female; and he remembereth the heathen; and all are alike unto God, both Jew and Gentile'.[60]

The ethnic theology of Mormonism is, in fact, highly distinctive. Mormons have been much preoccupied with the status of native Amerindians and of blacks. Mormons have tended to view these other races through the filters of their sacred texts and traditions, including not only the Book of Mormon but also the Christian Bible and their own treatments thereof. Alongside the Book of Mormon, Smith also provided revised versions of sections of the Bible, in the Book of Moses and Book of Abraham.[61] Thus Mormons gain exposure both to traditional biblical accounts of the peopling of the ancient world and to the supplementary Mormon narrative of the peopling of the Americas. As a result, Mormonism inspired a set of lineage-based preferences and prejudices, which superficially mimicked racism, but were not, strictly speaking, determined by colour or by conventional racial categories.

The Book of Mormon is particularly rich in ethnological and genealogical lore. Smith's revelation introduced Americans to a variety of unfamiliar tribes and peoples. According to the Book of Mormon, there had been two separate migrations of Old Testament Israelites to America. First, in the aftermath of the dispersion at Babel, the Jaredites had come to America around 2250 BC. The Book of Mormon was, however, the record of the second Israelite migration of around 600 BC led by Lehi, of the tribe of Joseph. Lehi, it was said, had led a party of Israelites across the Arabian peninsula to the Persian Gulf, and from there they had set sail across the Indian and Pacific Oceans, eventually settling in the Americas. The descendants of Lehi had split into two groups, the righteous Nephites, whose sacred history was narrated in the Book of Mormon, and the benighted Lamanites. When the resurrected Christ had appeared in America, it was to the Nephites that he had made himself known. The Nephites had enjoyed a high civilisation and had used a language and script known as 'reformed Egyptian'. This Nephite civilisation had persisted in America until around 400 AD when the Nephites were wiped out by the Lamanites at the battle of Cumorah Hill, in upper New York state, near which Smith had found the golden plates. The plates, it transpired, recorded the entire history of the rise and fall of the virtuous Nephite people of Israel in America.[62]

The plates also made quite clear the identity and provenance of native Amerindians. They too were a remnant of the ancient Israelitish people in America. Here Smith's translations meshed with the recent speculations of Ethan Smith (1762–1849; no relation) in his *View of the Hebrews* (1823), where he argued that the 'Red Indians' were descended of the Ten Lost Tribes of Israel. Mormons contend not only that native Americans – including the indigenous people of Central and South America as well as North American Indians – are of Lamanite stock, but also Polynesians. Mormon attitudes to these various peoples were determined by the ambiguous moral categories of the Book of Mormon in which the Lamanites are beloved fellow-Israelites, yet also unrighteous, heathen backsliders who had fallen from holiness.[63]

The position of blacks in Mormon ethnology is even more problematic. Smith's versions of the stories of Cain and Ham in *The pearl of great price* reinforced a suspicion of these lineages, from which black Africans were held to descend. Black Africans were for a hundred years from the late nineteenth to the late twentieth centuries held to be of the cursed lineage of Cain, a doctrine which – like polygamy – has since been formally overturned by the church, but which persists in the 'folklore' of ordinary Mormons. Another belief which was current in contemporary biblical folklore related that the wife of Ham had been a descendant of Cain. As a result of their accursed Cainite lineage, blacks were barred from the Mormon priesthood. The Mormon priesthood is not like the priesthood in other branches of Christianity, but instead resembles the adult male laity of other churches. Mormon males are usually admitted to the priesthood at the age of twelve. Thus, the disqualification of blacks from the priesthood effectively barred them from full adult male participation in the life of the church. Although not literally a restriction on church membership, the exclusion of blacks from the priesthood came very close in practice to a denial of active membership. Race was not in itself the basis of this system of religious segregation. Indeed, the priesthood was opened to dark-skinned Polynesians (Lamanites) before it was opened to black Africans. African (Cainite–Hamite) descent rather than colour per se, it was decided, determined exclusion from the priesthood. The stumbling block was the supposed biblical lineage of blacks from those notorious sinners Cain and Ham, with African descent deemed *prima facie* evidence of a 'cursed lineage', whose beginnings were set out in Genesis. This explains why Mormons did not discriminate against Polynesians, who were often darker than African-Americans, but who were not considered to belong to the pedigree of Cain. Indeed, Mormons quite properly denied that skin colour was part of the rationale for the exclusion of blacks from the priesthood, and were able to point to the lack of any ban on participation by non-white, but equally – and crucially – non-Cainite, Maori, Samoan and Tongan Mormons. Only in

June 1978 under the inspired church presidency of Spencer W. Kimball (1895–1985) did the Latter-Day Saints end their bar upon African-Americans and other peoples of African origin.[64]

British Israelism also made its mark upon Mormonism, in particular upon its obsession with biblical lineages. This influence, as Armand Mauss has shown, was at its most pronounced in the late nineteenth and early twentieth centuries. Mormonism has shared the obsession of Anglo-Israelism with the dispersal and identification of the Ten Lost Tribes of Israel, though the emphasis within Mormonism has been upon the presence of the Lost Tribes in the sacred space of America. The Mormon fascination with genealogy and family trees not only pertains to individuals, but also focuses on tribal lineages within the house of Israel. Today, this aspect of Mormonism is most visible in Mormon philo-Semitism. The Jews are a favoured lineage in Mormon Israelism, which, it should be noted, has nothing in common with the anti-Semitic Israelism of Christian Identity. Indeed, Mormon millennialism anticipates a literal in-gathering of Israel at two centres – in Palestine itself and at the new Zion in America.[65]

However, the British Israelite dimension of Mormonism was once more obvious. Traditionally, Mormon doctrine has identified adherents of the religion as literal, biological descendants of the ancient tribes of Israel, particularly the tribe of Ephraim. Thus nineteenth-century Mormon religion was not only doctrinal, but also embodied an ethnic identity. This is because Mormons considered themselves to be a gathered remnant of the Lost Tribes of Israel, most notably that of Ephraim. Mid-nineteenth-century Mormon recruitment in north-west Europe was predicated upon the recovery and gathering of the Lost Tribe of Ephraim at the new Jerusalem in America. The Ephraimites – identified with the Germanic peoples of northern and western Europe – are thus one of the most favoured lineages among Mormons, in sharp contrast, for example, to the disfavoured lineage of Cainites (Africans).[66]

Lamanites, or native American Indians, occupy an intermediate position in this ethical hierarchy of lineages. Mormon attitudes to the native American Lamanites, was, and remains, somewhat ambivalent and inflected with racialism. The significance of lineage identity notwithstanding, racial transformation – both as curse and as promise – stands at the heart of the Mormon interpretation of their sacred history. According to I Nephi 12:23, after the Lamanites 'had dwindled in unbelief they became a dark and loathsome, and a filthy people, full of idleness and all manner of abominations'. Indeed, the Book of Mormon appears to echo racialist misreadings of the curses pronounced upon Cain and Ham:

And he had caused the cursing to come upon them, yea, even a sore cursing, because of their iniquity. For behold they had hardened their hearts against him, that they had become like unto a flint; wherefore, as they were white, and exceeding fair and delightsome, that they might not be enticing unto my people the Lord God did cause a skin of blackness to come upon them. And thus saith the Lord God: I will cause that they shall be loathsome unto thy people, save they shall repent of their iniquities.

And cursed shall be the seed of him that mixeth with their seed; for they shall be cursed even with the same cursing. And the Lord spake it, and it was done. (II Nephi 5:21–3)

According to Alma 3:6, 'the skins of the Lamanites were dark, according to the mark which was set upon their fathers, which was a curse upon them because of their transgression and their rebellion against their brethren, who consisted of Nephi, Jacob, and Joseph, and Sam, who were just and holy men'. Whiteness was clearly equated with righteousness and God's favour. Nevertheless, these distinctions were the temporary product of a curse, not biological divisions. Moreover, they served a divine purpose. Alma 3:8 explained the religious rationale of the racial distinction imposed upon the Lamanites: 'And this was done that their seed might be distinguished from the seed of their brethren, that thereby the Lord God might preserve his people, and that they might not mix and believe in incorrect traditions which would prove their destruction.' Indeed, in III Nephi 2:14–16 the Lamanites who were reunited with the Nephites were liberated from the temporary curse under which they had suffered, 'and their skin became white like unto the Nephites' (v. 15). Was racial difference an accidental in this narrative?

A further significant ambiguity emerges when Jacob denounces the Nephites for their backsliding, and not only warns them that they might appear darker than the Lamanites in the sight of God, but then appears explicitly to reject judgement based on the colour of one's skin, which in itself is a symbolic reminder rather of the sins of one's ancestors (Jacob 3:8–9):

O my brethren, I fear that unless ye shall repent of your sins that their skins shall be whiter than yours, when ye shall be brought with them before the throne of God.

Wherefore, a commandment I give unto you, which is the word of God, that ye revile no more against them because of the darkness of their skins; neither shall ye revile against them because of their filthiness; but ye shall remember your own filthiness, and remember that their filthiness came because of their fathers.

Although the Book of Mormon contains anti-Lamanite passages, it is not consistently prejudiced against the Lamanites. Theirs is a double-edged story. According to the Mormon *Doctrine and covenants*, the Lamanites would eventually 'blossom as the rose'.[67] Indeed, the Lamanites also stood heirs to a promise of racial and moral redemption by way of a future 'Christian' mission to the Indians foretold in the Book of Mormon (II Nephi 30:5–6):

And the gospel of Jesus Christ shall be declared among them; wherefore they shall be restored unto the knowledge of their fathers, and also to the knowledge of Jesus Christ, which was had among their fathers.

And then shall they rejoice; for they shall know that it is a blessing unto them from the hand of God; and their scales of darkness shall begin to fall from their eyes; and many generations shall not pass away among them, save they shall be a white and delightsome people.

Not that Amerindians will come to be appreciated as Amerindians. Rather the Lamanite 'remnant of our seed' (II Nephi 30:4) will come to learn that they are 'descended of the Jews'.

The treatment of the Lamanites in the Book of Mormon has had real-life consequences in the history and sociology of Mormon–Amerindian interaction. Mormon proselytising campaigns have been shaped by the church's distinctive ethnological system. Brigham Young, indeed, had an unrealised vision – which went well beyond proselytising – of Mormon–Indian intermarriage, a process which would lead to the reincorporation of the remnant of Lamanite Israel with Mormon Israel. However, the category of Lamanite was an unstable one with shifting boundaries. Towards the end of the nineteenth century, Mormons began to perceive native Americans more directly as Indians, and, consequently, to neglect them. Early twentieth-century Mormons forgot about the missionary imperative to restore the Lamanite remnant of the house of Israel to the true faith. The mission to the Indians languished, and there were no Lamanite projects between the 1880s and the 1940s. Nevertheless, things changed when Spencer Kimball became an apostle of the church in 1943 and was given direction of Indian affairs. Under the inspiration of this rising Mormon leader, who felt Mormons held special responsibilities towards the Lamanites, from the 1950s Mormons began to renew their interest in outreach to the Lamanite–Indian peoples.[68]

Brigham Young University became the leading university for North American Indian graduations, with graduation rates for native Amerindian students reaching five times higher than the national average for this ethnic group. Between 1950 and 1985 more than 500 Amerindians from about as many as seventy-five different tribes had gained degrees from BYU. According to BYU's own promotional materials, the university was by 1975 contributing more of its own funds to native Amerindian education than all the rest of the universities in the United States combined. There is no reason to suspect the substance of such boasts; but, unlike other supporters of native Amerindian education, Mormon commitment did not rest on any relativistic commitment to multiculturalism or even to a pragmatic desire to see native Amerindians assimilate economically to the standards of the white United States. Rather, Mormons were driven by the theological imperative to redeem the Lamanite. Indeed, some Mormons expressed concern at inter-racial marriages involving Indians, for this kind of assimilation to white America served only to dilute the 'blood of the children of the covenant'. Lamanite exogamy undermined purity of Israelite lineage.[69]

The Mormons clearly valued native Americans – though not as the upholders of a distinctive cultural tradition which ought to be valued on its own terms for what it meant to indigenous Amerindians. Rather Mormon philanthropy and outreach were predicated upon prizing native Americans for something quite extraneous to native American culture – their supposed descent from the Lamanites described in the Book of Mormon. An unconscious racism lurked under the mantle of pro-Indian philanthropy. Mormons did not want to know about native Americans as they really were: the Book of Mormon provided the essential framework for understanding Lamanite ethnography, history and identity. As Mauss notes, Mormons considered native Americans 'first and foremost as divinely destined objects of missionary endeavor', not as peoples with their own distinctive history.[70]

Although Mormons knew who the Lamanites were, they supplemented the revealed word of the Book of Mormon with archaeological researches. Indeed, the roots of a peculiar Mormon fascination with the high civilisations of Mexico and Central America lie in the sacred history of the Lamanites. Archaeological knowledge of Aztec and Maya civilisations is read as an external validation of the ancient history of America set out in the Book of Mormon. In 1979 a Foundation for Ancient Research and Mormon Studies (FARMS) was established. FARMS produced a translation of the *Popul Voh*, a pre-Columbian Mayan text, but only as an external pillar of religious truth. Mormons have established Lamanite missions in Central and South America and in Polynesia, which, in an unlikely convergence with the speculations of the non-Mormon explorer Thor Heyerdahl, they believe to have been settled from the Americas.[71]

Whereas Mormon attitudes to native Amerindians were integral to Mormon religion, the long tradition of excluding blacks from the priesthood was not. Nevertheless, until the 1970s priesthood denial was widely believed to be a fundamental ingredient of Mormon ecclesiology. Only in 1973 in a substantial painstaking work of revisionist scholarship published in *Dialogue* – an independent journal on the progressive wing of Mormon life – did Lester E. Bush Jnr expose the exclusion of blacks from the priesthood as an accidental accretion to the faith. According to Bush, there was no 'contemporary evidence' that Joseph Smith restricted priesthood eligibility on account either of one's race or – what black racial characteristics revealed to the world – one's biblical lineage.[72]

In the beginning Mormonism was, in this respect at least, colour-blind, for it had its origins in New York and Ohio in an American region far removed from the slaveholding states. Like many northerners of his time, Smith disliked both slavery and abolitionism. While he believed in Negro equality, he had no truck with miscegenation. The survival of the faith dictated a cautious navigation through the turbulent politics of slavery which dominated mid-nineteenth-century American life. This involved a degree of oscillation between pro- and anti-slavery positions, including neutrality. Despite the prevalence within early Mormonism of a 'Northern' distaste for Southern slaveholding ways, accusations in Missouri, in the wake of Nat Turner's slave rebellion, that Mormons were stirring up slaves led to a certain amount of prudent backtracking. In 1835 the church published a statement which denounced proselytising of bond-servants without the permission of their masters.[73]

However, it does seem likely that a *lineage* bias – as distinct from an explicitly racial bias – was present in the Mormon scriptures from the start. In a penetrating and original work of scholarship, *The refiner's fire: the making of Mormon cosmology 1644–1844* (1994), John L. Brooke demonstrated the role of the occult fringe of early modern European thought, in particular the Hermetic and Masonic traditions, on the worldview of Mormonism's founder, Joseph Smith. Brooke shows how the Masonic tradition might have had some bearing on the construction of Mormonism's unusual brand of ethnology. Some Freemasons subscribed to a distinctive brand of biblical interpretation, which related sacred history with the antiquity of the Masonic craft. After the Fall of

Man, they claimed, Adam had retained a special kind of divine knowledge which constituted the core of the Masonic tradition. However, from Seth and Cain, the surviving sons of Adam, there had descended two morally distinct races of men, the one good, the other evil, with each, moreover, bearer of rival versions of Masonic knowledge, one authentic, the other spurious. Authentic Masonry – really a kind of theology and theory of the universe, not just a knowledge of the building craft – descended from Noah to Solomon and was enshrined in Freemasonry; the other was transmitted by Ham to the pagan religions of antiquity with which he was associated in early modern antiquarianism. Brooke argues that this Masonic 'two-seed tradition' would play a role in shaping Mormon attitudes to the 'seed of Adam' and the 'seed of Cain', especially as it related to Mormon conceptions of the restored Old Testament priesthood. Smith did, of course, subscribe to the popular view that Africans were the descendants of Ham and, as such, implicated in the curse pronounced by Noah. However, at this stage there was no connection between the cursed lineage of Ham and the qualifications required for the Mormon priesthood. Indeed, a black convert to Mormonism, Elijah Abel, was admitted to the priesthood in 1836.[74]

Historians of Mormonism have noticed how the incipient racialism of Smith's era hardened into the racialist orthodoxy of Brigham Young's time. Even the flight to the Salt Lake valley would implicate Mormons in the debate over the extension of slavery into the western parts of American territory. As a movement Mormonism was harried for its novelty and, most obviously, for its teachings on polygamy. As a result its leaders had to be cautious in their politics at a time when the burning question in the United States concerned the future of slavery. The electoral platform of the Republican Party in the campaign of 1856 denounced two relics from the barbaric past which ought to be abolished: slavery and polygamy.[75]

It was Young who reformulated a widespread non-doctrinal folklore – shared by Joseph Smith – which identified Africans as the descendants of Ham into a compelling church policy which excluded blacks from the priesthood because they belonged to the cursed lineage of Cain. Young believed that the mark of Cain consisted in a 'flat nose' and 'black skin'. The first record of priesthood denial on the basis of African descent comes only in 1849. By 1852 Brigham Young had invoked a Mormon one-drop rule whereby the possession of 'one drop' of the seed of Cain rendered a Mormon male ineligible for the priesthood.[76]

The pearl of great price, composed of Smith's renderings of the Books of Abraham and Moses, formally became part of the Mormon canon of scripture in 1880.[77] These books advanced highly racialised readings of the curses inflicted upon Cain and Ham, and their descendants:

For behold, the Lord shall curse the land with much heat, and the barrenness thereof shall go forth forever; and there was a blackness came upon all the children of Canaan, that they were despised among all people. (*Pearl of great price*, Moses 7:8)

And Enoch also beheld the residue of the people which were the sons of Adam; and they were a mixture of all the seed of Adam save it was the seed of Cain, for the seed of Cain were black, and had not place among them. (*Pearl of great price*, Moses 7:22)

However, the crucial passage, from the perspective of Mormon eccle-siology, comes in the Book of Abraham, where Noah 'cursed him [Ham] as pertaining to the Priesthood' (*Pearl of great price*, Abraham 1:26).

Only from the 1880s did Mormons begin to impress Joseph Smith's recently canonised work into the justification of priesthood denial to blacks. Remarks on Cain and Ham in *The pearl of great price* were subjected to a broad, creative and racialising exegesis which resoundingly ensnared the Prophet Joseph Smith in the theology of priesthood exclusion. Mormons came to believe that Cain had turned black after murdering his brother, as were his descendants, among whom one Egyptus had married Ham. Both the lineages of Cain and Ham had been excluded from the patriarchal priesthood in scriptural times, a proscrip-tion which the Mormon church quite legitimately continued in the restored church. According to Nowell Bringhurst, the books of Moses and Abraham 'represent a "harder" Mormon line taken against blacks than that earlier assumed toward the Indians in the *Book of Mormon*'. Nevertheless, the *Pearl*'s late nineteenth-century interpreters imported a further degree of racialism into the book than was warranted by the original. In parallel with American culture, Mormonism assumed its most overtly racialist stance in the late nineteenth century.[78]

A further belief also developed among Mormons – a sort of Mormon karma – that skin colour was an indication of righteousness (or otherwise) in the pre-mortal life. Blacks, it came to be believed, had sinned in the pre-mortal existence. A key figure in the consolidation of this ultra-racialist tenet was Joseph Fielding Smith (1876–1972), who became an apostle in 1910 and for much of the twentieth century was recognised as an authoritative interpreter of Mormon doctrine, briefly holding the presidency of the church in his mid-nineties. He held the view that aptitudes had been divinely conferred in the pre-mortal life both on individuals and on groups. The pre-mortal life had also been a sort of testing ground for the allocation of God's spirit children to favoured or disfavoured mortal lineages. A British Israelite sympathiser, Fielding Smith argued that the pre-mortal lineage of Ephraim had been highly meritorious, and had deserved the blessings it obtained in the mortal life. By contrast, of course, the lineage of Cain and Ham had been the least deserving of merit, and its destiny in mortal history was therefore a lesser one.[79]

The rise of Spencer Kimball, with his more latitudinarian conception of Mormon ethnology, has seen the gradual eclipse of the racialist ideas associated with Fielding Smith and his influential son-in-law, the apostle and theologian Bruce McConkie. Moreover, the success of the civil rights movement at home and the opportunities of worldwide missionary growth presented compelling anti-racist challenges to the ossified Mormon ethnology of the first two-thirds of the twentieth century. The current trend in Mormonism leads away from the old white ethnocentrism, towards universalism. Nevertheless, contemporary Mormonism is still weighed down with the baggage of the past. It remains a very 'white' religion, notwithstanding its missionary outreach to people of colour at home and abroad. Mormon iconography is saturated with images of the people of the book as a white, fair-skinned race. Moreover, the Mormons have a very corporeal conception of divinity, and their Christ remains whiter than white.[80]

THEOSOPHY

Nineteenth-century racialism also left its imprint in the doctrines of Theosophy. This might well occasion some surprise, for Theosophy is a form of spirituality founded upon an ecumenical and explicitly anti-racist platform. Indeed, Theosophy proclaims itself a religion of global racial and religious reconciliation. Yet despite this overt anti-racialist message, Theosophy betrays its origins in the racialist atmosphere of the late nineteenth century and is saturated in the language and ideas of Victorian ethnology. Although Theosophy, it should be clear, was not a racialist organisation, its scriptures contained both a decidedly anti-racist spirituality and a counter-current of racialist thinking. For Theosophists, the story of humanity, it transpires, is a narrative of root-races. Nor was the racial dimension of Theosophy an altogether silent legacy, invisible as it is in modern Theosophical self-consciousness. Scholars have begun to

recover a powerful synergy between occult and racialist theories in the late
nineteenth and early twentieth centuries. For instance, the Nazi fascination with Tibet, to which an expedition was sent in 1938, was underpinned by Theosophical influences.[81] Nor should we forget that the
'Svastica' (or swastika), a sign of mystical conception among the early
Aryans, makes a somewhat sinister appearance in Theosophical anthropology.[82] Today's Theosophists would be appalled by such connections,
given their associations with New Age mysticism. Nonetheless, while
superficially Theosophy appears largely a blend of eastern religious doctrines and western esoterism, its neglected metaphysical and pseudo-scientific underpinnings retain the inflections of the evolutionism and
racialism of late nineteenth-century science. In particular, Theosophical
anthropology remains tied, albeit loosely, to a fossilised scientific racism.

The Theosophical Society was set up in New York in 1875. Its guru was
a Russian spiritualist, Madame Helena Petrovna Blavatsky (1831–91),
whose ideas would enjoy such wide currency and a religious embodiment
in Theosophy in large part because of the organisational gifts of
the movement's American co-founder, Colonel Henry Steel Olcott
(1832–1907). Blavatsky claimed to be the chosen heir of the Masters of
Wisdom, an apostolic succession of initiates who had maintained an
esoteric wisdom tradition through the ages. The society's system of beliefs
was embodied in the 'scriptures' of Theosophy, Blavatsky's two principal
works, *Isis unveiled* (1877) and *The secret doctrine* (1888). At the core of
Blavatsky's doctrinal system resided a body of anti-materialist metaphysics. Consciousness, she proclaimed, was the ground of our being.[83]

The wisdom of the East played a significant part in Theosophy.
Blavatsky had travelled in Tibet, Ladakh and India during 1856–7.
Inspired with a global mission and conscious of the central role of
Hinduism in the recovery of divine wisdom, Blavatsky and Olcott moved
to India, where the Theosophical Society based its headquarters at Adyar,
near Madras. Blavatsky claimed to be disseminating truths found in an
ancient eastern text entitled the *Stanzas of Dzyan*, which she had read and
translated at a remote Himalayan monastery. From her initiation into the
secrets of the *Stanzas of Dzyan*, Blavatsky acquired a cosmology, a cyclical
theory of development through sequences of birth, decay and revival. The
story of mankind, according to Blavatsky, follows a similar cyclical pattern. Blavatsky had also been exposed – supposedly – to the truths preserved by priest-kings in the subterranean city of Shamballah in the Gobi
desert, which was peopled by post-Atlantean survivors of the fourth
root-race. Following the example of their founding guru, Theosophists

ascribed particular value to the non-European Other. Indeed, the society aimed to bring about a universal brotherhood incorporating all races and religions.

Blavatsky did not conceive of Theosophy as an antagonist or rival of existing religions; rather, she believed, Theosophy complemented religion by providing the means for understanding the core truths of the world's various religions in their proper light. Blavatsky regarded the Christian scriptures as an embodiment of truth – albeit not on its own terms. Theosophy contemplated truth as a much larger jigsaw puzzle, of which the Bible constituted one very significant piece. Thus she acknowledged up to a point the authority of the Bible on spiritual (and ethnological) matters, but regarded it as only a portion of a greater truth, further pieces of which might be found in the relics of the other great religions and civilisations of antiquity, particularly in India. One of the roles of Theosophy was to reconstruct the totality of human history out of the venerable fragmentary relics bequeathed to the fifth root-race (the current stage of humanity). Divine knowledge had once been unitary, according to Theosophists, but is now fragmented, found dispersed throughout the world's religions. It is the purpose of Theosophy to knit together the wholeness of truth from a disjointed and incoherent plurality of religions. In this respect, Theosophy is underpinned by a kind of ecumenism and a desire for a global reconciliation of theologies. Divine wisdom had been communicated to humankind, refracted through the diverse cultural trappings which disguised the fundamental one-ness of all religions. Blavatsky regarded the world's major religions as conveying aspects of a greater truth. Nevertheless, Christianity and the great religions of Asia had forgotten the real truths which had originally inspired them, submerged under the doctrinal rubbish of later cultural accretions. Blavatsky disdained the parochial and solipsistic delusions that underpinned religious divisions. Instead she traced the conflicts that raged among the major world religions to their source: 'Truth is known but to the few; the rest, unwilling to withdraw the veil from their own hearts, imagine it blinding the eyes of their neighbours.' Theosophy, on the other hand, made sense of the accumulated wisdom of the ages. Comparative religion was an integral part of a Theosophical method aimed at purifying and syncretising religion. Blavatsky paid especial honour to the vatic dimension of spirituality, for it was the seers and mystics of the world's religions who had possessed the vision to penetrate beyond the surface illusion of things. These mystical initiates had perceived the deeper truths of reality which lay beyond the realm of matter. Theosophy would enhance this partial attainment of spirituality by leading humankind to a higher consciousness of ultimate reality.[84]

In spite of her adherence to an unchanging, timeless and coherent body of wisdom, Blavatsky was both eclectic and trendily up-to-date in her concerns. Her *oeuvre* reveals a magpie garnering of modish late nineteenth-century themes and issues, including evolution and race. Indeed, much of the second volume of *The secret doctrine* was devoted to the subject she termed 'Anthropogenesis'. Blavatsky took the view that the 'occult sciences' had an important function: to mediate between the prevalent but influential errors of both Darwinian anthropology and a narrowly conceived reading of the biblical account of the origins of mankind. How might one steer a middle course between the arid materialism of Darwinian evolution and the narrow doctrinal defensiveness of traditionalist Christianity? Ancient tradition, it seemed, held the key to unlocking the secrets of the cosmos, nature and the story of humanity. 'Tradition', declared Blavatsky, 'is left contemptuously unnoticed by sceptic and materialist, and made subservient to the Bible in every case by the too zealous churchman.' The first man, according to all the philosophies of ancient times, so Blavatsky believed, had evolved out of prior spiritual beings.[85]

Blavatsky was an opponent of the version of evolution espoused by Darwinian materialists, but she was otherwise well disposed towards the general case for evolution. Blavatsky subscribed to a purposive evolution whose goals were spiritual rather than biological. Blavatskian evolution accords with the cosmological law of cyclical decay and renewal by way of sequential rounds of racial degeneracy and revival. Within the Theosophical scheme of evolution, there was an interpenetration of the spiritual and physical, which, by a cyclical law of nature, ensured the unfolding of man's latent divinity. Evolution had occurred out of spiritual stuff. Matter was only a part of nature; spirit was an intrinsic and essential part of the ultimate reality. The Blavatskian critique of the materialist bias in Darwinian evolution depended upon a predominantly spiritualist definition of the nature of man. The 'objective, physical body' comprised only one-third of the 'triune' human being. The 'real human' was located in man's 'vitalizing astral body (or soul)', while these two elements of man were, Blavatsky insisted, 'brooded over and illuminated by the third – the sovereign, the immortal spirit'.[86]

Mankind had not evolved, Blavatsky insisted, from animal savagery to high civilisation. She found this scheme of evolution implausible. Mankind had not followed such a course unaided or from such a lowly starting point. Rather, human development had begun on earth with the reception here of spiritual life-forms from prior worlds. The incarnation on earth of wise beings from previous worlds was a vital first step in the unfolding process of human evolution on earth. Darwin's big mistakes were to concentrate on biological evolution to the exclusion of spiritual developments, and thus to neglect the spiritual transformations which preceded physical developments and in so doing to mistake a part of the evolutionary process of transformation for the whole. Blavatsky also claimed that there had been a variety of methods of procreation before the onset of normal human reproduction. This transition from one system of reproduction to another was part of her larger non-materialist theory of evolution from spiritual to more corporeal forms of being. Clear sexual differentiation had accompanied the passage from spiritual to corporeal beings. The third and fourth root-races, for example, had no longer been 'androgynous' or 'sexless semi-spirits'.[87]

Race played a central part in this evolutionary narrative. The core tenets of Theosophic anthropogenesis, according to Blavatsky, were the 'simultaneous evolution of seven human groups on seven different portions of the planet'; the birth of the astral before the physical body; and the view that the creation of man preceded that of every mammalian, including other anthropoids, on the planet. This last belief appeared to run in direct contradiction not only to evolutionary theory but also to the word of scripture; however, Blavatsky insisted that her revision was a correct reading of Genesis 2 where Adam was formed in verse 7 and the beasts in verse 19. According to Blavatsky, Genesis was really 'a compilation of the universal legends of the universal humanity'.[88]

Blavatsky was strongly influenced in her theory of mankind by her reading of Louis Jacolliot's *The Bible in India* (1870) and of George Smith's *Chaldean account of Genesis* (1876). In a similar vein Blavatsky aimed to produce a reconciliation between the book of Genesis and the theogonies of other major religions and civilisations. Genesis was part – not the whole – of a larger picture which had been revealed – and not exclusively – to the patriarchs. Christianity participated in the greater truth, but did not monopolise it. Indeed, orthodox theology tended to distort glimpses of a deeper truth which could be found in the Christian scriptures and in those of other ancient religions. The Bible provided only a narrow snapshot of human antiquity, its story of origins focusing almost exclusively on the emergence of the fifth root-race. Whereas the Puranas referred to an earlier phase of human development, the Bible, 'neatly skipping the pre-Adamic races, proceeds with its allegories concerning the fifth race'. Read esoterically, both the Puranas and the Jewish scriptures appeared to be 'based on the same scheme of evolution'. Blavatsky's story of racial evolution depended in part upon an allegorical reading of Genesis: 'The rib is bone, and when we read in Genesis that Eve was made out of the rib, it only means that the race with bones was produced out of a previous race or races, which were boneless.' In other words, the earliest root-race had been ethereal.[89]

Indeed, Blavatsky was at bottom an accommodationist, attempting not only to effect a concordance between the world's great religions, but also between those aspects of the greater underlying truth captured by such antagonists as Christians and Darwinians. In its early mentions of wholly physical and wholly spiritual creatures, after which came the union of the physical and the spiritual in the Adamite race, the Bible, Blavatsky believed, encoded a version of Darwinian evolution and the Theosophical transformation of races. In effect, Blavatsky set out for Theosophists a distinctive system of polygenesis which did not resemble those put forward either by secular critics of Christian monogenesis or by revisionist defenders of Christian anthropology. Theosophy promoted a halfway house between full-blown polygenesis and Christian monogenesis:

Strictly speaking, esoteric philosophy teaches a modified polygenesis. For, while it assigns to humanity a oneness of origin, in so far that its forefathers or Creators were all divine beings – though of different classes or degrees of perfection in their hierarchy – men were nevertheless born on seven different centres of the continent of that period. Though all of one common origin, yet ... their potentialities and mental capabilities, outward or physical forms, and future characteristics, were very different.

Nevertheless, the pre-Adamism inherent in Genesis seemed to provide a crucial bridge between Darwinian evolution and scriptural truth, as it might be properly interpreted in the light of Theosophical method:

The whole Darwinian theory of natural selection is included in the first six chapters of the book of Genesis. The 'man' of chapter 1 is radically different from the 'Adam' of chapter 2, for the former was created 'male and female' – that is, bi-sexed – and in the image of God; while the latter, according to verse seven, was formed of the dust of the ground, and became 'a living soul' after the Lord God 'breathed into his nostrils the breath of life'. Moreover, this Adam was a male being, and in verse twenty we are told 'there was not found a helpmeet for him'.

Indeed, Blavatsky claimed that Genesis contained mentions not only of these two races, but also in chapter 4 of two other races, the 'sons of God' and a race of giants.[90]

Man would, in the fullness of time, Blavatsky believed, move through seven root-races, each centred on a different continent. Theosophy embodied an elaborate system of racial and evolutionary classifications. This racial system rested upon a theological basis. The first, second and early third root-races had been, in the words of one Theosophist, 'not, strictly speaking, human'. Each root-race was further subdivided into seven sub-races. Within the ethnological scheme of Theosophy, the Teutonic family was, for example, the fifth sub-race of the fifth root-race. Blavatsky believed she was living through the fifth – Aryan – root-race. The first spiritual race had inhabited an astral continent; the following three races had been based on terrestrial continents – near the North Pole, in the Indian Ocean and then the Atlantic – which had now disappeared beneath the waves. Races had evolved in distinct phases embodying varying degrees of spiritual and physical essence. The first race of mankind was wholly spiritual – a race of self-born, boneless, formless spiritual beings. Next followed the second race, the Hyperborean race of the North Pole. The Hyperboreans had not existed in a bodily form nor had they reproduced in a physical way. Sexual reproduction had come only with the third, Lemurian race.[91]

Clearly, race played a significant part in Theosophical religion, which ran against the universalist grain of Theosophical aspirations. Within the Theosophical system of evolving root-races, the white race was celebrated as a higher type of humanity, an embodiment of the current fifth root-race. In the contemporary world the fifth root-race, the Aryan, now prevailed. Each root-race had different psychic and intellectual potential. Despite her universalist ideals, Blavatsky also extended to the psychic realm the common nineteenth-century assumption that racial groups had differing capacities for religious belief and worship. According to Blavatsky, 'Races of men differ in spiritual gifts as in color, stature, or any other external quality; among some peoples seership naturally prevails, among others mediumship.' There was also an element of racial prophecy in Theosophy. Blavatsky believed that in the contemporary United States a new root-race was being formed which would carry forward the spiritual progress of the human race. This sixth root-race to come was predicted to have its centre – it should occasion scant surprise – in California.[92]

The Theosophical system of evolution – with its phased chronology of root-races – categorised certain extant ethnic and racial groups as archaisms. Racial extinction and the present redundancy of pre-Aryan races which had survived from the Lemuro-Atlantean eras were integral elements in this Theosophical narrative. Included within Theosophical

ethnology was a scale of racial anachronism. The Theosophical significance of races within the epochal round of the fifth root-race
depended on the chronological provenance of a particular ethnic group.
Some of the lesser races of the modern world were, it seemed, archaic
remnants of earlier root-races:

> The Secret Doctrine teaches that the specific unity of mankind is not without
> exceptions even now. For there are, or rather still were a few years ago,
> descendants of these half-animal tribes or races, both of remote Lemurian and
> Lemuro-Atlantean origin. The world knows them as Tasmanians (now extinct),
> Australians, Andaman Islanders, etc.

In Theosophical taxonomy the Turanians and Dravidians were types of
the previous fourth root-race, while some Australian aborigines were held
to be archaic remnants of the third, Lemurian root-race. As representatives of earlier evolutionary types, these ethnic groups symbolised a racial
redundancy, their evolutionary purpose having been accomplished in a
previous era. Blavatsky argued that the fertile cross-breeding of Europeans
with Tasmanians was impossible not just because of 'physiological law',
but from a 'decree of karmic evolution'. By the lights of Theosophical
evolution, it appeared that the contemporary world was inhabited both
by purposive races of the fifth root-race, whose racial mission lay ahead of
them, and also by pathetic racial anachronisms, survivors from bygone
phases of evolution, their mission spent.[93]

Fashionably eclectic, Blavatsky appropriated some of the findings of
Indo-European philology for Theosophy, corrupting these in the process.
The Theosophical taxonomies of root-races and sub-races seemed to
resemble, albeit loosely, the categories of nineteenth-century philology.
The Atlantean sub-races included various non-Aryan peoples, such as
Dravidians, Toltecs, Lapps, Turanians, Mongolians and original Semites,
while the Aryan included as sub-races the Hindu Aryan, the 'Aryan
Semite', the Iranian, the Celtic and the Teutonic. Blavatsky upheld some
of the insights of the Aryan thesis, but added her own characteristically
eccentric twist to the conventional Aryan–Semitic distinction. The
Semites were in Blavatsky's scheme of ethnology a branch of the Aryan
race. The Semites were 'later Aryans – degenerate in spirituality, and
perfected in materiality'. The Semitic languages, moreover, were,
according to Blavatsky, 'the bastard descendants of the first phonetic
corruptions of the eldest children of the early Sanskrit'. The Semites were
in fact seen by Theosophists as a bridge between the fourth and fifth

root-races. The later Semites, on the other hand, 'though retaining much of their old physical type', were deemed to be 'truly Aryan'. 'The Aryan Road', Theosophists believed, was 'a stage in the race-scheme of things'.[94]

Geology – or rather a sort of geomancy – also played a central part in the unfolding history of the root-races. Myths of sunken continents loom large in Theosophical ethnology. The fourth root-race had flourished on the lost Atlantic continent of Atlantis, and before that the third root-race had been composed of the inhabitants of the continent of Lemuria, which had stretched from Madagascar to Ceylon and Sumatra, covering much of what was now the Indian Ocean, and the inhabitants of Atlantis. Curiously, the Lemurian idea enjoyed a respectable scientific pedigree at the point when it was appropriated into Theosophical science. The distinguished German evolutionary biologist Ernst Haeckel assigned a prominent place to Lemuria in his scheme of racial evolution. Haeckel conjectured that the ape-like ancestors of the Aryan race had migrated to Eurasia from the lost continent of Lemuria. Indeed, Haeckel's ethnology was a curious amalgam of evolutionary science and racial mysticism of the sort which appealed to Blavatsky. Haeckel distanced himself from mainstream religion, partly out of dislike for the corrupting effects which he believed Christianity had inflicted upon the noble Aryan ancestors of the German nation.[95]

The races of the world could be easily mapped on to Theosophical ideas of evolution and shifting continental geography. In *The lost Lemuria* (1904), the Theosophist W. Scott-Elliot identified the Lemurian root-race as Negroid. The Lemurians had eventually intermarried with the Rmoahals, the first sub-race of Atlanteans. Scott-Elliot claimed that the 'degraded remnants of the third root race who still inhabit the earth may be recognised in the aborigines of Australia, the Andaman islanders, some hill tribes of India, the Tierra-del Fuegans, the Bushmen of Africa, and some other savage tribes'.[96] Philology also featured in the system. Scott-Elliot argued that Chinese was the sole lineal descendant of the stunted languages of Lemuria. Theosophical theories of root-races, sunken continents and race evolution were also imported wholesale in the Anthroposophical movement founded by Rudolf Steiner (1861–1925).[97]

More recently, a variant of Blavatskian biology has surfaced in the anti-Darwinian theories of Michael A. Cremo and Richard L. Thompson. Members of the Krishna Consciousness movement, Cremo and Thompson have argued in their *Hidden history of the human race* (1999), which is published by Bhaktivedanta Book Publishing and dedicated to His Divine Grace A. C. Bhaktivedanta Swami Prabhupada, that anatomically modern humans have been around for millions of years. Cremo and Thompson contend that the scientific community has suppressed or neglected evidence for the great antiquity of the human race, such as the apparent human footprints – quite different from marks left by Australopithecine feet – found in volcanic ash deposits at Laetoli in Tanzania which are believed to have been 3.6 million years old. Stratigraphic anomalies lie at the heart of the Krishna Consciousness critique of conventional evolutionary chronology. Cremo and Thompson list numerous examples – some from the reports of nineteenth-century excavations – of anatomically modern skeletal remains found in very old geological contexts. They do not deny that other hominids have existed; rather, they insist that these other hominids have coexisted with man for tens of millions of years. Ultimately, of course, the findings of Cremo and Thompson accord with the revelations of Vedic literature on the great antiquity of the human race. Cremo and Thompson argue that, as Blavatsky once believed, the reconciliation of evolutionary biology with Vedic perspectives would serve only to enhance our understanding of human development.[98]

CHAPTER 8

Black Counter-Theologies

Racialised religion has not only been a white phenomenon. Many of the features of white theology over the past two centuries have been replicated by black theologians. Not only have black theologians participated, naturally enough, in the defence of monogenist orthodoxy against polygenist heresies whose logical tendencies appeared to be racialist; in addition, they have appropriated some of the less attractive elements of nineteenth-century racialism in the (otherwise perfectly reasonable) defence of the black race against white slurs. The predicament of black Americans in particular was an awkward one. Whether enslaved or formally subordinate or informally marginalised, blacks realised that they were not recognised as the equal of white Americans within a nominally Christian society. Why did white Americans ignore the teachings of the gospel? Why did the unequivocal message of Acts 17:26 – 'And [God] hath made of one blood all nations of men for to dwell on all the face of the earth' – not resonate with a Bible-reading people? Understandably, black Chrsitians responded in divergent ways to this dilemma. Whereas one stream of black culture – the tradition associated with the rhetoric of Martin Luther King Jnr – emphasised the universalist message of the gospel and black equality and kinship with whites, another current reflected black disenchantment with the hypocrisy of white Christianity and instead promoted separatism and an ethnocentric reading of scripture which highlighted the special role of the black race within the unfolding drama of sacred history.[1] Quite apart from the exigencies of theology, social practices also impacted upon black religion. During the nineteenth century, separate racial denominations seemed a more likely prospect for the untrammelled expression of black Christianity than integrated churches. In 1816 Richard Allen (1760–1831) set up the African Methodist Episcopal Church which brought together black Methodists from the middle states of the eastern seaboard. Along similar lines, James Varick (1750–1827) of New York city founded the African Methodist Episcopal Zion Church.

Thus, although black theologians saw the anti-racist potential in the white man's Christianity and opened it up – in practice – as a colour-blind, multiracial faith (which it had been all along in principle), there was also a great temptation towards a black vindicationist hermeneutic which rejected out of hand the corrupting whiteness of white Christianity. Instead this was to be replaced with an uplifting racial narrative of black achievement and chosenness. For black vindicationists, the western theological tradition had involved white ethnic impersonation and the consequent erasure of blacks from a central role in scripture. In particular, black theologians have argued that the historic Christ had borne little resemblance to the pseudo-Christ of the dominant western tradition of religious art and sculpture.

One of the most influential proponents of a racialised Christianity was Henry McNeal Turner (1834–1915), a bishop in the African Methodist Episcopal Church. In his denominational journal *Voice of Missions*, Turner used his editorial platform to question a monopolistic white appropriation of the Deity:

We have as much right Biblically and otherwise to believe that God is a Negro, as you buckra, or white, people have to believe that God is a fine looking, symmetrical and ornamented white man. For the bulk of you, and all the fool Negroes of the country, believe that God is a white-skinned, blue-eyed, straight-haired, projecting-nosed, compressed-lipped and finely-robed white gentleman, sitting upon a throne somewhere in the heavens. Every race of people since time began who have attempted to describe their God by words, or by paintings, or by carvings, or by any other form or figure, have conveyed the idea that the God who made them and shaped their destinies was symbolized in themselves, and why should not the Negro believe that he resembles God as much so as other people? We do not believe that there is any hope for a race of people who do not believe that they look like God.[2]

Racial uplift, Turner believed, was an essential ingredient of a vibrant black Christianity.

Yet vindicationism of this sort also reflected wider ideological currents in American culture. During the nineteenth century, in particular, black racial apologists were exposed to the same currents of racialist thought as their white detractors, and it should occasion no surprise that racialist inflections appeared in black as well as in white theology. Thus black America spawned its own forms of racial religion. Just as whites insinuated Caucasian or Aryan readings into scriptural interpretation, so some black Americans imparted their own black African spin to sacred history. A good example of this came in the work of the classicist Edward Wilmot Blyden (1832–1912), born of slave parents of Ibo origin in St Thomas in the Danish West Indies, who came via the United States to a chair at Liberia College. During the 1860s Blyden studied Arabic, which he had added to the curriculum of Liberia College, and in 1886 abandoned the Presbyterian ministry to become a freelance proponent of a non-sectarian religion which included a warm appreciation of the positive role played by Islam in African religiosity and race relations. Blyden never actually converted to Islam, though that would have been the logical terminus of his racialist understanding of religion. He wondered 'why the religions of the Indo-Europeans' seemed to 'transcend with difficulty the limits of race'. It was a profound puzzle 'why the grand Semitic idea of the conversion to Divine truth of all the races of mankind, and their incorporation into one spiritual family, seems, under European propagandism, to make such slow progress'. Race held the answer. Despite receiving a 'Semitic religion', the Aryan peoples of Europe nevertheless 'gave it, in a great degree, the colouring of their own minds'. The 'Aryan genius still asserted itself'. Blyden – like several other exponents of the new philology – regarded religion as a manifestation of race. Basically, he believed that Aryans were materialists with a tendency to materialise any religion, however spiritual, with which they came into contact. This problem did not arise in the case of Islam, which was not riddled with racial contradictions. Where Christianity was the Semitic religion of an Aryan people, Islam was a Semitic religion which flourished within the Semitic race: 'The Mohammedan religion, on the other hand, an offshoot from the Semitic mind, disregarding all adventitious circumstances, seeks for the real man, neglects the accidental for the essential, the adventitious for the integral. Hence it extinguishes all distinctions founded upon race, colour, or nationality.'[3]

In certain respects, black racialised religion constituted a mirror image of its white counterparts. Nevertheless, there was no monolithic black interpretation of scripture. Moreover, black theologians – even at their most racially assertive – tended not to challenge the basic contours of scriptural history and ethnology. Polygenesis held little allure for black racialists. Indeed, sacred ethnology went unchallenged in principle among blacks. The central points of contention within the black theological tradition – as we shall see – usually concerned points of detail about the lineage of Ham. It is important to recognise the significance of theology as an autonomous factor in black religious life. Theology was not simply the maidservant of racial pride. Rather, blacks also struggled to defend the authority of scripture.

Nineteenth-century black monogenist ethnologists – just like their white counterparts – participated in an intellectual battle to rebut polygenist arguments. In the case of black monogenists, the intellectual debate had an added edge; for monogenesis offered a means of confounding a principal support for slavery and white supremacy. However, black monogenists were also concerned to defend the authority of Christian scripture as something worth defending for its own sake. Monogenesis was not an epiphenomenon of a deeper and more pressing racial struggle. Religious truth was as important to black Christians as racial truth. Hosea Easton (1787–1830), pastor of the Methodist Episcopal Zion Church in Hartford, Connecticut, argued that whatever differences existed between races were 'casual or accidental'. There were, he insisted 'no constitutional differences'; rather, colour was 'the result of the same laws which variegate the whole creation'.[4] James McCune Smith (1813–64), a black physician who had obtained a medical degree from the University of Glasgow in 1837, after rejections from American medical schools, advanced an environmentalist strain of monogenesis which was nearly akin to the prevailing monogenist orthodoxy found in the medical world of later Enlightenment Scotland.[5] Frederick Douglass denounced the polygenist threat of Nott, Gliddon, Agassiz and Morton to the authority of scripture. According to Douglass, 'the credit of the Bible' was 'at stake'. Douglass went on to link pro-slavery arguments to the religious scepticism of the polygenists.[6] The historian, politician and Baptist minister George Washington Williams (1849–91) began his *History of the Negro race in America* (1882) with a defence of monogenesis.[7] Joseph Hayne (b. 1849), a black cleric and physician from Brooklyn, contended that there was 'no part of the inspired Word of God that teaches the non-unity of the human race'.[8]

Similarly, black scriptural ethnologists – like their white counterparts – tried to make sense of obscure passages in the Bible which sat awkwardly with monogenist truth. For instance, the black physician and journalist Martin Delany (1812–85) concluded that the 'descendants of Adam must have been very numerous' because 'we read of peoples which we cannot comprehend as having had an existence'. In particular, the narrative of Cain's journey to the land of Nod, on the east of Eden, where he found a wife who bore his son Enoch, was pregnant with mysterious lacunae. As Delany noted, until this point readers of the Bible had been aware of only one woman, Eve, 'who did not even have a daughter, so far as Moses has informed us in Genesis'.[9]

Polygenesis was not the only major error with which black theologians were confronted. There was also the need to correct racialist misinterpretations of the curses pronounced upon Cain and Ham, which for many white racists betoken divine legitimation of black slavery, or at the very least inferiority. Indeed, curse denial was one of the dominant themes of nineteenth-century black theological literature. In his *Text book of the origin and history etc of the colored people* (1841), the Presbyterian minister James Pennington (1807–70) exploded the legends of black descent from both Cain and Ham. Pennington insisted that Noah had been descended from Adam's third son Seth, not from Cain. Therefore, he concluded, when Noah and his three sons and their respective wives entered the Ark, 'they left the posterity of Cain to perish in the flood'. Nor did the story that blacks were cursed by Noah stand up to detailed scrutiny. Pennington acknowledged that blacks were descended from Noah's son Ham, but not from Ham's son Canaan at whom Noah's curse had been directed. Rather blacks were descended from two of Ham's other three sons, namely Cush and Mizraim. Africans are not Canaanites, argued Pennington; therefore they should be released from slavery which had no scriptural warrant whatsoever. Indeed, Pennington also questioned whether the curse was intended to reach beyond Canaan himself to his posterity. Genesis 9:27 said simply that God would enlarge Japhet who would dwell in the tents of Shem, and that 'Canaan shall be his servant.' There was no mention of the curse extending to the descendants of Canaan. Moreover, playing upon the prevailing anti-Catholicism among white Protestant Americans, Pennington traced unscriptural justifications of slavery back to the superstitions and corruptions of Roman Catholic Europe: 'Have the ministers of the sacred office at the south who interpret the Bible in support of slavery, ever thought that they are preaching a doctrine first invented by a bishop of the Romish church!?' Free, Protestant interpretation of the scriptures provided no sanction for black slavery.[10]

In 1852 the black Episcopalian minister Alexander Crummell (1819–98) published an essay entitled 'The Negro race not under a curse'. According to Crummell, the curse described in Genesis was narrowly and particularly restricted only to the descendants of Canaan. It had not, as many whites mistakenly believed, been a general curse applicable to all the descendants of Ham. Black Africans, Crummell insisted, were not descended from Canaan.[11] In a tit-for-tat response to white slurs on the Hamitic line, some black writers also denigrated the achievements of Japhet's white descendants.[12] Indeed, far from rejecting the white-imposed association of the black African race with Noah's irreverent son, many nineteenth-century black Americans took pride in belonging to the lineage of Ham, readily accepting – and projecting – a Hamitic identity. Here the glorious civilisation of ancient Egypt – in lieu of conventional white associations of Hamitic ancestry with the curse of servitude – assumed enormous importance in raising black self-esteem.[13] Black writers identified Ham's son Mizraim as the founder of the Egyptian people. Unsurprisingly, black champions of their race's ancient Egyptian heritage were frustrated by the white Eurocentric assumptions of contemporary Egyptology. Was there a white academic conspiracy to decouple the glorious achievements of Egyptian civilisation from the black Hamitic people which sustained it? Henry Highland Garnet (1815–82), a Presbyterian minister and active opponent of slavery, complained that 'the modern world seems determined to pilfer Africa of her glory'. Garnet insisted that the ancient Egyptians were Hamitic Africans, that Moses had married a black Ethiopian, and that those fathers of Christian theology, Cyprian, Origen and Augustine, had been black.[14] Rufus Perry (1833–95) denounced the stereotypical white Egyptologist who

delights to robe all ancient Egypt in white. The old monarchs are made to conform in figure to the Grecian and Roman mould, and in color to the Shemitic race of Asia, and to the Anglo-Saxon. The black mummy is aroused from his ancient sleep and transformed by the art of Pythagorean metempsychosis into a white mummy with a look of disdain upon its former self. The Negro is not in it.

Perry boasted that 'we may justly claim for the Negro race all of Egypt's pristine greatness'.[15] The glories of Hamitic Egypt remained a potent inspiration for twentieth-century black nationalism. George Wells Parker (1882–1931) founded the Hamitic League of the World, a non-Garveyite black nationalist organisation whose objective was to puff the indispensable role played by Hamites in the rise of civilisation.[16]

The confident black assumption of a Hamitic identity was part of a wider reappropriation of scripture from its white interpreters. In *Light and truth* (1844), Robert Benjamin Lewis of Maine, who came of mixed African and Amerindian origins, argued that the Bible should be read as a narrative of black achievement. Indeed, argued Lewis, not only were the descendants of Ham black, so too were the Shemites. While Hamites had been black, with 'frizzled or curly hair', the peoples descended from Shem had also been black, but with long, straight hair. Lewis identified the posterity of Noah as 'colored people'. More particularly, Lewis insisted that Moses had been black, as had various other figures in the Old Testament narrative. Had not Job – in the book of Job 30:30 – declared

'My skin is black upon me'? Had not Jeremiah, in the book of Lamentation 5:10, proclaimed that 'Our skin was black like an oven'? Did not these remarks – along with the Song of Solomon's 'I am black but comely' – suggest that the Hebraic peoples of the Old Testament had – at the very least – been coloured or that they had regularly intermarried with black peoples? Furthermore, Lewis argued that Christian theology was a product of the black intellect. Had not some of the primary figures of the patristic era been Africans, such as Tertullian, Cyprian, Origen and Augustine himself? Lewis also claimed that the genealogy of Christ was a lineage of colour.[17]

This idea was developed and elaborated by various black writers, including W. L. Hunter, whose *Jesus Christ had Negro blood in his veins* (1901) had gone through nine editions by 1913. Hunter identified four black women in Christ's genealogy, at Matthew 1:3, I Chronicles 2:3–4, Joshua 2:21 and I Kings 3:1. This finding was sufficient for him to declare 'clear proof that Jesus Christ came nearer being a black man than a white man, or at least a very dark man'. As a result, Hunter wondered mischievously how whites – with their unacknowledged 'religion of race prejudice' – would react to the Second Coming:

What will the negro-hating white Christians do when He comes to take charge of His church, and they find that He is a black Savior? Will the white man worship a black Savior? Yet, that is what they do every day in the week, and must forever do or have no Savior at all, for we have proven . . . that the incarnate Savior was nearer a black than a white man . . .

In the course of his researches into Christ's genealogy, Hunter also identified the first-ever priest Melchizedek as black, and similarly the prophet Amos.[18]

Similarly, James Morris Webb, in *The black man the father of civilization proven from biblical history* (1910), argued that there had been no curse on Ham, that both Moses and Solomon had married black women, and that David's great-grandfather Booz had been born of a Hamitic woman, Rachab. This Hamitic marriage anticipated several black Canaanitish marriages in the lineage of Christ, whose veins, Webb insisted, had run with Ethiopian blood, whose hair had been woolly, and who in early twentieth-century racial classification would have been designated as a Negro.[19]

Indeed, some black writers championed a racially exclusive version of Christianity, one which assigned a central role to blacks – and blacks alone – in the providential unfolding of sacred history. In his *Principia of ethnology* (1879), Martin Delany detected a hitherto neglected African dimension to the Christian story. When Herod ordered the slaughter of the innocents, where did the angel of the Lord tell Joseph to take the infant Jesus? According to Matthew 2:13, the holy family was to flee to Egypt: 'only in Africa could the son of God be saved'. Moreover, Delany also contended that when Christ collapsed under the weight of the cross he was to carry up the hill of Calvary – with the awful prospect this entailed of 'the will of God thwarted, and the plan of salvation checked' – there appeared a black African, 'a man of Cyrene, Simon by name (Simon Niger)' who was compelled to carry the cross: 'So the African was the first bearer of the cross of Jesus Christ.' Delany wondered whether this was an 'accident' or a 'providence of God', concluding that it was 'yet another evidence of the favor of Providence to this race', which was charged with a special 'mission'.[20]

This racial mission was set out with greater clarity in 1884 by Bishop James Theodore Holly (1829–1911) of the African Methodist Episcopal Church in an article on 'The divine plan of human redemption, in its ethnological development'. Each of the racial stocks descending, respectively, from Shem, Japhet and Ham was responsible for a particular role in God's grand design for humanity:

In the development of the divine plan of human redemption the Semitic race had the formulating, the committing to writing and the primal guardianship of the holy scriptures during the Hebrew dispensation. The Japhetic race has had the task committed to them of translating, publishing and promulgating broadcast the same holy scriptures ... But neither the one nor the other of those two races have entered into or carried the spirit of those scriptures. This crowning work of the will of God is reserved for the millennial phase of Christianity, when Ethiopia shall stretch out her hands directly unto God.

According to Holly, the 'Hamitic race' was destined to assume practical leadership in the next phase of the divine scheme.[21]

Nevertheless, the idea of black racial mission not only led to a sense of racial superiority: in the case of Alexander Crummell it also became entangled with a theological case for the ethnic cleansing of inferior, morally flawed peoples. Indeed, in Crummell's Thanksgiving address of 1877, 'The destined superiority of the Negro', he appeared to endorse racial extinction and divinely ordained genocide as a core element in 'God's disciplinary and retributive economy in races and nations', for the providential system of racial destiny and chosenness threw up losers as well as winners. On some occasions, God would chastise peoples who had lapsed into immoral or pagan declension as a means of goading them to religious renewal and moral reformation; but on others he would go much further, and abandon particularly unfavoured races and nations. Crummell spelled out the facts of history as he saw them: 'Some peoples God does not merely correct; He destroys them.' Genocide was integral to the providential patterning of human history:

The history of the world is, in one view, a history of national destructions. The wrecks of nations lie everywhere upon the shores of time. Real aboriginal life is rarely found. People after people, in rapid succession, have come into constructive being, and as rapidly gone down; lost forever from sight beneath the waves of a relentless destiny . . . On the American continent, tribe after tribe [has] passed from existence; yea, there are Bibles in Indian tongues which no living man is now able to read. Their peoples have all perished! When I am called upon to account for all this loss of national and tribal life, I say that God destroyed them. And the declaration is made on the strength of a principle attested by numerous facts in sacred and profane history; that when the sins of a people reach a state of hateful maturity, then God sends upon them sudden destruction.

Crummell evinced no sympathy for other non-white peoples caught up in the convulsions consequent upon the expansion of Europe. Awareness of the righteous workings of providence in the affairs of races and nations steeled Crummell against an ill-informed compassion:

Depravity prepares some races of men for destruction . . . Such was the condition of the American Indian at the time of the discovery of America by Columbus. The historical fact abides, that when the white man first reached the shores of this continent he met the tradition of a decaying population. The New Zealand population of our own day presents a parallel case. By a universal disregard of the social and sanitary conditions which pertain to health and longevity, their physical constitution has fallen into absolute decay; and ere long it must become extinct. Indeed, the gross paganism of these two peoples was both moral and physical stagnation; was domestic and family ruin; and has resulted in national suicide! It came to them as the effect, the direct consequence of great penal laws established by the Almighty, in which are wrapped the punishment of sin.

Crummell believed that God studied racial and national characters in the hope of identifying 'latent germs of virtues' which might be nurtured and trained in order that these favoured peoples might do the work of providence. Among such chosen peoples, Crummell counted the Greeks, Romans, Scandinavians and the Saxons. In this particular respect, Crummell mimicked – without a trace of irony or subversion – the white voices of Saxonist racialism. However, the Negroes promised to be the divinely favoured race of the future. Indeed, the black experience of slavery had, Crummell insisted, not been 'retributive', but 'preparative', a time of trial and endurance which had served as 'the grand moral training of the religious tendencies of the race'. Blacks, he foresaw, stood on the 'pathway of progress to that superiority and eminence which is our rightful heritage, and which is evidently the promise of our God!'[22]

The temptation to read the Bible in ethnological terms was exacerbated by the messianic appeal to black nationalists of the Afrocentrist ideology of Ethiopianism. The apocalyptic ideology of Ethiopianism involved a black nationalist vision of Africa redeemed – not only released from the bondage of white colonialism, but also sanctified. The destiny of the race had a profound theological significance, for the regeneration of Africa was part of God's plan for humanity. Consider the promise found in Psalms 68:31 – 'Princes shall come out of Egypt; Ethiopia shall soon stretch out her hands unto God.' This much-cited verse was the principal text of black Ethiopianist exegesis. Ethiopianism was also couched in terms of an ethnic narrative of Exodus, of how a people had been uprooted from its homeland and how it might be restored to its original patrimony. The Bible, of course, presented stories of deliverance from bondage which proved inspirational to downtrodden blacks. In particular, Ethiopianists sought in the stories of Old Testament Israel an uplifting parallel between the ancient Hebrew experience and that of African-Americans displaced by slavery. In this way, Ethiopianist ideas contributed to a kind of black Zionism, whose focus was initially on an African Zion – Ethiopia. However, with the rise of black Judaism in the twentieth century, black nationalists would also begin to dream of their restoration to an Israelite homeland.[23]

Ethiopianism found its most concrete institutional expression in Marcus Garvey's black nationalist organisation, the Universal Negro Improvement Association, which flourished in the early 1920s before Garvey's conviction for mail fraud. In addition to its Ethiopianism, the manifesto of the UNIA exemplified the tensions between universalism and ethnocentrism that bedevilled black theology. This statement of Garveyite doctrine incorporated both the adherence to an implicitly monogenist idea of human brotherhood alongside an aspiration to achieve the physical separation of the races. The primary allegiance of blacks, Garveyites believed, should be to their race, not to the United States. However, the realisation of black nationhood was to come not in a national homeland for blacks carved out of the United States, but through a racial nation-state in Africa. The ultimate goal of Garveyism was African redemption, an Exodus to the mother-continent, which was foremost a black nationalist enterprise, yet also had a deeper spiritual significance. Garvey was often described explicitly as a modern Moses. Furthermore, Garveyite organisation was affiliated to churches. Meetings of local chapters of the UNIA were scheduled to follow church services, and black religiosity provided a vital platform for the first phase of black nationalism in the United Sates. In particular, the African Orthodox Church was a Garveyite church with a close, though ambiguous, relationship with the UNIA. The UNIA itself engaged explicitly with religious issues, and its fourth convention in August 1924 witnessed an extensive discussion of the white racialisation of Christianity and the need to end this 'spiritual enslavement' by reinterpreting scripture along black vindicationist lines.[24]

Such was the power of the Exodus idea and the corresponding strength of the black identification with the plight of the Old Testament nation of Israel that Arnold Josiah Ford (1876–1935), the author of much of the UNIA hymnal and co-author of its national anthem, 'Ethiopia, Land of our fathers', encouraged Garvey to consider incorporating Judaism within the theological core of Garveyism. Ford would leave the Garveyite movement to form his own synagogue, and helped to foster – as will be seen later – a culture of Black Judaism.

Nowadays the most conspicuous form of black Ethiopianism is Rastafarianism, a strain of black religiosity which emerged in twentieth-century Jamaica. Outsiders tend to know Rastafarianism by way of some of its more distinctive features. Rastafarians smoke ganja (marijuana), to them a sacred weed which grew out of King Solomon's grave, and which confers divine inspiration upon its smokers, liberating their minds from bondage to Babylon; they wear their hair in dreadlocks, which symbolise the mane of the Lion of Judah; and they are associated with reggae music. However, less well known are the racial elements in Rastafarian religion. Rastafarianism identifies all black people as the true children of Israel, and they regard the Bible as the history of the black African race, a history which has been appropriated and perverted by Europeans in order to deceive and oppress black people. While it had deeper roots in Garveyism and the African-inspired myalist (a type of witchcraft) rituals of nineteenth-century Jamaica's Native Baptist movement, the critical moment in the emergence of Rastafarianism came in 1930 with the coronation of Haile Selassie (1892–1975) – Ras (Prince) Tafari – as emperor of Ethiopia.

Haile Selassie's titles included 'The Lion of Judah', and he claimed to be 225th in the long line of Ethiopian kings which ran from the biblical union of the Queen of Sheba and King Solomon. Independently, various figures, including Leonard Percival Howell, Joseph Nathaniel Hibbert and Henry Archibald Dunkley, founded Rastafarian groups in Jamaica which promoted Ethiopianism and worship of Haile Selassie as the new Messiah, a black Christ. According to Rastafarian doctrine, Africans were held in bondage in 'Babylon' – a term for the evil white powers of oppression which included not only the British Empire, but also the Italians who had invaded the holy land of Ethiopia, an event which Rastafarians believed to have been foretold in the Book of Revelation. Against the misery of exile in the Babylonish world, Rastafarians held out the promise of an Ethiopian Zion. When Haile Selassie visited Jamaica in 1966, an emotional crowd of around 100,000 people congregated to welcome the living black God.[25]

During the second half of the twentieth century, black theology entered the mainstream of American religious discourse, albeit as a dissident voice, but one which resonated with liberal tendencies in white churches and divinity schools, and bore a marked affinity with other emerging streams of liberation theology.

The most uncompromising spokesman on behalf of a theology of negritude was Bishop Albert Cleage Jnr of Detroit, Michigan. Cleage established the Central United Church of Christ in 1953 as a black nationalist place of worship, and in 1968 he published his manifesto *The black Messiah*, which was translated into fourteen languages. Here Cleage insisted that Jesus was black and the leader of a revolutionary movement against white Roman oppression. What was the ethnological composition of the biblical nation of Israel? Cleage claimed that Israel had been 'a mixed blood, non-white nation'. More precisely, the 'Nation Israel' had been composed of 'a mixture of Chaldeans, Egyptians, Midianites, Ethiopians, Kushites, Babylonians and other dark peoples, all of whom were already mixed with the black people of Central Africa'. Cleage explained the confusion whereby 'the Jews you see in America today are white'. He identified 'most of them' as 'the descendants of white Europeans and Asiatics who were converted to Judaism about one thousand years ago'. On the other hand, those Jews who had 'stayed in that part of the world where black people are predominant, remained black'. Cleage identified Jesus as a zealot, a black leader of an underground movement which preached a message of rebellion against the white Roman Empire and racial separatism. Nor had Jesus come to proclaim a gospel of universal love. According to Cleage, Jesus' purpose was somewhat different and more secular: 'Jesus was trying to rebuild the Black Nation Israel and to free it from Rome, the white oppressor.' However, Paul and later the theologians of a white European Christendom had corrupted the original anti-white message bequeathed by the black Jesus.[26]

Black Jesus, black God? If God created man in his own image, Cleage speculated, then what must God look like? God must partake, he reasoned, of all the various racial hues found in the world: 'God must be a combination of this black, red, yellow and white. In no other way could God have created man in his own image.' By the logic of the American one-drop rule, reasoned Cleage subversively, God was black:

So if we think of God as a person (and we are taught in the Christian religion to think of God as a person, as a personality capable of love, capable of concern, capable of purpose and of action) then God must be a combination of black, yellow and red with just a little touch of white, and we must think of God as a black God. So all those prayers you've been sending up to a white God have been wasted. In America, one drop of black makes you black. So by American law, God is black, and by any practical interpretation, why would God have made seven-eighths of the world non-white and yet he himself be white? That is not reasonable. If God were white, he'd have made everybody white. And if he decided to send his son to earth, he would have sent a white son down to some nice white people. He certainly would not have sent him down to a black people like Israel.

In time Cleage became even more committed to the Black Christ and the cause of black nationalist religion. In 1970 he re-named his church the Shrine of the Black Madonna and assumed a Swahili name Jaramogi Abebe Agyeman.[27]

The leading mainstream proponent of black liberation theology in the United States has been James H. Cone of the Union Theological Seminary in New York. Cone first came to prominence with his explosive book *Black theology and black power* (1969). Cone pronounced a racialised gospel: blacks are a 'beautiful people' and 'a manifestation of god's presence on earth'. However, Cone stops just short of a literal reading of a black Jesus. Nevertheless, in his early, black power phase, he articulated an ethnocentric version of Christianity, whose rhetorical excesses, if not the subtleties in the theology, bear affinity with the extremes of black nationalism:

The assumption that one can know God without knowing blackness is the basic heresy of the white churches. They want God without blackness, Christ without obedience, love without death. What they fail to realize is that in America, God's revelation on earth has always been black, red, or some other shocking shade, but never white. Whiteness, as revealed in the history of America, is the expression of what is wrong with man. It is a symbol of man's depravity. God cannot be white, even though white churches have portrayed him as white. When we look at what whiteness has done to the minds of men in this country, we can see clearly what the New Testament meant when it spoke of the principalities and powers. To speak of Satan and his powers becomes not just a way of speaking but a fact of reality. When we can see a people who are being controlled by an ideology of whiteness, then we know what reconciliation must mean. The coming of Christ means a denial of what we thought we were. It means denying the white devil in us.

The degenerationist biblical anthropology of the Fall, in this view, appears to coincide with the anthropology of race.[28]

In *A black theology of liberation* (1970), Cone claimed that Christianity was at bottom a religion of liberation. Theology, by extension, he defined as 'a rational study of the being of God in the world in light of the existential situation of an oppressed community, relating the forces of liberation to the essence of the gospel, which is Jesus Christ'. Theology, Cone believed, could only be authentically Christian if it were directed towards the relief of oppression. In the twentieth-century United States, this meant an identification with the sufferings of the black population. White Christians needed to learn – literally – to 'hate' their whiteness, to acknowledge the failure of white-inflected churchmanship to 'relate the gospel of Jesus to the pain of being black in a white society' and, thus, to aspire to a 'black' witness in their Christianity. 'In order to be Christian theology', argued Cone, 'white theology must cease being white theology and become black theology by denying whiteness as an acceptable form of human existence and affirming blackness as God's intention for humanity.' Cone explicitly denied that God was 'color-blind'. Cone had no truck with sentimental racial neutrality: 'in a racist society, God is never color-blind. To say God is color-blind is analogous to saying that God is blind to justice and injustice, to right and wrong, to good and evil.' Although Cone does not quite endorse Cleage's literal interpretation of Christ's racial blackness, nevertheless in his theology of liberation Cone reveals Christ as symbolically and theologically black, the historical Jesus as ethnically non-white. Christ's 'blackness', according to Cone, 'clarifies the definition of him as the Incarnate One. In him God becomes oppressed humanity.' Symbolically, the oppressed Christ represents an adversarial religion, which, if interpreted correctly, should in the present stand as a rebuke to the values of the dominant white culture of the United States in the twentieth century. Yet Cone is careful not to align himself too obviously with a crude racial literalism which is oblivious of the theological significance of Christ's incarnation as 'the oppressed one':

It seems to me that the literal color of Jesus is irrelevant, as are the different shades of blackness in America. Generally speaking, blacks are not oppressed on the basis of the depths of their blackness. Light blacks are oppressed just as much as dark blacks. But as it happens, Jesus was not white in any sense of the word, literally or theologically. Therefore, Albert Cleage is not too far wrong when he describes Jesus as a black Jew; and he is certainly on solid theological grounds when he describes Christ as the Black Messiah.

Thus, while Cone considers Jesus to have been black by the one-drop rule, he implies that ethnological speculation of this sort misses the greater and deeper truth of Christ's incarnation as one of the oppressed.[29]

Cone was outspoken in his condemnation of white theology, which was not so much a system unfortunately riddled with error as an evil and explicit rejection of the true Christianity of racial liberation. Not only did white theology involve a distortion of Christ's true message of liberation, but its refusal to unmask 'the satanic nature of racism' implicates it in its diabolic project. 'American white theology', Cone proclaimed, was 'a theology of the Antichrist insofar as it arises from an identification with the white community, thereby placing God's approval on white oppression of black existence'.[30]

Nevertheless, Cone does appear to have moderated his earlier position. In *God of the oppressed* (1975), Cone continues his argument that black theology must arise out of black experience and must reflect upon the black racial experience of oppression. However, in this work he insists that a true black theology must not be limited by race. Indeed, Cone criticised those strains of black theology which do no more than furnish black politics with a form of divine legitimation. Keenly aware of Feuerbach's powerful nineteenth-century critique of religion as mere human projection, Cone recognises that an authentic black theology must transcend the subjectivity of its immediate social context. Otherwise black theology is, like white theology, little more than a smokescreen for the promotion of racial interests. Cone has argued that 'the authenticity of black theological discourse is dependent upon its pointing to the divine One whose presence is not restricted to any historical manifestation'. Black theologians must distinguish between mankind's flawed human understanding of God and God's own word as found in the scriptures.[31]

Despite its central focus on questions of race, black theology has been far from monolithic. Indeed, a dissident figure emerged within the realm of black theology, who challenged the central failings he detected within the canonical arguments of Cleage and Cone. William Jones maintained that Cleage and Cone had failed to make theodicy – the branch of theology that reconciles the suffering of humankind with the ultimate goodness of God – the crucial point of departure for their systems of black theology. Just as a Jew might wonder, in the aftermath of the Holocaust, not only whether the Jews were indeed God's chosen people, but whether God himself might be an anti-Semite, so blacks, faced with the enormous and disproportionate sufferings of the black race in early modern and modern history (not least relative to 'white non-suffering'), might legitimately ask the question: 'Is God a white racist?' As a result, the issue of theodicy – a racial theodicy – needed to be at the heart of black theology. Otherwise, how could one construct a viable and coherent system of theology while troubled by – at the very least – a niggling suspicion that the deity was a racist? Black theology, Jones perceived, needed to be much more than simply a theological counter-measure deployed against traditional 'white theology', a hitherto unrecognised theology of racism and oppression. Such an approach, oblivious of the dangers of an unresolved racial theodicy, was potentially riddled with major contradictions. An authentic and coherent black theology needed to wrestle at the outset with the explosive issue of 'divine racism'. Could blacks be sure that God was not a white supremacist? Could blacks be sure that God favoured the liberation of blacks? Was it possible to construct a viable and robust black liberation theology, asked Jones, 'without a foundational theodicy which refutes the charge of divine racism?'[32]

A black racial consciousness has also become apparent in divinity schools. Its leaders, foremost among whom is Cain Hope Felder, are highly critical of the dominant 'Eurocentric' tradition of 'biblical exegesis'. Accepted definitions of 'normative hermeneutics', Felder notes, encapsulate 'white, male Eurocentric' notions of method and subject. Instead, the new school of African-American biblical scholarship reminds white scholars that the ancient Near East contained a mixture of ethnicities and skin colours, which constitute legitimate matter of academic enquiry. Tellingly, Felder claims that there has existed a major unacknowledged gulf between racial attitudes in the biblical world and modern 'Eurocentric' interpretations of the biblical past, which were suffused with racialist assumptions. Negative attitudes to blacks were not to be found in the Bible; however, they were abundant in 'postbiblical' interpretation. Felder wishes to highlight the 'contrast between the biblical world before color prejudice and our postbiblical Western history of translation and interpretation that have marginalized blacks in antiquity while sacralizing other groups'. 'We must remind our people', urges Felder, 'that there is a glorious and rich history of people of color in antiquity; and there has been a carefully orchestrated effort in Western historiography to hide this fact.' Christ's supposed whiteness provides a highly significant case in point. Felder argues that 'many Palestinian Jews of Jesus' time could be easily classified as Afro-Asiatic, despite the fact that European artists and American mass media have routinely depicted such persons as Anglo-Saxons'. Of course, divinity schools do not tend to be scenes of racist conspiracy; however, the less strident claim that biblical studies – like other areas of scholarship – have since the nineteenth century been inflected by racialist assumptions has considerable plausibility.[33]

Black Judaism and black Islam also emerged from the rich sectarian creativity of American Protestant culture, their respective claims to Judaic and Islamic identities notwithstanding. Moreover, these new hybrids also drew upon and inverted the prevailing racialist outlook in contemporary white culture. Black Judaism and black Islam consciously positioned themselves outside the fold of the white man's Christian religion. If Christianity were white, they concluded, then logically black religion had to be non-Christian. Nevertheless, some of the black Jews remained ambivalent on the subject of Jesus, regarded by some as a black Jew, and often integrated elements of Christianity within their supposed Judaism.

Identification with Judaism – founded upon Ethiopianist parallels between the plight of displaced African-American blacks and the exiled Jews of the Old Testament – reinforced the ethnic and nationalist dimensions of black religiosity. The implicit message of black Judaism in its various forms was that blacks were a special chosen people, who – as Jews – deserved to return to their homeland. As well as drawing upon and modifying Ethiopianism, black Judaism also mimics the white racialist exegesis of British Israelite literature. Just as British Israelites connected a white Anglo-Saxon present to a sacred Hebrew lineage and, by the same token, exposed the purportedly fraudulent claims of modern Jews to be the lineal descendants of Old Testament Hebrews, so black Jews sacralise their ethnic identity by invoking an ancient black Hebraic lineage, while also questioning the validity of supposed Jewish pretensions to descent from the black nation whose history is recounted in the Old Testament.

The origins of black Judaism appear to reside partly in the vindicationist tradition of identifying biblical characters as black. In addition, ethnographic work during the late nineteenth and early twentieth centuries among the Falashas of Ethiopia lent credible anthropological support to the case for black Judaism. The visit of Joseph Halevy to the Falashas in 1867 was followed in 1904 by the investigations of Jacques Faitlovitch, who aimed to reconnect the Falashas with the mainstreams of Judaism. Faitlovitch's researches inspired fascination among American blacks with the black Jews of Ethiopia, and the ex-Garveyite Arnold Ford, who met Faitlovitch in 1929, would travel to Ethiopia in Faitlovitch's footsteps in 1930.

Black Judaism has taken a number of forms, some of them syncretic and more nearly Christian than Jewish. One of the earliest forerunners of black Judaism was the movement inaugurated in the late nineteenth century by William Christian, the founder of the Church of the Living God. Christian, a Baptist, reinterpreted the Bible in black terms, contending that Abraham, David, Job and Jeremiah, as well as Christ himself, were all black. By 1985 Christian's organisation had 42,000 members and was more distinctively Pentecostalist than Judaic. More properly Judaic – despite its overtly Christian title – was an organisation known as the Church of God and Saints of Christ, founded in Kansas in 1896 by Prophet William S. Crowdy (1847–1908), another Baptist, who had served in the Union Army during the American Civil War. The Church of God and Saints of Christ grew initially in Kansas and surrounding states, where it quickly acquired twenty-nine congregations. Later, its centre of gravity shifted to the East Coast, with bases in Belleville, Virginia, and Washington, DC. According to Crowdy, blacks were Jews. In a direct inversion of white Saxonist Israelism, Crowdy claimed that blacks were the Ten Lost Tribes of Israel. All Jews had been black originally. There was, however, more to Crowdy's religion than a mere system of racial exegesis: he also effected a synthesis of Jewish and Christian ritual. Crowdy's church of black Jews adopted rites drawn from both the Old and New Testaments. At communion no wine was used, only water and unleavened bread. The Passover was observed and so was the Jewish calendar. Circumcision was also practised. Nevertheless, the black Jews of Belleville also participated in foot washing, after Christ's example, and baptism.[34]

The Church of God (also known as the Black Jews) was the Philadelphia creation of Prophet Frank S. Cherry (d. 1965). Cherry claimed that black people had been the original inhabitants of earth. Black people were, moreover, the Israelites of the Bible descended from Jacob, who had been black. The black Jews of the Church of God conjured up a sacred history of race which reversed the equation of blackness and punishment associated with the narratives of Cain and Ham. Instead, they traced the inferior white colouring of European-Americans to another biblical figure, Gehazi, who was cursed for his sin in II Kings 5:27 – 'The leprosy therefore of Naaman shall cleave unto thee, and unto thy seed for ever. And he [Gehazi] went out from his [Elisha's] presence a leper as white as snow.' The story of Gehazi underpinned claims that white inferiority was a divinely ordained condition. Moreover, the tale of Gehazi also provided a convenient explanation of the ethnic origins of white Jews. Despite his purported 'Judaic' affiliations, Cherry expressed contempt for white Jews who reject Jesus (who had also been black). Within this syncretic faith, the Bible and Talmud were both used and Christian hymns were sung, but Christmas and Easter were not celebrated. Passover was celebrated as a substitute for communion.[35]

The Commandment Keepers Congregation of the Living God, or the Black Jews of Harlem, founded their distinctive ethnoreligious identity upon claims to be Ethiopian Hebrews or Falashas. They recognise Judaism as the one true religion, and are strictly kosher; however, their idea of Judaism is a racialised one. The inspirational leader of the Commandment Keepers was Rabbi Wentworth Matthew (1892–1973), who drew heavily upon West Indian support. The movement involved the fusion in 1930 of two post-Garveyite organisations, Matthew's congregation of Commandment Keepers with his friend Arnold Ford's synagogue of Beth B'nai Abraham, which Ford had set up in 1924. Matthew, who had been born in Lagos and moved to New York via St Kitts, had been a Pentecostalist minister with the quasi-Judaic Church of the Living God, but had founded his own church, the Commandment Keepers, in 1919 and had moved thereafter in a steadily Judaising direction under the influence of his friend Ford. It was the departure of Ford to Ethiopia in 1930 to study the Falashas at first hand that prompted the merger of Ford's synagogue with Matthew's Commandment Keepers, and ensured the further Judaising of the latter. In 1935 Matthew announced that his followers were in fact Falashas, whose Falasha identity had been suppressed during centuries of slavery. Blacks, the Commandment Keepers claim, are descendants of the marriage of King Solomon with the Queen of Sheba. Matthew asserted that blacks were the real Jews, being Falashas, that the patriarchs of the Old Testament had been black and that Christianity was a white man's religion, not that it stopped him retaining elements of early – and presumably, therefore, more authentically black – Christianity, including foot washing, in the rituals of the Commandment Keepers. Nevertheless, Rabbi Matthew maintained some links with white Jews, on the grounds that they did not reject out of hand the Commandment Keepers' claim to be Falashas.[36]

The Original Hebrew Israelite Nation emerged in mid-1960s Chicago where Ben Ammi Carter and Shaeah Ben-Yehuda organised the A-Beta Hebrew Center. In 1967 the Nation attempted to move back to its purported homeland in Israel, but its returnees were instead diverted to Liberia. However, in 1969 the Israeli authorities relented and the Nation was admitted. By 1980 there were around 1,500 members of the Nation in Israel. However, the Nation, which continues to operate in the United States as well as in Israel, constitutes an unwelcome guest in the Israeli homeland. Not only has the Nation instituted polygamy in Israel, but its beliefs that blacks are the true Hebrews, that Jews have usurped an authentically black Hebraic identity and that the land of Palestine is the true homeland of the black Hebrew nation are somewhat unsettling for its reluctant hosts.[37]

Black Islam also has a rich heritage which predates the formation of Nation of Islam. Indeed, Wilson Jeremiah Moses notes that the Moorish Science Temple and Nation of Islam appear to be the heirs of a nineteenth-century tradition of biblical interpretation which identified blacks with an Asiatic provenance. Noble Drew Ali (né Timothy Drew, 1886–1929) founded the Moorish Temple of America in Newark, New Jersey, in 1915 after a purported trip to the King of Morocco. Ali taught black Americans that they were Moors, descendants ultimately of the scriptural Moabites of Canaan. In addition, Ali announced that, while Christianity was the religion of the white man, Islam was the creed appropriate to the Moorish race. However, despite his racial aversion to Christianity, Ali formulated his Moorish doctrine eclectically, not only out of shards of authentic Quranic wisdom, but also from the Christian scriptures and from the esoteric mysteries of eastern philosophy. Ali's movement had collapsed by around 1930 but its values were perpetuated in the mission of Wallace Fard (b. 1877–93?–d. after 1934) who created the Lost-Found Nation of Islam. Fard presented himself as a prophet from Arabia who had come to direct black Americans to their ancestral religious fold within Islam. Fard suggested the adoption of the surname X in repudiation of the European surnames commonly held by blacks, which were not only spuriously related to a genuine African family history but also served as reminders of a slave heritage. Fard disappeared mysteriously in 1934 and the leadership of his movement, Nation of Islam, was assumed by Elijah Muhammad, formerly Elijah Poole (d. 1975). Under Elijah Muhammad, the movement grew, possibly achieving 50,000 adherents by about 1960. During the 1960s, the admission of the celebrated boxer Cassius Clay (Muhammad Ali) to the ranks of Nation of Islam significantly boosted its profile among blacks – and fearful whites.[38]

Nation of Islam – the principal begetter of whose doctrine was Wallace Fard – proclaimed Islamic credentials, but used a vague and distantly apprehended *idea* of Islam largely to confer historic legitimacy on a full-frontal critique of Christianity as the white man's religion. Indeed, the theological distinctiveness of Nation of Islam resided not in its Islamic pretensions, but in a religious anthropology more analogous to other manifestations of the creative 'Protestant' fringe of American culture, such as Mormonism. On closer inspection, the syncretic elements of Nation of Islam theology are apparent. The religion constitutes a bizarre synthesis of black nationalism, anti-Catholicism and fantastic pseudo-scientific lore derived from an early twentieth-century fascination with science fiction and the possibilities of flying saucers and extraterrestrial life, as well as some biblical and Quranic elements.[39]

Nation of Islam was founded as a religion of racial destiny. Indeed, racialism was interwoven with the very creation of the universe, for the original self-created man of the universe – Allah or God – was black and had created other people in his image. Thus earth had at first been peopled with blacks, the original race. However, the black people – divided into thirteen tribes but sharing a common nationhood based on skin colour, Islamic religion and righteousness – had not been found in Africa, but in Asia. Indeed, the Nation's religious anthropology insisted upon the Asiatic identity of the black race and went further in purveying a strain of anti-African prejudice. Whites were responsible for identifying blacks as Africans when they were properly Asiatics, in order to undermine the genuine links between blacks and the high civilisations of Egypt and the Near East. In the Nation's sacred history, Asiatic blacks had only colonised Africa in a much later period. One tribe had been exterminated, but the twelve tribes – an obvious borrowing from the twelve tribes of Israel – had lived in peace and harmony. The leading tribe was the tribe of Shabazz (pronounced Sha-boz), a people of black skin and straight hair who had settled the Nile valley and established Egyptian civilisation. A golden age persisted until the appearance of the evil scientist Yacub, whose role in the Nation's theology was akin to that of the serpent in Genesis or of Lucifer in Christian and Islamic scriptures.[40]

Yacub was the begetter of the 'tricknology' which was to ruin the idyllic life of the original black people. In the course of his scientific work, the evil Yacub managed to differentiate the black and brown germs which formed the essence of the black race, and was able to separate out the distinctive black germ until he had the material with which to create a different race. This element in the Nation's theology, at least in so far as it was propagated by Elijah Muhammad's leading lieutenant, Malcolm X, drew upon a crude rendering of Mendelian genetics and the assumption that there existed distinct racial chromosomes. On the island of Pelan, Yacub and after him his followers had carried out racial experiments to cleanse the black stock of remaining traces of blackness. Eventually, over generations the white man was created artificially through scientific experiment and selective breeding on the enclosed island community. The world now contained both an aboriginal black race and a scientifically engineered race of 'white devils' who were programmed for evil and tyranny. The primary characteristic of the white devils was their penchant for tricknology. Born out of trickery and deceit, these moral flaws were the central ingredients of the white man's racial character. Tricknology was a system of deceit which underpinned the white man's oppression of the black. It underscored the Nation's depiction of history as a tale of stark moral contrasts between a righteous aboriginal black race and a subhuman and artificial race of white devils. Tricknology was behind the apparent superiority of the white man.[41]

Eventually Allah had sent a mulatto prophet Musa (Moses) to try to uplift the degraded white people of Europe. Later, another prophet, the black man Jesus – who had been human, not divine – had preached authentic Islam to the benighted whites. However, the whites – who included the Jews – had failed to appreciate the righteous message of Jesus and had had him murdered. Moreover, the conspirators had then deified Christ as a means of diverting attention from Christ's Islamic message, including knowledge of the one black God, Allah. Christianity was not the religion of the dead prophet Jesus, but a deceptive form of priestcraft: Christians were really cheated into worshipping the pope in lieu of Christ, a resounding echo of the traditional Protestant definition of the Antichrist. Indeed, in the eyes of the Nation, the papacy constituted the citadel of white pseudo-Christian tricknology.[42]

Thereafter, sacred history was a history of tricknology, oppression and degradation, encompassing the rise of white Europe – which had purloined the achievements and technologies of Islamic civilisation – the discovery of America, the enslavement of blacks and their transportation to the New World, and the moral degradation of the black race in modern America. Ethically blacks had lapsed, assimilating to the values of the dominant white devils of America and forgetting the moral truths and prohibitions of Islam. The twentieth century was to be a time of ethnic and religious renewal and rediscovery under the guidance of a new prophet. The tribe of Shabazz in the United States would relearn its Islamic religion and regain its original Arabic names. This reformation needed to be accomplished with reasonable haste, for Nation also subscribed to a prophecy that the Last Days were imminent. Only then would blacks be in a position – identified and shepherded to safe havens – to survive the divine judgement which would be visited on the modern white United States and its allies by means of an armed space ship known as the Mother Plane. On the destruction of the old white-dominated world system, the Black Nation would then be in a position to rebuild civilisation on a righteous Islamic blueprint.[43]

Some black Muslims, such as Malcolm X, found in Nation of Islam a bridge towards a genuine understanding of Islam proper. Malcolm X was the son of a Baptist minister, the Reverend Earl Little, who had organised on behalf of Garvey's UNIA. Within Nation of Islam, Malcolm came to reject the Christianity in which he had grown up. Nothing, he contended, had done more to advance the deceitful oppressions of tricknology than Christianity, 'the white man's religion'. According to Malcolm X, 'The holy Bible in the white man's hands and his interpretations of it have been the greatest single ideological weapon for enslaving millions of non-white human beings.' Indeed, the central deceit propounded by Christians was its narcotic quietism, the belief that the remedy of the world's ills lay in a future afterlife. Heaven was a tool of white tricknology to dull the anger of oppressed blacks. Malcolm X denounced the lie that Christ was a blond, blue-eyed white man. Furthermore, he claimed that he had never met any 'intelligent white man who would try to insist that Jesus was white'. The primary objective, as Malcolm X saw it, of Nation of Islam was to undo the brainwashing accomplished by 'our white slave-master's Christian religion'.[44]

Although Nation of Islam presented itself as a special religion for the black man, an antithesis of white Christian oppression, Malcolm X came to recognise the un-Islamic provenance of Nation's theology and rites. Indeed, Malcolm X's exposure to Islam proper, 'true Islam' as he called it, during his pilgrimage – or hajj – to Mecca in 1964 led to a major reorientation of his theology of race. The experience of brotherhood with Muslims of all shades of complexion, including 'fellow Muslims, whose eyes were the bluest of blue, whose hair was the blondest of blond, and whose skin was the whitest of white', convinced Malcolm X that there was a serious flaw in Nation of Islam's outright, unqualified demonisation of the white man. Moreover, Malcolm had also been told that the racial lineage of the descendants of the prophet Muhammad had included both blacks and whites. True Islam – unlike the spurious Nation of Islam, so Malcolm X believed – was a religion of universal brotherhood, embracing all races and colours, one of whose chief characteristics was 'color-blindness'. Orthodox Islam provided the United States with its best chance to tackle its racial problems. White Muslims, according to Malcolm, had through their religion of universal brotherhood erased white racial arrogance from their mental attitudes and behaviour. At the time of his assassination in 1965, Malcolm X, who had also changed his name to the more authentically Islamic seeming El-Hajj Malik El-Shabazz, had come to reject the unreservedly anti-white theology of Nation of Islam, but retained its critique of Christianity as the religion of the white man.[45]

Black Islam, like black Judaism, is – ultimately – an extreme manifestation of black Protestant Christianity, a form of religiosity with no apparent moorings in any real Islamic or Judaic tradition, yet which sought in non-European monotheism an authentic alternative to white-inflected American Protestantism. Black Hebrews and black Muslims ventured further than those black Christians who founded black denominations within the fold of Christianity. In all three types of response – black Christian denominationalism, black Judaism and black Islam – the primary motivation, quite understandably, given centuries of racial oppression, was a desire to create a form of black religiosity free of white racist contamination.

CHAPTER 9

Conclusion

When I embarked on this project several years ago, I had a suspicion – perhaps verging on a crude hypothesis – that the dethroning of biblical authority was a necessary prelude to the emergence of modern racism. Doctrinal racialism, it appeared, had not flourished in the early modern world, that era's terrible experience of race slavery notwithstanding, because, in large part, the message of the Christian scriptures constrained the development of polygenist ideas of multiple human origins.[1] The onset of a distinctive ideology of innate racial differences seemed – at least superficially – to be connected to the Enlightenment critique of the historical and scientific validity of the Old Testament and the wider development of a culture of secularism. Full-blown racialism, I conjectured, was a secularised doctrine, untrammelled by the monogenist anthropology clearly articulated (or so it seemed) in Genesis, and reiterated in the message of universal brotherly love found in the New Testament, and underpinned by the explicit statement of universal kinship found in Acts 17:26.

In the course of my researches I came to realise that, while the logic behind my initial course of reasoning was not unsound, the historical record – even in the field of ideology – is replete with unpredictable and apparently illogical developments. The human imagination is equally capable of interpreting the Christian scriptures in a racialist as in an anti-racialist manner. It often depends less, it seems, on the logic of the scriptures than on the objectives of the interpreter, or indeed on the logic of the system developed conjointly out of the scriptures and their theological accompaniment. Nor, of course, does secularisation inevitably lead to racism, not that I ever suspected this: rather, I suspected that liberation from the scriptures opens the *possibility* – no more than that – of a less constrained doctrine of racial difference grounded on a theory of polygenesis. As it transpires, polygenist theories of plural creations of races and theories of the pre-Adamic creations of other races did find their way into otherwise traditional readings of the scriptures. Genesis, it turned out, yielded both polygenist and monogenist lessons in anthropology.

Other commentators have shared my initial sense of a deep underlying connection between a de-Christianised outlook and doctrinal racism. In a section of the modern American *Interpreter's Bible* devoted to 'Race prejudice', the Bible's 'ultimate message' is declared to be 'the universal purpose of God which destroys race pride and passion'. This is confidently contrasted with the Hitlerian 'paganism of race and blood and soil'.[2] However, as we have seen in the course of this book, it is not clear that so sharp a divergence can be drawn between benign biblical and sinister secular–pagan influences on the race question. Racists, it seems, will reach for any tool, including the Bible, to justify racial segregation or subordination. By the same token, certain passages of the Bible have provided not only reassurance but also inspiration for racists. Clearly, the Bible has, after all, established a solid ideological platform for the construction of certain racist beliefs and practices.

This book does not, therefore, advance any grand overarching thesis about the relationship of race and theology. As we have seen, the Christian pre-Adamites of the late nineteenth century were no less racialist at bottom than Enlightenment critics of monogenesis. There is, it transpires, no simple or reductive way of categorising a person's racialist sentiments on the basis of his or her doctrinal preferences. Nevertheless, doctrinal preference *was* a crucial determinant of racial attitudes, albeit not in any simple or straightforward way. Traditions of scriptural interpretation, varied as these were on matters of ethnological origins and relationships, played an enormous role in constructing and shaping the discourse of race in the early modern and modern eras.

On the other hand, the nineteenth and early twentieth centuries witnessed a countervailing force – the impact on religion of a powerful race concept. In this period, intelligentsias – Christian as well as secular – began to view race as a hitherto neglected panacea to problems in the human sciences. As a result, religions themselves came to be seen as epiphenomena of deeper racial characteristics, which in turn generated long-term anti-racialist reactions within western Christianity. The second half of the twentieth century has seen the abandonment of the racialised worldview of the nineteenth century. Within the mainstream churches, theology acts as a highly visible constraint upon racist temptations. Of course, within modern liberal Christianity the issues of sacred ethnology which once exercised nineteenth-century theologians have become intellectually redundant. In particular, liberal theologians read many of the historical passages of scripture which appear to treat of ethnological questions not in a literal manner, but symbolically. As a result of such non-literalist readings, the ethnological implications which would logically ensue from a literal rendering of scripture are dissipated.

Nevertheless, most of the mainstream liberal churches have taken an uncompromising stand in campaigns against racism, notably against the South African system of apartheid. Indeed, mainstream clerics have enthusiastically promoted the ethical message of Acts 17:26. Despite the declining ethnological significance of the Bible in twentieth-century culture, it would be a mistake to neglect the theological roots of anti-racism. Certainly, anti-racism draws upon a variety of secular and naturalistic arguments, including the scientific insights of biology and anthropology as well as sociological arguments for multiculturalism. Nevertheless, the churches have also contributed enormously to the twentieth-century liberal critique of racism.

Anti-racism is a hybridised ideology which draws significantly on both scriptural and naturalistic positions. The latter tendency is enshrined not only in the orthodoxies of modern anthropology, which took a significant cultural turn under the influence of Franz Boas, but has also received the imprimatur of UNESCO. Between 1950 and 1967, four committees of leading scientists, including anthropologists and biologists, produced Statements on Race under the auspices of UNESCO. The first UNESCO Statement on Race, issued in Paris in July 1950, exiled notions of racial polygenesis beyond the bounds of recognised science:

Scientists have reached general agreement in recognizing that mankind is one: that all men belong to the same species, Homo sapiens. It is further generally agreed among scientists that all men are probably derived from the same common stock; and that such differences as exist between different groups of mankind are due to the operation of evolutionary factors of differentiation, such as isolation, the drift and random fixation of the material particles which control heredity (the genes), changes in the structure of these particles, hybridization, and natural selection.

Genetically, the likenesses within the family of mankind were much more striking and of much greater significance than any minor differences. Moreover, genetic variability was not the result of any 'fundamental difference' between groups. Indeed, the term 'race' was itself scientifically misleading, and the expression 'ethnic groups' was one with which scientists were more comfortable. Race had become a problematic term, threatened with proscription from the vocabulary and agenda of mainstream science. The second Statement, of 1951, reiterated the main thrust of the 1950 statement, while clarifying a few particular points. It stressed, for instance, that there was 'no evidence for the existence of so-called "pure" races'. The fourth UNESCO Statement of 1967 dealt both with the cultural problem of racism as well as the biological problem of race, and clearly established the pseudo-scientific basis of racial pre- judice: 'Racism falsely claims that there is a scientific basis for arranging groups hierarchically in terms of psychological and cultural characteristics that are immutable and innate.' Biology did not justify racism.[3]

Late twentieth-century theologians endorsed the judgements of their peers in the sciences. At the fourth assembly of the World Council of Churches held in Uppsala in 1968, there emerged a clear definition of the theological offence of racism:

Racism is a blatant denial of the Christian faith. (1) It denies the effectiveness of the reconciling work of Jesus Christ, through whose love all human diversities lose their divisive significance; (2) it denies our common humanity in creation and our belief that all men are made in God's image; (3) it falsely asserts that we find our significance in terms of racial identity rather than in Jesus Christ.

The fifth assembly, held in Nairobi in 1975, contrasted the unequivocal anti-racism of the 'biblical message' with the 'demonic character' of racism. The assembly denounced racism as a sin against God. Racism had also become a heresy. Apartheid drew particularly fierce denunciations from the World Council of Churches. In its Vancouver assembly of 1983 it issued a denunciation of 'any theological justification of apartheid as a heretical perversion of the gospel'. Now, any strain of theology that even presumed to 'condone' apartheid was deemed to be a heresy. Indeed, in 1982 at the World Alliance of Reformed Churches conference in Ottawa, the Dutch Reformed Church was suspended from membership of that body.[4]

The international campaign against the South African system of apartheid foregrounded the theological critique of racism championed by Desmond Tutu, the Anglican archbishop of Cape Town. Tutu stressed that he rejected apartheid on the basis of a respectable Christian tradition that predated the bogeys – in the eyes of mainstream white South Africa – of both Marxism and the African National Congress. On the other hand, Tutu reminded white South Africa that, however subversive his message, his ideological pedigree was impeccable. 'Whites brought us the Bible', he declared, 'and we are taking it seriously.' Tutu placed critical importance on Genesis 1:26 which made clear that human personhood was created in the image of God. Moreover, where apartheid taught the lesson of 'the fundamental irreconcilability of people because they belong to different races', the Bible, Tutu reminded South Africans, instructs us 'quite unequivocally that people are created for fellowship, for togetherness, not for alienation, apartness, enmity and division'. The crux of this matter resided in Genesis II. Tutu recognised the need to address the Dutch Reformed Church's separatist account of the Babel narrative. God had not willed separation between peoples, insisted Tutu, despite the Dutch Reformed reading of the confounding of language and dispersal of peoples in the aftermath of Babel as divine correctives of a sinful tendency to blur human distinctions. Tutu acknowledged in that church's 'perverse exegesis' of Genesis II a superficial and misleading 'justification for racial separation, a divine sanction for the diversity of nations'. Somehow, in the topsy-turvy world of Dutch Reformed hermeneutics the 'divine punishment for sin' had been transformed into 'the divine intention for humankind'. Rather, Tutu interpreted the consequences of human arrogance in the building of the Tower of Babel as a tragic shattering of human community and communication. Tutu stressed that Christ's purpose was to effect reconciliation – not only between man and God, but also between men. Ethnic reconciliation was part of Christ's mission. In Tutu's interpretation of the New Testament, Christ 'came to restore human community and brotherhood which sin destroyed. He came to say that God had intended us for fellowship, for *koinonia*, for togetherness, without destroying our distinctiveness, our cultural otherness.' In its repudiation of this 'central verity' of the faith, apartheid was intrinsically 'unchristian and unbiblical'.[5]

Christianity has clearly played a significant role in the ideological assault upon racism. The connection between the anti-polygenist traditions of the early modern era and the modern Christian critique of racialist ideas is, though undoubtedly real, a slender one, for the older idioms of scriptural ethnology have, largely, fallen into desuetude. Issues of monogenesis, polygenesis, pre-Adamites, the curse upon Ham, the genealogies of the Noachids and the identity of the Lost Tribes of Israel, which once convulsed the theological realm, have been shunted to the margins of its discourse, to become, for the most part, the hobbyhorses of harmless Casaubons who continue the campaign of the nineteenth century to reconcile sacred history with the insights of evolutionary biology.[6]

In some areas, however, race retained an inescapable theological dimension into the second half of the twentieth century. As late as 1958, only 4 per cent of American whites approved of inter-racial marriage.[7]

Fears of miscegenation provided a compelling social backdrop for continuing discussion in the United States of the divine significance of racial differences, including the contentious issue of Noah's curse upon the Canaanite lineage of Ham.[8] More recently, American culture wars, accompanied by what appears to be an accelerating retreat from Darwinism – whether into full-blown Creationism or into Intelligent Design – tend to enhance the cultural purchase of Old Testament chronology and biblical literalism, in the heartland at least. Standard monogenist readings of sacred history have the potential, of course, to inspire inter-racial philanthropy and a sense of the close kinship of the world's peoples. However, it would be unwise to discount the malleability of Genesis. In parts of the United States, hostility towards blacks and towards Jews sustains – and is sustained by – otherwise discredited lines of biblical interpretation. Notwithstanding the united stand of most mainstream churches against the sins of racism, we should not lose sight of the disturbing fact that some of the themes of sacred ethnology continue, on the eccentric fringes of Protestantism, to provide the doctrinal fuel of militant religions of race hatred.

Notes

CHAPTER 1

1 M. O'Brien, *Conjectures of order: intellectual life and the American South, 1810–1860* (Chapel Hill, NC, and London, 2004), p. 250.

2 J. Diamond, 'Race without color', *Discover* (Nov. 1994), 83–9, at 87.

3 S. M. Garn, *Human races* (1961: 3rd edn, Springfield, IL, 1971), pp. 47–8; S. Molnar, *Human variation: races, types, and ethnic groups* (2nd edn, Englewood Cliffs, NJ, 1983), p. 125.

4 D. G. Blackburn, 'Why race is not a biological concept', in B. Lang (ed.), *Race and racism in theory and practice* (Lanham, MD, and Oxford, 2000), pp. 11–12; A. F. Corcos, *The myth of human races* (East Lansing, MI, 1997), p. 94.

5 Diamond, 'Race', 86; Garn, *Human races*, p. 40.

6 W. C. Boyd, 'Genetics and the human race', *Science* 140, no. 3571 (7 Jun. 1963), 1057–64, at 1059–60; Molnar, *Human variation*, p. 138.

7 Diamond, 'Race', 86, 89; Blackburn, 'Race', p. 14; J. Shreeve, 'Terms of estrangement', *Discover* (Nov. 1994), 57–63, at 58; Molnar, *Human variation*, pp. 1, 132–3.

8 K. Kidd, 'Races, genes and human origins: how genetically diverse are we?', in A. W. Galston and E. J. Shurr (eds.), *New dimensions in bioethics* (Boston, MA, 2001), pp. 14, 19; S. Olson, *Mapping human history* (2002: London, pbk, 2003), p. 63; Corcos, *Myth of human races*, pp. 107, 202.

9 S. Jones, *The language of the genes* (1993: rev. edn, London, 2000), p. 262; Shreeve, 'Terms', 58; Blackburn, 'Race', p. 12; M. W. Lewis and K. E. Wigen, *The myth of continents: a critique of metageography* (Berkeley, Los Angeles and London, 1997), p. 122.

10 M. de Saint-Méry, *Description topographique, physique, civile, politique et historique de la partie française de l'isle Saint-Domingue* (eds. B. Maurel and E. Taillemite, 3 vols., Paris, 1984), I, pp. 86–101.

11 François Bernier, 'Nouvelle division de la terre, par les différentes espèces ou races d'hommes qui l'habitent, envoyée par un fameux voyageur', *Journal des sçavans* (1684), no. 12, 133–40; M. Banton, *Racial theories* (1987: 2nd edn, Cambridge, 1998), pp. 20, 22; *The anthropological treatises of Johann Friedrich Blumenbach* (1865: repr. Boston, 1973), pp. 99–100, 209–11, 264–76; Oscar

Peschel, *The races of man and their geographical distribution* (London, 1876), p. 321; W. Z. Ripley, *Races of Europe* (London, 1900).

12 Garn, *Human races*, pp. 155–78; Boyd, 'Genetics'.

13 L. Cavalli-Sforza, *Genes, peoples and languages* (London, 2001), p. 30.

14 K. Prewitt, 'Racial classification in America', *Daedalus* (winter 2005), 5–17, at 6–9; K. L. Williams, 'Multiracialism and the civil rights future', *Daedalus* (winter 2005), 53–60; Corcos, *Myth of human races*, pp. 133–5; Blackburn, 'Race', p. 22.

15 M. A. Elliott, 'Telling the difference: nineteenth-century legal narratives of racial taxonomy', *Law and Social Inquiry* 24 (1999), 611–36, at 617, 619–23.

16 J. Snow, 'The civilization of white men: the race of the Hindu in *United States v. Bhagat Singh Thind*', in H. Goldschmidt and E. McAlister (eds.), *Race, nation, and religion in the Americas* (New York, 2004).

17 F. M. Snowden Jnr, *Before color prejudice: the ancient view of blacks* (1983: Cambridge, MA, and London, 1991).

18 J. E. Chaplin, *Subject matter: technology, the body and science on the Anglo-American frontier, 1500–1676* (Cambridge, MA, and London, 2001).

19 G. Marshall, 'Racial classifications: popular and scientific', in C. L. Brace and J. Metress (eds.), *Man in evolutionary perspective* (New York, 1973), p. 367; F. Dikotter, *The discourse of race in modern China* (1992: London, pbk, 1994), pp. 137–8.

20 T. W. Allen, *The invention of the white race* (2 vols., London, 1994–7); L. P. Curtis Jnr, *Apes and angels: the Irishman in Victorian caricature* (rev. edn, Washington, DC, 1997); A. Vaughan, 'From white man to redskin: changing Anglo-American perceptions of the American Indian', *American Historical Review* 87 (1982), 917–53.

21 M. F. Jacobson, *Whiteness of a different color* (Cambridge, MA, and London, 1998), pp. 2, 6–8.

22 C. Kidd, 'Teutonist ethnology and Scottish nationalist inhibition, 1780–1880', *Scottish Historical Review* 74 (1995), 45–68; C. Kidd, 'Race, empire and the limits of nineteenth-century Scottish nationhood', *Historical Journal* 46 (2003), 873–92.

23 M. Meijer, *Race and aesthetics in the anthropology of Petrus Camper (1722–1789)* (Amsterdam, 1999).

24 D. De Giustino, *Conquest of mind: phrenology and Victorian social thought* (London, 1975); R. Cooter, *The cultural meaning of popular science: phrenology and the organization of consent in nineteenth-century Britain* (Cambridge, 1984); Anders Retzius, 'On the bony frame of the head in different nations', *Edinburgh Medical and Surgical Journal* 74 (1850), 99–114; N. Stepan, *The idea of race in science: Great Britain 1800–1960* (Oxford, 1982).

25 M. Staum, *Labeling people: French scholars on society, race, and empire 1815–1848* (Montreal, 2003), p. 126; T. F. Gossett, *Race: the history of an idea in America* (1963: new edn, Oxford and New York, 1997), p. 81; J. Sawday, 'New men, strange faces, other minds: Arthur Keith, race and the Piltdown affair', in

W. Ernst and B. Harris (eds.), *Race, science and medicine* (London, 1999); John Beddoe, *The races of Britain* (1885: repr. London, 1971), p. 5.

CHAPTER 2

1 C. Kidd, *British identities before nationalism* (Cambridge, 1999), ch. 8.
2 C. Kidd, 'Identity before identities: ethnicity, nationalism and the historian', in J. Rudolph (ed.), *History and nation* (Lewisburg, PA, 2006).
3 Alexander Winchell, *Preadamites; or a demonstration of the existence of men before Adam* (2nd edn, Chicago, 1880), p. 43; Dominick McCausland, *The builders of Babel* (London, 1871), pp. 21, 138, 294.
4 M. Staum, *Labeling people: French scholars on society, race, and empire 1815–1848* (Montreal, 2003), pp. 44–5; M. Adhikari, 'The sons of Ham: slavery and the making of coloured identity', *South African Historical Journal* 27 (1992), 95–112, at 95; H. F. Augstein, 'Linguistics and politics in the early nineteenth century: James Cowles Prichard's moral philology', *History of European Ideas* 23 (1997), 1–18, at 5.
5 E. R. Sanders, 'The Hamitic hypothesis: its origin and functions in time perspective', *Journal of African History* 10 (1969), 521–32.
6 H. F. Augstein, 'From the land of the Bible to the Caucasus and beyond: the shifting ideas of the geographical origin of humankind', in W. Ernst and B. Harris (eds.), *Race, science and medicine* (London, 1999).
7 F. Dikotter, *The discourse of race in modern China* (1992: London, pbk, 1994), pp. 72–5.
8 A. Smedley, *Race in North America: origin and evolution of a worldview* (Boulder, CO, 1993), pp. 154–5.
9 G. Stocking, *Victorian anthropology* (New York, 1987), pp. 69, 74–5; Stocking, 'Reading the palimpsest of inquiry', in Stocking, *Delimiting anthropology* (Madison, WI, 2001), pp. 170–1; M. Banton, *Racial theories* (1987: 2nd edn, Cambridge, 1998), pp. 44–5, 68; M. Biddiss, *Father of racist ideology: the social and political thought of Count Gobineau* (New York, 1970), pp. 118–19.
10 Ebenezer Sibly, *An universal system of natural history* (7 vols., London, 1794–1803), I, pp. 309–10.
11 John Mitchell, 'An essay upon the causes of the different colours of people in different climates', *Philosophical Transactions* 43 (London, 1746), 102–50, at 146–7.
12 Thomas Jarrold, *Anthropologia: or, dissertations on the form and colour of man* (London, 1808), p. 243.
13 William Apess, *A son of the forest* (1829), in B. O'Connell (ed.), *On our own ground: the complete writings of William Apess, a Pequot* (Amherst, MA, 1992), pp. 10, 34; R. S. Sugirtharajah, *The Bible and the Third World* (Cambridge, 2001), pp. 87–90.
14 Martin Delany, *Principia of ethnology: the origin of races and color* (1879: Baltimore, MD, 1991), p. 11.

15 John Hunter, 'On the colour of the pigmentum of the eye in different animals' (1786), in Hunter, *Works* (5 vols., London, 1835–7), IV, pp. 277–9.

16 James Cowles Prichard, *Researches into the physical history of mankind* (5 vols., London, 1826–47), I, pp. 138–9, 149, 151.

17 Hugh Miller, 'Unity of the human races' (*The Witness*, 13 Jul. 1850), republished in Miller, *Essays, historical and biographical, political and social, literary and scientific* (7th edn, London and Edinburgh, 1875), pp. 387–97, at p. 396.

18 Winchell, *Preadamites*, pp. 242–3.

19 John Painter, *Ethnology: or the history and genealogy of the human race* (London, 1879), p. 21.

20 See ch. 5.

21 *Clearer light; or, the teachings of the Bible, respecting the Creation, the original inhabitants of the earth, the diversities of the human race, and other questions of the day* (London, 1874), pp. 38–44.

22 John Overton, *The genealogy of Christ, elucidated by sacred history* (2 vols., London, 1817), I, ch. 2, esp. p. 125.

23 Dominick McCausland, *Adam and the Adamite: or, the harmony of scripture and ethnology* (London, 1864), pp. 253–7.

24 Marcus Garvey, *Life and lessons* (eds. R. A. Hill and B. Bair, Berkeley, Los Angeles and London, 1987), p. 269.

25 D. E. Mungello, *Curious land: Jesuit accommodation and the origins of Sinology* (Studia Leibnitiana supplementa 25, Stuttgart, 1985); A. Grafton, *New worlds, ancient texts* (1992: pbk edn, Cambridge, MA, 1995); P. Rossi, *The dark abyss of time* (transl. L. Cochrane, Chicago, 1984); H. Trevor-Roper, 'James Ussher, Archbishop of Armagh', in Trevor-Roper, *Catholics, Anglicans and Puritans* (London, 1987).

26 Samuel Shuckford, *The sacred and prophane history of the world connected* (3 vols., London, 1728–37), I, pp. 29, 102; II, p. 68. For Shuckford's publishing history, see B. Feldman and R. D. Richardson, *The rise of modern mythology* (Bloomington, IN, 1972), p. 71. see also John Webb, *An historical essay endeavoring a probability that the language of the empire of China is the primitive language* (London, 1669), pp. 31–2, 43, 60–8; *An universal history, from the earliest account of time to the present* (7 vols., London, 1736–44), I, p. 116 fn.

27 Simon Berington, *Dissertations on the Mosaical creation, deluge, building of Babel and confusion of tongues* (London, 1750), pp. 458–62.

28 Mitchell, 'Essay', 146.

29 Claude-Nicolas Le Cat, *Traité de la couleur de la peau humaine en général, de celle des nègres en particulier, et de la métamorphose d'une de ces couleurs en l'autre, soit de naissance, soit accidentellement* (Amsterdam, 1765), p. 6.

30 Josiah Priest, *Slavery as it relates to the Negro, or African race* (Albany, NY, 1843), pp. 27, 33, 133, 137.

31 N. Leask, 'Francis Wilford and the colonial construction of Hindu geography, 1799–1822', in A. Gilroy (ed.), *Romantic geographies: discourses of travel 1775–1844* (Manchester, 2000), p. 206; T. Trautmann, *Aryans and British India* (Berkeley and Los Angeles, 1997), pp. 90–2.

32 T. Ballantyne, *Orientalism and race: Aryanism in the British Empire* (Houndmills, 2002), pp. 166–7.

33 James Boswell, *Life of Johnson* (Oxford, 1980), p. 284.

34 Robert Burns, 'The ordination', in Burns, *Poems and Songs* (ed. J. Kinsley, Oxford, 1969), p. 171.

35 Alexander McLeod, *Negro slavery unjustifiable* (Glasgow, 1804), p. 24.

36 T. V. Peterson, *Ham and Japheth: the mythic world of whites in the antebellum South* (Metuchen, NJ, and London, 1978), p. 102.

37 *Human relations and the South African scene in the light of scripture* (Dutch Reformed Church, Cape Town, 1974), pp. 5, 15–20.

38 Thomas Browne, *Pseudodoxia epidemica* (2 vols., Oxford, 1981), I, p. 519; Richard Kidder, *A commentary on the five books of Moses* (2 vols., London, 1694), II, p. 250; Thomas Stackhouse, *A new history of the Holy Bible* (2 vols., London, 1733), I, pp. 460–1.

39 John Bryant Clifford, *The Anglo-Israelites* (London, 1879), pp. 12–13.

40 *Human relations*, p. 95.

41 Priest, *Slavery*, p. 335; Thomas Smyth, *The unity of the human races proved to be the doctrine of scripture, reason and science* (from the American edn, rev. and enlarged, Edinburgh, 1851), p. 110.

42 C. A. Clegg III, *An original man: the life and times of Elijah Muhammad* (New York, 1997), pp. 53–4.

43 Albert Cleage, *The black Messiah* (Kansas City, 1968), p. 40.

44 T. Parfitt, *The Lost Tribes of Israel: the history of a myth* (London, 2002).

45 Asahel Grant, *The Nestorians: or the Lost Tribes* (London, 1841).

46 L. E. Huddleston, *Origin of the American Indians: European concepts, 1492–1729* (Austin, TX, 1967), esp. pp. 84, 87–8, 113, 129–32, 135.

47 Parfitt, *Lost Tribes*.

48 See ch. 7.

49 M. Barkun, *Religion and the racist right: the origins of the Christian Identity movement* (rev. edn, Chapel Hill, NC, and London, 1997).

50 W. R. Telford, 'Jesus Christ movie star: the depiction of Jesus in the cinema', in C. Marsh and G. Ortiz (eds.), *Explorations in theology and film* (Oxford, 1997), p. 132; W. Barnes Tatum, *Jesus at the movies: a guide to the first hundred years* (Santa Rosa, CA, 1997); J. O. Thompson, 'Jesus as moving image', in S. E. Porter, M. A. Hayes and D. Tombs (eds.), *Images of Christ ancient and modern* (Sheffield, 1997).

51 Madison Grant, *The passing of the great race* (4th edn, New York, 1926), p. 230.

52 Buckner H. Payne, *The Negro: what is his ethnological status?* (2nd edn, Cincinnati, 1867), p. 47.

53 Leask, 'Wilford', p. 210.

54 J. B. S. Carwithen, *A view of the Brahminical religion and its confirmation of the truth of the sacred history* (London, 1810), p. 29.

55 Godfrey Higgins, *Anacalypsis* (London, 1878 edn), pp. 39–40, 59, 159–60, 163, 173–5, 178, 182–3, 195, 396–9.

56 Sarah Titcomb, *Aryan sun-myths the origin of religions* (London, 1889), p. 122.

57 Louis Jacolliot, *The Bible in India: Hindoo origin of Hebrew and Christian revelation* (1869: transl. London, 1870), esp. pp. 100–4, 186, 230, 234, 247, 285, 297, 299.

58 W. E. B. DuBois, *Darkwater: voices from within the veil* (London, 1920), 'Jesus Christ in Texas', pp. 123–33, at pp. 125–6.

59 Countee Cullen, *The Black Christ and other poems* (London and New York, 1929).

60 George Alexander McGuire, 'What is that in thine hand?', reprinted in R. Burkett (ed.), *Black redemption: churchmen speak for the Garvey movement* (Philadelphia, 1978), p. 176; *The Marcus Garvey and Universal Negro Improvement Papers* (ed. R. A. Hill, 7 vols., Berkeley, Los Angeles and London, 1983–90), V, pp. 625, 630.

61 James H. Cone, *Black theology and black power* (New York, 1969), p. 68.

62 Cleage, *Black Messiah*, p. 72.

63 M. Olender, *The languages of paradise: race, religion and philology in the nineteenth century* (transl. A. Goldhammer, Cambridge, MA, 1992), pp. 14, 69–71; I. Hannaford, *Race: the history of an idea in the West* (Baltimore, 1996), p. 253.

64 Emile Burnouf, *The science of religions* (transl. Julie Liebe, London, 1888), pp. 193, 195–6.

65 Houston Stewart Chamberlain, *The foundations of the nineteenth century* (transl. J. Lees, 2 vols., London, 1911), I, pp. 205–12.

66 Grant, *Passing of the great race*, p. 227.

67 R. Steigmann-Gall, *The holy Reich: Nazi conceptions of Christianity, 1919–1945* (Cambridge, 2003), pp. 19–20, 22, 31–2.

68 N. Goodrick-Clarke, *The occult roots of Nazism: secret Aryan cults and their influence on Nazi ideology* (1985: New York, 1992), pp. 158, 180.

69 S. Heschel, 'When Jesus was an Aryan: the Protestant church and antisemitic propaganda', in R. P. Ericksen and S. Heschel (eds.), *Betrayal: German churches and the Holocaust* (Minneapolis, 1999); Heschel, 'Nazifying Christian theology: Walter Grundmann and the Institute for the Eradication of Jewish Influence on German Church Life', *Church History* 63 (1994), 587–605; Heschel, *Abraham Geiger and the Jewish Jesus* (Chicago and London, 1998).

70 *Hitler's table talk 1941–4* (transl. N. Cameron and R. H. Stevens, 1953: 2nd edn, London, 1973), 21 Oct. 1941, midday, pp. 76–8; C. Bennett, *In search of Jesus* (London and New York, 2001), pp. 173, 240, 244.

71 The story of the Iberian and Roman Catholic Atlantic is a very different one. See e.g. A. Pagden, *The fall of natural man: the American Indian and the origins of comparative ethnology* (Cambridge, 1982).

CHAPTER 3

1 R. Tuck, *Natural rights theories* (Cambridge, 1979).
2 C. Kidd, *British identities before nationalism* (Cambridge, 1999).

3 M. T. Hodgen, *Early anthropology in the sixteenth and seventeenth centuries* (Philadelphia, 1964).

4 J.-C. Müller, 'Early stages of language comparison from Sassetti to Sir William Jones (1786)', *Kratylos* 31 (1986), 1–31.

5 Hodgen, *Early anthropology*; A. Grafton, *Defenders of the text: the traditions of scholarship in an age of science, 1450–1800* (1991: Cambridge, MA, pbk, 1994); Grafton, *New worlds, ancient texts: the power of tradition and the shock of discovery* (1992: Cambridge, MA, pbk, 1995); P. Rossi, *The dark abyss of time* (transl. L. Cochrane, Chicago, 1984).

6 C. Kidd, *British identities*, ch. 2.

7 J. E. Chaplin, *Subject matter: technology, the body and science on the Anglo-American frontier, 1500–1676* (Cambridge, MA, and London, 2001), p. 166.

8 P. Harrison, *The Bible, Protestantism, and the rise of natural science* (1998: Cambridge, pbk, 2001).

9 Richard Cumberland, *Origines gentium antiquissimae; or, attempts for discovering the times of the first planting of nations* (London, 1724), p. 143; Harrison, *Bible, Protestantism and the rise of natural science*, p. 224; F. Egerton, 'The longevity of the patriarchs: a topic in the history of demography', *Journal of the History of Ideas* 27 (1966), 575–84; P. Almond, *Adam and Eve in seventeenth-century thought* (Cambridge, 1999), pp. 19–27.

10 John Gill, *An exposition of the Old Testament, in which are recorded the original of the several nations of the world, and of the Jewish nation in particular* (4 vols., London, 1763–5), I, p. 64.

11 *The ancient patriarchs' peregrination; or a map of the first inhabited countries there were in the world; containing a description of the passages and proceedings from the Flood to the family of Jacob* (1600), in *A second collection of scarce and valuable tracts* (4 vols., London, 1750), I, p. 243.

12 Francis Lee, *Apoleipomena* (2 vols., London, 1752), II, pp. 32–3, 39, 50, 67.

13 Peter Heylyn, *Cosmography* (London, 1670 edn), p. 8.

14 Simon Patrick, *A commentary upon the first book of Moses, called Genesis* (London, 1695), pp. 226–7, 231.

15 John Webb, *An historical essay endeavoring a probability that the language of the empire of China is the primitive language* (London, 1669); R. Ramsay, 'China and the ideal of order in John Webb's *An historical essay*', *Journal of the History of Ideas* 62 (2001), 483–503.

16 Simon Berington, *Dissertations on the Mosaical creation, deluge, building of Babel and confusion of tongues* (London, 1750), pp. 458–63.

17 William Wotton, *A discourse concerning the confusion of languages at Babel* (London, 1713), pp. 36, 41.

18 Joseph Charles, *The dispersion of the men at Babel considered, and the principal cause of it enquired into* (London, 1755).

19 L. E. Huddleston, *Origins of the American Indians: European concepts 1492–1729* (Austin, TX, 1967).

20 R. H. Popkin, *Isaac La Peyrère (1596–1676)* (Leiden, 1987), pp. 33, 35; Almond, *Adam and Eve*, pp. 49–51.

21 Popkin, *La Peyrère*, pp. 14, 80–1; R. Popkin, 'The philosophical bases of modern racism', in Popkin, *The high road to Pyrrhonism* (1980: Indianapolis, 1993), p. 92; Rossi, *Dark abyss*, p. 138; R. Popkin, *The history of scepticism from Erasmus to Spinoza* (Berkeley and Los Angeles, 1979); A. Grafton, 'Isaac La Peyrère and the Old Testament', in Grafton, *Defenders of the text*; Grafton, *New worlds, ancient texts*, pp. 237–42; N. Malcolm, 'Hobbes, Ezra and the Bible', in Malcolm, *Aspects of Hobbes* (2002: Oxford pbk, 2004), p. 393.

22 Popkin, *La Peyrère*, p. 7.

23 See the translations, La Peyrère, *A theological system upon that presupposition that men were before Adam* (London, 1655); La Peyrère, *Men before Adam* (London, 1656).

24 Popkin, *La Peyrère*, p. 3.

25 R. Popkin, 'The philosophy of Bishop Stillingfleet', *Journal of the History of Philosophy* 9 (1971), 303–19, at 305.

26 Edward Stillingfleet, *Origines sacrae* (London, 1662), p. 534.

27 Mathew Hale, *The primitive origination of mankind, considered and examined, according to the light of nature* (London, 1677), esp. bk II, pp. 182–3, 190, 195–7.

28 Richard Kidder, *A commentary on the five books of Moses* (2 vols., London, 1694), I, p. 6.

29 Nathaniel Lardner, *An essay on the Mosaic account of the Creation and the Fall of man* (1753), in Lardner, *Works* (11 vols., London, 1788), XI, pp. 244–5.

30 Thomas Browne, *Pseudodoxia epidemica* (2 vols., Oxford, 1981), I, pp. 324–33, 377–9, 468–83, 507–32.

31 *Athenian Mercury*, vol. III, no. 29, Q. 6; I, no. 9, Q. 1; I, no. 26, Q. 2; I, no. 20, Q. 17; II, no. 23, Q. 8; II, no. 27, Q. 4; I, no. 12, Q. 2; I, no. 26, Q. 8; I, no. 10, Q. 2; I, no. 24, Q. 5; I, no. 30, Q. 9; II, no. 1, Q. 12; III, no. 17, Q. 5; IV, no. 15, Q. 4.

32 William Whiston, 'An exposition of the curse upon Cain and Lamech: shewing that the present Africans and Indians are their posterity', in Whiston, *A supplement to the literal accomplishment of scripture prophecies* (London, 1725), pp. 106–34, at p. 126.

33 *Ibid.*, pp. 109, 111–12, 117–19, 121, 126–7, 130.

34 *Ibid.*, pp. 124, 127, 130–1.

35 Thomas Stackhouse, *A new history of the holy Bible* (2 vols., London, 1733), I, p. 192.

36 F. Manuel, *The eighteenth century confronts the gods* (Cambridge, MA, 1959); D. A. Pailin, *Attitudes to other religions: comparative religion in seventeenth- and eighteenth-century Britain* (Manchester, 1984).

37 Browne, *Pseudodoxia*, I, p. 550.

38 C. Kidd, *British identities*, pp. 42, 53–5.

39 J. G. A. Pocock, *Barbarism and religion*, vol. II, *Narratives of civil government* (Cambridge, 1999), p. 358.

40 Gill, *Exposition*, I, pp. 33, 62.

41 Matthew Bridges, *Testimony of profane antiquity* (London, 1825), p. 116.

42 G. Fredrickson, *Racism: a short history* (Princeton, 2002), pp. 42, 45–6, 51–2.

43 E. Morgan, *American slavery, American freedom* (New York, 1975); D. B. Davis, 'Constructing race: a reflection', *William and Mary Quarterly* 3rd ser. 54 (1997), 7–18. The most sophisticated exception to the consensus is W. Jordan, *White over black: American attitudes towards the Negro, 1550–1812* (Chapel Hill, NC, 1968).

44 Heylyn, *Cosmography*, p. 1016.

45 John Mitchell, 'An essay upon the causes of the different colours of people in different climates', *Philosophical Transactions* 43 (London, 1746), 102–50, at 146.

46 Ignatius Sancho, *Letters* (ed. V. Carretta, Harmondsworth, 1998), pp. 86, 93, 109, 111, 138, 143, 180; Olaudah Equiano, *The interesting narrative* (ed. V. Carretta, Harmondsworth, 1995), pp. 40–5.

47 K. Thomas, *Man and the natural world: changing attitudes in England 1500–1800* (1983: Harmondsworth, pbk, 1984), p. 135.

CHAPTER 4

1 See e.g. M. Foucault, *Discipline and punish: the birth of the prison* (London, 1977); Foucault, *Madness and civilization* (London, 1965); J. L. Talmon, *The origins of totalitarian democracy* (London, 1952); E. Voegelin, *From Enlightenment to revolution* (Durham, NC, 1975); A. Macintyre, *After virtue* (London, 1981); J. Gray, *Enlightenment's wake* (New York and London, 1995).

2 E. C. Eze (ed.), *Race and the Enlightenment: a reader* (Cambridge, MA, and Oxford, 1997).

3 Eze, 'Introduction', in Eze, *Race and the Enlightenment*, p. 4.

4 J. Immerwahr, 'Hume's revised racism', *Journal of the History of Ideas* 53 (1992), 481–6; E. C. Eze, 'Hume, race and human nature', *Journal of the History of Ideas* 61 (2000), 691–8.

5 E. Said, *Orientalism* (Harmondsworth, 1978); L. Poliakov, *Le mythe aryen* (1971: new edn, Brussels, 1987); L. Wolff, *Inventing eastern Europe: the map of civilization on the mind of the Enlightenment* (Palo Alto, 1994).

6 G. L. Mosse, *Towards the final solution: a history of European racism* (London, 1978), esp. pp. 1–3, 17.

7 H. F. Augstein, 'Introduction', in Augstein (ed.), *Race: the origins of an idea, 1760–1850* (Bristol, 1996), p. xxxii.

8 G. Fredrickson, *Racism: a short history* (Princeton, 2002), p. 57. See also M. Banton, 'The classification of race in Europe and North America: 1700–1850', *International Social Science Journal* 39 (1987), 45–60, at 45.

9 Y. Slezkine, 'Naturalists versus nations: eighteenth-century Russian scholars confront ethnic diversity', *Representations* 47 (1994), 170–95, at 172. I am indebted to Simon Dixon for this reference.

10 R. H. Popkin, 'The philosophical basis of eighteenth-century racism', in H. E. Pagliaro (ed.), *Studies in eighteenth-century culture: racism in the eighteenth century* (Cleveland and London, 1973), p. 253; R. H. Popkin, *Isaac La Peyrère (1596–1676)* (Leiden, 1987). See also D. R. McKee, 'Isaac de la

Peyrère, a precursor of eighteenth-century critical deists', *Publications of the Modern Language Association of America* 59 (1944), 456–85; Fredrickson, *Racism*, p. 47.

11 See e.g. R. B. Sher, *Church and university in the Scottish Enlightenment: the Moderate literati of Edinburgh* (Princeton, 1985).

12 See e.g. B. W. Young, *Religion and Enlightenment in eighteenth-century England* (Oxford, 1998). See also D. Livingstone, 'Geographical inquiry, rational religion and moral philosophy: Enlightenment discourses on the human condition', in Livingstone and C. Withers (eds.), *Geography and Enlightenment* (Chicago, 1999).

13 M. Meijer, *Race and aesthetics in the anthropology of Petrus Camper (1722–1789)* (Amsterdam, 1999).

14 J. F. Blumenbach, *Anthropological treatises* (transl. T. Bendyshe, London, 1865); Augstein, 'Introduction', p. xvii; E. Mayr, *The growth of biological thought* (Cambridge, MA, 1982), pp. 374, 526, 688, 872–3.

15 G. Stocking, *Victorian anthropology* (New York, 1987), chs. 1, 2.

16 M. Duchet, *Anthropologie et histoire au siècle des Lumières* (1971: Paris, 1995), pp. 286–9.

17 Jean Buffon, 'Variétés dans l'espèce humaine' (1749), in Buffon, *Histoire naturelle* (selection ed. J. Varloot, Paris, 1984), pp. 142–3.

18 Duchet, *Anthropologie*, p. 263.

19 R. K. Harrison, *Introduction to the Old Testament* (1969: London, 1970), pp. 11–12.

20 J. Redwood, *Reason, ridicule and religion: the age of Enlightenment in England 1660–1750* (1976: London, 1996).

21 Charles Blount, *The oracles of reason* (London, 1693), pp. 8, 10–11.

22 Josiah King, *Mr Blount's Oracles of reason, examined and answered* (Exeter, 1698).

23 *Two essays, sent in a letter from Oxford, to a nobleman in London* (1695), in *A third collection of scarce and valuable tracts* (4 vols., London, 1751), III, pp. 291–308.

24 John Harris, *Remarks on some late papers, relating to the universal deluge* (London, 1697), p. 66.

25 John Mitchell, 'An essay upon the causes of the different colours of people in different climates', *Philosophical Transactions* 43 (1746), 102–50, esp. 114, 122, 126, 130–2, 134, 146–7.

26 Oliver Goldsmith, *A history of the earth and animated nature* (8 vols., London, 1774), II, pp. 240, 242.

27 See e.g. R. Meek, *Social science and the ignoble savage* (Cambridge, 1976); C. Berry, *Social theory of the Scottish Enlightenment* (Edinburgh, 1997).

28 William Robertson, *History of America*, in William Robertson, *Works* (London, 1831), pp. 784, 786–7.

29 Richard Millar, 'How far can the varieties of the human species that are observable in the different countries of the world, be accounted for from physical causes?', Archives of the Royal Medical Society, Bristo Square, Edinburgh, MS Records vol. XIX (1785–6), 144–77, at 149.

30 David Hume, 'Of national characters', in Hume, *Essays, moral, political and literary* (ed. E. F. Miller, Indianapolis, 1987), pp. 208 fn, 629–30.

31 For Kames's brush with heresy in the 1750s, see Sher, *Church and university*, pp. 65–8, 72–3.

32 Henry Home, Lord Kames, *Sketches of the history of man* (2 vols., Edinburgh, 1774), II, pp. 70–2.

33 *Ibid.*, II, pp. 72, 75.

34 *Ibid.*, II, p. 76.

35 *Ibid.*, I, pp. 12, 15.

36 *Ibid.*, I, pp. 38–9.

37 *Ibid.*, I, p. 39.

38 *Ibid.*, I, pp. 39–40.

39 *Ibid.*, I, pp. 39–40, 43.

40 Reverend Henry Cooke to Thomas Smyth, 25 Oct. 1850, 'Introductory letters', p. 5, in Thomas Smyth, *The unity of the human races proved to be the doctrine of scripture, reason and science* (from the American edn, rev. and enlarged, Edinburgh, 1851).

41 John Anderson, 'Discourses of natural and artificial systems in natural history; and of the varieties in the human kind', Strathclyde University Library, Glasgow, Special Collections, MS 9, ff. 23, 30–1, 33.

42 James Beattie, *An essay on the nature and immutability of truth in opposition to sophistry and scepticism* (1771: repr. London, 1996), pp. 507–12; Beattie, *Elements of moral science* (1790–3: 2 vols., Edinburgh, 1807), II, pp. 56, 74.

43 Beattie, *Elements*, II, pp. 56–7.

44 *Ibid.*, II, pp. 60–3.

45 William Charles Wells, *Two Essays . . . and An Account of a female of the white race of mankind, part of whose skin resembles that of a Negro; with some observations on the causes of the differences in colour and form between the white and Negro races of men* (London, 1818), pp. 426, 432, 435–6.

46 Archives of the Royal Medical Society, Bristo Square, Edinburgh: Millar, 'Varieties', XIX (1785–6), 144–77; Benjamin Smith Barton, 'An essay towards a natural history of the North American Indians. Being an attempt to describe, and to investigate the causes of some of the varieties in figure, in complexion etc among mankind', XXIII (1788–90), 1–17; James Buchan, 'Whether are moral and physical causes sufficient to account for the varieties which occur in the human species?', XXVI (1790–1), 302–22; John Bradley, 'Whence the varieties of the human species?', XXVII (1791–2), 95–105; E. Holme, 'To the operation of what causes are we to ascribe the variety of complexion in the human species?', XXIX (1792–3), 366–82; R. E. Taylor, 'What are the causes of the variety of complexion in the human species?', XXXI (1793–4), 274–88; William Webb, 'Are the diversities among mankind the effect of physical and moral causes?', XXXII (1794–5), 134–67; R. D. Mackintosh, 'Upon what do the physical varieties of the human body in different characters depend?', XLII (1798–9), 31–69; Alexander Robertson, 'Do the varieties which we observe among mankind arise from the action of

moral and physical causes, or are there different races of men?', XL (1798–9), 201–17; Joseph Reade, 'What are principally the causes of variety in the human species?', XLIV (1800–1), 99–114; James Cowles Prichard, 'Of the varieties of the human race', LVIII (1807–8), 87–133; Richard Dyett, 'Is there any original difference of intellectual ability amongst mankind?', LVIII (1807–8), 215–36; Nicholas Pitta, 'What is the influence of climate on the human species? And what are the varieties of men which result from it?', LXVI (1811–12), 283–307.

47 Taylor, 'Causes'; Alexander Robertson, 'Varieties'.
48 Pitta, 'Climate', 287.
49 Alexander Robertson, 'Varieties', 202, 217.
50 Taylor, 'Causes', 288.
51 Prichard, 'Varieties', 124; Holme, 'Operation', 370; Buchan, 'Causes', 311; Alexander Robertson, 'Varieties', 213; Taylor, 'Causes', 278–9.
52 Bradley, 'Varieties', 99.
53 Holme, 'Operation', 374.
54 Mackintosh, 'Varieties', 39–40; Bradley, 'Varieties', 97–8; Prichard, 'Varieties', 112.
55 Millar, 'Varieties', 154, 163–4.
56 Mackintosh, 'Varieties', 46.
57 Pitta, 'Climate', 291, 302.
58 Prichard, 'Varieties', 100.
59 Mackintosh, 'Varieties', 57.
60 Pitta, 'Varieties', 289.
61 Barton, 'Essay', 11–13, 16.
62 H. May, *The Enlightenment in America* (Oxford, 1976).
63 M. Noll, *Princeton and the republic, 1768–1822: the search for a Christian Enlightenment in the era of Samuel Stanhope Smith* (Princeton, 1989).
64 Samuel Stanhope Smith, *An essay on the causes of complexion and figure in the human species* (Bristol, 1995), pp. 26–32, 144.
65 *Ibid.*, pp. 144–5.
66 *Ibid.*, pp. 163–5.
67 T. F. Gossett, *Race: the history of an idea in America* (1963: new edn, Oxford and New York, 1997).
68 James Adair, *The history of the American Indians* (London, 1775), esp. pp. 3, 11–12, 15, 18–19, 34, 37, 96, 118–19, 124, 132–4, 218; A. F. C. Wallace, *Jefferson and the Indians* (Cambridge, MA, 1999), p. 137; Bernard Romans, *Concise natural history of East and West Florida* (New York, 1775), quoted in D. Boorstin, *The lost world of Thomas Jefferson* (1948: Boston, 1964), pp. 68–9; Thomas Jefferson to John Adams, 27 May 1813, *Adams–Jefferson Letters* (ed. L. J. Cappon, 2 vols., Chapel Hill, NC, 1959), II, pp. 323–4.
69 Thomas Jefferson, *Notes on the State of Virginia*, in S. K. Padover (ed.), *The complete Jefferson* (1943: repr. New York, 1969), p. 636.
70 *Ibid.*, p. 665.
71 Gossett, *Race*, p. 41.

72 W. Stanton, *The leopard's spots: scientific attitudes toward race in America 1815–1859* (Chicago and London, 1960), pp. 12–13; B. Dain, *A hideous monster of the mind: American race theory in the early republic* (Cambridge, MA, and London, 2002), pp. 23–5.

73 E. Gray, *New World Babel: languages and nations in early America* (Princeton, 1999), pp. 129–30.

74 John Pinkerton, 'An essay on the origin of Scotish poetry', in Pinkerton (ed.), *Ancient Scotish poems* (2 vols., London, 1786), I, p. xxiv.

75 *Ibid.*, I, pp. xxv–xxvi.

76 John Pinkerton, *Dissertation on the Scythians and Goths* (London, 1787), pp. 26, 33.

77 William Coxe and William Owen Pughe, *A vindication of the Celts* (London, 1803), pp. iii, 2.

78 Thomas Price, *An essay on the physiognomy and physiology of the present inhabitants of Britain* (London, 1829), pp. v, vii–ix, 25.

79 Edward King, *Morsels of criticism: tending to illustrate some few passages in the Holy Scriptures, upon philosophical principles* (2nd edn, 3 vols., London, 1800), III, pp. 85, 93, 101, 113.

80 Charles White, *An account of the regular gradation in man* (London, 1799), pp. 52–6, 58–9, 61–3, 119–24, 132, 134, 136–7.

81 Thomas Jarrold, *Anthropologia: or, dissertations on the form and colour of man* (London, 1808), pp. 9, 55–67, 207.

82 See e.g. the environmentalist monogenesis of Ebenezer Sibly, *An universal system of natural history* (7 vols., London, 1794–1803), I, pp. 132–3, 187, 189–90, 290–5, 298–302, 305, 307, 311–12.

83 William Paley, *A view of the evidences of Christianity* (1794: 11th edn, 2 vols., London, 1805), II, pp. 291, 294.

84 G. Cannon, *The life and mind of Oriental Jones* (Cambridge, 1990).

85 William Jones, 'On the chronology of the Hindus', in Jones, *Works* (6 vols., London, 1799), I, pp. 288, 313; Jones, 'Third anniversary discourse', 2 Feb. 1786, in *Works*, I, p. 29.

86 Jones, 'Ninth anniversary discourse', 23 Feb. 1792, in *Works*, I, pp. 135, 137–8.

87 M. Olender, 'Europe, or how to escape Babel', *History and Theory* 33 (1994), 5–25, at 17.

88 John Bird Sumner, *A treatise on the records of the creation* (2 vols., London, 1816), I, pp. 313, 317.

89 *Ibid.*, I, pp. 294, 296–8, 302, 304–6, 310–11.

90 John Mason Good, *The book of nature* (3rd edn, 3 vols., London, 1834), II, pp. 77–81, 83, 85–6, 91–3.

91 T. Keegan, *Colonial South Africa and the origins of the racial order* (London, 1996), p. 91. See the 'sedimentation' of older forms of racial discourse together with Scottish stadial theory in an Enlightenment which did not consider physical features the 'primary register' of human difference, in R. Wheeler, *The complexion of race: categories of difference in eighteenth-century British culture* (Philadelphia, 2000), esp. pp. 5–9, 290, 301.

92 P. Corsi, *The age of Lamarck: evolutionary theories in France 1790–1830* (transl. J. Mandelbaum, London, 1998), pp. 221–2; F. Schiller, *Paul Broca* (1979: Oxford, 1992).

CHAPTER 5

1 William Robertson Smith, *Lectures on the religion of the Semites: first series: the fundamental institutions* (Edinburgh, 1889); J. G. Frazer, *The golden bough* (1890: various editions).
2 R. K. Harrison, *Introduction to the Old Testament* (1969: London, 1970), pp. 13–17.
3 William Robinson, *The first chapter of the Bible* (Cambridge, 1856), p. 3.
4 Paton J. Gloag, *The primeval world: a treatise on the relations of geology to theology* (Edinburgh, 1859), p. 81; Andrew Taylor, *The geological difficulties of the age theory* (Edinburgh, n.d.), p. 16.
5 Sir Charles MacGregor, *Notes on Genesis* (London, 1853), pp. 10–11.
6 Thomas Chalmers, 'Remarks on Cuvier's theory of the earth' (Christian Instructor, 1814), in Chalmers, *Works* (25 vols., Glasgow, 1836–42), XII, pp. 349–72.
7 See e.g. Isabella Duncan, *Pre-Adamite man* (London, 1860); E. Fancher, 'Was Adam the first man?', *Scribner's Monthly* (Oct. 1871), 578–89.
8 Hugh Miller, *The testimony of the rocks* (Edinburgh, 1856).
9 John Pye Smith, *On the relation between the Holy Scriptures and some parts of geological science* (London, 1839).
10 James Sime, *The Mosaic record in harmony with the geological* (Edinburgh, 1854), pp. 42–4, 56–8.
11 Moses Stuart, *Critical history and defence of the Old Testament canon* (1845: London, 1849), pp. 2, 364; Stuart, *Philological view of the modern doctrines of geology* (Edinburgh, 1836), pp. 7, 9.
12 Edward Hitchcock, *The religion of geology and its connected sciences* (London, 1851), pp. 4, 155–7; Hitchcock, *The connection between geology and the Mosaic history of the Creation* (Edinburgh, 1836), pp. 14–15.
13 John W. Draper, *History of the conflict between religion and science* (24th edn, London, 1904), pp. 57–8.
14 Philip Henry Gosse, *Omphalos: an attempt to untie the geological knot* (London, 1857), pp. 123, 334, 336, 354.
15 George Campbell, 8th Duke of Argyll, *Primeval man* (London, 1869), pp. 105–6, 108, 127.
16 Thomas Smyth, *The unity of the human races proved to be the doctrine of scripture, reason and science* (from the American edn, rev. and enlarged, Edinburgh, 1851), pp. 46, 48–9, 54.
17 James Allin, *God as revealed in his works* (London, 1857), p. 10.
18 Pye Smith, *Relation*, p. 74.
19 Donald Macdonald, *Creation and the Fall* (Edinburgh, 1856), p. 373.

20 John Laidlaw, *The Bible doctrine of man or the anthropology and psychology of scripture* (Edinburgh, 1895), pp. 215–16.
21 John William Dawson, *The origin of the world according to revelation and science* (London, 1877), p. 263.
22 Reginald Poole, 'Editor's preface', in [Edward Lane,] *The genesis of the earth and of man* (ed. Poole, 2nd rev. and enlarged edn, London and Edinburgh, 1860), p. xxi.
23 Daniel Wilson, 'The unity of the human race', *Canadian Journal* 3 (1855), 229–31, at 230.
24 John Bathurst Deane, *The worship of the serpent traced throughout the world* (London, 1830).
25 Matthew Bridges, *Testimony of profane antiquity* (London, 1825).
26 George Smith, *The patriarchal age* (London, 1847), pp. 311–12, 315, 401–2.
27 George Rawlinson, *The historical evidences of the truth of the scripture records* (London, 1859), pp. 74–5.
28 John Pratt, *Scripture and science not at variance* (2nd edn, London, 1858), pp. 59–60.
29 Dawson, *Origin*, p. 320; Dawson, *The meeting place of geology and history* (London, 1894), pp. 64, 215.
30 James Cowles Prichard, *The eastern origin of the Celtic nations* (Oxford, 1831); Prichard, *Researches into the physical history of mankind* (5 vols., London, 1826–47); H. F. Augstein, 'Linguistics and politics in the early nineteenth century: James Cowles Prichard's moral philology', *History of European Ideas* 23 (1997), 1–18; Augstein, *James Cowles Prichard's anthropology* (Amsterdam, 1999).
31 Daniel Wilson, *Prehistoric man: researches into the origin of civilisation in the Old and New World* (2 vols., Cambridge, 1862), I, pp. 44, 56–7; Daniel Wilson, 'Unity of the human race', 229, 231; Daniel Wilson, 'Review of Nott and Gliddon, *Indigenous races of the earth*', *Canadian Journal* ns 2 (1857), 208–16, at 209; Daniel Wilson, *Prehistoric annals of Scotland* (2nd edn, 2 vols., London, 1863), I, p. 4; M. Ash, 'Old books, old castles, and old friends: the making of Daniel Wilson's *Archaeology and prehistoric annals of Scotland*', in E. Hulse (ed.), *Thinking with both hands: Sir Daniel Wilson in the old world and the new* (Toronto, 1999), pp. 72–3; B. Trigger, '*Prehistoric man* and Daniel Wilson's later Canadian ethnology', in Hulse, *Thinking with both hands*, pp. 86–7, 92–3, 97; B. McCardle, '"Heart of heart": Daniel Wilson's human biology', in Hulse, *Thinking with both hands*, pp. 101–2, 105–7.
32 Pye Smith, *Relation*, pp. 71, 74, 302, 319.
33 Sharon Turner, *The sacred history of the world* (8th edn, 3 vols., 1848), II, p. 155.
34 Charles Caldwell, *Thoughts on the original unity of the human race* (1830: 2nd edn, Cincinnati, 1852), esp. pp. viii, xi, 49, 117–20; William Van Amringe, *An investigation of the theories of the natural history of man* (New York, 1848), esp. pp. 47, 63, 73–6.
35 Alexander Kinmont, *Twelve lectures on the natural history of man* (Cincinnati, 1839), esp. pp. 172, 213–14.

36 J. R. McKivigan and M. Snay, 'Introduction', in McKivigan and Snay (eds.), *Religion and the antebellum debate over slavery* (Athens, GA, 1998), pp. 16–17; R. W. Fogel, *Without consent or contract: the rise and fall of American slavery* (New York and London, 1989), pp. 274–5.

37 Stuart, *Critical history*, pp. 2, 47.

38 John Henry Hopkins, *A scriptural, ecclesiastical and historical view of slavery* (New York, 1864), pp. 7, 48, 69.

39 M. Noll, 'The Bible and slavery', in R. M. Miller, H. S. Stout and C. Reagan Wilson (eds.), *Religion and the American Civil War* (New York and Oxford, 1998), p. 44. See also H. Shelton Smith, *In his image but . . .: racism in Southern religion, 1780–1910* (Durham, NC, 1972), pp. 129–36; E. Fox-Genovese and E. D. Genovese, *The mind of the master class: history and faith in the Southern slaveholders' world view* (Cambridge, 2005), pp. 473–527.

40 Howell Cobb, *A scriptural examination of the institution of slavery in the United States* (n.p., 1856), pp. 12, 83.

41 Noll, 'The Bible and slavery', pp. 43–4; Noll, *America's God: from Jonathan Edwards to Abraham Lincoln* (Oxford, 2002), pp. 386–400; E. Brooks Holifield, *Theology in America: Christian thought from the age of the Puritans to the Civil War* (New Haven and London, 2003), pp. 498–500.

42 Theodore Dwight Weld, *The Bible against slavery: an inquiry into the patriarchal and Mosaic systems* (4th edn, New York, 1838), p. 66.

43 Fred A. Ross, *Slavery ordained of God* (1857: repr. Miami, FL, 1969), 'Speech delivered at Buffalo, before the General Assembly of the Presbyterian Church', 27 May 1853, p. 25.

44 Thornton Stringfellow, *Scriptural and statistical views in favor of slavery* (4th edn, Richmond, VA, 1856), pp. 8–9.

45 W. S. Jenkins, *Pro-slavery thought in the Old South* (Chapel Hill, NC, 1935), p. 206; T. V. Peterson, *Ham and Japheth: the mythic world of whites in the antebellum South* (Metuchen, NJ, and London, 1978), p. 102; S. Haynes, *Noah's curse: the biblical justification of American slavery* (New York, 2002); Fox-Genovese and Genovese, *The mind of the master class*, pp. 521–6.

46 Josiah Priest, *Slavery as it relates to the Negro, or African race* (Albany, NY, 1843), p. 27.

47 Louis Agassiz, Response to Nott, *Proceedings of the American Association for the Advancement of Science* 3 (1850), p. 107; E. Lurie, *Louis Agassiz: a life in science* (1960: Baltimore, MD, 1988), p. 260; L. Menand, *The metaphysical club* (New York and London, 2001), p. 113.

48 Louis Agassiz, 'The diversity of origin of the human races', *Christian Examiner* (Jul. 1850), 110–45, at 111, 113.

49 *Ibid.*, 111–12, 120, 134, 138.

50 M. O'Brien, *Conjectures of order: intellectual life and the American South, 1810–1860* (Chapel Hill, NC, and London, 2004), pp. 240–1, 247–8.

51 George Fitzhugh, *Cannibals all! or slaves without masters* (ed. C. Vann Woodward, Cambridge, MA, 1960), pp. 199–200; Fitzhugh, 'Southern

thought', *De Bow's Review* (Oct. 1857), 347; H. Wish, *George Fitzhugh: propagandist of the Old South* (Baton Rouge, 1943), p. 298.

52 Josiah Nott and George Gliddon, *Types of mankind* (4th edn, Philadelphia, 1854), pp. 555–6; O'Brien, *Conjectures*, p. 242.

53 Nott and Gliddon, *Types of mankind*, pp. 55, 573, 555–8, 559.

54 *Ibid.*, pp. lxxvi, 412, 465.

55 Peterson, *Ham*, p. 70.

56 Shelton Smith, *In his image but* ..., pp. 160–5. For science in the South, see e.g. D. Gilpin Faust, *A sacred circle: the dilemma of the intellectual in the Old South, 1840–1860* (Baltimore, MD, and London, 1977); L. D. Stephens, *Science, race, and religion in the American South: John Bachman and the Charleston circle of naturalists, 1815–1895* (Chapel Hill, NC, and London, 2000).

57 John Bachman, *The doctrine of the unity of the human race* (Charleston, SC, 1850), pp. 8, 156–7, 212; Stephens, *Science, race, and religion*, pp. 180–1.

58 J. L. Cabell, *The testimony of modern science to the unity of mankind* (1858: 2nd edn, New York, 1859), pp. 266–7.

59 Samuel Davies Baldwin, *Dominion; or, the unity and trinity of the human race* (Nashville, TN, 1858), esp. pp. 17, 22–3, 266, 270, 277, 411, 432, 462.

60 Thornwell quoted in Noll, 'The Bible and slavery', pp. 51–2; O'Brien, *Conjectures*, p. 1152.

61 Samuel Cartwright, 'The prognathous species of mankind' (1857), reprinted in E. McKitrick (ed.), *Slavery defended: the views of the Old South* (Englewood Cliffs, NJ, 1963), pp. 139, 143.

62 Samuel Cartwright, 'Unity of the human race disproved by the Hebrew Bible', *De Bow's Review* (Aug. 1860), 129–36, at 129–30; Adam Clarke, *The holy Bible ... with a commentary and critical notes* (6 vols., London, 1836 edn), I, pp. 50–3.

63 Buckner H. Payne, *The Negro: what is his ethnological status?* (2nd edn, Cincinnati, 1867), pp. 3–5, 7–11, 21–2, 26–7, 30, 36, 45, 48. The story can be followed in J. D. Smith (ed.), *Anti-black thought 1863–1925* (11 vols., New York and London, 1993), vols. V and VI, which contain reprints of many of the relevant tracts. See also J. D. Smith, *An old creed for the new South: proslavery ideology and historiography, 1865–1918* (Westport, CT, 1985), pp. 43–4.

64 D. G. Phillips, *Nachash: what is it?* (Augusta, GA, 1868), pp. 35, 38–9, 48.

65 *The Adamic race* (New York, 1868), pp. 59, 67–8.

66 Sister Sallie, *The color line* (Memphis?, 1875?), pp. 40, 59.

67 A. Hoyle Lester, *The pre-Adamite, or who tempted Eve?* (Philadelphia, 1875), pp. 13, 18–19, 77.

68 Charles Carroll, *The tempter of Eve* (St Louis, 1902), pp. 388–9, 398–9, 402, 407–33, 470, 499. See also M. Stokes, 'Someone's in the Garden with Eve: race, religion and the American Fall', *American Quarterly* 50 (1998), 718–44, at 727.

69 Robert Young, *The Negro: a reply to Ariel* (Nashville, TN, 1867), pp. 4–5.

70 G. Stocking, *Victorian anthropology* (New York, 1987), pp. 240–8; T. Ellingson, *The myth of the noble savage* (Berkeley and Los Angeles, 2001), pp. 239–89; J. C. D. Clark, *Our shadowed present* (London, 2003), p. 94. See also G. Feeley-Harnik, '"Communities of blood": the natural history of kinship in nineteenth-century America', *Comparative Studies in Society and History* 41 (1999), 215–62, at 218.

71 John William Colenso, *The Pentateuch and Book of Joshua critically examined* (4 vols., London, 1862–3), I, 'Preface', pp. vi–viii; P. Hinchliff, 'Ethics, evolution and biblical criticism in the thought of Benjamin Jowett and John William Colenso', *Journal of Ecclesiastical History* 37 (1986), 91–110.

72 Colenso, *Pentateuch*, I, p. 10; for arithmetical absurdities, see esp. I, chs. 4–6, 10, 12, 21; J. Rogerson, *Old Testament criticism in the nineteenth century* (London, 1984), pp. 221–3, 226–7; A. N. Wilson, *God's funeral* (1999: London, pbk, 2000), p. 137.

73 Colenso, *Pentateuch*, IV, p. 241.

74 *Ibid.*, IV, pp. 241–2.

75 John William Colenso, *On missions to the Zulus in Natal and Zululand* (London, 1865), pp. 8–9.

76 *Ibid.*, p. 9.

77 William Holden, *The past and future of the Kaffir races* (London, 1866), pp. 4–6.

78 J. Secord, *Victorian sensation* (Chicago, 2000).

79 P. J. Bowler, *Theories of human evolution: a century of debate, 1844–1944* (Baltimore, MD, 1986), pp. 58, 132–4; M. Banton, *Racial theories* (1987: 2nd edn, Cambridge, 1998), p. 81.

80 J. L. Altholz, 'The mind of Victorian orthodoxy: Anglican responses to *Essays and Reviews*, 1860–1864', in G. Parsons (ed.), *Religion in Victorian Britain*, vol. IV, *Interpretations* (Manchester, 1988), pp. 28–9.

81 D. N. Livingstone, 'Preadamites: the history of an idea from heresy to orthodoxy', *Scottish Journal of Theology* 40 (1987), 41–66; Livingstone, *The Preadamite theory and the marriage of science and religion, Transactions of the American Philosophical Society* 82 pt 3, 1992.

82 George Harris, 'The plurality of races, and the distinctive character of the Adamite species', *Anthropological Review* 5 (1867), 175–87.

83 [Lane], *The genesis of the earth*, pp. 62–3.

84 Duncan, *Pre-Adamite man*; S. Snobelen, 'Of stones, men and angels: the competing myth of Isabelle Duncan's *Pre-Adamite man* (1860)', *Studies in the History and Philosophy of Biology and Biomedical Sciences* 32 (2001), 59–104.

85 Dominick McCausland, *Adam and the Adamite; or, the harmony of scripture and ethnology* (London, 1864), pp. 182–3, 229, 264.

86 *Ibid.*, p. 291.

87 Alexander Winchell, *Preadamites; or a demonstration of the existence of men before Adam* (2nd edn, Chicago, 1880), p. v.

88 *Ibid.*, pp. 190–1.

89 *Ibid.*, p. 285.

90 *Ibid.*, pp. 472–3.

91 *Ibid.*, p. 285.

92 *Ibid.*, pp. 156, 282.

93 Reuben A. Torrey, *Difficulties and alleged errors and contradictions in the Bible* (London, [1908]), pp. 31–9; G. M. Marsden, *Fundamentalism and American culture: the shaping of twentieth-century evangelicalism 1870–1925* (New York and Oxford, 1980), pp. 37, 60, 118–19.

94 George Dickison, *The Mosaic account of Creation, as unfolded in Genesis, verified by science* (Edinburgh, 1902?), pp. 3, 124–5, 127–8, 150, 164–5, 174, 212. Dickison was also the author of *The second advent, including the return of the twelve tribes of Israel to their own land, and the millennium* (Edinburgh and London, 1913).

95 See e.g. Arthur Johnes, *Philological proofs of the original unity and recent origin of the human race* (London, 1843); C. S. Wake, 'The psychological unity of mankind', *in Memoirs read before the Anthropological Society of London III* (London, 1870), pp. 134–47.

CHAPTER 6

1 See e.g. J. R. Beard's article, 'Head', in John Kitto (ed.), *A cyclopaedia of biblical literature* (2 vols., Edinburgh, 1845), I, p. 819, whose subject was the science of craniology as devised by Camper and Blumenbach. According to Beard, comparative craniology demonstrated that the 'different families of mankind are marked by peculiarities of construction in the head'.

2 Archibald Sayce, *The races of the Old Testament* (London, 1891), pp. 3, 15–18, 22, 24, 172–3.

3 Archibald Sayce, 'The white race of ancient Palestine', *The Expositor* 3rd ser. 8 (1888), 48–57.

4 C. R. Conder, *Bible accuracy as shown by monuments* (London, 1903), pp. 20–1.

5 S. Kelley, *Racializing Jesus: race, ideology and the formation of modern biblical scholarship* (London and New York, 2002).

6 James Freeman Clarke, *Ten great religions: an essay in comparative theology* (London, 1871), pp. 2–3, 15.

7 C. A. Bayly, *The birth of the modern world 1780–1914* (Oxford, 2004), p. 343.

8 J. P. Lesley, *Man's origin and destiny sketched from the platform of the sciences* (London, 1868), p. 295.

9 Alexander Winchell, *Preadamites; or a demonstration of the existence of men before Adam* (2nd edn, Chicago, 1880), pp. 156, 181.

10 James Cowles Prichard, *Researches into the physical history of mankind* (5 vols., London, 1826–47), IV, pp. 549–50, 609–10, 612.

11 E. Leach, 'Anthropology of religion: British and French schools', in N. Smart, J. Clayton, S. Katz and P. Sherry (eds.), *Nineteenth-century religious thought in the West*, vol. III (Cambridge, 1985).

12 W. Robertson Smith, *Lectures on the religion of the Semites: first series: the fundamental institutions* (Edinburgh, 1889), p. 33.

13 For Max Müller, see K. Jankowsky, 'Friedrich Max Müller and the development of linguistic science', *Historiographia Linguistica* 6 (1979), 339–59; G. Beckerlegge, 'Professor Friedrich Max Müller and the missionary cause', in J. Wolffe (ed.), *Religion in Victorian Britain*, vol. V, *Culture and empire* (Manchester, 1997); J. Kitagawa and J. S. Strong, 'Friedrich Max Müller and the comparative study of religion', in Smart et al., *Nineteenth-century religious thought*.

14 Isaac Taylor, *The origin of the Aryans* (London, 1889).

15 Ernest Renan, *Histoire générale et système comparé des langues sémitiques: première partie: Histoire générale des langues sémitiques* (4th edn, Paris, 1864), pp. 4, 16, 18, 21; Renan, *History of the people of Israel till the time of King David* (London, 1888), pp. 7–8, 39–41; M. Olender, *The languages of paradise: race, religion and philology in the nineteenth century* (transl. A. Goldhammer, Cambridge, MA, 1992), ch. 4.

16 Emile Burnouf, *The science of religions* (transl. Julie Liebe, London, 1888), pp. 190–1, 194; F. E. Faverty, *Matthew Arnold the ethnologist* (Evanston, IL, 1951), p. 170.

17 Burnouf, *Science of religions*, pp. 74, 196.

18 *Ibid.*, pp. 53–4, 62, 74, 198.

19 *Ibid.*, pp. 50, 77, 80, 197.

20 Albert Réville, *Prolégomènes de l'histoire des religions* (2nd edn, Paris, 1881), pp. 114–15, 126. A. S. Squire's English translation was published in 1884.

21 Christian Bunsen, *Outlines of the philosophy of universal history, applied to language and religion* (2 vols., London, 1854), quotation at II, p. 195.

22 F. Max Müller, *Chips from a German workshop* (4 vols., London, 1867–75), I, pp. 343–4, 360; Max Müller, *Physical religion: the Gifford lectures delivered before the University of Glasgow in 1890* (new edn, London, 1898), pp. 220–1.

23 Max Müller, *Chips*, I, pp. 362, 367.

24 F. Max Müller, *Lectures on the origin and growth of religion* (new edn, London, 1882), p. 287; Max Müller, *Chips*, I, pp. 351–2.

25 Max Müller, *Chips*, II, pp. 9–10, 17.

26 F. Max Müller, *Lectures on the science of language* (2nd ser., London, 1864), pp. 404–5.

27 *Ibid.*, p. 413; Max Müller, *Chips*, II, p. 17.

28 Max Müller, *Chips*, I, pp. 356–7.

29 Max Müller, *Science of language*, p. 425; Max Müller, *Chips*, I, p. 358.

30 George Cox, *The mythology of the Aryan nations* (2 vols., London, 1870), I, p. 97.

31 C. F. Keary, *Outlines of primitive belief among the Indo-European races* (London, 1882), pp. x–xi, 108–10.

32 Robert Brown, *Semitic influence in Hellenic mythology* (London, 1898), pp. 20–1, 87, 92; Brown, *Poseidon: a link between Semite, Hamite and Aryan* (London, 1872).

33 Dominick McCausland, *The builders of Babel* (London, 1871), pp. 21, 24, 125–6, 201–2.

34 F. W. Farrar, *Families of speech* (London, 1870), pp. 129–30.

35 John William Dawson, *The origin of the world according to revelation and science* (London, 1877), pp. 254–5; Dawson, *The meeting place of geology and history* (London, 1894), pp. 131, 133.

36 Dawson, *Origin of the world*, pp. 14–16; Dawson, *Fossil men and their modern representatives* (London, 1880), pp. 278, 333–4.

37 T. H. Huxley, 'The interpreters of Genesis and the interpreters of nature' (1885), pp. 161–2, and 'The evolution of theology: an anthropological study' (1886), pp. 288, 316–17, both in Huxley, *Science and Hebrew tradition* (London, 1893), vol. IV of Huxley's *Collected essays*.

38 Charles Loring Brace, *The races of the Old World* (London, 1863), p. 32.

39 Dunbar Heath, 'On the great race-elements in Christianity', *Anthropological Review* 5 (1867), xix–xxviii.

40 Alexander Lindsay, 25th Earl of Crawford and 8th Earl of Balcarres, *The creed of Japhet, that is of the race popularly surnamed Indo-Germanic or Aryan* (privately published, 1891).

41 Robert Knox, *Races of men* (London, 1850), pp. 3–4, 69.

42 Henry Milman, *History of Latin Christianity* (3rd edn, 9 vols., London, 1872), I, pp. 10, 328–30; IX, pp. 355–6.

43 *Ibid.*, I, p. 330; IX, pp. 231–53, 353. See also George Cox, *Latin and Teutonic Christendom* (London, 1870).

44 Taylor, *Origin of the Aryans*, pp. 246–9.

45 Charles Kingsley, *The Roman and the Teuton* (Cambridge and London, 1864), pp. 9–10; Faverty, *Arnold ethnologist*, pp. 102–3.

46 A. G. Richey, *A short history of the Irish people* (Dublin, 1887), pp. 132, 298–9.

47 John Rhys, 'Race theories and European politics', *New Princeton Review* 5 (1888), 1–17, at 14–15.

48 J. A. Cramb, *The origins and destiny of imperial Britain* (London, 1915), pp. 58–9, 69–70, 134.

49 John Lothrop Motley, *The Rise of the Dutch Republic* (1855: 3 vols., London and New York, 1906), I, pp. 13–18, 226.

50 Clarke, *Ten great religions*, pp. 395–6.

51 Josiah Strong, *Our country* (ed. J. Herbst, Cambridge, MA, 1963), p. 201.

52 Madison Grant, *The passing of the great race* (4th edn, New York, 1926), pp. 185, 227–30; B. Regal, *Henry Fairfield Osborn: race and the search for the origins of man* (Aldershot and Burlington, VT, 2002), pp. 116–17.

53 J. M. Robertson, *The Saxon and the Celt: a study in sociology* (London, 1897), pp. 92–7, 204.

54 J. M. Robertson, *A short history of freethought, ancient and modern* (3rd rev. edn, 2 vols., London, 1914), I, pp. 64–5, 121, 248, 413, 431.

55 S. R. Pattison, *Gospel ethnology* (London, 1887), pp. 4, 20, 217.

56 Clarke, *Ten great religions*, pp. 16–18, 20–1, 24, 29–31.

57 John Nicol Farquhar, *The crown of Hinduism* (London, 1913), pp. 34, 77.

58 *Ibid.*, pp. 67, 72, 75–6, 421, 457.

CHAPTER 7

1 For the British Israelite phenomenon, see J. Black, *New forms of the old faith* (London, 1948), ch. 12; H. Davies, *Christian deviations* (1954: London, 1972), ch. 8; J. Wilson, 'British Israelism: the ideological restraints on sect organisation', in B. R. Wilson (ed.), *Patterns of sectarianism: organisation and ideology in social and religious movements* (London, 1967); O. M. Friedman, *Origins of the British Israelites: the Lost Tribes* (San Francisco, 1993); T. Parfitt, *The Lost Tribes of Israel: the history of a myth* (London, 2002).

2 Parfitt, *Lost Tribes*, p. 85; Asahel Grant, *The Nestorians: or the Lost Tribes* (London, 1841).

3 Parfitt, *Lost Tribes*, pp. 39–40; T. F. Stunt, 'Brothers, Richard', *Oxford dictionary of national biography* (Oxford, 2004); Friedman, *Origins*, p. 15.

4 John Finleyson, *The last trumpet and the flying angel* (London, 1849), pp. 20, 32.

5 J. Wilson, 'British Israelism', p. 353.

6 John Wilson, *Lectures on our Israelitish origin* (5th edn, London, 1876), pp. v, 117, 371.

7 *Ibid.*, pp. vii, 274, 321.

8 *Ibid.*, pp. 23, 189–90.

9 *Ibid.*, pp. 282, 368.

10 *Ibid.*, pp. 25–6, 28.

11 J. Wilson, 'British Israelism'.

12 A. M. Hyamson, 'Anglo-Israelism', in J. Hastings (ed.), *Encyclopaedia of religion and ethics* (13 vols., Edinburgh, 1908–26), I, pp. 482–3.

13 H. Herbert Pain, *Englishmen Israelites* (London, 1896), p. 7.

14 J. Wilson, 'British Israelism', p. 345.

15 Pain, *Englishmen Israelites*, p. 162; D. S. Katz and R. H. Popkin, *Messianic revolution: radical religious politics to the end of the second millennium* (Harmondsworth, 1999), p. 180.

16 A. M. Rainey, *The distribution of Shem, Ham and Japheth* (London, [1881]), p. 6.

17 Edward Hine, *Forty-seven identifications of the British nation with the Lost Ten Tribes of Israel* (London, 1874), p. 2.

18 *The Ten Tribes* (London, [1882]), p. 7.

19 T. K. de Verdon, *The veil lifted from all nations* (London, 1872), p. 42.

20 Rainey, *Distribution*, pp. 3–5.

21 C. M., *Israel in Britain: the collected papers on the ethnic and philological argument* (London, 1876), pp. 20, 27, 30–1.

22 John Pym Yeatman, *The Shemetic origin of the nations of western Europe* (London, 1879), pp. 1–2, 20–1.

23 J. Muspratt Williams, *The Sakai, and not the Scuths of Herodotus, the descendants of the Israelites, and our ancestors* (London, n.d.), pp. 12–19.

24 H. W. J. Senior, *The British Israelites; or, evidences of our Hebrew origin* (London, 1885), p. 11.

25 M. Carew, *Tara and the Ark of the Covenant* (Dublin, 2003).
26 E. Reisenauer, '"That we may do Israel's work": racial election in British imperial thought', *Proceedings of the South Carolina Historical Association 1999*, 97–112, at 104.
27 *Where are the Ten Tribes?* (London, 1872), pp. 18–19.
28 John Gilder Shaw, *Israel notwithstanding* (London, 1879), p. 84.
29 Edward Hine, *The English nation identified* (Warrington, 1872), p. 26; Hine, *Forty-seven identifications*, p. 27.
30 Charles Totten, *Our race* (London, [1895]), p. xv.
31 J. R. Goff Jnr, *Fields white with harvest* (Fayetteville, AR, and London, 1988), pp. 3–5.
32 N. Bloch-Hoell, *The Pentecostal movement* (Oslo, 1964), p. 18.
33 Charles Parham, *A voice crying in the wilderness* (1902: 4th edn, 1944), in *The sermons of Charles F. Parham* (New York and London, 1985), pp. 83–4, 106–7.
34 Goff, *Fields*, pp. 108–10; G. Wacker, *Heaven below: early Pentecostals and American culture* (Cambridge, MA, and London, 2001), p. 230.
35 R. M. Anderson, *Vision of the disinherited: the making of American Pentecostalism* (New York and Oxford, 1979), pp. 188, 190–1; Wacker, *Heaven below*, p. 232.
36 Wacker, *Heaven below*, p. 231; M. Barkun, *Religion and the racist right: the origins of the Christian Identity movement* (rev. edn, Chapel Hill, NC, and London, 1997), p. 21.
37 R. Kyle, 'The Worldwide Church of God', in C. Partridge (ed.), *Encyclopedia of new religions* (Oxford, 2004), pp. 64–5.
38 Herbert Armstrong, *The United States and British Commonwealth in prophecy* (Pasadena, 1967), p. 15.
39 *Ibid.*, pp. 2, 15, 20, 34, 36.
40 *Ibid.*, pp. 23, 53, 115.
41 J. A. Aho, *The politics of righteousness: Idaho Christian patriotism* (Seattle and London, 1990), p. 98; Barkun, *Religion*, pp. 150–1.
42 Barkun, *Religion*, chs. 5–9; Aho, *Politics of righteousness*, pp. 53–4, 85, 89; Katz and Popkin, *Messianic revolution*, chs. 6–8; J. G. Melton, *The encyclopedia of American religions: religious creeds* (Detroit, 1988), p. 633.
43 J. G. Melton, *Biographical dictionary of American cult and sect leaders* (New York and London, 1986), pp. 218–19; Barkun, *Religion*, pp. 161–2.
44 Barkun, *Religion*, pp. 14, 31–40, 85, 91, 156, 158, 165–8.
45 *Ibid.*, pp. 60–3, 70.
46 *Ibid.*, pp. 77–9.
47 Aho, *Politics of righteousness*, ch. 4; Barkun, *Religion*, pp. 150–1, 177, 181, 183–4.
48 H. L. Bushart, J. R. Craig and M. Barnes, *Soldiers of God: white supremacists and their holy war for America* (New York, 1998), p. 37.
49 Aho, *Politics of righteousness*, pp. 18–19, 93; Bushart et al., *Soldiers of God*, pp. 37, 41, 78.
50 'Statement of beliefs of Aryan Nations/Church of Jesus Christ Christian', in Bushart et al., *Soldiers of God*, p. 84; Aho, *Politics of righteousness*, p. 24.

51 Aho, *Politics of righteousness*, pp. 97–8.

52 Melton, *Creeds*, p. 633; Barkun, *Religion*, p. 188.

53 'Interview with Dan Gayman', in C. Swain and R. Nieli (eds.), *Contemporary voices of white nationalism in America* (Cambridge, 2003), pp. 208, 217, 219.

54 *Ibid.*, pp. 210–12, 222.

55 N. Goodrick-Clarke, *Black sun: Aryan cults, esoteric Nazism and the politics of identity* (New York and London, 2002), pp. 249–55; Melton, *Creeds*, pp. 647–8.

56 M. Gardell, *Gods of the blood: pagan revival and white separatism* (Durham, NC, and London, 2003), p. 167; Goodrick-Clarke, *Black sun*, p. 259.

57 Gardell, *Gods of the blood*, esp. p. 220.

58 R. N. Ostling and J. K. Ostling, *Mormon America* (New York, 1999).

59 D. M. Quinn, *Early Mormonism and the magic world view* (Salt Lake City, 1987), pp. 219–20.

60 All references taken from The Book of Mormon (Salt Lake City, 1961 edn).

61 A. L. Mauss, *All Abraham's children: changing Mormon conceptions of race and lineage* (Urbana and Chicago, 2003); N. G. Bringhurst, *Saints, slaves, and blacks: the changing place of black people within Mormonism* (Westport, CT, and London, 1981); L. E. Bush Jnr, 'Mormonism's Negro doctrine: an historical overview', *Dialogue: A Journal of Mormon Thought* 8 (1973), 11–68; P. L. Barlow, *Mormons and the Bible* (Oxford, 1991).

62 D. Davies, 'Mormon history, identity and faith community', in E. Tonkin, M. McDonald and M. Chapman (eds.), *History and ethnicity* (London, 1989); Bringhurst, *Saints*, p. 4; T. F. O'Dea, *The Mormons* (1957: Chicago, 1964), pp. 22–3.

63 J. L. Brooke, *The refiner's fire* (Cambridge, 1994), p. 163; Bringhurst, *Saints*, pp. 6–7; Mauss, *All Abraham's children*, chs. 3–5; L. J. Arrington and D. Bitton, *The Mormon experience* (New York, 1979), ch. 8.

64 *The pearl of great price* (Salt Lake City, 1952 edn); M. L. McNamara, 'Secularization or sacralization: The change in LDS church policy on blacks', in M. Cornwall, T. B. Heaton and L. A. Young (eds.), *Contemporary Mormonism: social science perspectives* (1994: Urbana and Chicago, 2001); Bringhurst, *Saints*, pp. xvii, 174, 178, 234–5.

65 Mauss, *All Abraham's children*, pp. 164–5.

66 *Ibid.*, pp. 24, 26–7; Bringhurst, *Saints*, p. 129.

67 *The doctrine and covenants of the Church of Jesus Christ of Latter-Day Saints* (Salt Lake City, 1952), 49:24.

68 Mauss, *All Abraham's children*, p. 82; B. A. Chadwick and S. L. Albrecht, 'Mormons and Indians: beliefs, policies, programs, and practices', in Cornwall et al., *Contemporary Mormonism*.

69 Mauss, *All Abraham's children*, pp. 89–90, 136–7; Chadwick and Albrecht, 'Mormons and Indians'.

70 Mauss, *All Abraham's children*, pp. 84, 93–4, 109.

71 *Ibid.*, pp. 142–5.

72 Bush, 'Mormonism's Negro doctrine', 21.

73 *Ibid.*, 13.

74 Brooke, *Refiner's fire*, pp. 164–7; Quinn, *Early Mormonism*, p. 167; Bush, 'Mormonism's Negro doctrine', 17.

75 Bringhurst, *Saints*, p. 113.

76 Bush, 'Mormonism's Negro doctrine', 25–6; Bringhurst, *Saints*, p. 124.

77 Mauss, *All Abraham's children*, p. 238.

78 Bringhurst, *Saints*, pp. 43, 150–1; Bush, 'Mormonism's Negro doctrine', 35.

79 Mauss, *All Abraham's children*, pp. 29–30.

80 Bringhurst, *Saints*, p. 167.

81 C. Hale, *Himmler's crusade: the true story of the 1938 Nazi expedition to Tibet* (London, 2003), pp. 21–30.

82 Helena Petrovna Blavatsky, *The secret doctrine: the synthesis of science, religion, and philosophy* (2nd edn, 3 vols., London, 1888–97), II, pp. 99, 101.

83 S. Cranston, *HPB: the extraordinary life and influence of Helena Blavatsky, founder of the modern Theosophical movement* (New York, 1993).

84 H. Blavatsky, *Isis unveiled* (2 vols., New York, 1884 edn), I, p. 307;. J. Oppenheim, *The other world: spiritualism and psychical research in England, 1850–1914* (1985: Cambridge, pbk, 1988) pp. 167, 180, 189–90.

85 Blavatsky, *Secret doctrine*, II, p. 263.

86 Blavatsky, *Isis unveiled*, II, p. 588.

87 Blavatsky, *Secret doctrine*, II, p. 125.

88 Blavatsky, *Isis unveiled*, II, p. 217.

89 Blavatsky, *Secret doctrine*, II, pp. 193, 251–2.

90 Blavatsky, *Secret doctrine*, II, p. 249; Blavatsky, *Isis unveiled*, I, p. 303.

91 *The Christ of the Aryan Road* (London, 1927), p. 13; T. Besterman, *A dictionary of Theosophy* (London, 1927), p. 125; W. Williamson, *The Great Law: a study of religious origins and of the unity underlying them* (London, 1899).

92 Blavatsky, *Isis unveiled*, II, p. 588.

93 Blavatsky, *Secret doctrine*, II, pp. 195–6.

94 Blavatsky, *Secret doctrine*, II, p. 200; Williamson, *Great Law*, pp. 244–5.

95 B. Regal, *Henry Fairfield Osborn: race and the search for the origins of man* (Aldershot and Burlington, VT, 2002), pp. 6–7.

96 W. Scott-Elliot, *The lost Lemuria* (London, 1904), pp. 24, 28, 31.

97 Rudolf Steiner, *Atlantis and Lemuria* (transl. A. Blake, London, 1923), pp. 21, 50–69.

98 M. A. Cremo and R. L. Thompson, *The hidden history of the human race* (Los Angeles, 1999).

CHAPTER 8

1 See esp. W. J. Moses, *Afrotopia: the roots of African American popular history* (Cambridge, 1998); Moses (ed.), *Classical black nationalism* (New York, 1996); Moses, *Black messiahs and Uncle Toms: social and literary manipulations of a religious myth* (University Park, PA, and London, 1982); S. Howe,

Afrocentrism (1998: London, 1999); M. Bay, *The white image in the black mind: African-American ideas about white people, 1830–1925* (Oxford, 2000).

2 Quoted in S. Prothero, *American Jesus* (New York, 2003), p. 214.

3 Edward Blyden, *Christianity, Islam and the Negro race* (1887: Edinburgh, 1967), pp. 242–4.

4 Hosea Easton, *A treatise on the intellectual character and the civil and political condition of the colored people of the U. States* (Boston, 1837), in G. R. Price and J. B. Stewart (eds.), *To heal the scourge of prejudice: the life and writings of Hosea Easton* (Amherst, MA, 1999), p. 67.

5 Bay, *White image*, pp. 58–63. For McCune Smith's intellectual career, see B. Dain, *A hideous monster of the mind: American race theory in the early republic* (Cambridge, MA, and London, 2002), pp. 237–63.

6 Bay, *White image*, pp. 68–9; Moses, *Afrotopia*, pp. 110–11.

7 Howe, *Afrocentrism*, p. 40.

8 Joseph Hayne, *The Amonian or Hamitic origin of the ancient Greeks, Cretans and all the Celtic races* (2nd edn, Brooklyn, NY, 1905), p. 69.

9 Martin Delany, *Principia of ethnology: the origin of races and color* (1879: Baltimore, MD, 1991), p. 10.

10 James Pennington, *Text book of the origin and history etc of the colored people* (1841: repr. Detroit, n.d.), pp. 8–17, 44.

11 Moses, *Afrotopia*, p. 100.

12 Easton, *Treatise*, p. 80.

13 Howe, *Afrocentrism*; Moses, *Afrotopia*, esp. ch. 3; Dain, *Hideous monster*, ch. 4.

14 Henry Highland Garnet, *The past and the present condition, and the destiny, of the colored race* (Troy, NY, 1848), pp. 6–7, 12.

15 Rufus L. Perry, *The Cushite or the descendants of Ham* (Springfield, MA, 1893), pp. viii–ix, 68.

16 Moses, *Afrotopia*, pp. 88–9; *The Marcus Garvey and Universal Negro Improvement Association Papers* (ed. R. A. Hill, 7 vols., Berkeley, Los Angeles and London, 1983–90), I, pp. 552–3.

17 R. B. Lewis, *Light and truth* (Boston, 1844), esp. pp. 13, 192, 313–15, 351–4, 362–7.

18 W. L. Hunter, *Jesus Christ had Negro blood in his veins* (9th edn, Brooklyn, 1913), pp. 13–16, 22, 30, 40.

19 James Morris Webb, *The black man the father of civilization proven from biblical history* (Seattle, 1910), pp. 6–8, 10–12, 18.

20 Delany, *Principia*, pp. 76–8.

21 James Theodore Holly, 'The divine plan of human redemption, in its ethnological development', *AME Church Review* 1 (1884), 84–5, quoted in T. H. Smith, *Conjuring culture: biblical formations of black America* (New York and Oxford, 1994), pp. 236–7.

22 Alexander Crummell, *Destiny and race: selected writings 1840–1898* (ed. W. J. Moses, Amherst, MA, 1992), pp. 194–5, 197–8, 203, 205.

23 Moses, *Afrotopia*, p. 26.

24 *Garvey Papers*, see esp. V, pp. 625–6, 665–7; Moses, *Black messiahs*, pp. 136–7.

25 L. G. Murphy, J. G. Melton and G. L. Ward (eds.), *Encyclopedia of African-American religions* (New York and London, 1993), pp. 632–7.

26 Albert Cleage, *The black Messiah* (Kansas City, 1968), pp. 3, 41, 72; *Detroit News*, 22 Feb. 2000. I should like to thank my former student Kirsten Phimister for alerting me to Cleage's obituary.

27 Cleage, *Black Messiah*, pp. 42–3.

28 James H. Cone, *Black theology and black power* (New York, 1969), p. 150.

29 James H. Cone, *A black theology of liberation* (1970: New York, 1990), pp. 1, 4, 6, 9, 114, 121, 123.

30 *Ibid.*, pp. 6, 20.

31 James H. Cone, *God of the oppressed* (New York, 1975), p. 84.

32 William Jones, 'Theodicy and methodology in black theology: a critique of Washington, Cone and Cleage', *Harvard Theological Review* 64 (1971), 541–57, esp. 541–5. Jones amplified these ideas in *Is God a white racist? A preamble to black theology* (1973: Boston, 1998).

33 Cain Hope Felder, 'Introduction' and 'Race, racism and biblical narrative', both in Felder (ed.), *Stony the road we trod: African American biblical interpretation* (Minneapolis, 1991), pp. 1, 6, 127, 136.

34 J. R. Washington Jnr, *Black sects and cults* (1972: Lanham, MD, 1984), pp. 132–3; Murphy et al., *Encyclopedia*, pp. 172–3, 215.

35 H. A. Baer, 'The role of the Bible and other sacred texts in African-American denominations and sects', in V. L. Wimbush (ed.), *African-Americans and the Bible: sacred texts and social textures* (New York and London, 2000), p. 96; Prothero, *American Jesus*, p. 218; Washington, *Black sects*, p. 133; Moses, *Black messiahs*, p. 185; Murphy et al., *Encyclopedia*, pp. 156, 161–2.

36 Washington, *Black sects*, p. 134; *Garvey Papers*, VII, pp. 451–2; Moses, *Black messiahs*, pp. 137, 186; Murphy et al., *Encyclopedia*, p. 204.

37 Murphy et al., *Encyclopedia*, pp. 90, 563.

38 Moses, *Afrotopia*, p. 14; D. Remnick, *King of the world: Muhammad Ali and the rise of an American hero* (New York, 1998).

39 C. A. Clegg III, *An original man: the life and times of Elijah Muhammad* (New York, 1997).

40 *Ibid.*, pp. 41–73.

41 See Malcolm X, *Autobiography* (London, 2001 edn), pp. 269–70: 'Mr Muhammad's teaching about how the white man had been created led me to *Findings in Genetics* by Gregor Mendel ... [which] helped me to understand that if you started with a black man, a white man could be produced; but starting with a white man, you never could produce a black man – because the white chromosome is recessive. And since no one disputes that there was one Original Man, the conclusion is clear.'

42 Clegg, *Original man*, pp. 41–73.

43 *Ibid.*

44 Malcolm X, *Autobiography*, pp. 286, 343.

45 *Ibid.*, pp. 430, 448–9, 453, 455.

CHAPTER 9

1 Of course, there remains a powerful counter-current of dissent to this position, and one which is not to be lightly dismissed. See e.g. W. D. Jordan, *White over black: American attitudes towards the Negro, 1550–1812* (Chapel Hill, NC, 1968); F. G. Wood, *The arrogance of faith: Christianity and race in America from the colonial era to the twentieth century* (New York, 1990). However, there might be more common ground here than is at first apparent. It is certainly not the argument of my book to suggest that Christians were immune to *racist* temptations; whether Christianity fostered *racialist* doctrines is another matter, though one complicated, obviously, by the curse upon Ham's son Canaan and the existence of slavery in the biblical world.

2 *Interpreter's Bible* (12 vols., New York and Nashville, 1951–7), I, p. 559.

3 A. Montagu, *Statement on Race: an annotated elaboration and exposition of the four Statements on Race issued by the United Nations Educational, Scientific and Cultural Organisation* (3rd edn, New York, 1972), pp. 7, 9, 145, 158.

4 A. van der Bent (ed.), *Breaking down the walls: World Council of Churches statements and actions on racism 1948–1985* (Programme to Combat Racism, World Council of Churches, Geneva, 1986), pp. 34, 53, 85, 87.

5 D. Tutu, 'The divine imperative' (1982), pp. 62, 65, 72, and 'Letter to State President P. W. Botha, 8 April 1988', pp. 144–5, both in Tutu, *The rainbow people of God* (London, 1994).

6 See e.g. A. Rendle Short, *Modern discovery and the Bible* (London, 1942), esp. pp. 80–1; B. Ramm, *The Christian view of science and scripture* (London, 1965), esp. pp. 214–16, 220, 234, 236; R. J. Berry, *Adam and the ape: a Christian approach to the theory of evolution* (London, 1975), esp. pp. 40, 42, 49–50.

7 J. L. Hochschild, 'Looking ahead: racial trends in the United States', *Daedalus* (winter 2005), 70–81, at 76.

8 See e.g. the contrasting views of T. B. Maston, *The Bible and race* (Nashville, TN, 1959), pp. 30–1, 105–17; Maston, *Segregation and desegregation: a Christian approach* (New York, 1959), pp. 80, 99–100; and H. Ezell, *The Christian problem of racial segregation* (New York, 1959), esp. pp. 9–10, 13–19.

Index